Bertha M. C. Gardiner

King and Commonwealth

A history of Charles I. and the great rebellion

Bertha M. C. Gardiner

King and Commonwealth
A history of Charles I. and the great rebellion

ISBN/EAN: 9783337213121

Printed in Europe, USA, Canada, Australia, Japan

Cover: Foto ©ninafisch / pixelio.de

More available books at **www.hansebooks.com**

KING AND COMMONWEALTH

A HISTORY
OF
CHARLES I. AND THE GREAT REBELLION

BY

B. MERITON CORDERY

AND

J. SURTEES PHILLPOTTS

HEAD MASTER OF BEDFORD SCHOOL
FORMERLY FELLOW OF NEW COLLEGE, OXFORD

Nothing extenuate
Nor set down aught in malice

PHILADELPHIA
JOS. H. COATES AND CO.
1876

PREFACE.

The aim in writing this short history has been to give within a moderate compass a lively idea of the feelings and motives at work in what was perhaps the most important epoch of our national history. With this aim it seemed best to treat the main events with all that fulness of detail, which assists the imagination in realizing the past, and to omit such minor actions as seemed not essential to the understanding of the main facts. The same rule has been followed in dealing with the military history. For this, personal visits have been made to the battle-fields, and some rough sketches of the ground have been added. No constitutional question has been touched without a preliminary attempt to put the growth and forms of the Constitution before the reader in such a manner as to encourage him to form a judgment for himself.

In a joint work it is difficult to define exactly the part taken by each writer, but my own share in the book may be described rather as that of editor than author; it has, in fact, been mainly confined to matters of style and arrangement, with criticisms on events and on constitutional questions. My coadjutor, who kindly undertook the subject at my suggestion, wrote the first draft of the whole book, and is not only responsible for the accuracy of the facts, but deserves all the credit of research into original documents at the British Museum and Bodleian libraries.

While for facts our endeavour has always been to go to contemporary records, yet it is impossible that any one can write on this period without feeling more obligation to the labours of Mr. Forster than can be adequately expressed in foot-notes. Acknowledgement is also due for many suggestive ideas not only to Hallam and other writers on the time, but to Mr. Freeman for the light he has thrown on the early history of the English constitution, and to Mr. Bagehot for his vivid description of its practical working at the present time.

I cannot conclude without expressing our thanks to Mr. R. W. Taylor for some corrections in the proof, to the Rev. C. E. Moberly for revising the earlier chapters, and above all to the Bishop of Exeter, whose occasional hints have given the kind of help that can only be given by one who has not only an accurate knowledge of the facts, but a thorough grasp of the constitutional questions at issue.

J. SURTEES PHILLPOTTS.

CONTENTS.

CHAPTER	PAGE
I. CONSTITUTIONAL INTRODUCTION. — GOVERNMENTS OF ELIZABETH AND JAMES I.	1
II. CHARLES' FIRST PARLIAMENTS.—IMPEACHMENT OF BUCKINGHAM.—PETITION OF RIGHT (1625—1629)	29
III. ELEVEN YEARS OF ARBITRARY GOVERNMENT (1629—1640)	51
IV. MEETING OF LONG PARLIAMENT AND TRIAL OF STRAFFORD (1640—1641)	82
V. GRAND REMONSTRANCE.—IMPEACHMENT OF FIVE MEMBERS (1641—1642)	99
VI. FIRST YEAR OF THE WAR.—BATTLES OF EDGEHILL AND NEWBURY (1642—1643)	123
VII. RISE OF INDEPENDENTS. — BATTLE OF MARSTON MOOR.—SELF-DENYING ORDINANCE (1643—1645)	148
VIII. NASEBY.—END OF WAR (1645—1646)	179
IX. PRESBYTERIANS, INDEPENDENTS, ERASTIANS, AND THEIR THEORIES	199
X. TRIUMPH OF THE ARMY OVER PARLIAMENT.—DEATH OF THE KING (1647—1649)	212
XI. SOCIAL STATE OF ENGLAND	248

CHAPTER	PAGE
XII. TRIUMPHS OF THE COMMONWEALTH BY LAND AND SEA (1649—1652)	277
XIII. FALL OF REPUBLICANS, AND BAREBONE'S PARLIAMENT (1651—1653)	303
XIV. THE FIRST THREE YEARS OF THE PROTECTORATE (1654—1656)	328
XV. THE LAST TWO YEARS OF THE PROTECTORATE (1656—1658)	347
XVI. RICHARD CROMWELL.—ANARCHY.—THE RESTORATION (1658—1660)	367
APPENDIX	386
INDEX	394

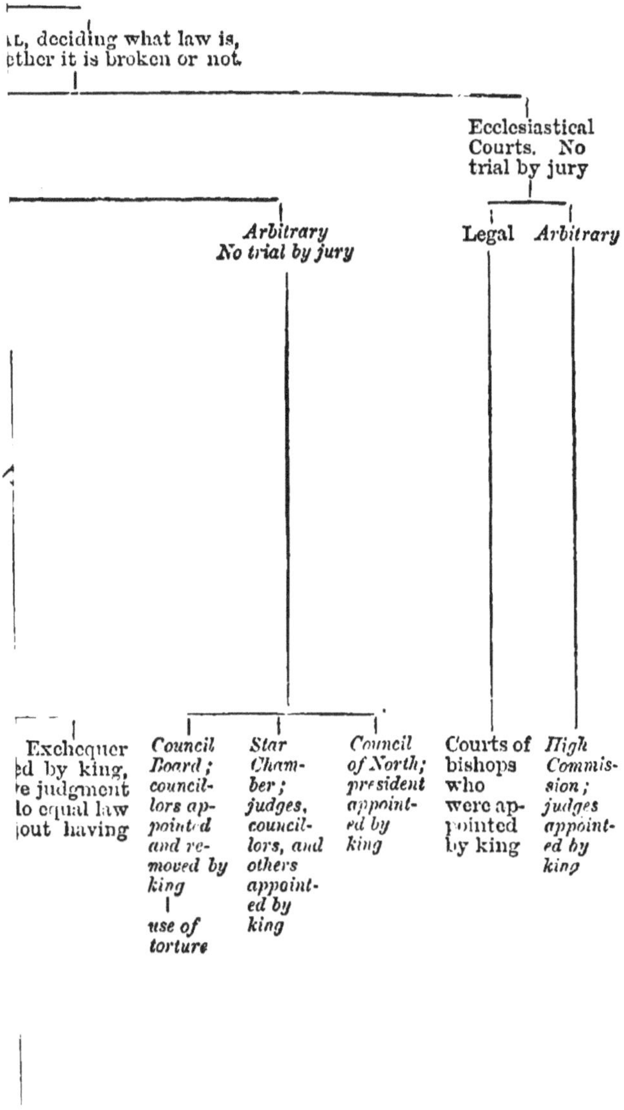

ᴌ, deciding what law is,
ether it is broken or not.

Ecclesiastical
Courts. No
trial by jury

Arbitrary
No trial by jury

Legal *Arbitrary*

Exchequer
ed by king,
e judgment
to equal law
out having

Council
Board;
council-
lors ap-
pointed
and re-
moved by
king

use of
torture

Star
Cham-
ber;
judges,
council-
lors, and
others
appoint-
ed by
king

Council
of North;
president
appoint-
ed by
king

Courts of
bishops
who
were ap-
pointed
by king

High
Commis-
sion;
judges
appoint-
ed by
king

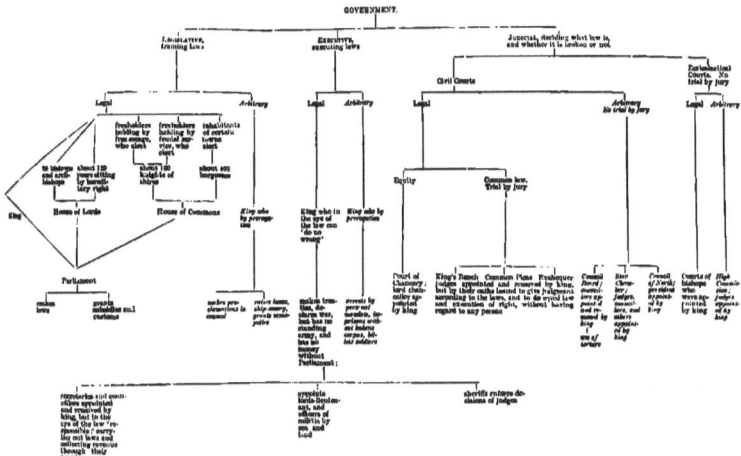

KING AND COMMONWEALTH.

CHAPTER I.
CONSTITUTIONAL INTRODUCTION.—GOVERNMENTS OF ELIZABETH AND JAMES I.

No people ever was and remained free, but because it was determined to be so; because neither its rulers nor any other party in the nation could compel it to be otherwise. If a people—especially one whose freedom has not yet become prescriptive—does not value it sufficiently to fight for it and maintain it against any force which can be mustered within the country, it is only a question in how few years or months that people will be enslaved.—MILL, DISSERTATIONS AND DISCUSSIONS.

A PEOPLE, to be free, must take part in, or possess control over, the three powers of government, Legislative, Executive, Judicial. As to the first, if they are to be masters of their persons and properties, neither laws must be made nor taxes imposed without their consent; secondly, ministers of the executive, whether councillors of state, tax-collectors, military or police officers, must be personally responsible to the law courts, or they may infringe with impunity the laws the people have secured; lastly, though persons and properties be protected by laws, and though ministers be liable to prosecution, this protection is nominal only, unless the judges who interpret the laws, are sufficiently independent of the executive. *Three functions of government, I. Legislative, II. Executive, III. Judicial*

I. Englishmen of the seventeenth century shared in the legislative power with the sovereign, who could make no laws without consent of the two Houses of Parliament. Their properties were protected from arbitrary seizure, their persons from arbitrary imprisonment, by two statutes, the Magna Charta, first granted by King John, and the Confirmatio Chartarum, first granted by Edward I. *I. Legislative. Liberties of Englishmen in 16th and 17th centuries.*

1

These together provide, first, that no person shall be put in prison without legal warrant, or kept there without being brought to trial according to the laws of the land ; that is, that the question of law shall be decided by the established judge of the law ; secondly, that the question of fact, whether a man accused at the suit of the crown, has, or has not, committed the crime laid to his charge, shall be decided by a jury of twelve of his countrymen ; and lastly, that no taxes of any sort shall be imposed without consent of Parliament.

<small>Classes represented in Parliament.</small> Several classes of the nation shared indirectly in the government by being represented in Parliament. In the Upper House sat the temporal and spiritual lords of the realm in their own right. To the Lower House all the fifty-two counties of England and Wales, with the exception of Durham, returned two members each, elected by freeholders possessed of lands or tenements to the annual value of 40s.* The term <small>Freeholders including feudal tenants and yeomen.</small> freeholder included two classes, holders of land by knight's service, and holders of land by free socage.† The first class was composed of feudal tenants, gentlemen by birth, who had originally held land in return for military service, and whose tenure was still subject to several irksome burdens. The second class was composed of yeomen, men of ignoble blood, but with a tenure dating from feudal times. The Normans of the conquest would have thought it beneath them to hold land by any other than a military tenure. But in many cases they permitted the despised Saxons to remain in possession of their lands, sometimes on condition of performing agricultural services which soon took the form of a fixed annual rent ; sometimes on condition merely of taking an oath of fealty and paying occasional fines. Thus in England there sprang up in quite early times an independent class who were owners of the soil, and though not of gentle birth, sat on juries, voted at county elections, and attended the courts in which freeholders met together to transact the business of their county.

* Money was about four times its present value, that is, one shilling then could purchase as much food or other necessaries of life as four shillings now; so this would now represent land which would bring in £8 a year as rent and cost say £250 to buy.

† Socage is probably derived from Saxon *soc*, "liberty," "privilege," "franchise." *Socagers* were bound to attend the court of the lord to whose *soc* or "right" of justice they belonged.

Besides county representatives, the House of Commons contained over four hundred members, returned according to usage by certain privileged towns. These were the classes possessed of political rights. Below these were the whole mass of the unenfranchised—hired labourers, tenants at will, and copyholders.* These were the descendants of those Saxons whom the Normans had reduced to a state of serfdom; and, unlike freeholders, were incapable either of sitting on juries or voting at elections. For the last hundred years, however, they had nearly all been free, and were protected in person and property by the same laws as freeholders. {Burgesses. Copyholders and hired labourers unrepresented.}

All classes being thus possessed of the same liberties, their common freedom gave them common interests, and caused them to unite in spite of social distinctions, and oppose the establishment of arbitrary government.

In France the political condition of the people was inferior to that of the English, and this mainly from want of union and fellow-feeling between the different ranks into which French society was divided. There was no class answering to the English yeomanry; the feudal tenants were a noble and privileged class, and were divided by this barrier of privilege from their unfortunate inferiors in rank, on whom the main burden of direct taxation fell; as the inequalities of taxation increased, the different classes became more and more isolated, and thus the kings, never meeting with combined resistance from the whole body of their subjects, came by degrees to usurp absolute power, to impose taxes at will, and to govern without the aid of any national assembly. {No privileged class.}

II. A people are little benefited by the possession of good laws, unless those laws are respected and obeyed by those who are entrusted with the execution of them. The executive power was then, as now, exercised by ministers of the crown. But in the course of two centuries the position of these ministers has been totally changed. The queen's ministers are now in such close harmony with the Parliament, that they have been defined as a committee of the {II. Executive Power now exercised by a committee of the legislature.}

---

* The *copyholder* held land of the lord of the manor, subject to certain restrictions and agricultural services enumerated in the *copy* of the roll of the estate. So long as he performed those services he might not be dispossessed.

legislature.* Chosen out of the predominant party in Parliament, they conduct the government only so long as they can command a majority of votes in the Lower House. If their measures are outvoted, they have no choice but to resign office, or by obtaining a dissolution, to appeal to a new Parliament for renewal of the support which is their only claim to power.

Executive in 16th century exercised by the crown. In the sixteenth century, on the contrary, the executive power lay entirely in the hands of the king, who settled all questions of administration, made peace and war, appointed and dismissed officers of state, and expended the revenue, uncontrolled by the representatives of the people. Yet, great as was the power thus exercised by the crown, two safeguards were provided against its abuse. The first was *Two safeguards. (1) No army in England.* negative, the absence of a standing army in England. In France absolute power was upheld by an army, recruited in part by foreigners, and officered solely by nobles; this army the king found no difficulty in maintaining, as he imposed taxes at pleasure. No such right, however, belonged to English monarchs, who were without the funds necessary for the support of a standing army; and it was only by means of a standing army, possessed with an 'esprit de corps' of its own, and divided in interest from the people, that arbitrary government could be permanently established. The House of Commons always originated money bills; they held, therefore, the purse-strings of the nation, and were careful only to grant supplies sufficient for the ordinary purposes of government.

* Though this is substantially true as a contrast to the position of the ministry in the 16th century, it would be a great mistake to disregard the influence of the *forms* under which the constitution works. (I.) Even now the control of the Commons is not so great as it seems. The ministers are not mere delegates, for Parliament controls rather than directs; it has no right to tell the Queen's ministers what to do, though it can veto their proposals, and censure them for their acts when done; the initiative remains with the cabinet. (II.) The influence of the crown is more than it seems. (i.) It has a voice in discussing despatches which settle foreign policy. (ii.) Though it cannot exclude from office a man who has made himself indispensable to the nation, it has, no doubt, a negative voice in the selection of the less conspicuous members of the cabinet, and thus exercises a real, though imperceptible, influence on the attitude of rising politicians.

The *form* is always of vast importance in constitutional questions. The popular influence, which seems to be the substantial power, is the wind that fills the sails and gives the motion; but the exact direction of the motion must still depend in a large measure on the helmsman. The shipwreck of the 17th century came from an attempt to sail in the teeth of the wind. A skilful helmsman may do much by gaining and losing tacks, but the Stuarts were not skilful.

The principles of the constitution contained a second and positive safeguard against the abuse of the regal power. Great lawyers had long since declared that the king, like his subjects, was bound to respect the laws. "The king," Bracton wrote as early as the thirteenth century, "also hath a superior, namely God, and also the law, by which he was made a king." It was not likely, however, that the subject would have either the power or the desire to arraign sovereigns themselves before courts of law. A fiction of the lawyers intervened and gave a better means of securing the same end. This fiction was that the "king could do no wrong." From this it followed that if wrong was done, the ministers, and not the king, must have advised and executed the wrong; ministers could not screen themselves behind the king's name; if they broke the laws in the performance of their functions, though it was at the king's bidding, they were still liable to be sued by the injured parties in a court of justice.

(2) Responsibility of king's ministers.

Still these safeguards had not been found sufficient to prevent the executive from violating the law. In the first place, several powers, sometimes simply oppressive, sometimes actually illegal, were regarded as belonging to the crown in right of the royal prerogative. By these both the subject's property and liberty were endangered. Thus the king, though he dared not tax without consent of Parliament, used to borrow large sums under the name of loans, which were seldom repaid. Both the king and his council imprisoned without showing legal cause. Proclamations were made by the King in Council, which, though regarded as temporary measures only, were in matter of fact laws, and sometimes had penalties attached to them for disobedience. So again, though the use of torture was not lawful by the common law, and contrary to several statutes, State prisoners were constantly put to the rack on the strength of warrants signed by the king.

Liberties not secure. (1) Illegal powers exercised by crown.

In the second place, though the law allowed the subject to seek redress, the redress was rarely attainable. Few dared to incur the king's displeasure by attacking the conduct of his servants, and if they did, juries were often intimidated,* judges were often corrupt. The strength of the chain is the

(2) Judges dependent upon crown.

* Under the Tudors, juries had been fined and imprisoned for deciding against the crown. If they decided for the crown, though unjustly, they could not be punished, because they could not have been tampered with by the sovereign!

strength of its weakest point. The weak point of the English constitution lay in the dependence of the judges upon the crown; unless the interpreters of the laws were independent, no law could ever effectually secure the liberties of the people.

(3) Arbitrary courts. And in the third place, besides the common law courts, other courts of justice existed, in which the accused was neither tried by jury nor sentenced according to known laws.

III. Judicial. Omitting the Court of Chancery, which had no jurisdiction in political cases, there were then, as now, three chief courts of justice, the King's Bench, the Common Pleas, and the Exchequer, all of which sat at Westminster; four or five judges belonged to each, who in all cases were bound to give judgment, not according to their own pleasure, or the will of the king, but according to the law of the realm, whether statute or common law.*

Since the Act of Settlement in 1702 the common law judges hold office for life, receive salaries fixed by law, and can only be dismissed from office if convicted of some offence, or in consequence of an address of the two Houses of Parliament. But in the seventeenth century they only held office at the pleasure of the king, and being dependent in part upon his bounty for their salaries, were regarded as the servants of the court.†

But these courts at any rate acknowledged the known laws, and tried prisoners by jury. Of a very different character was the Court of Star Chamber, so called because its sittings were held in a room leading out of Westminster Hall, of which the walls were decorated with stars. The germ of this court lay in a jurisdiction exercised from the time of Edward III. by the king's Common Council, which was accustomed to call to account offenders too powerful to be brought to submit to the ordinary courts of law. Then came a second stage. An Act of Parliament was passed in the reign of Henry VII. (1491), forming a court of justice, composed of certain members of the

* The common law consists of customs handed down from Norman times, and of the judgments of judges founded upon those customs; statute law of acts of Parliament.

† Thus in James' time the Admiralty judge acknowledges the receipt of instructions, "by which I understand his Majesty's resolution to continue Sir John Eliot in prison. I am glad I did forbear to deliver my opinion of the state of his cause, lest perhaps it might have differed somewhat."—Forster's Eliot, i. ii. 4.

council, and entrusted with powers of judging cases of riots, the bribing of juries, and other specified offences. This second stage gave a parliamentary sanction to the court, but limited its powers and specified its persons. It was out of this chrysalis that the Court of Star Chamber emerged. By the end of Henry the Eighth's reign, it had reached its third, or final stage, in which it boasted parliamentary sanction, at the same time that it repudiated the conditions under which that sanction had been given. The limits of persons and of offences had both disappeared. The powers formerly vested only in the members of the court of Henry VII. had silently passed into the hands of the whole body of the Common Council,* while its jurisdiction had been extended beyond the offences specified by the statute to cases of breach of trust, fraud, and libel.

Besides the Court of Star Chamber, there was a second court, the Court of High Commission, which deprived the subject of the protection granted him by the common law, and of trial by jury. After Henry VIII. quarrelled with Pope Clement VII. about a divorce from Catherine of Arragon, Parliament passed an Act of Supremacy, declaring the king the supreme head of the Church. This was re-enacted when Elizabeth came to the throne (1558), and an addition made to it, granting the queen power to appoint persons to exercise jurisdiction in ecclesiastical affairs, as, for instance, in the reformation of heresies and abuses. Elizabeth, therefore, was acting within her powers when, in 1583, she erected a permanent commission, consisting of twelve bishops, privy councillors, and others; but she undoubtedly was straining her power when she gave this court an authority—not granted her by the statute—to try suspected persons by juries, or *by any other means they could devise*, and to punish by fine and imprisonment. Thus, while the Court of Star Chamber, by judging cases of libel, deprived the subject of liberty of speech, the Court of High Commission deprived him of liberty of conscience. Both alike, therefore, soon came to be hated by the people; both were distinctly contrary to Magna Charta, for in neither was the accused tried by jury or by the laws of the land; both were contrary to the first axioms of jus-

* The king had two councils: his Privy Council, which advised with him in all State matters, and his Common Council. In the Common Council sat, not only all members of the Privy Council, but also some of the common law judges, and others added at the pleasure of the king.

tice, the separation of accuser and judge, for in these courts the ministers of the crown first prosecuted a man in their capacity of councillors, and then themselves passed sentence upon him as judges.

Queen Elizabeth was not disposed to yield up any powers, legal or illegal, that had been exercised by her predecessors on the throne. She, however, was careful not to strain them beyond what the temper of the nation would bear. Though she often violated the rights of individuals, she never attacked those of large numbers at once, and always kept on good terms with her parliaments, by making concessions at times when a refusal would have caused ill-feeling. But notwithstanding the tact with which her government was conducted, as the people increased in knowledge and wealth, they grew more and more sensitive to infringements of their rights, and gave signs that through their representative, the House of Commons, they would soon call upon the crown to resign the powers it had usurped to the great detriment of the subject's liberty.

Caution with which Elizabeth exercised her power.

That the legislature should make laws, and the executive break them, was a sufficient cause in itself to produce a rupture between the two powers. The probability, however, of such a rupture was greatly increased by the fact that a second cause of quarrel existed between the crown and the Parliament—religious differences. In England, the Reformation had been, no doubt, a popular movement, as it had been abroad; but it was controlled and directed by a monarchy which had but a partial sympathy with its aims. The consequence was an exceeding moderation. The king was made head of the Church in place of the pope; the monasteries were dissolved; the clergy were allowed to marry; the doctrine of purgatory was denied, as was that of a physical change in the elements at the sacrament; images and crosses were removed from churches; the people were allowed to read the Bible in their own tongue; an English liturgy was composed; and the English sovereigns, heads of the Church, said, as it were, to the people, 'Thus far shall ye go, and no farther.' But no sooner had the princes finished their work, than a new set of reformers arose, preaching another, fuller, more popular reformation.

The Reformation directed by the English kings.

The main principle of the reformers was to get rid of those

superstitious observances which marred the freedom of the worshipper's communicating with his Maker; they did not believe in the necessity of priestly intervention, nor in the special sanctity of prayers in a foreign tongue. On the continent, this principle had been carried much further than in England; and when exiles, who had fled the country during the persecutions of Mary's reign, returned home from Flanders, Strasburg, or Geneva, they regarded the English Church as hardly deserving the name of reformed. 'How many signs of Romish superstition,' they said, 'are left in the prayer-book, and the services ! What abuses yet remain in administration ! Look at the plurality of benefices. How can one man be in a dozen places at a time ? Are the clergy still to flaunt the priestly surplice and gaudy popish vestments, foolish and abominable apparel, in which the Catholic priests pretend to make mere water holy, to achieve a miraculous transformation of bread and wine, or to conjure the devil out of persons and places possessed ? Is the communion-table not to stand, table-like, in the body of the church, but to be set up in the chancel like the altar of the papists ? Shall the sign of the cross in baptism, the bowing at the name of Jesus, the ring in marriage, the keeping of saints' days, all these remains of popish superstitions, be observed in a church that calls itself reformed ! Surely the snake is only scotched, not killed.' *Popular reformers attack popish ceremonies.*

Elizabeth, on the contrary, while she regarded the authority of her bishops as a support to the power of the crown, also hoped, by disallowing further change in church ceremonies, to conciliate Catholics. Her ecclesiastical power was absolute. She, therefore, refused to give the Puritans satisfaction even in matters of form. If the Puritan minister would officiate at the services of the Church, he must wear vestments he abhorred ; if he would baptize a child, he must make the sign of the cross ; if he would join two people in marriage, he must use the ring ; in all points, he must conform exactly to the minutiæ of the rubric. *No toleration allowed by Elizabeth.*

The Act of Supremacy was a double-edged sword, cruel to Puritans and Catholics alike. All clergymen holding benefices, all laymen holding office in the State, who refused to take an oath, when tendered, recognizing the queen as head of the Church, were to be deprived of their benefices or *Act of Supremacy.*

offices (1558). The Act of Uniformity forbade ministers, beneficed or not, to use any other than the established liturgy; for the first offence, they forfeited all their goods and chattels; for the second, they suffered a year's imprisonment; for the third, imprisonment for life; while fines were imposed upon laymen who stayed away from their parish church on Sundays or holidays (1559).

Act of Uniformity.

But persecution, instead of suppressing the reformers, only increased their numbers and animosity. From attacking ceremonies, they went on to attack the authority of the bishops. If the Holy Scriptures, they said, contain all things necessary for salvation, then where in them is to be found mention of that proud hierarchy of archbishops, bishops, and priests, by which the English Church is governed? Turning their eyes towards Scotland, they there saw established a church on a Presbyterian model, governed by assemblies of ministers and lay elders on less hierarchical principles than the Episcopal. For this model they claimed the authority of a Divine Right, as being the original form of church government established by the will of God in the time of the apostles.

Reformers desire establishment of Presbyterian Church.

To the queen, this new programme of reform, attacking, as it did, not only episcopal authority, but her own prerogative as head of the Church, was still more distasteful than that which had required merely a reform of ceremonies.

An established church may be either self-governed or governed by the State. The Episcopal Church was a State church in the fullest sense of the term; archbishops and bishops, like ministers of state, were appointed by the sovereign; no laws to regulate the conduct of the laity in spiritual matters could emanate from any source but the queen in Parliament; and, in fact, there was no spiritual authority distinct from the State. On the other hand, the Presbyterian Church prided itself on being self-governed. According to this system, every parish had its minister, its deacon, and its lay elder, together forming a little court of justice, or kirk session, which called parishioners to account for spiritual and moral offences, such as drunkenness, scolding, or Sabbath-breaking; and punished by censures, fines, or imprisonment. So many parishes formed a presbytery; so

Episcopal Church dependent upon the State.

Presbyterian Church independent of State control.

DIVINE RIGHT OF KINGS.

many presbyteries formed a province, and both presbytery and province possessed a distinct judicial assembly, composed of lay elders and ministers. Lastly, there was a general assembly of the church, composed of all the ministers of parishes, together with a sprinkling of lay elders, and to this body appeals were made from the judicial decisions of the lesser assemblies. The orders and regulations made by the general assembly of the church were binding upon the whole nation, clergy and laity. This church had been established in Scotland by rebellion, and its ministers did not hesitate to set up their own authority in opposition to that of king and State. "Disregard not our threatening," they said to James VI., "for there was never yet one in this realm, in the place where your grace is, who prospered after the ministers began to threaten him."

Of these two systems, the Episcopal form of church government, though less popular, was also less tyrannical than the Presbyterian. The powers of English bishops were far more limited than those of Scottish assemblies. The Church of Scotland, however, which gave power to the ministers of the people, instead of to courtly prelates, suited the enthusiasm of the age, and naturally recommended itself to the more earnest reformers on this side the border. Rejoiced to find that Elizabeth regarded the Presbyterians as rebellious fanatics, the bishops on their side now set up a counter claim of Divine Right in favour of the Episcopal Church as administered by the queen; and, in return for the privilege of fining, imprisoning, and ejecting nonconformists, taught the people that kings rule by Divine Right, as the viceregents of God upon earth, and that opposition to the commands of princes is disobedience to the commands of God. *Episcopal Church less tyrannical than the Presbyterian.* *Bishops support the power of the crown.*

But Puritan ministers, though deprived of their livings, could not be silenced. They thought the whole state of society and religion in England needed to be penetrated with a new spirit. Themselves eager readers of their Bibles, zealous preachers, active reformers, filled with true missionary zeal, they found that the court and nobility cared little for serious matters, and that noblemen and gentlemen spent their time in gaming, in dancing, in attending grand shows, or in fighting on the continent. They aimed at a social as well as a religious *Puritans cannot be suppressed.*

reform. Printing had largely increased the numbers of readers and writers, and had at the same time extended the range not only of serious but also of profane literature. It was an age of poets. There were two hundred living in the last part of the century, Spenser and Shakespeare amongst them. The middle classes followed the same kind of amusements as their superiors, frequenting the bear-garden, the bowling-green, the gaming-house, and the theatre. The country people had their wakes and fairs and festivals. Amidst so much rioting and pleasuring the Puritans saw few ministers competent to lead the people to more serious paths. The clergy, so far from checking the freedom of society, were as eager in the pursuit of amusement as their parishioners: before the Reformation their incapacity had been the reproach of the Catholic Church; it was now equally the reproach of the newly established Church. Many Catholics, rather than lose their livings, had taken the oaths required of them—were they reformed? While they passed their time in taverns, gaming and drinking, they were not likely to acquire the new art of preaching. "Dumb dogs," said the Puritans, are "left to guard the Church, while we are turned out." In many villages no sermon was heard "from year's end to year's end." Such a church seemed to invite reform; and the Presbyterians were ready for the task. Persecution not going far enough to extirpate the reformers, only attracted the minds of others to the consideration of the questions in dispute, and discussion led to more advanced views on reform. Episcopacy was generally the religion of the upper classes. Presbyterian opinions prevailed amongst the middle ranks; and now the very poorest of the nation began also to have their special ideas on religious questions. Men, women, and children, poor people who had nothing to support them but their handicrafts and trades, would in summer-time meet in the fields outside London at five o'clock in the morning, and in winter in private houses, in order to worship after their own fashion. Every congregation, they maintained, however small, ought to be left free to settle its own affairs, without interference from either bishops or assemblies. Amongst these latest reformers were several distinct sects, which, without holding the same doctrines, agreed in their general view of church government; and being taught by weakness to combine together in spite of minor differences of opinion, were the

Sectarians.

first to raise the flag of 'liberty of conscience.' More cruelly used than Presbyterians, many of these sectarians fled the country for Holland, where they established churches on their own principles. Those who stayed in England ran the risk of imprisonment for life.

In spite, however, of persecution, the reformers were devotedly loyal to the queen. For though, through political motives, she persecuted Puritans at home, abroad she supported the Protestants in the fierce conflict they were waging with Catholicism. *Elizabeth supports Protestant cause on continent.* On one side were arrayed the pope, the King of Spain, the Emperor of Austria, the Catholic princes of Germany; on the other, Sweden, Denmark, Holland, and the Protestant German princes; and it was chiefly owing to the support of England that this side was able to maintain its ground against the Catholics.

The popes had long desired to force back into their fold the country that was thus recognized as the head of Protestant States. Pius V. had said he wished he could shed his blood in an expedition against England; and now Gregory XIII. urged on Philip II. of Spain to attempt the conquest of the heretic kingdom. He could not have found a prince or nation more suited for his purpose. The Spaniards and English hated one another with a national as well as a religious hatred. A love of enterprize and discovery had spread rapidly amongst all classes during Elizabeth's long reign. Adventurers, led often by noblemen and gentlemen, sailed to America and the West Indies, making fruitless efforts to discover gold mines, or to found colonies. On these expeditions they burnt the settlements and seized the treasure ships of the Spaniards, who, being *Enmity between Spain and England.* already possessed of Mexico, Peru, and much of the West Indies, regarded themselves as sole lords of the New World, and were quite prepared for a war to the knife with the intruders.

It was thus to fight the battle at once of the pope and of the nation that the Invincible Armada sailed from Spain. It sailed to take vengeance on a heretic queen, who, while supporting the Dutch in rebellion, disputed the claims of Philip to the possession of two continents. It came threatening England with conquest and Protestantism with destruction. But storms and winds and the courage of English seamen shattered and destroyed the Armada (1588). The triumph of England was the salvation of the Protestant cause. The invaded now becoming the invaders, burned Spanish galleons in the very harbours of Spain.

Her foreign policy a chief cause of Elizabeth's popularity.

With the people success will go far to justify even a tyrannical government. Hence it was that, although storms were rising, and the political atmosphere was charged with electricity, no violent contention ever arose between Elizabeth and her subjects. The occasional illegal acts committed by her government, the cruel sentences passed upon Puritans by the courts of High Commission and Star Chamber, were forgiven because she pursued a foreign policy that accorded with the wishes of the nation, and caused England to be feared and respected. The bonds of loyalty seemed strong because they had not been tried too severely. It is a principle in mechanics that girders should not be strained beyond the limits of perfect recovery. An excessive tension may not only cause danger for the moment, but may be a source of permanent weakness. Such a tension came when the nation was ruled by monarchs who had neither the capacity to lead their Parliaments nor the temper to follow them.

James I., his character.

On the death of Elizabeth the great Tudor line was extinct.* James VI. of Scotland, who outwardly united the two kingdoms, failed to unite his subjects to himself. He was thought cowardly, conceited, pretentious. It was believed that flattery was the readiest road to his favour; he certainly suffered himself to fall under the control of unworthy favourites, so that his court received the character of being the head-quarters of riot and vice, if not of far darker crimes.

* Henry VII., 1492—1509.

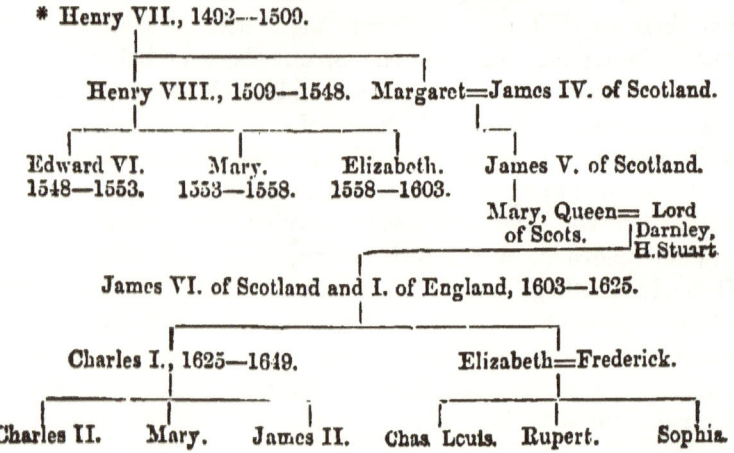

The members of the Commons refused to grant the money of the nation to be lavished on such favourites or wasted in such riot. James, therefore, did not trouble himself with often meeting the representatives of the peop'e. Holding the theory that he was possessed of absolute power, he ventured to try to carry that theory into practice. A few instances will show the manner in which the liberties of the subject were violated by his government.

His first Parliament granted him for life duties on exports and imports, called tonnage and poundage (1604). These duties were fixed at a certain rate ; for instance, there was a duty of 2s. 6d. on every hundred-weight of currants imported into the country. James, of his sole authority, trebled this duty, and afterwards, without asking the consent of Parliament, imposed heavy taxes upon almost all merchandise. In principle there is no distinction between the illegal levying of a direct or an indirect tax. The ignorant, however, are much more struck by that which comes plainly before them. Hence, had James attempted to raise a direct tax, such as the subsidies granted in Parliament, which were levied on land and articles of personal property, he would have aroused far more indignation than he did by the imposition of illegal customs. The subsidy must have been paid directly into the hands of the tax-gatherer, whereas the illegal duties were paid in the first instance by the merchants, and the fact that these merchants repaid themselves out of the profits of the consumer by raising prices, was not obvious to the vulgar. The people, however, really suffered in purse as well as in right, and Parliament would have been wanting in its duty, if it had not protested against this interference with the property of the subject.

James imposes illegal taxes.

The person of the subject was no safer than his property.

It is contrary to the common law of England to force any man to criminate himself. The Courts of High Commission and Star Chamber, however, did not follow the procedure of the common law courts, and were in the habit of tendering the prisoner an oath, technically called the oath *ex officio,* to answer truly all questions put to him. Two Puritans, for refusing to take this oath, were imprisoned by the Court of High Commission. The common law allowed every man committed to prison upon a criminal charge, to apply to the court of King's Bench for a so-called writ of *habeas corpus,* directing the

Illegal commitments.

gaoler to produce his prisoner and the warrant upon which he was committed, before the court on a stated day.* The judge, upon view of the warrant, discharged the prisoner, released him on bail, or sent him back to prison to await his trial, according as the charge against him was no offence in the eye of the law, or a bailable offence, or one for which no bail could be received.

The two Puritans in question were brought before the judges of the King's Bench on a writ of *habeas corpus.* Fuller, their counsel, argued that they ought to be released, because the High Commissioners had not been empowered *by law* to imprison, or fine, or administer the oath *ex officio.* This argument struck at the root of the authority of the High Commission, and Fuller was himself summoned before the court, on the ground that he had slandered the king's authority. He refused, like his clients, to take the oath, "to answer truly all questions put to him," and applied to the Court of King's Bench for a prohibition to stay the proceedings. It was by means of such prohibitions that the common law courts were accustomed to prevent the ecclesiastical courts from meddling with cases which properly came under the cognizance of the common law. The judges sent the prohibition, but at the same time signified that they should not interfere, if the High Commissioners charged the prisoner with heresy and schism. The Puritan advocate was accordingly convicted of heresy, fined £200, and committed to prison. The common law judges would not interfere in his favour, though he appealed again to them, and he seems, eventually, to have regained his liberty only by submitting, and paying the fine.†

Marginal note: Arbitrary procedure of Court of High Commission.

The Courts of Star Chamber and High Commission, however illegally their jurisdiction was acquired and conducted, at least brought definite charges against the accused, and allowed him a

* *Habeas corpus ad subjiciendum* are the first words of the writ to the gaoler, meaning that he is to *have the person* (of the prisoner) to produce before the court (so *habeas corpus ad testificandum* are the first words of a writ for producing a prisoner to give evidence). The writ was anciently called *corpus cum causâ,* because it required the return of the *cause* of detention, as well as of the *body* imprisoned. The principle of the writ was contained in the Magna Charta of King John, which enacted that "no freeman should be imprisoned but by lawful judgment of his peers or by the law of the land." It was used between subject and subject in the time of Henry VI., and against the crown in that of Henry VII., so that it was fully recognized as law long before the re-enactments in the reign of Charles I., and the *Habeas Corpus Act* of Charles II., 1679.

† Gardiner, Hist. of Eng. (1603—1616), i. 445.

form of trial. The King's Council went even further than this, and constantly committed political opponents of the government, without bringing any charge against them, or allowing them the benefit of a trial. The imprisonment extended from weeks, or months, to years, and the writ of *habeas corpus*, which ought to have protected any subject from such an outrage, was rarely obtainable. In the case of Arabella Stuart, the causeless displeasure of the king formed the ground of a life-long imprisonment. This lady, who was first cousin to James, married, through pure affection, a distant relation, William Seymour, a descendant of Mary, the youngest daughter of Henry VII. James, jealous of the union of two relations, both of whom had a distant claim to the crown, confined Seymour in the Tower, and placed Arabella in confinement at Lambeth. Both made their escape, with the intention of meeting at Leigh, near Blackwall, on board a French vessel, which was engaged to carry them across the Channel. Arabella arrived before her husband, and, in spite of her entreaties, her attendants, in fear of pursuit, forced the captain to sail. Seymour, on his arrival, finding the French vessel gone, hired a collier, and was landed in safety at Ostend. Arabella was not so fortunate. When within sight of Calais, a vessel, sent from Dover in pursuit, overtook the fugitive, and carried her back to England. On her arrival, she was immediately committed to the Tower, whence she wrote to the two chief justices, imploring them to secure her a trial by the usual writ of *habeas corpus*: " And if your lordships may not, or will not, grant unto me the ordinary relief of a distressed subject, then, I beseech you, become humble intercessors to his Majesty, that I may receive such benefit of justice as both his Majesty by his oath hath promised, and the laws of this realm afford to all others, those of his blood not excepted. And though, unfortunate woman! I can obtain neither, yet, I beseech your lordships, retain me in your good opinion, and judge charitably, till I be proved to have committed any offence, either against God or his Majesty, deserving so long restraint or separation from my lawful husband." Arabella's just demand remained ungranted. Her marriage was no crime at law, and had she been brought before the judges, they could hardly have done less than order her release. The idea of attempting to change the succession would have been ludicrous, if true, but there was no ground for suspicion of political motive in the marriage to give a shadow of excuse for her restraint. Separated from her husband, and broken-hearted, Arabella lost her reason, and, after some four years of confinement, at last died in the Tower.

The Countess of Shrewsbury, Arabella's aunt, was brought up before the council, on the charge of being an accomplice in her niece's escape. Refusing to implicate herself, by answering in any way to a charge so unknown to the law, she bravely replied, that, if the council had a charge against her, she would be ready to answer before her peers. Such an appeal to the hated liberties of the subject was not suffered to pass unpunished, and for several years her name appears in the list of unhappy inmates of the Tower.

It was not only the king's animosity which was to be dreaded, but the greed of the court. The interests of the nation were bought and sold by courtiers and ministers. Several of James' council were in receipt of salaries from the King of Spain. Others were in a nefarious league with the pirates who then preyed on our shipping. The story of Sir John Eliot and Captain Nutt sheds a flood of light on various judicial and executive anomalies of the reign. In 1623 Eliot was Vice-admiral of Devon. Amongst his duties were those of boarding pirate vessels, and deciding upon the lawfulness of prizes. Captain Nutt, an English pirate, who, at the head of several ships, had for three years past ranged the seas between the coasts of England and America, was notorious alike for audacity and cruelty. Sailing to Torbay and landing in force whenever he came ashore, he dared the vice-admiral to seize him, and boasted of the pardons he had already obtained. Armed with a copy of one of these pardons, conditional on the captain's surrendering himself within a certain time, Eliot risked his life and went on board the pirate vessel. There was little doubt that the time within which the pardon was valid was already past, but Nutt, acting probably on the supposition that Eliot could only be influenced by mercenary motives, agreed to surrender himself, and to pay a fine of £500, together with six packs of calves' skins. If the pardon were good, the fine would be shared between the vice-admiral, Eliot, and the lord-admiral, Buckingham. Directly the man was ashore, Eliot placed him under arrest, and then wrote an account of the whole transaction to the council. He took occasion to point out how the pirate, even while treating, had audaciously seized a Colchester brig, laden with woods and sugar to the value of some £4000, but left the question of the validity of the pardon entirely to their lordships' decision. The first result of this was, that Eliot received a letter from Conway, the under-secretary of state, highly commending him for his good service, and intimating that he should before long receive the honour of kissing the king's hand. Within a few days Eliot repaired to London, not, however, to kiss the king's hand, but to become a prisoner in the Marshalsea, and answer in the Court of Admiralty charges preferred against him by the Council Board. The pirate, Nutt, to give his court friends an excuse for shielding him, had the audacity to come forward as the accuser of his captor, alleging that Eliot, both by letter and message, had urged him to sail to Dartmouth and make prizes of divers ships that were there, laden with goods and money out of Spain; and that it was not until thus encouraged that he had ventured on seizing the Colchester brig. The letter Nutt was unable to produce; the charges were denied both by Eliot and his officers. The judge of the Admiralty, in his reports to the council, did not venture to express an opinion in regard to Eliot, but pointed out how the lord-admiral's interests might be neglected, if the vice-admiral were kept long absent from his post in Devon. But while Buckingham at the time was in Spain, Eliot's enemy, and Nutt's friend, Sir John Calvert, the principal secretary of state, was in England. It was through his influence that the council had proceeded against Eliot. The pirate had rendered him some service in the establishment of a colony in Newfoundland, and if his word may be believed, this was his sole motive for seeking to blacken the character of the vice-admiral, and obtain a pardon from the king for that "unlucky fellow, Captain Nutt." It was no wonder Eliot felt angry and used stronger language in writing to Secretary Conway than he usually employed. "I cannot so much yet undervalue my integrity, to doubt that the words of a malicious assassin, now standing for his life, shall have reputation equal to the credit of a gentleman." Nutt, however, by means of his powerful friend, obtained his pardon and, in addition, a grant of £100 out of the ship and goods seized at Torbay. The duration of Eliot's imprisonment is uncertain; probably he remained in the Marshalsea until the following October, at which time Charles and Buckingham returned from Spain. In the following month he was canvassing for a seat in the last of James' parliaments.*

While person and property were thus dealt with, it was hardly likely that there should be any recognition of the later rights of freedom of speech and freedom of thought. Presbyterians and sectarians were forced to fly the country, in order to escape imprisonment. Puritan preachers were ejected from their livings. Puritan writers were prosecuted in the Star Chamber. James himself made a jest of the fines inflicted on them ;—"it were no reason that those that will refuse the airy sign of the cross after baptism should have their purses stuffed with any more solid and substantial crosses."† But persecution that does not go far enough to extirpate its victims defeats its own ends. Sympathy was felt for the Puritans, their opinions spread, and the division between the two parties grew wider and wider. Clergymen who found favour at court adopted doctrines approaching to those of Rome, and supported the power of the crown by teaching the duty of passive obedience, and the doctrine of the Divine Right of kings. Clergymen who found favour with the people taught that in the plain words of Scripture is to be found all that the Christian needs for his guidance; and denounced to their hearers, as sinful and displeasing to God, popish ceremonies and doctrines, and the worldly court-life, with its drinking, swearing, acting, fine dressing, and dancing.

Puritans persecuted.

Thus, at the end of James' reign, men of very various opinions were all alike designated Puritans. There was the sectarian, who desired that each separate congregation should be allowed its own special form of worship; the Presbyterian, who desired to see a church similar to that of Scotland established in England; the churchman, who objected to popish ceremonies and doctrines; the patriot, who, from opposing tyranny in the State, came to mistrust a church that taught the duty of passive obedience to kings' commands; and, lastly, the earnest man, who, by merely leading, in his own person, a pure life, seemed to reprove

Word Puritan designates men of various opinions.

---

* Forster : Life of Sir J. Eliot, i. 2.
† Ellis Orig. Letters, iii. 450: Coins were called crosses from the stamp of the cross on the reverse, as sovereigns from the king's head on the obverse.

the manners of the court; all these became alike objects of the scoffs and jeers of the king's friends, and were classed together as factious hypocrites and Puritans.

But neither James' pretensions to absolute power, nor his actual infringement of the constitution, nor the persecution of Puritans, nor the vices of his court, did so much to alienate the affection of his subjects, as did the conduct of his foreign policy. The Thirty Years' War had now begun. Matthias, Emperor of Germany, ruler of Austria, Hungary, and Bohemia, was childless. To secure the succession, he caused his cousin Ferdinand, archduke of Styria, to be crowned as next king of his great kingdoms of Bohemia and Hungary.* This prince had been brought up by the Jesuits, and was so ardent a Catholic that he said he would sooner beg his bread from door to door, than that the Catholic Church should suffer injury. He had long since driven the Protestants out of his own duchy of Styria. Sooner than accept such a fanatic as their king, the Bohemians, of whom the majority were Protestants, rose in rebellion, and offered the crown to one of their own persuasion, Frederick, prince of the Palatinate,† who

^{James' foreign policy cause of division between himself and his subjects.}

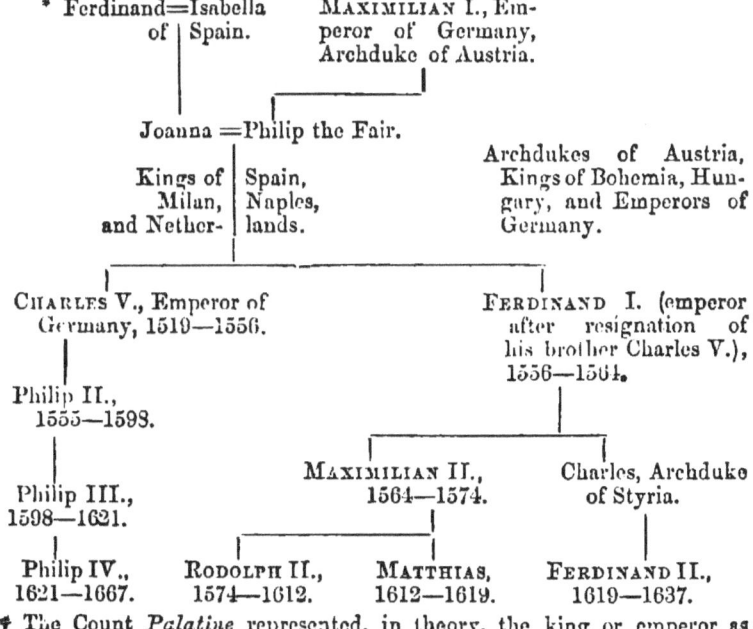

* Ferdinand=Isabella of Spain.

† The Count *Palatine* represented, in theory, the king or emperor as

accepted the dangerous gift, and was crowned King of Bohemia (August, 1619).

Thirty Years' War. This was the origin of the great religious struggle between Catholics and Protestants, which is called the Thirty Years' War. Frederick, the Protestant champion, had for his enemies, Ferdinand, elected Emperor of Germany on the death of Matthias (1619); the Catholic princes of the German empire; and Philip III. of Spain.

The Austrian Emperors of Germany, and the Kings of Spain, Milan, and the Netherlands, being near relations, always acted in one another's interests. Jealousy of the united power of Spain and Austria inclined France to prefer political to religious considerations, so that it usually supported the Protestant princes in withstanding the encroachments of the emperors; but it was useless at the present time for Frederick to look for help to a country torn by civil dissensions, and governed by a minor.

From James, his Protestant father-in-law, whose daughter, Elizabeth, he had married amidst the rejoicings of the English (1613), as well as from his fellow Protestant princes of the empire, he might, not without reason, hope for support, in a war nominally undertaken in the interests of the Protestant cause.

James, however, hating war, had made peace, on his accession, with the old Catholic enemy, Spain, and declared his intention to the French ambassador, of "avoiding war as his own damnation." But, on the breaking out of the Thirty Years' War, the king found himself placed in a dilemma. For he must either give up his theory of non-intervention, or suffer England to fall from the proud position to which Elizabeth had raised her, as head of the Protestant States. Even now, when we recognize the full evil of war, it seems hardly generous in those themselves possessed of liberty to refuse assistance to a free people maintaining their freedom against foreign armies. To English Protestants, in whose minds the remembrance of the Armada was still fresh, it seemed at once both base and foolish to look on

---

judge in his own *palace*. Barons, especially those of frontier provinces, had similar royal judicial privileges delegated to them. Such provinces were called palatine. In Germany there was an upper and lower Palatinate; the lower *Palatinate* comprised the upper part of the rich Rhine valley, with Heidelberg for its capital, and conferred a vote at the election of the emperors of Germany.

with indifference, while a Protestant people were deprived of liberty of conscience by armies composed of foreigners and Catholics. Protestant Europe was one country, and a blow struck at one Protestant State was regarded as a blow struck at the interests of all Protestant States.

James, however, acting in opposition to the wishes of his subjects, refused to support his son-in-law. In the first place, he desired to avoid hostilities with Spain, in the interests of a match that he had been negotiating for the past six years between the Prince of Wales and Philip the Third's daughter, to whose dowry he cannily looked as a means of paying his debts, without applying to Parliament for aid. He had just executed England's greatest captain, Sir Walter Raleigh, to please Philip. In the second place, he disliked the idea of assisting subjects in rebellion against their prince. In favour of the first motive, there was nothing to be said. Who could uphold a King of England in relying on foreign gold for the support of his government, rather than on the goodwill of his subjects? In favour of the second more might be urged, though not from James' point of view. The Bohemian nobles, the authors of the rebellion, were rapacious and lawless, and without the moral qualities necessary for the conduct of a revolution and the establishment of a free government. A state of anarchy in Germany was foreseen as the probable result of their success, and even several Protestant princes refused to assist Frederick in weakening the imperial power, by which alone some sort of law was maintained between the different States that composed the empire. Accordingly, neither England nor France took part in the struggle ; the Protestant princes made peace for themselves (July, 1620) ; and Frederick was defeated and driven out of Bohemia (Nov., 1620). When the armies of Spain and Austria proceeded to invade the Palatinate, Frederick's hereditary dominions, James summoned a Parliament, with a half-formed resolve of breaking with Spain, and taking an active part in the war (1620).

James' reasons for refusing to assist his son-in-law.

It was impracticable for England to maintain a large army in the Palatinate, and even the attempt would have required supplies far larger than the country was disposed to grant. James was aware of these facts, and therefore the slower to enter upon hostilities. It must be allowed that the Commons acted unrea-

Commons press James to enter on spirited policy, but slow to grant necessary funds.

sonably. The country gentlemen, who came up to Westminster once in five or six years, were not enlightened by newspapers, and had no means of acquainting themselves with the intricate course of foreign politics, or of forming any correct estimate of the probable cost of a war. Now, while knowledge of their own incapacity prevented them from pretending to direct operations, their Protestant zeal caused them to press James to assist his son-in-law, and their ignorance to suppose that this could be done at comparatively a small expense to the country. Elizabeth had always had the skill so to direct the blow that it should inflict the greatest injury to her adversary at the least possible cost to herself. She would have seen that the sea was England's field of fame, and would never have marched an army to Heidelberg. Had she still sat on the throne, perhaps a dash upon some Spanish port might have rendered the Protestants a material assistance, by drawing Philip's armies off from Germany. But her foreign policy, when not marred by misplaced parsimony or favouritism, had been marked by her exceptional genius, and it was unreasonable to expect her commonplace successor to strike out a line of action at once spirited, effective, and economical. It was probably fortunate for England that he never heartily made the attempt.

The Parliament was asked for money sufficient to maintain for the winter some regiments of English volunteers, engaged in defending Heidelberg, the capital of the Palatinate. But the Commons, before voting money, desired to see the king commit *Commons petition James to marry his son to a Protestant princess.* himself to a decided policy, and prepared a petition, begging him to marry his son to a Protestant princess, and to make war on Spain. James, hearing beforehand of the contents of the petition, wrote a letter, forbidding the House to meddle with his son's match; and adding, as a warning to those who should disregard the royal command, that, "as for liberty of speech, he was free to punish any man's misdemeanours in Parliament, both during and after their sitting." In meddling with matters of peace and war, the Commons were not so sure of their ground, but liberty of speech* they regarded as a precious inheritance from their

---

* Even in Edward the Third's time, the Commons seem to have been allowed to debate on many things concerning the king's prerogative; and

PARLIAMENT OVERRIDDEN.

earliest ancestors. A second petition was at once prepared, begging his Majesty, "such a wise and just king, to recognise liberty of speech, their ancient and undoubted right." James replied by saying "he would not infringe their privileges, only he did not like their style of speaking—how could any privileges be their undoubted right and inheritance, when these were all derived from the grace and permission of his ancestors and himself?"

The Commons, too wise to let such doctrine as this pass unchallenged, entered a protest in their journals (18 Dec., 1621), to the effect that, 'Their liberties and privileges were the undoubted birthright of the subjects of England; the State, the defence of the realm, the Church, the laws and grievances were proper matters for them to debate; members have liberty of speech, and freedom from all imprisonment for speaking on any matters touching Parliament business.' James, in the full assembly of his council, and in presence of the judges, caused the journal-book to be brought before him, and, with his own hand, erased this protestation, declaring it to be invalid, void, and of none effect. *Commons enter in their journals declaration of their privileges.*

The dissatisfaction of the nation at the king, and his Spanish Catholic match, was greatly increased after the dissolution of this Parliament (6 Jan., 1622). Abroad, the Protestants were being defeated, persecuted, crushed. Frederick was driven, not only out of Bohemia, but out of *Protestants defeated.*

Henry IV. promised to take no notice of any reports made to him of their proceedings before such matters were brought before him by the advice and assent of *all* the Commons. A Parliament, or "speaking-house," would be a poor guardian of liberties without itself having liberty of utterance. The principle was well stated nearly half a century after this (1667): "No man can doubt but whatever is once enacted is lawful; but nothing can come into an Act of Parliament but it must be first affirmed or propounded by somebody; so that if the Act can wrong nobody, no more can the first propounding. The members must be as free as the Houses; an Act of Parliament cannot disturb the State; therefore the debate that tends to it cannot; for it must be propounded and debated before it can be enacted."—May's Parl. Practice, 102.

Besides freedom of speech on subjects of Parliamentary debate, the principal privileges of Parliament were:

The right of both Houses of judging and punishing their own members for any misdemeanour committed in Parliament.

The right of the Commons of determining any disputed election.

The right of members of both Houses to enjoy freedom from arrest, and exemption from all legal process, while Parliament was sitting, except on charges of treason, felony, and breach of the peace.

his hereditary dominions, the Palatinate, and forced, with his family, to take refuge in Holland, and live on the alms of the Prince of Orange. Protestants were banished from Austria Proper. In Bohemia, the Protestant faith and civil liberty disappeared together. In the Palatinate, the Protestant worship was suppressed. In France, the government was in arms against the Huguenots, and succeeded in wresting one stronghold from them after another. Spain seized the hopeful opportunity to renew the war with Holland.

<small>Spanish marriage spoken, written, preached against.</small> The Puritan pulpits "rang against the Spanish marriage." In vain James told the bishops to prevent the clergy from preaching on such topics; in vain he issued proclamations, forbidding the people to talk; their voices could no more be restrained than a "mountain torrent." Pamphlets were written and published which risked the ears, if not the lives of their authors. Most malignant of all, <small>Tom Tell-Truth.</small> "Tom Tell-Truth" attacked the king and his government on every side.

"I, a poor unknown subject," says the pamphleteer, "who hear the people talk, will undertake that discontinued but noble office of telling your Majesty the truth. Some there are that find fault with your government, even to wishing Elizabeth were alive again, for we have lost by change of sex. Great Britain, say they, is a great deal less than little England was wont to be. The excess of peace hath long since turned virtue into vice, and health into sickness.

"The Spaniards and the Duke of Bavaria play with your Majesty as men do with little children, at handy-dandy, which hand will you have? and give them nothing. The very losers at cards fall a cursing and swearing at the loss of the Palatinate; and, when told of your Majesty's proclamation not to talk about State affairs, answer in a chafe, 'You must give losers leave to speak.'

"You sent my Lord of Doncaster into France to mediate peace. It would have been better had the money spent on that embassage been given to the poor Huguenots; they may well call England the 'Land of Promise.' The princes that serve the Pope send arms; you—that should fight the battles of the Lord—ambassadors.

"No need for your Majesty to fear the Puritan religion; if a king will be absolute and dissolute, it is a wonder he will suffer any other; for it may be observed in some parts of Christendom* that let a king ruling over a Protestant people be never so wicked in his person, nor so enormous in his government, let him stamp vice with his example, let him remove the ancient bounds of sovereignty, and make every day new yokes and new scourges for

* *I.e.*, in England.

his poor people, let him take rewards and punishments out of the hand of justice, and distribute them without regard to right or wrong; in short, let him so excel in mischief, ruin, and oppression, as Nero compared with him may be held a very father of the people. Yet, when he hath done all that can be imagined to procure hate and contempt, he may go boldly in and out to his sports, clothed in his quilted garments, stiletto-proof, he shall not need to take either the less drink when he goes to bed, or the more thought when he riseth.

"His minions, a pack of ravenous curs, think all other subjects beasts, and only made for them to prey upon; they may revel and laugh, when all the kingdom mourns. His poor Protestant subjects shall only think he is given them of God for the punishment of their sins, for the preachers shall praise him and make the pulpit a stage of flattery, He ought to be obeyed, not because he is good but because he is their king. The subject is tied to such wonderful patience and obedience as doth almost verify that bold speech of Machiavel, when he said, 'Christianity made men cowards.'"*

James, after quarrelling with his Parliament, eagerly renewed the Marriage Treaty with Spain. He hankered more than ever after the Infanta's dower, and hoped, by means of Philip's interest with the Emperor, to secure the restoration of the Palatinate to Frederick. The Spaniards, on their side, were ready for a treaty which would secure them from a war with England while fighting in Germany. Following the suggestion of the Spanish ambassador, Charles undertook a secret journey to Spain, intending to conclude the treaty in person, and return home with his bride by his side (Feb., 1623). He was accompanied only by his father's favourite, George Villiers, Marquis (afterwards Duke) of Buckingham. *Charles and Buckingham go to Spain.*

Philip IV. took advantage of this foolish act to raise his demands, and obtained the consent of both James and Charles to secret articles, in which they engaged never to put the laws against Catholics into force, and to obtain the consent of Parliament to their repeal within three years. The promise was worthless; for James well knew the Parliament would never consent.

Wearied by the delays caused by the Spaniards, Charles returned home (Oct., 1623) before the time agreed on for the performance of the marriage ceremony, and afterwards wrote to the Earl of Bristol, with whom he had left his proxy, that there was to be neither marriage nor friendship, unless Philip consented to restore the Palatinate to Frederick by force of arms. This demand broke off the *Marriage Treaty with Spain broken off.*

* Somers' Tracts. II. 487—9.

treaty; for whatever delusive hopes Philip had held out to James, he had never undertaken to do more than endeavour, by his interest with the Emperor, to effect a peace favourable to Frederick. "We have a maxim of State," said a Spanish minister, for once speaking the truth, "that the King of Spain must never fight the Emperor."

Money voted by Parliament to carry on war with Spain. Buckingham, who had quarrelled with the Spaniards, was now eager for war. James found his favourite would leave him no peace till he summoned a Parliament, which he did sorely against his will, and then Buckingham, with Charles by his side to confirm his story, gave the two Houses a false account of what had taken place in Spain, declaring that the Spaniards broke off the match because the prince would not become a Catholic. James' court was not a good school for training a young prince in the duties of veracity; and it was certainly unfortunate for Charles' character that the circumstance of his first introduction to Parliament should have been of so ambiguous a nature. However, the story thus supported was believed for the time, and the question of peace and war with Spain being submitted to the Commons' consideration, they voted a subsidy of £300,000 to defend the coasts and help Holland. The same year four regiments crossed the Channel to assist the Dutch in fighting the Spaniards in the Netherlands (1624).

French Marriage Treaty. While the nation desired a Protestant alliance, the king only thought of a dowry. James now proposed to marry his son to another Catholic princess, Henrietta, sister of Louis XIII., King of France. He died, however, before the marriage took place, after a reign of twenty-three years (25th March, 1625). Though a French marriage was hailed as a deliverance after the Spanish project, yet the history of the next twenty years will perhaps seem to justify the Commons' antipathy to any Catholic marriage.

CHAPTER II.

CHARLES' FIRST PARLIAMENTS.—IMPEACHMENT OF BUCKINGHAM.—PETITION OF RIGHT.—(1625-1629).

How shall we do for money for these wars?
RICHARD II.

LITTLE was known of the new king, who was only twenty-four years old when he came to the throne, and had seldom appeared in public. His manners were grave and cold; he loved order and propriety. "I will have no drunkards in my bedchamber," he said, and turned out of office one of Buckingham's own brothers. The courtiers followed the lead of their master, and led outwardly decorous lives.*

But all hopes that were entertained of good agreement between king and people were doomed to a speedy end. Charles, who from his earliest years had heard taught at his father's court the doctrine of the Divine Right of kings, regarded it as the duty of Parliament submissively to vote supplies and carry out the wishes of the monarch, without questioning his government or bargaining for redress of grievances. His subjects, on the other hand, still smarting at James' disregard of the laws of the land and the privilege of Parliament, were determined to make the new king acknowledge the limits which the laws set to the prerogative of the Crown. {Certainty of quarrel between King and Parliament.}

An immediate cause of quarrel between Charles and the nation lay in the ascendancy of Buckingham, whose popularity had faded almost as soon as born. For if he had broken off the Spanish match on the grounds alleged by himself, he had since brought about the king's marriage with another Catholic, Henrietta Maria, sister of Louis XIII. It is rare for a favourite to

* Birch, I. 12;—Hutch. Mem.

remain supreme during the life of one master; still more rare for him to gain the affection of a second. Disappointment that Buckingham had not been ruined on the death of James now intensified the hatred felt by all classes towards him. Almost every officer employed by the Government was his creature, and at his command. "He on whom the duke smiled, was advanced; he on whom he frowned, cast down."* The highest nobles in the land found that, to stand well in the eyes of the king, they must court the favour of this haughty minion —this upstart country squire. Buckingham himself was ill-fitted to exercise power. Handsome, of fascinating manners, courageous and not implacable, he was yet vain withal, insolent, reckless, no genius, and utterly selfish; a man who would embroil his country in war to salve a wound of vanity, and then, after pledging his country's word, break it again to satisfy a change of whim. Such was the adviser with whom Charles met his first Parliament—a Parliament he soon summoned, as he was preparing a fleet for an expedition carefully kept secret from the country, and found himself in urgent need of money to fit this out. (18th June.)

Buckingham hated; his character.

Charles' first Parliament.

A dreadful plague was raging in London, of which the people were dying by thousands a week, so that the Houses were anxious to finish their business quickly and end the session. A bill for two subsidies,† amounting to something short of £200,000, was brought into the Lower House, and the members understanding from a message sent by the king

---

* Strafford, Letters and Despatches, I. 28.

† A subsidy was an income tax of 4s. in the pound upon the annual value of lands, and a property-tax of 2s. 8d. in the pound upon the actual value of goods. Those whose lands were not worth 20s. a year, or whose personal property was less than £3 in value, were not taxed. These subsidies were levied by commissioners, appointed by the Chancellor of the Exchequer from amongst the inhabitants of the county or borough. The assessment was made with great laxity; owing to this fact and to a constant rise in the money-value of lands, and goods (the price of wheat for instance, doubling in Elizabeth's reign, the real state of the subsidy was very much less than the nominal. A tenth or a fifteenth was generally voted in addition to the subsidy. These were originally the real tenth or fifteenth of all the movables or personal property of the subject. Each county or borough was responsible for a certain sum, which was levied by commissioners, appointed by its representatives in the Commons. Since the last valuation had been made in the reign of Edward III., in that of Charles I., when the purchasing power of money had decreased five times, the tenths and fifteenths instead of being taxes of 2s. and of 1s. 4d., were more like taxes of 5d. and 3d., in the £ respectively.

that he was satisfied with the amount, and would allow them to re-assemble at some more convenient season, began to disperse in large numbers to their homes. The House was already emptied of two-thirds of its members, when the Bill of Tonnage and Poundage, granting the king the custom duties, came before it.

Although the usual practice since the reign of Henry V. had been to grant the customs for life, the Commons, owing to the thinness of their House, and their wish for time to regulate the scale of duties, only granted them to Charles for a year, delaying to make him a life grant until the next session of Parliament. The bill reached the Upper House;* but Charles taking the contents as an insult, did not care to get it passed. The Parliament, however, might have adjourned without greater causes of discontent than the favour shown to Catholics and the rejection of the Tonnage and Poundage Bill, had not Buckingham deliberately fomented a quarrel. *[margin: Commons limit to a year the Bill of Tonnage and Poundage.]*

At the calling of James' last Parliament, when the match with Spain was broken off, the duke had allied himself with the popular leaders. Now, wishing to be entirely free of their control, especially in the conduct of the fleet, he determined to bring about a rupture with the Parliament and so effect a dissolution. Accordingly, on the day when the two Houses adjourned, and the king's assent was given to the bill for two subsidies, the members heard, to their dismay, that they were required, within a fortnight's time, to meet again at Oxford, a town where the plague had not yet appeared. (10th July.) *[margin: First Parliament adjourned to Oxford.]*

Short as the interval was between the two sessions, events were not wanting to breed suspicion and distrust. Dr. Montague, a clergyman, censured by the Commons for publishing books upholding the Divine Right of kings, and teaching confession, the use of images, and other Roman doctrines, had been appointed chaplain to the king. Charles had agreed in the French Marriage Treaty not to put the laws against Catholics into force; and these conditions, kept secret at the time, were now beginning to be divulged. The customs were still levied, though the king had no legal claim to them, having failed to carry the Bill for Tonnage and Poundage. The national fleet was not allowed to defend the nation; reserved for the king's high purposes, which were still unrevealed, it might not move to *[margin: Causes of discontent.]*

* This has been proved by Forster's Life of Sir John Eliot, i. v. 6.

clear the channel of the Turkish pirates, now ravaging the coasts, plundering merchant vessels, and carrying off captives by hundreds. There was an ugly story abroad, that eight ships had been actually lent the French king to assist him in blocking up the Huguenots, brother Protestants, in Rochelle. And now, as a crowning cause of discontent, the Parliament was re-assembled, at an unusual place, at the hottest time of a plague-smitten season (Aug 1st), and asked for sums that the king's ministers should have shown were necessary before. Long journeys were no light matter in those days, when roads were so bad that a coach and four could often go little more than four miles an hour. The members regarded the demand now made upon them almost as an insult, and felt convinced that Charles and Buckingham preferred this patent disregard of their convenience to revealing their whole policy at first. Thus, instead of granting a second supply, the House began to debate upon the abuses of the administration, and to point at the duke as the cause of them.

"Strange, the adjournment for only a few days, and that meeting there in Oxford! As it could not be that the king should have such mutability in himself, was not the real cause manifest to them? To have the whole kingdom hurried in such haste for the will and pleasure of *one subject!* All this was beyond example and comparison."*

Parliament dissolved. On this, Charles carried out Buckingham's intention, and dissolved the Parliament at once (12th Aug.). There had been good cause for the caution displayed by the Commons in granting supplies. In the spring, Charles and Buckingham, keeping their purpose concealed even from the Privy Council, pressed seven merchant vessels, and sent them with a ship of war under Captain Pennington's command, to be employed by Louis XIII. in blocking up the Huguenots in Rochelle.

Charles lends Louis ships to use against Rochelle. The sailors, however, showed their spirit. Learning at Dieppe their destined service, masters and men persisted in sailing back to the Downs, swearing that they would be hanged or thrown overboard before they would fight; while Pennington, who fully shared the feelings of the crews, wrote to the king, asking to be removed from command. In reply, however, he was only peremptorily ordered back to the French coast, and received a royal warrant authorizing him to

* See Forster's Life of Sir John Eliot, i. vi. 4.

compel obedience, "even unto the sinking of the ships." The men, being now told that the civil war in France was at an end, and that they were to be employed against Genoa, an ally of Spain, were with difficulty a second time persuaded to sail. At Dieppe, however, the truth could no longer be concealed. One vessel sailed back to the Downs, and the rest of the crews deserted their ships, leaving them to be manned by Frenchmen. A gunner—the only Englishman who took part in the service—was killed by a shot before Rochelle. Sailors desert the vessels.

This story was the common talk of the nation at the time of the dissolution of Parliament. An expedition so unpopular was especially unfortunate when the king was bent on going to war with Spain. No English king could hope to carry on war without obtaining large parliamentary grants, unless he was prepared to resort to illegal means of raising money. James had disliked Parliaments, and therefore, with good reason, clung to peace. Peace was still open to Charles, for war had not been declared; but he preferred breaking the law to breaking his resolution. Money was raised in the form of loans.

By these means, a fleet of ninety vessels was collected. It sailed in the autumn (4th Oct.). Buckingham, though lord-admiral, was too wise to command in person. Sir Edward Cecil, created Viscount Wimbledon for the occasion, was sent as deputy, to take the blame in case of failure. Success those who knew the state of the fleet hardly ventured to hope for. The agents the duke employed in manning, provisioning, and furnishing the vessels, had shamefully embezzled the funds, so that victuals were bad, men sick, and ships leaky, even at starting. Wimbledon received secret instructions to seize shipping and stores in the Spanish harbours, and to capture a fleet of richly laden merchantmen, returning home from the West Indies. Charles had great hopes that his exchequer would be replenished with Spanish bullion. Fleet sails against Spain.

Wimbledon, however, after entering the harbour of Cadiz and surprising a fort, found his troops disorderly, and finally returned to England without having fought an enemy or made a prize (Nov., Dec.). Disease broke out on the voyage home; hundreds perished at sea; hundreds were landed in a dying condition, solely, as it was said, through the bad food supplied for both soldiers and sailors. Upon the success of Returns home disgraced.

this expedition Buckingham's reputation was staked. It had been planned by him, by his advice its destination had been kept secret from Parliament, and he was justly regarded as the real author of the disgrace.

Charles summons a second Parliament. Meantime the loans had fallen short; the seamen came up to London clamouring for their pay; the royal exchequer was empty. There was no escape, and Charles had to summon a second Parliament, which met only some six months after the dissolution of the first (6th Feb., 1626).

The illegal methods of raising money, the employment of English ships for crushing French Protestants, the fiasco of the fleet, were all set down to Buckingham.

Buckingham advised to conciliate the country. The duke received hints of what was coming. "The office of high-admiral," wrote a friendly counsellor, "requires one whole man to execute it. Your grace hath another sea of business to wade through, and the voluntary resigning of this office would fill all men, yea, even your enemies, with affection." Buckingham, Lord High-Admiral of England and Ireland, Governor-General of seas and navy, Master of the Horse, Warden of the Cinque Ports, refused to resign one of these or his other titles to popular clamour.

But while Charles asked for a subsidy, the Commons appointed a committee to search into grievances. The committee soon satisfied themselves that all evils found their head and source in Buckingham. On this the king tried threats. " I must let you know," he wrote in a letter to the House, "that I will not allow any of my servants to be questioned amongst you, much less such as are of eminent place and near unto me. The old question was, What shall be done to the man whom the king will honour? But now it hath been the labour of some to seek what may be done against him whom the king thinks fit to honour. .... I wish you would hasten my supply, or else it will be worse for yourselves, for if any ill happen, I think I shall be the last that shall feel it."

Buckingham impeached. The Commons, undaunted, impeached the duke for high crimes and misdemeanours (22nd April). In cases of parliamentary impeachment, the House of Commons is accuser, the House of Lords judge. The earliest case occurred towards the end of Edward the Third's reign (1376). From the time of Henry VI. there was no impeachment for nearly two centuries (1449—1621), till the practice was revived in the reign of James I., when two of the king's ministers were impeached for bribery and corruption—Bacon, lord chancellor, in 1621 ; the Earl of Middlesex, lord treasurer, in 1624. In times when the Parliament and the crown, the law and the prerogative, were struggling for mastery, and when the crown dismissed and appointed at pleasure both judges and ministers of State, such a power was a most useful weapon in the hands of the Commons. Now, since the trials of Warren Hastings (1791) and Lord Melville (1805), the right of impeachment has ceased to be exercised, because the relation of all parties has changed. The law has gained the victory over the prerogative. Courts of justice are independent, and ministers of the crown only hold office at the pleasure of the Commons.

The reverse of all this might have been affirmed at the time when Buckingham was impeached. The special allegations against him were his holding many offices at the same time, selling places of judicature, lending ships to Louis to be used against Rochelle, with various other offences, in all thirteen. *True charge against Buckingham.* But the Commons did not, in fact, impeach Buckingham for any particular crime. Their quarrel with him was that he alone possessed the royal ear, and that he counselled Charles to commit illegal acts at home, and pursue a wavering course of foreign policy, detrimental to the interests of the Protestants. The English nation has always been intolerant of tyranny at second hand. It seemed to them now monstrous that the wishes of people and Parliament should be over-ruled by the fancies of one unworthy favourite. They determined, therefore, to impeach the duke, as the only constitutional means then possessed of securing the change of ministry they desired.

"What vast treasures he has gotten," said Sir John Eliot, conducting the impeachment before the Lords, " what infinite sums of money, and what a mass of lands ! If your lordships please to calculate, you will find it all amounting to little less than the whole of the subsidies which the king has had within that time. A lamentable example of the subjects' bounties so to be employed ! His profuse expenses, his superfluous feasts, his magnificent buildings, his riots, his excesses, what are they but the visible evidences of an express exhausting of the State, a chronicle of the immensity of his waste of the revenues of the crown ? No wonder, then, our king is now in want, this man abounding so. And as long as he abounds, the king must still be wanting. . . . *Speech of Sir John Eliot.*

"Of all the precedents I can find, none so near resembles him as doth Sejanus, and him Tacitus describes thus: that he was *audax, sui obtegens, in alios criminator : juxta adulatio et superbia.** If your lordships please to measure him by this, pray see in what they vary. He is *bold*, and of such a boldness, I dare be bold to say, as is seldom heard of. He is *secret* in his purposes, and more, that we have showed already. Is he a *slanderer?* Is he an *accuser?* I wish this Parliament had not felt it, nor that which was before. As for his *pride and flattery*, what man can judge the greater? . . And now, my lords, I will conclude with a particular censure given on the Bishop of Ely in the time of Richard I. That prelate had the king's treasures at his command, and had luxuriously abused them. His obscure kindred were married to earls, barons, and others of great rank and place. No man's business could be done without his help. He would not suffer the king's council to advise in the highest affairs of state. He gave *ignotis personis et obscuris* the custody of castles and great trusts. He ascended to such a height of insolence and pride, that he ceased to be fit for characters of mercy. And therefore, says the record, of which I now hold the original, *per totam insulam publicè proclametur ;*—PEREAT QUI PERDERE CUNCTA FESTINAT; OPPRIMATUR NE OMNES OPPRIMAT"† (10th May).

Charles visits the House of Lords, When Charles heard that Eliot had compared the duke to Sejanus, he exclaimed, "He must intend me for Tiberius!" and with the defendant by his side, went to the Upper House, and tried to overawe the duke's judges by informing the Lords that he had given orders for punishment of some insolent speeches spoken to them yesterday, and that he could himself be a witness to clear the duke of every charge brought against him (11th May). He was as good as *and imprisons two members of the Commons.* his word, and the same day committed to the Tower two of the managers of the impeachment, Sir Dudley Digges and Sir John Eliot. The Lords, of whom many were concealed enemies of the favourite, let the king speak and depart in silence. The Commons agreed to do no business until their members were restored to the House.

Charles angrily dissolves the Parliament. Charles might have ended the struggle by a dissolution, but as he still hoped to obtain a supply, he preferred to release the two members. Finding, however, that the Commons would not grant money, unless the duke was first removed from office, he determined to put a stop to the impeachment, by dissolving the Parliament. "No, not a minute!" he said to the Lords, who came in person to petition him to stay the

* Tac. Ann. iv. 1. † Forster's Life of Sir J. Eliot, i. vii. 6.

dissolution, and the next day he carried out his purpose (15th June).

The people had been anxiously watching the course of events within the House. "This is the king's last Parliament," they said, aware of Charles' indignation at the impeachment of his minister. "And now that the Parliament is dissolved, and the duke still in power, what will follow next?" "Is it not time to pray? Unless God show us the way out, we are but in an ill case."* {Fears entertained in the country.}

Charles did not keep his subjects long in doubt of his intentions. In fact, a series of measures followed, attacking more classes and more interests within a shorter period than had been ever known in English history.

Although Charles was already engaged in war with Spain, and had not received a penny from his last Parliament, he had still the temerity to enter into war with France. Several causes of quarrel existed between himself and his brother-in-law, Louis XIII. Shortly before the death of James, Cardinal Richelieu, Louis' chief minister, had effected a league between France and the Protestant powers (1624). The French were to fight the armies of Austria and Spain, while the King of Denmark, Christian IV., assisted by men and money from France, was to lead the Protestant forces of Germany for the recovery of the Palatinate. {Coalition of Protestant powers against Spain and Austria.} The fleets of England and Holland were to attack Spain, while the Turks were engaged to fall upon Hungary. But as soon as Louis had reduced the Huguenots in Rochelle by the aid of the ships borrowed from Charles, he deserted his allies, and made peace with Spain (March, 1626). The reason of this sudden change in French policy was that the Huguenots, regardless of the interests of their co-religionists, seized the moment when France was about to engage in foreign war, to rise in arms against the government. The English contingent had already been fitted out with the money granted in James' last Parliament. But Louis now refused permission for these troops to pass through France on their way to join the German army, so that they were obliged to take a long sea passage to Zealand. Disease broke

* Ellis. 3rd Series, 227, 228.

out, and 5000 men out of the 14,000 men perished before they saw the face of a foe.*

Christian IV., thus left unsupported, was defeated at Lutter (27th August, 1626), and the armies of the emperor, Ferdinand II., were soon overrunning the north of Germany (1627-8). Charles, who had agreed in his marriage treaty not to put the laws against Catholics into force, and had afterwards lent Louis ships, expecting, in return, to receive aid for the recovery of the Palatinate, naturally felt aggrieved at the conduct of the French government. Moreover, Buckingham had some personal disagreement with Richelieu, which was believed to be his only motive for breaking the peace between the two nations.

War with France. The war was unpopular in England, because the French, through their well-known jealousy of Spain and Austria, were regarded as the natural allies of the German Protestants. But Charles and Buckingham were ill advised enough to hope that, by merely declaring themselves friends of the Huguenots, they would be carried along on a flood-tide of popularity, and thus be able to raise money enough by illegal means for the support of two wars at once. A general loan was demanded; every man, rich or poor, was required to give in the same proportion as he had been rated in the last subsidy granted by Parliament. This so-called loan was in fact nothing less than a tax laid on land and property, without consent of Parliament. Henry VIII., the most absolute of the Tudor sovereigns, once endeavoured to raise money by means of a general loan; but even in his time the attempt produced widespread discontent; a serious insurrection broke out in Suffolk, and the imposition was withdrawn (1525). Since that time a steady increase in wealth and knowledge had for more than a century been strengthening the middle classes, and confirming their attachment to their liberties. Leaders were now to be found in the House of Commons, ready boldly to point the attention of the nation to acts of arbitrary power, and to brave the consequences of the royal displeasure. It was

Money raised by illegal means.

---

* Vessels were not then required, as they happily are now, to have on board a sufficient supply of lime juice, or other preventives against consequences of a salt diet. Hence the fatal ravages of scurvy in those times. The symptoms of this disease are described as—discoloured spots, swelled legs, extraordinary lassitude and dejection, sudden death resulting on the least motion or exertion of strength. See G. Anson's Voyage, I. x.

hardly likely, therefore, that an act from which Henry VIII. and Cardinal Wolsey had shrunk, should fail to rouse indignation when attempted by Charles and his detested favourite.

Opposition arose on all sides from rich and poor. The prisons were full of gentlemen who refused to lend. Lincolnshire "almost rebelled;" Shropshire "utterly denied." Several gentlemen, on being brought before the Council Chamber, refused to kneel, for fear of seeming to acknowledge that they were in any way responsible for a legitimate refusal of an illegitimate demand. In London, only two or three in a parish would pay, and that though goods were seized, and the duke threatened, saying, "Sirrah, take heed what you do; did not you speak treason at such a time?" Charles himself was reported to be so inflamed against refusers, that he was "vowing a perpetual remembrance, as well as a present punishment."* {Opposition to loan offered by all classes.}

Five gentlemen, imprisoned for refusing the loan, applied to the Court of King's Bench for a writ of *habeas corpus*.† The judge sent a writ to the gaoler, commanding him to produce his prisoners before the court, with the warrant on which they had been imprisoned. The gaoler replied that they were committed by a warrant from the king's council, by the special command of his Majesty, but that no special cause of imprisoment was mentioned. Accordingly, the question was pleaded before the judges of the King's Bench, whether or not the king had power to commit his subjects to prison without alleging any crime against them. The court was crowded, and shouts of applause were raised at the arguments of the prisoners' counsel. The judges, however, gave judgment in favour of the king, and the five gentlemen were remanded to prison. {Judgment of Court of King's Bench concerning personal liberty of subject.}

The poor, who refused the loans, were pressed into the service of the army and navy. On some districts an extra imposition was laid, called "coat and conduct money," for fitting out the soldiers. The rich had soldiers quartered on them, who acted as though the king's soldiers were as much above the law as their master. Not content with killing and carrying off oxen and sheep from the owners' grounds, they murdered and robbed upon the highways, "nay, in fairs and markets, for to meet a poor man coming from the market {Disorderly conduct of soldiers.}

* Straff. Letters, I. 38; Birch. 190, 154, 157, 164.   † See p. 16.

with a pair of shoes, and take them from him, was but a sport and merriment." The highways became so insecure, that, to suppress disorders, Charles issued commissions to execute martial law. The ordinary course of justice was then set aside, and the commissioners tried and sentenced the soldiers under forms more summary than those of the common law. In spite, however, of the crimes committed, the remedy seemed to the nation worse than the disease. Standing armies and courts-martial being alike unknown to English statute or common law, Charles had no more legal power to issue commissions to try soldiers by martial law than he had to try civilians.* To increase the general indignation, the clergy received orders to preach up the duty of passive obedience and the divine right of kings. Those who looked out for promotion complied, but the preachers were regarded as mere lacqueys of the court. It was adding insult to injury, first to take the people's properties illegally, and then to tell them that submission was a duty, pleasing to God.

Commissions issued for execution of martial law.

Clergy preach duty of passive obedience.

At last, at the expense of so much bitterness between king and commons, a fleet of 100 vessels was fitted out, and sailed for France (27th June). Buckingham took the command himself; a landing was effected on the Isle of Rhé, and the Huguenots in Rochelle were persuaded to trust to the honour of the English, and try the event of war against Louis XIII. once more. But, after two months had been spent in an unsuccessful siege of the fortified town of St. Martin,† Buckingham made a disastrous retreat along a narrow causeway, beset on either side with salt pits and ditches. So many officers and soldiers were slain, so many taken prisoners, that not above half the number of those who sailed returned to their homes. Beside the cries of private mourning

Expedition of Buckingham to Rochelle.

---

* Kings of England had indeed always exercised the right of issuing ordinances of war for the regulation of their armies. But this military law had been confined to military offences committed on actual service, while these 'soldiers, mariners, and other dissolute persons,' were (1) not on actual service, and (2) had committed offences which were cognizable at the courts of common law; hence fears were naturally entertained that so tempting a method of procedure would be extended to civilians. Since England has had a standing army, a Mutiny Act is annually passed, allowing courts-martial for punishment of military offences, and reserving the crown power to frame further articles in case of actual war.

† For map, see p. 46.

were heard those of public indignation. Buckingham was believed to have gone to Rochelle in a pet, merely to gratify his spleen against Louis, without caring either for the Huguenots or his troops; and the people, in whose minds the remembrance of Elizabeth's triumphs was still fresh, went back to King John's time to find a parallel disgrace, describing it as "the shamefullest overthrow the English have received since we lost Normandy."

A clamour was raised for a Parliament. The coasts were infested; pirates entered the harbours, and sailed up the rivers; the very fishermen were afraid to put out; trade was decaying, for merchants refused to build vessels only to be pressed into the king's service; the sailors came round about the palace at Whitehall, crying out for pay. Charles had pledged himself to relieve Rochelle, the siege of which, by Louis, was the only outcome of his intervention; but how he was to carry on two wars, in the face of all these difficulties, was a question to puzzle the wisest head. The lords of the council were afraid to try forced loans again, and Charles, though, as he truly said, he did "abominate the name," consented to follow their advice, and send out the summons for another Parliament. *Charles summons a third Parliament.*

The House was filled with patriots, elected against court candidates by overwhelming majorities. Eliot, Pym, Coke, Selden, Wentworth, were all there; and Oliver Cromwell, a young man of twenty-nine, took his seat for the first time as member for the town of Huntingdon. *Enemies of court in large majority.* Charles opened this, his third Parliament, with threats (17th March). "If you," he said, "should not do your duties in contributing what the State at this time needs, I must, in discharge of my conscience, use those other means which God hath put into my hands." The threat only made the Commons more determined to put an end to the loans, billeting of soldiers, and imprisonments, "those other means" which had caused such just and bitter resentment.

Debates on granting the king a supply, and on finding a remedy for grievances, advanced hand in hand. The decision of the judges, that the king might not commit a subject to prison, *except at his pleasure,** was thought a wanton outrage on the intelligence of the nation. According to this theory, the laws were only binding on the king so long as he graciously chose not

* Forster's Life of Sir J. Eliot, ii. ix. 2.

to act in right of his royal prerogative, so that Acts of Parliament, regarded for centuries as the bulwarks of public liberty, were rendered absolutely meaningless.

Judgment of King's Bench canvassed in Commons. "To have my body pent up in a gaol," exclaimed an indignant patriot, "without remedy of law, and to be so adjudged . . If this be law, why do we talk of liberties? Why do we trouble ourselves with a dispute about law, franchises, property of goods, and the like? What may a man call his own, if not the liberty of his person? I am weary of treading these ways."

A security was needed that the old laws should be kept in force, and the king's prerogative be prevented from trampling them under foot. "We must vindicate—what?" said Wentworth, "new things? No! our ancient, lawful, and vital liberties! We must reinforce the laws made by our ancestors. We must set such a stamp upon them as no licentious spirit shall dare hereafter to invade them."

The Commons, however, still believed the king would feel bound in conscience to respect a law which he passed himself; *Petition of Right.* and, under this impression, drew up a bill, in the form of a Petition of Right, to serve as a new guarantee for the preservation of liberty. They called their bill the Petition of Right, because it was but a confirmation of old laws, of rights already possessed. The Petition demanded :

1st. That no freeman be required to give any gift, loan, benevolence, or tax without common consent by Act of Parliament.

2nd. That no freeman be imprisoned or detained contrary to the laws of the land.

3rd. That soldiers and mariners be not billeted in private houses.

4th. That commissions to punish soldiers and sailors by martial law be revoked, and no more issued.

The Upper House, which the king had partially packed by the creation of several new lords, proposed to add to the petition the following saving clause :—" We humbly present this petition to your Majesty, with due regard to leave entire that sovereign power wherewith your Majesty is entrusted for the protection of your people." The Commons, however, refused to accept the amendment, which conceded the very point at issue. "All our petition," said Pym, "is for the laws of England; this power seems to be another power distinct from the power of the law. We can-

Saving clause proposed by Lords, rejected by Commons.

not leave him a sovereign power, for he was never possessed of it." After several conferences between the two Houses, the Lords yielded and passed the petition in the form desired by the Commons (27th May). Charles, being in want of money, did not venture in any direct manner to refuse his consent, but when the petition was read before assembled King, Lords, and Commons, the lord keeper read out, instead of the usual words by which the royal assent is signified, a new form, "that the king wished that right should be done, and that he held himself in conscience as much obliged to maintain their just rights and liberties as his own prerogative" (2nd June). The Commons were engaged in preparing a remonstrance against the evil advisers by whose counsel this worthless answer had been given, when a message came from the king, forbidding the House to meddle with affairs of State (5th June). There followed a prolonged silence. Not to meddle with affairs of State, meant that they must endure the ascendancy of the duke, and see the name of England despised abroad from a policy which was at once meddlesome, feeble, and fickle; while at home outrages were done to the dearest liberties of their country, which it was their bounden duty to defend. Some members sat down in tears, dumb through grief; others mingled their speech with tears; some hundred wept in all, they felt so much was at stake. "Let us palliate no longer," cried the old lawyer, Sir Edward Coke, "if we do, God will not prosper us. I think the Duke of Buckingham is the cause of all our miseries—that man is the grievance of grievances; it is not the king but the duke"—(a great cry of "'Tis he, 'tis he!" "Yea, yea!" "Well moved, well spoken")—"that saith, 'We require you not to meddle with State government or the ministers thereof'" (5th June).

Charles' first answer to Petition of Right.

Charles forbids House of Commons to meddle with affairs of State.

Two days later, Charles yielded, the Petition of Right was read a second time, and the reply given in the usual form: "*Soit droit fait comme il est désiré*" (7th June).

King's second answer to Petition of Right.

The Commons, on their side, passed a bill for five subsidies, after which Parliament was prorogued (26th June).

While Parliament was sitting, another fleet which was sent to Rochelle, returned without raising the siege. "What wonder!" said the people; "was not the commander Buckingham's brother-in-law?" No allowance had been made for the shallowness of that sandy coast: Lord Denbigh, finding his ships drew too much water to approach the city, seemed only too glad of an excuse for sailing away at once. It was believed that the expedition had been got up, not to save Rochelle, but merely to blind the eyes of Parliament. One of the duke's household, called Dr. Lamb, was set upon by the rabble in the streets of London, and so brutally knocked about that he died the same night. The city magistrates could not, or would not, find the offenders. The people sang,

"Let Charles and George do what they can,
The duke shall die like Dr. Lamb."

Felton murders Buckingham. Felton, described as a gentleman of low stature, few words, and melancholy spirit, after pondering over a remonstrance of the Commons, declaring Buckingham the cause of all the evils under which the kingdom suffered, conceived it his duty to rid his country of an enemy. The duke was at Portsmouth, preparing to set sail immediately in command of another fleet for the relief of Rochelle. He was in company with several officers, French and English, when, in passing through a dark lobby leading from a breakfast-room into a hall, he was stabbed to the heart. "The villain hath killed me!" he cried, pulled out the knife, staggered to a table, and fell dead in the arms of the bystanders (23rd Aug.). No one had seen the blow struck, and suspicion was falling on the Frenchmen, when Felton stepped forward out of the crowd and said, "I am the man who did the deed, let no one suffer who is innocent." The people could not restrain their joy; healths were drunk to the murderer, verses written in his honour. Crowds gathered to see him on his way to London and the Tower, greeting him as the slayer of the Philistine. "Now, God bless thee, little David," "The Lord be merciful unto thee," "The Lord comfort thee," were the cries that reached his ears.

Judges declare use of torture against the common law. On being brought before the council and threatened by Bishop Laud with the rack, unless he revealed the names of his associates, he replied that he alone was author of the deed, and that as for the rack, he could not say whether torture might make him accuse his lordship, or which of their lordships. The threat was not put into execution. The judges unanimously declared the use of torture was contrary to the common law of England, and the king did not think it prudent to override their decision. Felton was hanged at Tyburn. To the last he felt little remorse for the murder. Though he confessed he had done wrong in shedding blood, he could not be brought to doubt but that good would result to Church and State from his act.

The duke was only thirty-five. Charles called him "his martyr," and never forgave those who opposed him during life, or spoke ill of him after death. His fate shows the truth of the common maxim that those who are above the law are above the protection of law; but the crime was the crime of a fanatic. Not a shadow of suspicion rests on the popular leaders. They were at once too far-sighted and too honourable. Acts of treachery and violence, whatever the immediate advantage gained, are sure in the long run to recoil to the injury of the side that practises them. Sooner or later, violence is condemned by public opinion, for in a constitutional struggle, the mass of the nation have really more the feelings of a jury than of parties to a case. It is only by winning a favourable judgment from the large and wavering masses, that any party, which has no armed force behind it, can obtain a sure and final triumph. Violent partisans are always to be found ready to approve and employ all means without distinction to advance their ends; but the English leaders knew that the statue of Wingless Victory can only stand in the shrine of law and right. *Popular leaders not implicated in the crime.*

The fleet, which now sailed under Lord Lindsay, was as unsuccessful as though Buckingham himself had lived to command it. While Charles delayed, Richelieu's genius and energy were at work. The city was gradually shut in on the land side by a line of circumvallation extending nine miles, while a vast mole of nearly a mile in length was raised across the roadstead. After two unsuccessful attempts to force their way through the mole, the English returned without having placed a morsel of food within reach of the starving inhabitants. The town had a strong position between the sea and the marshes on the rocky promontory from which it got its name of the "little rock." Originally a colony of serfs, who had fled from the oppressions of their feudal lords, it had a tradition of political as well as of religious freedom. Once a fief of the English kings, and now much dearer as a stronghold of Protestantism, the English were deeply interested in its heroic resistance, and regarded themselves and their country as irretrievably disgraced, when, after 16,000 were said to have died of famine, the city at last surrendered at discretion (8th Oct., 1628).

Fall of Rochelle. The fall was a fatal blow to the cause of the Huguenots. Liberty of conscience was still left them, but their fortresses were destroyed, their assemblies, their privileges, their organization by churches abolished. Instead of being a power within the state, they became a sect.*

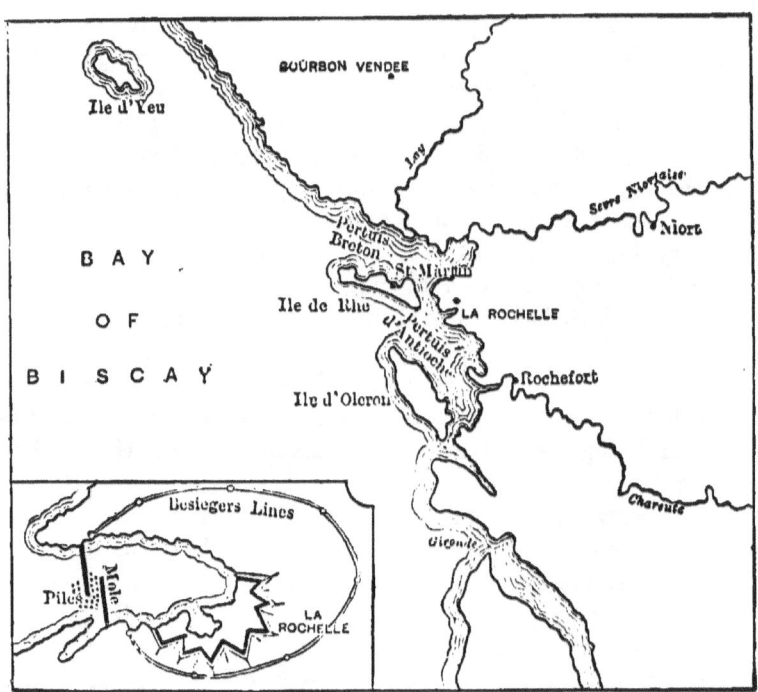

The English, after this defeat of their religion, could not console themselves for long with the victory they had obtained over the government in the Petition of Right. At first the people in London rung bells and made bonfires, believing their liberties to be now secured; but their mistake was soon proved. Notwith-

* Lavallée, Hist. de France.

standing the king's distinct promise to respect the rights enumerated in the Petition, the customs were still levied. A merchant, a member of the Commons, who refused to pay £200 duty, had his goods seized to the value of £5000. "If all the Parliament were in you, we would take your goods," said the custom-house officers. Men who ventured on speaking or writing against the introduction of Catholic ceremonies and doctrines into a Protestant church, were brought before the Star Chamber on charges of libel, fined, cast into prison, and, in some cases, mutilated. Bishop Laud, a cruel persecutor of Puritans, was translated to the see of London (July). Clergymen, tried and censured by the last Parliament for publishing books and sermons maintaining the right of the king to take his subjects' goods without their own consent, were now rewarded with bishoprics or rich livings. Charles did not seem to realize the alteration he had made in his position by giving his consent to the Petition of Right. Previously, no special tie bound him to act by law. No special charge of deceit, therefore, could be brought against him if, like his father, he tried to exalt his position into that of a French king, free arbitrarily to tax and imprison his subjects. But now a victory had been fairly won by patriots armed only with the legal weapons of the constitution, and by confirming the old charters by a new statute, he had pledged his word to their observance ; by infringement now, he would lose the confidence as well as the affection of his subjects. *Petition of Right broken by ministers.*

Meantime the place of Buckingham was filled. The name of Sir Thomas Wentworth had hitherto been counted among the chief leaders of the opposition. But his subsequent conduct seemed to show that his actions had been dictated by pride rather than by patriotism. Haughty and ambitious, scorning to hold a second place, he had chosen to rise to influence as an enemy of the court, rather than lower himself and sue for favour to Buckingham. Promotion, however, is sure to be offered to a dangerous opponent, who will sacrifice principles to place. A month before Buckingham's death, Wentworth was raised to a barony. Thus when Felton made the first place vacant, Charles had already enlisted in his service a man, whose great abilities and commanding nature rendered him far more competent to be his adviser in the exercise of arbitrary government than the vain *Sir Thomas Wentworth fills Buckingham's place in council.*

and frivolous favourite he had lost. Wentworth made no conditions as to the policy to be pursued; thus he left his party, not to forward their views in office, but simply to gratify his inordinate ambition. He appointed a meeting with his old friend and companion, Pym, at Greenwich, and there discoursed to him "of the dangers they were like to run by the courses they were in, and what advantages they might have, if they would listen to some offers which would probably be made to them from court." "You need not use all this art," replied Pym, "to tell me that you have a mind to leave us. But remember what I tell you. You are going to be undone. And remember also, that though you leave us now, I will never leave you, while your head is upon your shoulders."

Second session of Charles' Third Parliament. Thus Wentworth, now Viscount Wentworth, and a member of the Privy Council, at the next session of Parliament sat amongst the king's ministers in the Upper House, ready to throw all the weight of his abilities and eloquence upon the side of arbitrary power (20th Jan.).

The Commons immediately began to debate upon their grievances. 'The goods of merchants had been seized for refusing to pay illegal customs. Further, though no man ought to lose life or limb but by the law, the Star Chamber sentenced men to lose their ears.' "Next it will be our arms, and then our legs, and so our lives." Charles, not content with thus breaking his royal promise, had descended to subterfuge. Though by the king's own orders the Petition of Right, with the proper answer, had been entered in the journals of the House, yet copies had subsequently been dispersed over the country, with the first evasive answer annexed, as well as the second. It was found that the printer had received royal orders to suppress the true copies, and make a new impression. 'Noblesse oblige,' but such doubtful dealing could only bring obloquy on the sovereign. The strength of loyalty lies in sentiment, and this was a fatal omen of the future for king and commons.

Commons inquire into illegal acts of ministers and officers of executive. Meantime Charles sent message after message bidding the House pass a bill, granting him the customs, for this was in fact the only purpose for which he had called the Parliament. "Let the merchants have their goods restored," said the Commons, "before the bill is passed." "Kings," said one, "ought not, by the law of God, thus to oppress their subjects. I know we have a good king, and this is the advice of his wicked ministers, but there is nothing can be more dishonourable unto him." They proceeded to question those ministers; they demanded of the king's attorney-general by whose warrant he had discharged Catholic priests; they demanded of the farmers of the customs on what warrants they had seized the goods of merchants who refused to pay illegal duties; they demanded of the judges on what grounds they had refused to let the merchants have their cause tried at law. No acts could have given more dire offence to Charles. Other Houses of Commons had attacked some single minister of state, but none had ever ventured on questioning the conduct of the king's servants at large. An immediate dissolution being fully expected, the popular leaders determined not to separate, without first passing a vote against the illegal levying of the customs. On the 2nd of March Eliot rose to address the House. The Speaker, Finch, a thorough courtier, rose also, and saying that he had the king's orders for an immediate adjournment, left his chair. Two members, Denzil Hollis and Valentine, standing on either side, forced him back to his seat, and held him down, whilst Eliot made a short speech, in which he declared it to be the duty of the House to maintain religion and the rights of the subject, and brought forward a declaration to that effect, which he desired the Speaker to put to the vote. But Finch, with tears, refused to receive it or put it to the vote, declaring that he had the king's command to the contrary. Again he tried to rise from his chair, and again was forced down by Hollis and Valentine. "God's wounds," said Hollis, "he should sit there until it pleased them to rise." "You are the disgrace of your country, and the blot of a noble family," cried one of his own kinsmen. The king's councillors, coming forward to rescue the Speaker, were forcibly driven back to their seats. Blows were given, and sword hilts handled. "Let all," said Strode, "who desire the declaration read and put to the vote, stand up." Whereupon the majority of the House started to their feet, and Eliot flung down the paper before them. At this moment a messenger from the king came to the door, with orders to the sergeant to withdraw with the mace, which, by custom, always

The Speaker refuses to put Eliot's declaration to the vote.

Tumult in the House. King's messenger refused admittance.

4

lies on the Commons' table, while the House is proceeding with business. No sooner, however, had the sergeant laid his hand upon the mace, than a cry was raised to lock the door, and Sir Miles Hobert turned the lock, and put the key in his pocket. Eliot then read a protest against any who should levy or pay customs. "And for myself," he said, "I protest further, as I am a gentleman, if my fortune be ever again to meet in this honourable assembly, where I now leave, I will begin again." While he was speaking, the gentleman usher of the black rod, sent by Charles to pronounce a dissolution, vainly knocked at the door for admittance. And now Hollis, standing by the Speaker's chair, with a paper containing three resolutions in his hand, called out, that he put the question, "that they were traitors who should introduce Popery; that they were traitors who should levy the customs, ungranted by Parliament; that they were traitors who should voluntarily pay them." "Ay, ay," was shouted on all sides. The door was unlocked, and the members rushed out, carrying away in the stream a third messenger waiting outside from the king (2nd March).

The next day Charles signed a proclamation for a dissolution. The Commons "had," he said, "tried to erect an universal overwhelming power to themselves, which belongs only to us, and not to them." They had in fact tried to gain control over the executive power. So far the charge was true. The nation was weary of entering upon wars without its own approval or consent; of giving money for one object, and seeing it spent on another; of seeing good laws not only violated by ministers of the crown, but rendered nugatory by the quibbles of time-serving judges. The Petition of Right was already a dead letter. Judges, ministers, custom-house officers, all acted as though the king's consent to such a law had never been given. The Commons saw that it was but a vain guarantee against tyranny to 'have a king's word to the contrary.' They were on the right track when they sought to make the officers of the executive personally responsible, as according to the principles of the constitution they had always been. Charles, on his side, published a proclamation against Parliament, threatening "certain vipers of the Commonwealth" with condign punishment, and declaring it "presumption for any one to prescribe to him any time for the calling of that assembly."

CHAPTER III.

ELEVEN YEARS OF ARBITRARY GOVERNMENT.—1629—1640.

KPEΩN. ἄλλῳ γὰρ ἤ μοι χρή γε τῆσδ' ἄρχειν χθονός;
AIMΩN. πόλις γὰρ οὐκ ἔσθ' ἥτις ἀνδρός ἐσθ' ἑνός.
KPEΩN. οὐ τοῦ κρατοῦντος ἡ πόλις νομίζεται;
AIMΩN. καλῶς ἐρήμης γ' ἄν σὺ γῆς ἄρχοις μόνος.
CREON. For my behoof I have right to rule this land.
HAEMON. It is no state where all belongs to one.
CREON. Is not the state the sovereign's property?
HAEMON. A manless state how grand to rule—alone!—Soph. Ant. 739.

CHARLES had now made up his mind to govern without the aid of Parliament, and thus raise himself into the position of an absolute monarch. His education and his character had alike tended to blind his mind to the fact that, from the subjects' point of view, such an intention was criminal. Princes rarely converse with their fellows on an equal footing, or hear their own opinions and actions freely criticized. They are, therefore, apt to grow up prejudiced. Charles was especially unfortunate in this respect. In James' court, no man could maintain a footing who was not obsequious enough to let his own opinion follow that of his Majesty. The divine right by which kings rule, the superiority of the prerogative to the law, the subject's duty of passive obedience, were household words to the young prince. His social training was as bad as his political; the companions amongst whom he was thrown, were not only obsequious but immoral, and when he became king, his father's influence lived on in one of the most worthless of his favourites. Edward I., indeed, a king whose only thought was for his people's "security under fixed laws and customs" yet failed in inspiring his son with any such noble aims, though he banished the evil companions who were bent on marring that son's mind. But Charles was in all points a prince far superior to Edward II. Had he been trained by a father endowed with the noble qualities of Edward I., he might have run a peaceful course and lived and

Charles' education and character.

4—2

died in accord with his subjects. Charles' virtues, in fact, were his own, and displayed themselves in spite of his education. His manners and his tastes were refined, and his enemies were never able to deny that he was both a good husband and a good father. On the other hand, nature had bestowed on him no special gifts to counteract the evil effects of his political training. His character was cold and unbending, and he was without any generous sympathies, that might have brought him to recognize good in cause or man opposed to his own fixed ideas. Obstinate and opinionated when he came to the throne at twenty-four, so he remained to the last day of his life; no amount of experience proved sufficient to teach him the necessity of yielding to public opinion, or even of listening with patience to arguments that offended his high notions of what was due to himself as a king. With such an education and such a character, he was born in an evil time for himself. He had found a minister who could put his wishes into act, for Wentworth set himself, with all the energy of his nature, to the support of arbitrary government. Having shared in the counsels of the patriots, and knowing their deep-rooted love of liberty, this clear-sighted counsellor never deceived himself into thinking that any half measures were sufficient for success. On the Continent, many instances had proved that a standing army was the surest support to an arbitrary throne. With a fleet only and without such an army, Wentworth would say, a government had but 'one leg to stand upon.' To secure an army he must have money. At present much of the monies taken from the pockets of the people passed into those of courtiers and their dependents, instead of enriching the royal exchequer. It was easier to save money than to get it, and Wentworth, therefore, advocated economy in administration, in fact, the true financial policy of getting money's worth for money given. But Wentworth's advice was too good and his energy too great for his master. The minister was to be like the dwarf in the fairy tale, he was not to prescribe prudence but to save his employer from the results of imprudence. Advancing Wentworth as he did, Charles shrank from opposing the wishes of his wife and curtailing the perquisites of his friends. Under these conditions, the king's government might be violent, it could never be strong.

Advice of Wentworth too good for Charles.

Wentworth speedily concluded peace with France (April, 1629) and Spain (Nov., 1630). Experience had already proved that it was impossible to carry on war without applying to Parliament for aid. To provide for the expenses of the court and government was no easy matter, even when the country was at peace.

Charles' vain and passionate wife, Henrietta Maria, who in an ill-temper could dash her hands through the panes of a window, or turn a whole company out of her presence with one of her royal scowls, was not a queen to be easily guided by a minister. With some, however, her smiles were as potent as her frowns, and she soon won an ascendancy over her husband equal to that which Buckingham once exercised. To her, happiness meant a gay life at Whitehall, with a constant series of balls and masques, so that the expenses of the court rose rapidly, and soon reached sums far larger than those considered enormous in the time of James. Delighting, as she did, in the exercise of power and patronage, it was to the queen, and not to the king, or to Wentworth, that courtiers and their dependents applied, in order to obtain lucrative monopolies, offices, or pensions. The court offices were, indeed, regarded as a sort of booty. Fixed salaries there were none; but fees and perquisites were numerous, and every man's hand was open to a bribe. There was no shame felt in the matter. The Earl of Dorset, a member of council, and a judge in the Star Chamber, openly declared that he thought it no crime for a courtier to receive a reward from one for whom he procured a favour.

<small>Character of Henrietta Maria.</small>

<small>Charles' court and government corrupt.</small>

Out of the royal revenue* had to be provided, not only money sufficient to satisfy the desires of the court, but also to keep up the navy, to provide for the repairs of castles and forts, the expenses of ambassadors, and the salaries of officers of the executive.

---

* The king's ordinary revenue consisted—
  (1.) Of fines paid by feudal tenants.
  (2.) Of rents accruing from lands belonging to the crown.
  (3.) Of fines and fees paid in courts of justice.
  (4.) Of forfeitures of lands and goods for offences.
  (5.) Of the first-fruits and tenths of all spiritual preferments in the kingdom. The first-fruits or annates were the first year's whole profits by a valuation made in the thirteenth century (1288—1292). The decimæ were the tenth part of the annual profit of every living by the same valuation. These taxes, originally paid to the pope, were annexed to the crown by an act passed in the twenty-sixth year of Henry VIII. (By a statute of 2nd and 3rd Anne, the revenue of first-fruits and tenths has been vested in trustees for ever, to form a perpetual fund for the augmentation of poor livings.)
  (6.) Of the customduties, when granted to the king for life. To these however, Charles had no legal claim. See p. 31.

Since Parliamentary grants were out of the question and the ordinary revenue did not nearly meet the demand, a raid was made upon the property of all classes of society.

The nobility and gentry suffered as much as any. Holders of land on the borders of royal forests were accused of having encroached on the king's domains; the judges received orders to ferret out the weak points of titles, and when the cases came into court, to intimidate jurors into giving verdicts in the king's favour. Adverse verdicts entailed fines of ruinous amounts, and the legal rule that no prescription holds good against the crown was carried so far that even lands held by a title of three hundred years were reclaimed as royal property. By these means, the bounds of Rockingham Forest were increased from six miles to sixty. But 'depression of the nobility,' says Bacon, 'may make a king more absolute, but less safe.' These, and similar encroachments, only helped to cement the alliance between peers and commoners.

<small>Money raised by illegal means.</small>

There was an old feudal custom, long fallen into disuse, that on the accession of a new king, all who held land of him by knights' service, worth above the paltry sum of £20 per annum, should receive the order of knighthood, or pay a fine. Fines were now exacted from noblemen and gentlemen in all parts of the country, for having neglected to be knighted when Charles came to the throne. The fines levied were three or four times the amount at which the delinquents would have been rated for subsidies. The Catholics in return for their support were allowed to compound at an easier rate.*

The poor were also attacked. A statute, passed during the reign of Elizabeth, requiring that cottagers should have four acres of ground attached to their dwellings, had probably never been enforced, had certainly long since fallen into disuse: the poor householders were now held responsible, and complained that they were "mightily vexed," for commissioners were sent twenty miles round London to search out and fine those who had disobeyed the statute. The commissioners employed were "needy men of no fame, prisoners out of the Fleet," whose services, of course, could be cheaply bought; the money they collected mostly went to enrich two lords, who had received as a favour from the king, leave to put the commission into execution.

<small>Old laws raked up.</small>

* Ellis, Orig. Letters, ii. cclxxi.

If no old law could be raked up, Charles would act by proclamation. For instance, he forbade by proclamation the building of new houses, in or about London. Builders either bought licences, or else ran the risk of being called to account and punished for disregarding the proclamation.* Thus one man was fined £1000, and ordered to pull down forty-two dwelling-houses, stables, and coach-houses, by a certain time, on pain of paying a second £1000. Any classes who refused such black mail were severely dealt with. The innkeepers of London were inhibited from dressing any meat, because they declined to pay an excise duty on wine, when levied by the sole authority of the Council. They were soon glad to compound.

As a further means of raising money, the king granted or sold patents for the exclusive sale or manufacture of certain articles. The monopolists formed companies, of which all traders or manufacturers were forced to become members and obey the regulations. By these means taxes were laid on articles of every-day use and consumption, such as salt, corn, lace, tobacco, barrels, linen, cloth ; but most of the money so raised, while impoverishing the nation by raising the price of all necessaries, enriched, not the king, but his courtiers and their dependents. For instance, out of every £12 raised by the monopoly of wine, only £1 reached the exchequer, the other £11 stopping by the way amongst the vintners and the owners of the patent. If the companies sold bad articles, there was no redress. The poor women in London complained that the soap made by the company burnt the linen, scalded their fingers, and was full of tallow and lime. The soap-boilers were Catholics, and got the queen's laundress to subscribe to the goodness of the soap, but "she tells her Majesty she does not wash her linen with any other than Castile soap, and the truth is, most of the ladies that have subscribed have their linen washed with Castile soap." The Lord Mayor, whom the women followed about in the streets,

---

* Lawful proclamations were those—
(1) Issued by the crown in its purely executive capacity.
(2) Prohibiting acts already prohibited by law, or calling on the subject to perform some duty to which he was bound by law.
Unlawful proclamations were those usurping the legislative power, which the crown by right could only exercise in common with the two Houses of Parliament, as for instance, those granting individuals privileges against the rights of others, imposing duties not imposed by law, prohibiting under penalties acts which the law did not recognize as offences.

clamorously petitioning against the new soap, received a sharp reproof at the Council Board for giving too soft answers. The monopolies alienated London, which might have supplied the sinews of war to the king, as it eventually did for the Parliament. It was noted that "discontinuance of Parliaments brings up this kind of grain, which commonly is blasted when they come."

Besides being extortionate and arbitrary, the government was often cruel; and the common law judges, instead of administering justice impartially between subject and sovereign, allowed themselves to be made the instruments of oppression. Upon the dissolution of the last Parliament, several members of the Commons were imprisoned on warrants signed by the king, charging them with having stirred up sedition. Their counsel argued that sedition was a bailable offence, and that, therefore, they ought to be let free on bail. The judges, however, following the king's instructions, required the prisoners, not only to find bail for the present charge, but securities for their good behaviour in the future. As they refused to comply with these demands, which would have kept them under the thumb of the court and its judges, they were ordered back into prison.

Members of late Parliament committed illegally to prison.

These country leaders, who led the opposition in Parliament, risked much—property, liberty, life. Sir John Eliot, being of too noble a nature to be wrought upon either by corruption or intimidation, naturally became the victim of a government that always required submission before it relaxed its hold. He had long since been obliged to give away his property in trust for his children, to preserve himself and his family from ruin. An information in the King's Bench was now brought against Hollis and Valentine for raising a tumult in the Commons on the last day of the session, and against Eliot, for words spoken in the House. The three pleaded that the offences with which they were charged, being committed in Parliament, were not punishable in any other place. The most important of all privileges of Parliament, freedom of speech concerning matters of Parliamentary debate, was here called into question; and the prisoners' counsel brought forward many precedents to show that the liberties and privileges of Parliament could only be determined in Parliament, and not

Judgment of King's Bench on Eliot, Hollis, Valentine.

by any inferior court. The King's Bench, however, decided that it had a right to judge the alleged offences, though committed in Parliament, and condemned the defendants to be imprisoned during the king's pleasure; Eliot to pay a fine to the king of £2000, Hollis 1000 marks,* Valentine £500 (Feb. 12, 1630).†

In the course of twelve months' time, the other prisoners either consented to find sureties for good behaviour, or paid their fines, or were allowed to go at large on some excuse or other. Sir John Eliot alone refused to make any concession of principle, and was still closely confined in the Tower. Consumption attacked him, and his doctors prescribed air and exercise, but he was not allowed to pass out of the walls of his prison. "I am now," he writes, "where candlelight may be suffered, but scarce fire;" and this, though his lodgings had been changed to a dark gloomy chamber. He sent a petition to the king, informing him that he had fallen into a dangerous disease, and praying to be allowed to take some fresh air. Charles replied that the petition was not humble enough. Sir John sent a second by the hand of his son. "I am heartily sorry," he wrote, "I have displeased your Majesty, and beseech you once again to command your judges to set me at liberty, that when I have recovered my health, I may return back to my prison." But no order for release came: and the Lieutenant of the Tower offered to present a third petition with his own hand, and made no doubt but that Charles would grant it if Sir John would only write so as to acknowledge his fault, and humbly pray for pardon. "I thank you, sir," replied Eliot, "for your friendly advice, but my spirits are grown feeble and faint, which when it shall please God to restore unto their former vigour, I will take it into consideration." He did not mean to use the language of a culprit, and purchase his own life by betraying the cause of the nation. Death soon released him while still in the prime of his life (æt. 40). His son sent a petition to the king, begging that his father's body might be buried in his own county of Cornwall. Charles wrote under

[End of Sir John Eliot.]

* 1 mark = 13s. 4d.; therefore, 1000 marks, £666 13s. 4d.

† In 1667, only seven years after the Restoration, the Commons resolved that the judgment now given against Eliot, Hollis, and Valentine, though right as regarded the imputed riot, was illegal in extending to words spoken in Parliament; the Lords concurred in the vote and reversed the judgment. This decision established, once for all, the privilege of freedom of speech in Parliament, unlimited by any authority except that of the House itself.

the petition these words : " 'Let Sir John Eliot's body be buried in the church of that parish where he died.' And so he was buried in the Tower." Such was the fate of one of the purest-hearted of patriots (1632).

His history shows in an eminent degree the nobleness of the leaders of the opposition and the constitutional rectitude of their aims : with a true loyalty to his king, whom he tried in vain to urge into right courses, he won the leadership of the Commons, not more by his vivid eloquence than by the single-minded devotion of his character. There was a true pathos in his stoical bearing under suffering. In the solitude of his prison he bade his friends, 'for their own sakes forbear coming to visit him.' Dying in the Tower he appealed to his son at college not to let him 'receive by any misconduct of his that wound which no enemy could give—sorrow and affliction of the mind.' The limit he gently put to the intercessions of the friendly governor reminds us of the scene in Plato when Socrates put Crito's appeal aside by telling him that he heard the laws of his land remonstrating with him 'to think of right first, and of life and children afterwards.' Thus, unlike the Royalist victim of the Revolution, he departed 'as a sufferer and not a doer of evil.'* His country did not lose by his adherence to principle. In later times when the cause of liberty was in peril its defenders thought of Eliot and fought on.†

Illegal courts. Court of the North. Illegal judgments were now the curse of the nation. Where the common law courts could find no crime, the illegal courts came into action. North of the Humber, the Court of the North, of which Wentworth was president, took the place of the Star Chamber in the south. Its origin was even more questionable. Henry VIII., after an insurrection in 1536, issued a commission to the Archbishop of York and several gentlemen of the north, to examine into the grounds of the disorder, and to punish offenders in riots and conspiracies. But long after all traces of the insurrection had disappeared, the court remained, and its authority was gradually extended. The people dwelling north of the Humber complained that they were shut out from the protection of the common law courts at Westminster, and that their personal liberty and property were at the mercy of arbitrary judges, who sentenced according to their

* See p. 98, and Plato, "Crito," 54.
† See p. 105.

discretion. While the Court of the North was thus accused of encroaching even upon the civil jurisdiction of the Westminster courts, the Star Chamber was chiefly concerned with criminal cases, such as forgery, perjury, riot, libel, conspiracy, and every kind of misdemeanour. It adjudged any punishment short of death, as pillory, whipping, branding, cutting off the ears, fine, and imprisonment.

The customs were levied with rigour, though they had never been granted to Charles by statute.

Chambers, one of several merchants whose goods had been seized for refusing to pay illegal duties, vented his indignation by saying before the Council Board, "that the merchants in no part of the world were so screwed and wrung as in England ; that in Turkey they had more encouragement." The judges of the common law courts could have found no law by which to inflict a heavy punishment for a few hasty words. The judges of the Star Chamber, guided in their judgment by their discretion, declared the expressions used were likely to make the people believe that Charles' happy government was a Turkish tyranny, and sentenced Chambers to pay a fine of £2000, and to sign a submission. Chambers wrote under the submission these words : "I do utterly abhor and detest the contents of this submission, and never, till death, will acknowledge any part thereof." He was refused by the judges his habeas corpus, and remained a prisoner many years. *Sentence of Star Chamber on Chambers.*

Wentworth, as the councillor who possessed most influence in the government, incurred the hatred of all lovers of liberty, without gaining the friendship of the queen or the court. Regardless of the interests of courtiers and their dependents, he resolutely endeavoured, as far as he could obtain Charles' support, to govern with a view to increase the power of the crown. This administration required the surrender of illicit gains, and the punishment of criminals, however close their connection with men in high places. While, therefore, its vices incurred the odium of the country, its virtues incurred the odium of the court. However much a Somerset or a Buckingham may have been hated by rival aspirants to royal favour, it was the men who were hated and not their régime. Under them, so long as the interests of the favourite remained untouched, free licence was given to all to make their fortunes by the first means *Administration of Wentworth and Laud.*

that came to hand. The court and government of James had been thoroughly corrupt. The corruption of the courtiers under James had continued under Charles. But, where free rein was given him, Wentworth thus, not unaptly, describes the character of his administration : "Where I found a crown, a church, and a people spoiled, I could not imagine to redeem them from under the pressure with gracious smiles and gentle looks ; it would cost warmer water than so .... True it was, indeed, I knew no other rule to govern by but by reward and punishment ; and I must profess that where I found a person well and entirely set for the service of my master, I should lay my hand under his foot, and add to his respect and power all I might ; and that where I found the contrary, I should not dandle him in my arms, or soothe him in his untoward humour, but if he came in my reach, so far as honour and justice would warrant me, I must knock him soundly over the knuckles."* In Yorkshire, as president of the Court of the North, by preventing the proceeds of his trenchant measures from being filched by petty tax-gatherers, he succeeded in raising the royal revenue in the four northern counties to four or five times its previous amount. In London, Laud was also a zealous servant of the crown, and though ruthlessly trampling on recalcitrant merchants who refused to pay illegal customs, would try to remedy abuses and give ear to complaints, if trade were in any way injured for the advantage of a courtier.

In the year 1632 Wentworth was appointed Lord Deputy of Ireland. During the reigns of Elizabeth and James I., Ireland had for the first time been brought into complete subjection to English rule. English laws and English customs had been introduced into every province, and the Protestant Church established in place of the Catholic. The population was divided into three parts : 1st, the native Irish ; 2nd, the old English settlers in Dublin and the neighbouring counties of Kildare, Louth, and the two Meaths, which constituted 'the English pale'; 3rd, new English and Scotch settlers who had been planted upon lands taken from Irish rebels by Elizabeth and James.

Wentworth, Lord Deputy of Ireland.

State of Ireland. The Irish and old English settlers, forming a large majority of the population, were Catholics ; the new settlers Protestants. Though the Acts of Supremacy and Uni-

* Straff. Letters and Despatches, ii. 20.

formity had been enacted by an Irish Parliament, they were not fully put into force, because it was hardly possible to fine nonconformists, when 'in six parishes scarce six came to church.' Those, however, who refused to take the oath of supremacy when tendered, were shut out from holding any office in the State, or even from practising as lawyers. The people were ignorant and untaught. The Protestant clergy could not speak the same language as their flocks, and, while living with idle hands in a false position, had won for themselves an indifferent character. The Catholic bishops exercised far more power than the Protestant; the great lords, whether English or Irish, oppressed their tenants; the ministers of justice took bribes; the officers employed by the government, and the Protestant clergy, extorted large fees on every possible pretext; an undisciplined army was scattered over the country, living at free quarters; pirates from Dunkirk, Algiers, Spain, the Bay of Biscay, so infested the coasts, that the people were plundered in every creek; while the captains of the king's ships refused to move against them, alleging want of victuals, though the crews—'mere rabbles of disorderly people'—did the country more injury than the pirates themselves; meantime merchant vessels were run aground, rifled and burnt in sight of Dublin Castle; there was little trade; the taxes did not pay the expenses of the government, so that there was a debt of £100,000 owing by the crown.*

Wentworth was probably sent there because fair promises had been made to the Irish, which it was disagreeable to fulfil. The king hoped Wentworth's genius would keep Ireland quiet; he could not yet have hoped it would forge Ireland into a weapon to use against English liberty.† Wentworth set himself to work to rule despotically, but after he had put first his master's interest, he showed some regard for that of the people entrusted to him. No corruption was allowed; the fees received by the officers, high and low, in the government employ, were inquired into; judges were not allowed to act as mere instruments of great lords' oppression: the army was remodelled; discipline enforced; Wentworth saw every single man himself, though it numbered nearly 4000; the soldier paid for all he took; captains were made to understand that for the future they must perform garrison duty, must drill their troops, and provide them

* Straff. Letters and Despatches.   † See p. 89.

with good arms and horses, instead of appropriating the funds for their own uses. They soon found that the lord deputy was not the sort of man to jest with; they had either to do as they were told, or leave the service. The navy was unfortunately independent of his control. In Wentworth's own words, it grieved his heart that he had no power over the Admiralty. His grief indeed was no matter for wonder. The ship that was conveying over from England his wardrobe, furniture, and plate, was seized on the passage by that same Captain Nutt whom James I. and Secretary Calvert in 1623 let loose a second time upon the world.* As it was, to protect Dublin harbour from pirates, he fitted out a vessel at his own charge. He encouraged trade, but only so far as he thought the increase of Irish trade not detrimental to that of England. Thus in order to ensure to English manufacturers a readier sale for their cloths from the absence of Irish competition, he actually destroyed the woollen trade in Ireland. At the same time he introduced into Ulster the manufacture of linen from flax, erected looms, brought workmen from France and Flanders, and sent the first cargo of linen to Spain at his own risk. For this prohibitive policy in the supposed interest of England, Wentworth deserves no special blame. It is a blot attaching quite as much to the character of English parliaments as to that of English kings. What was special in that policy now, was the length to which it was carried. No deputy before Wentworth had been in possession at once of the necessary energy, determination, and disregard of human suffering, to uproot one branch of industry in the vain hope of seeing another spring up in a moment. Notwithstanding this suicidal act, the vigour of the government soon produced striking results; the debts of the crown were paid off, and in four years the customs were raised from £1200 to £40,000 and were still on the increase.

Yet the Irish felt no gratitude to the deputy, for if he protected them from the oppression of the government officers, and of their own aristocracy, he laid their property open to the rapacity of the king, and their personal freedom to his own vengeance.

The Irish had been required by Elizabeth and James to surrender their lands, in order to receive them back to hold by feudal tenure. The grants, by which the land had been restored, ought to have been enrolled in the Court of Chancery. But though the Irish of Connaught had paid £3000 for the purpose,

* See p. 18.

the enrolment had in many cases been neglected, and James' council had advised him on this pretext to forfeit the whole province, and to plant English Protestants on the lands thus taken from their rightful owners. When Charles came to the throne, the Irish, in terror of this project, proposed to support an army of 5000 men for three years, in return for fifty-three royal concessions or "graces." Of these the most important were, that the inhabitants of Connaught should be allowed to enrol their grants ; that the crown should lay claim to no estates that had been held for sixty years ; and that an Irish Parliament should be held to confirm these graces. Charles had agreed, signed the graces, and promised that a Parliament should be summoned to confirm them.

This Parliament was at last summoned by Wentworth, after the army had been supported for four, instead of for three years, the time originally agreed upon. It would seem hardly credible that neither the king nor his deputy, after having received the money, should have had the smallest intention of performing their part of the compact. Yet such was the case ; it was only with great reluctance that Charles allowed a Parliament, "that hydra, cunning as malicious," to be summoned at all. Wentworth, however, was confident that he should be able to manage it, by playing off the jealousies of Protestants against Catholics, and of Catholics against Protestants, and succeeded so well, that he persuaded the Parliament to grant the king six subsidies, giving the members to understand that after they had proved themselves such dutiful subjects, the king would be sure to grant them their desires. Never were men more deceived. The perfidious deputy, when sure of the money, turned round and told the Commons that most of the graces were prejudicial to the crown, and that it was his duty to beseech his Majesty not to grant them. They were helpless. A law called Poyning's Law had been passed in 1495, by which no bills could be introduced into the Irish Parliament except such as had been first allowed by the king and the English council. Hence the Irish House of Commons was not nearly so independent in action as the English, and the Parliament was dissolved without the most important graces having been passed into law.

Wentworth obtains a subsidy from Irish Parliament.

The consequences were soon experienced. Wentworth travelled west into Connaught, and inquired into defective titles (1635). The Council Chamber, an

Lands in Connaught forfeited to crown.

arbitrary court, answering the same purpose as the Star Chamber in England, fined the first jurors who declared against the crown £4000 each. After this example, little resistance was made. Some lands were declared to belong to the crown, that had been held for 300 years, and land-owners were glad to be allowed to pay a rent to the king for part of their lands, and to give up the rest for him to bestow on new Protestant settlers. This attack upon their property was far from being all that the Irish suffered. The deputy's pride and vindictiveness were unparalleled. Any who offended he marked out for destruction, and hunted down. Lord Mountnorris, vice-treasurer in Ireland, and a captain in the navy, was suddenly summoned, with several other officers in Dublin, to attend the deputy at a council of war (12th Dec., 1635). Mountnorris found himself accused of having said, six months before, at a dinner table, that a gentleman, struck by Wentworth, "had a brother that would not have taken such a blow." The court, composed mainly of councillors, then and there, in the presence of the deputy, sentenced the victim to be deprived of all office, and to be shot dead. The latter part of the sentence Wentworth only intended to be passed, not executed; the former he caused to be put in force, and prided himself on thus having humbled a man towards whom he had for a long time felt ill will.

Laws against Catholics not enforced. His ecclesiastical policy was somewhat less severe. Though the endowments of churches had been given to Protestant bishops and clergymen, every parish was allowed its priest and its mass-house, simply because Wentworth did not feel himself strong enough to put the Act of Uniformity into full force. When the English should be more thickly settled, when there should be in the country an army composed entirely of Protestants, strong enough to crush rebellion, he looked forward to forcing every Papist to conform to the Protestant worship.

Meantime the success of his Irish government did not lessen the number of the deputy's enemies at home. The queen and her tribe looked upon Ireland as a country where offices ought to be bestowed, as in England, upon her Majesty's recommendation. Wentworth begged the king that no office might be given away without the deputy's consent. Charles agreed, but ungenerously objected to make the denials himself. "You," he wrote, "must take upon you the refusing part." The disappointed courtiers displayed their spite by exclaiming against the deputy's pride and tyranny. True, they said, he refused to take bribes, but he was none the worse off, for he never gave any, as others refused his presents. If Wentworth's enemies in London might be believed, Mountnorris was actually shot, and people could even tell where the bullets had entered his body.

In spite of the great financial success of the Irish administration, the revenue raised in that country could not possibly be made to provide for the expenses of the English government. Hence although Wentworth carefully husbanded his surplus funds, and although so many illegal modes of taxation were resorted to in England, poverty prevented Charles from rendering the Protestant cause on the continent any effectual support either by arms or by negotiation.

The Thirty Years' War was still raging. The Emperor Ferdinand II., after his armies had overrun the north of Germany, nourished hopes, not only of rooting the Protestant doctrines out of Germany, but also of reducing the Catholic princes to dependence upon Austria (1628—1630). But at the moment when his power seemed greatest, the Protestants were saved by the break up of the Catholic camp. The Catholic princes of Germany feared they might lose their own independence if they suffered the emperor to overpower their Protestant fellows. The pope himself, Urban VIII., alarmed at the interference of Austria in Italy, joined the side of the French, and thus indirectly aided the Protestants. Finally Richelieu, still the chief minister of Louis XIII., eager as his successors for a divided Germany, called on Gustavus Adolphus, King of Sweden, to help in restoring the German princes to their ancient rights, by overthrowing the tyranny of the emperor.

Thirty Years' War.

Gustavus, with a small army of 30,000 men, defeated the Imperial general, Tilly, at Leipzig (Sept., 1631), and penetrated into the heart of Bavaria. At Lutzen he defeated the celebrated Wallenstein, and lost his own life (Nov., 1632). After his death every nation engaged was fighting for some special interest, and the war continued for seventeen years with varied success. Frederic, prince of the palatinate, died in 1632, still an exile from his dominions, but leaving his son to continue his claims.

The course of Gustavus was followed in England with deep interest. English and Scotch volunteers, after serving in the Swedish armies, returned home to note with grief that while they had been fighting in defence of the Protestant faith and political rights, their own country was falling subject to the sway of a religion that differed little from the Romish, and of a tyranny in the State that threatened to make government by Parliaments a thing of the past. Wentworth's influence, however, foiled the war-party; "Good my lord," he wrote to Laud in 1637, "if it be not too late, use your best to divert us from this war [with Austria]; it will necessarily put the king into all high ways possible, else will he not be able to subsist under the charge of it, and if these fail the next will be but the sacrificing those who have been his ministers."

Coasts of Britain infested by pirates. Not only, however, was Charles too poor to aid the Protestant cause, he could not even defend the coasts of his own kingdom. Dutch and French fishing vessels encroached on the English fisheries, refusing even to 'vail their flags' to the king's ships, while pirates from Algiers made descents upon the coasts of both England and Ireland, and carried off captives to be slaves to the Mussulman.

Ship-money. To raise a fleet, Charles ventured on a great strain of his prerogative. A lawyer, Noy, had found in the Tower some old writs, calling on the ports and maritime counties to provide ships for the public service. It was suggested by Finch, chief justice of the Common Pleas, that the same demand should now be made, not only on ports and maritime places, but also on inland counties, and that instead of causing each county to provide so many ships, a general tax under the name of ship-money, should be levied on land and property, in the same manner as a subsidy granted in Parliament.

People wondered, and even dependents of Wentworth ventured to express their dislike to the new imposition. "I would rather," one wrote, "pay ten subsidies in Parliament, than ten shillings this new-old-way of dead Noy's." None, however, had yet resisted illegal demands with impunity, and no immoderate opposition being offered, Charles gained yearly a sum of about £200,000 by this tax. He employed, indeed, the money on the object for which it was nominally raised. The Dutch fishers one year bought licences, and Rainsborough led an expedition against Salee on the coast of Algiers, whence he brought back from slavery 370 Englishmen and Irishmen (1637). So far the fleet restored England's supremacy, and the court gloried in the success of this high-handed policy. Privy councillors would laugh when the expression 'Liberty of the subject' was used before them; they said that the taxes and monopolies in England were nothing compared with those endured by other kingdoms, and that the people ought to be thankful for the general happiness of England, which grew rich in long years of peace while cruel wars devastated the continent and its inhabitants perished from famine. The facts were true enough, but it offers no satisfaction to sufferers to be told that others suffer more. The English people, who prided themselves on the free constitution of their country, felt as though an insult were offered them when their condition was compared with that of the slavish peasant of France, who could call nothing his own.* Gentlemen, freeholders, artisans, would talk and argue about their rights, and regret their old government by Parliaments. The students at the Inns of Court were noted for their loyalty, but even they, in getting up a masque in the queen's honour, could not forbear having a sly cut at the government. After the well-mounted masquers, with their gold and silver lace, their cloth of tissue, their silver spangles, followed the antimasquers, cripples, and beggars, on "poor lean jades;" amongst them a fellow with a bunch of carrots upon his head, and a capon upon his fist, who begged a patent of monopoly as the first inventor of the art to feed capons fat with carrots; after him came riding a man on a little horse with a great bit, who begged a patent that none might use any bits but such as were made by him. The crowd in the streets applauded, understanding a covert reproach at the monopolies, which raised the prices of the commonest necessaries of life.

Marginal note: Discontent general in country.

---

* During the reign of Henri IV. the prisons of Normandy were full of prisoners unable to pay the tax on salt. So many died, that 120 corpses were taken out at a time. The Parliament of Rouen begged his Majesty to take pity on his people; but the king, who had been informed that the tax was very productive, said he wished it to be continued, and seemed as though he would make a joke of the rest—'Semblait qu'il voulût tourner le reste en risée.'—Lavallée, iii. 57.

Judgment of Court of Exchequer in Hampden's case.

John Hampden, a gentleman of Buckinghamshire, was among the first to endanger his property and liberty in support of his country's rights. He refused to pay the twenty shillings at which a piece of his land was rated for ship-money. Charles consented to allow the case to be tried at law. He thought himself sure of the judges, for he had already obtained the signatures of all twelve to an extra-judicial opinion, publicly read in the Star Chamber, 'that his Majesty might command all his subjects to provide and furnish such number of ships with men, munition, and victuals, and for such time as he should think fit, for the defence and safeguard of the kingdom, and that he was the sole judge both of the danger, and when and how the same was to be prevented and avoided.'

The cause of Hampden was pleaded for twelve days before all the twelve judges of the Westminster courts, who by virtue of the Star Chamber opinion, stood in the same relation to the parties, as though previous to a trial for murder they had in a public and notorious manner declared their belief in the innocence of the accused. The whole nation, poor and rich, Puritans and Episcopalians, alike waited eagerly for the judgment.

Hampden's counsel brought forward what seemed an overwhelming weight of evidence. They could point to the various statutes from Magna Charta to the Petition of Right, that declared taxation, without consent of Parliament, illegal. Even if precedents to the contrary were to be found in times when "the government was more of force than of law," such, they argued, must give way before the authority of statute law. This was in fact unanswerable. But the crown lawyers maintained that absolute power —power to act without consent of Parliament — was innate in the person of the King of England. Some of the judges in giving sentence treated all constitutional statutes as waste paper. "Where Mr. Holborne," said Justice Berkeley, "supposed a fundamental policy in the creation of the frame of this kingdom—that in case the monarch of England should be inclined to exact from his subjects at his pleasure, he should be restrained, for he could have nothing from them but upon a common consent in Parliament—he is utterly mistaken herein. The law knows no such king-yoking policy. The law is itself an old and trusty servant of the king's; it is his instrument or means which he useth to govern his people by. I never read nor heard that lex was rex, but it is common and most true that rex is lex." " The king," said another, " may dispense with any law in cases of necessity." Out of the twelve judges only two pronounced in favour of Hampden ; one of these had intended to give his judgment on the side of the crown, but changed his mind through the persuasion of his wife, who bade him not to fear danger for himself or his family, for she would sooner suffer any want or misery with him, than that he should act against his conscience (1637-8).

But at the moment when the victory of the king seemed complete and courtiers were most exultant, danger was nearer than they thought. The decision gave universal discontent. It is hard to have your property taken from you illegally, but harder still to be told that that illegality is law. It was a Cadmean victory Charles had won ; the levying of ship-money was more difficult after the verdict than before, and he could not put thousands into prison for expressing discontent. Wentworth, wiser than his master, had not approved of the trial at all—"Hampden," like other opposers of tyranny, "had better have been whipped into his right senses ;" "if the rod be so used that it smarts not, I am the more sorry."

The nation hated the government of the State as arbitrary, corrupt, and cruel; it hated, however, still more the connivance at Popery, which characterized the government of the Church. During the reign of Elizabeth, several severe laws had been passed against Catholics, condemning priests and Jesuits to suffer death as traitors, forbidding the exercise of the Catholic worship, and ordering recusants who refused to attend service in the parish church, to pay a fine of £20 a month. But now these laws were not put into force ; fines were not regularly levied : if priests were arrested, they were at once discharged on warrants signed by the king or his secretaries. A Catholic chapel, built at Somerset House for Queen Henrietta's use, was publicly consecrated with three days' ceremonies, masses, and singing of litanies. Agents from the court of Rome actually resided in London ; they were known to everybody; their carriages rolled down the streets without any one daring to say a word against them. Many of the courtiers, some of the king's council, and even some of the bishops, were open or concealed Catholics ; court ladies constantly went over to Rome, and

Government of the Church.

the queen's Capuchin friars boasted that not a week passed but there were two or three conversions.

The king, however, all the time, had no thoughts of weakening his own prerogative by making the Church of England dependent on a foreign see. He was courting Rome to procure the pope's interest for the restoration of the palatinate to Charles, the eldest son of his sister, Elizabeth. The pope, on his side, was willing to keep on good terms with the heretical government, in order to save English Catholics from persecution. In itself this toleration was laudable. The motives, however, that influenced Charles to exercise it, were no enlarged views of religious toleration. He forbore to put the laws against Catholics in force, because the Catholics supported his pretensions to arbitrary power. The public law was set aside by a private agreement. At the same time, to make the contrast more bitter, Puritans, often guiltless of any crime at law, were suffered to pine away in prison under sentences of the courts of High Commission and Star Chamber.

Various causes afford excuse for the bitter and intolerant spirit *Excuse for intolerance of Puritans.* with which the Puritan regarded his Catholic fellow-countrymen. Many still lived who could recall to mind the events of 1588, when the Armada threatened the shores of England. Thousands still lived who remembered the discovery of the Gunpowder Plot. Jesuits had taught the doctrine, that heretic princes might be dethroned and murdered. Several attempts had been made upon Elizabeth's life. William the Silent, the heroic maintainer of Dutch liberty, had perished by the hand of a fanatic. The same fate had befallen the great Henri IV. of France. Diversity in the Church was thought incompatible with unity in the State. On the continent, not only did Catholics persecute Protestants, and Protestants Catholics, but one Protestant sect could not tolerate another; in England Presbyterians approved of the persecution of sectarians. In fact the principles of toleration had hardly as yet been enunciated, much less had they received a fair trial. It is experience alone that gives confidence, and few are bold enough to enter upon an untried course of action. The ordinary Englishman regarded the free toleration of Catholics as a crime both against his God and his country; as a Protestant he considered it a direct encouragement to the spread of idolatry and superstition; as a patriot, an opening for

Catholic priests to usurp political power, and bring England again into dependence upon a foreign jurisdiction.

There were, indeed, grounds for the fear, entertained by many, that a union would finally be effected between the Established Church of England and of Rome. Altars and images were restored to churches ; popish ceremonies were revived, popish doctrines taught ; the work of the Reformation was in part undone ; the worshipper was required to believe that all his church taught him was true and necessary for salvation, even though her teaching found no foundation in the Bible ; and again, in order to hold communion with God, he must seek the aid of priests and assist in ceremonies he regarded as superstitious. *Character of the Puritans.*

But though a Puritan, even if a Presbyterian or sectarian, could be forced to conform and attend his parish church, he could not be prevented from spreading his opinions and making them felt by others. For his manners and his conduct betrayed him, and they were such as to command approval. Morality was inculcated by the ministers of the Church, as much as by the more popular preachers, but practice is more than profession, and that Church was supported by a court which treated vice lightly and made a scoff of virtue. The genuine Puritan, on the contrary, was distinguished by his strict observance of the moral virtues. He sought in the Bible, but more especially in the books of the Old Testament, for the rules by which to guide his actions ; he gained a vivid conception of a personal God, with whom his own soul could enter into direct communion, and beneath whose displeasure it was fatal to fall ; and he felt with the Hebrew of the Old Testament, "he that keepeth the law, happy is he ; its ways are ways of pleasantness and all its paths are peace ; if thou hadst walked in its ways, thou shouldst have dwelt in peace for ever."

Imbued with such feelings, a certain seriousness of demeanour characterized the Puritan, and he not unnaturally preferred to pass his time in listening to sermons, in prayer, and in attending to the business of his calling, to idly seeking amusement at the theatre, the fair, or the dance, where he was sure to hear coarse and profane language spoken, and to fall into the society of drunkards. Confident that his conduct was approved by God, he could look down upon the unregenerate, and regard their scoffs with contempt. Amongst uneducated tradesmen and artisans, there were many fanatics, who refused to take part in any amusements, however innocent, and who almost seemed to court ridicule by their austere mode of life, their ostentatiously plain dress, their close-cut hair, and their frequent use of the words of scripture.

At the head of the Church stood Laud, Archbishop of Canterbury. A man more unsuited to assuage the religious passions of the times could hardly have held the position. However great a virtue in itself, sincere zeal, when untempered by charity, has produced the cruellest of persecutors. Some by nature are possessed of a largeness of mind that enables them to sympathize with the thoughts and feelings of others; while to some experience and education teach the duty, or at least the necessity of tolerating what they fail themselves to understand. Laud was sincere in his views, but nature had not generously gifted him with the quality of mercy. He came into power untutored by the experience won by working with others of different opinions. His abilities were only ordinary, and though his education was good for his time, it gave him learning rather than wisdom, and never succeeded in making up for the deficiencies of his heart. The new opinions seething around were nothing to him but a troublesome and dangerous fanaticism that required to be suppressed. Such sincere bigots placed in power have often wrought their country untold harm. They may by force succeed in stifling the new movement for years, perhaps for centuries; but, in either case, it is sure at last to break forth, possibly in some new form, and always with dangerous violence. Philip II., acting in the full belief that his work was sacred, drove freedom of thought out of Spain; hence, to this very day, the tyranny of extremes retards his country's advance and prosperity. Happily for England, Laud's success was of short duration. The reaction came in his lifetime, and he paid a heavy penalty for his rash attempt to force conformity upon a people panting for spiritual freedom.

<small>Character of Laud.</small>

The courts held by bishops, as well as the Court of High Commission, called to account ministers and laymen who did not attend church, or who failed to perform every ceremony exactly as ordained in the Prayer-book, or, indeed, as prescribed by Laud on his sole authority. A minister of Durham, for speaking in a sermon against the use of pictures and images, was degraded by the Court of High Commission, fined £500, and placed in prison, where he waited eleven years for the

<small>Puritans forced to conform.</small>

hour of release. The Court of Star Chamber, in which Laud himself sat as a judge, was always ready to support the cause of the Church. Three professional men, Prynne, a lawyer; Burton, a London minister; and Bastwick, a doctor, had written books inveighing against the bishops. On being brought before the Star Chamber, they were charged with felony, for having tried to stir up sedition, and sentenced to pay fines of £5000 each, to stand in the pillory in Palace Yard, Westminster, to have their ears cut off, and to be imprisoned for life. {Sentences of Star Chamber on Burton, Bastwick, Prynne.}

"So far," said Bastwick, addressing the crowd, surging round the pillories, "am I from base fear, or caring for anything that they can do, that had I as much blood as would swell the Thames, I would shed it every drop in this cause. Therefore, be not any of you discouraged, be not daunted at their power." "Had we," said Prynne, "respected (regarded) our liberties we had not stood here at this time." "Sir," said a woman to Burton, "there are many hundreds which, by God's assistance, would willingly suffer for the cause you suffer for this day." A mournful cry arose from the crowd, as the prisoners' ears were cropped, and many pressed forward to dip handkerchiefs into the blood streaming down the scaffold.

John Lilburne, a young man about twenty years old, was brought before the Star Chamber on a charge of being concerned in bringing seditious books over from Holland. He was required to swear, laying his hand upon the Gospels, to answer truly all questions put to him. He refused. "The oath," he said, "is of the same nature as the High Commission oath, which oath I know to be unlawful, and withal I find no warrant in the word of God for an oath of inquiry, and therefore, my lords, I dare not take it."* In accordance with his sentence, Lilburne was tied to a cart's tail and whipped from the Fleet prison to Westminster Yard, at every two or three steps receiving on his bare back a blow from a knotted treble-corded whip. The young enthusiast never flinched, but all the way quoted texts of Scripture, exhorting the crowd to resist the bishops. At Westminster Yard he bowed to his judges, whom he saw looking out at him from the Court of Star Chamber win- {Lilburne refuses illegal oath.}

* State Trials, 1.

dow, and then sitting in the bent painful attitude required by the pillory, continued his exhortations. "I will never take the oath, though I be pulled to pieces by wild horses; neither shall I think that man a faithful subject of Christ's kingdom, that shall at any time hereafter take it. My brethren, we are all at this present in a very dangerous and fearful condition, in regard we have turned traitors unto our God, in seeing His almighty great name and His heavenly truth trodden under foot, and yet we not only let the bishops alone in holding our peace, but most slavishly subject ourselves unto them, fearing the face of a piece of dirt more than the almighty great God of heaven and earth, who is able to cast both body and soul into everlasting damnation." He was still addressing the people in the same strain, when the warden of the Fleet came and placed a gag on his mouth.

Such were the means taken by the archbishop to crush the spirit of the Puritans, and by him not considered sufficiently "thorough." As if for the sole purpose of irritating his opponents, the king, by his advice, ordered a proclamation, called the Book of Sports, to be read by ministers after service, declaring that certain games, such as leaping, vaulting, and wrestling were lawful on Sundays. It had been originally published by James, but its reading not enforced. Now no minister might escape. Thirty who refused to obey in the diocese of Norwich—a stronghold of Puritanism—were suspended. Some temporized. A London minister read the proclamation, and after it the ten commandments. "Dearly beloved," he said, "you have heard the commandment of God and of man, obey which you please."

'Lecturers' put down. The Puritans raised subscriptions for purchasing from laymen their right of presentation to livings and for hiring lecturers to preach on afternoons in market towns. But Laud, not content with ordering that lecturers should wear the surplice and read the service, determined to break up the whole association. The trustees were declared by the Court of Exchequer to have misused the funds with which they were entrusted, and the whole were forfeited to the king, to be used for the good of the Church and the maintenance of conformable ministers. The Church, however, lost its hold on the people, when it lost the most earnest and most popular of its preachers. Into the livings of the ejected Puritans were put ignorant men or court clergy, who bade their people be passively obedient, while they lost their cherished liberties. Of such pastors Milton wrote, as—

" Blind mouths that scarce themselves know how to hold
A sheephook, or have learned aught else the least
That to the faithful herdsman's art belongs !
What recks it them ? What need they ? They are sped;
And when they list, their lean and flashy songs
Grate on their scrannel pipes of wretched straw ;
The hungry sheep look up, and are not fed,
But swoln with wind and the rank mist they draw,
Rot inwardly, and foul contagion spread ;
Beside what the grim wolf with privy paw*
Daily devours apace, and nothing said."

While Laud thus awoke the hate of Puritans by intolerance, he aroused that of the laity generally by endeavouring to raise the political importance of the Church. As a politician, he was both ambitious and unscrupulous, as might be expected of one who had risen to power at the heels of Buckingham. Courts held by bishops now sent out writs in their own names, instead of in that of the king. Clergymen were made justices of the peace in place of country gentlemen. Bishops sat in the king's council and in the Court of Star Chamber. Juxon, Bishop of London, was appointed by the king to the influential and coveted office of lord treasurer. "Now," wrote Laud in his diary, "if the Church will not hold themselves up under God, I can do no more."

In order to escape persecution and tyranny, new homes were sought in America. In Virginia a Church of England colony had been founded by adventurers in 1607. The earliest settlers in New England were the Pilgrim Fathers, a body of persecuted sectarians, who had sailed across the Atlantic in the "Mayflower," in 1620. Rhode Island was colonized in 1634, and liberty of conscience established. Lord Baltimore, a Roman Catholic, granted the same boon to all settlers in Maryland (1638). In the ten years preceding 1640, the number of emigrants to New England was estimated at 21,200. *Emigration to America.*

The Presbyterian Church had been long since established in Scotland by an act of the Scotch Parliament (1592). James I., however, had succeeded by not very creditable means in restoring Scotch bishops to the possession of their former titles, though to little of their former influence and position.

* For the conversions to Popery, see p. 69.

Charles and Laud now determined on setting up a church government in Scotland, to answer in all respects to that established in England. Canons, to regulate the Church of Scotland, were drawn up by the Scotch bishops, and afterwards revised by Laud, in which no place was left for the action of any Presbyterian assemblies. The following year, in place of "Knox's Liturgy," as the Service-book ordinarily used by the Scots was called, a new Prayer-book, nearly the same as the English, was ordered to be read in all churches, from the 23rd July, 1637. In St. Giles', the cathedral church of Edinburgh, no sooner had the dean opened the new liturgy, than all the lower order of people in the church began to scream, clap their hands, hiss and groan, making such a hideous outcry that no one could either hear or be heard. The cry was, "Sorrow, sorrow, for this dreadful day; they are bringing Popery amongst us." Sticks, stones, Bibles, stools, were hurled at the dean's head. In other places the Prayer-book received a like reception. By most it was looked on as little better than the mass itself. Its very exterior gave offence to the Presbyterian; the red and black type, the Gothic letters, pictorial capitals, and other illustrations, seemed to imply a revival of Catholic times. The nobles were afraid of being required to restore church property acquired at the Reformation; when not moved by religious fervour themselves, their interests made them at heart on the side of the rioters.

Episcopacy in Scotland.

The whole nation was enraged. When James I. had introduced changes into the Presbyterian form of church government, he had at least obtained the sanction of a corrupt church-assembly and parliament. But Charles was endeavouring to establish the Episcopalian Church in the place of the Presbyterian, upon his own sole authority, as though he were indeed an absolute monarch, able to make laws without the consent of his subjects.

The king, to whom a tumult raised by the rabble seemed no cause for alarm, sent orders that the new Service-book was still to be read. The lords of the Scotch council, however, dared not put his commands into execution. They were themselves assaulted in the streets of Edinburgh by an infuriated mob, and only rescued from death by the nobles and gentry, who now, following the example of the people, came flocking into the capital to sign an accusation against the bishops (18th Oct., 1637).

The tumults rapidly took the form of rebellion: a council was chosen, composed of members from the four classes, nobles, gentry, clergy, burgesses, which soon became a new power in the State, more formidable than the king's council (15th Nov., 1637); at last, a national league was formed under the name of the Covenant (a forerunner of the 'Solemn League and Covenant' with the English in 1643), binding the signers to reject the new canons and liturgy, and to defend their sovereign, their religion, their laws, and liberties (1st March, 1638). An assembly of the Church, which met at Glasgow, refused to dissolve at the instance of the Duke of Hamilton, the king's deputy (28th Nov., 1638), and proceeded to abolish liturgy, canons, and episcopacy itself. After thus defying the royal authority, the Covenanters prepared for war. The question of war had also to be debated in the king's council at home. The critical moment was now come, when the strength of the government was put to the test. "I am not for war," wrote one of the privy council; "in the exchequer there is but £200; the magazines are totally unfurnished; commanders are there none for execution or advice; the people are so discontented, there is reason to fear a greater part of them will be readier to join the Scots than to draw swords in the king's service." Wentworth, who did not despair so quickly as these panic-stricken councillors, began to increase the size of the army in Ireland, and to call for sterner measures against defaulters. Yet to advise Charles to do nothing by halves, to introduce episcopacy into Scotland, and to govern that country as he himself governed Ireland, was much like telling a man with a palsied hand to drive the nail home. The deputy, so proud of his Irish government, could not, or would not, read aright the signs of the times. Some of the council advised the calling of a Parliament, but Charles could not hear the proposal with patience. Money was therefore raised by loans and other illegal means. By the spring of 1639 an army of some 12,000 men was fitted out, and the king proceeded to York, followed, not only by his court, but by all the nobility and most influential gentry of the kingdom, whom he summoned to attend his person at their own charge, as had been customary in feudal times. He hoped by this display to overawe his needy Scottish subjects.

But the Scots were too much in earnest, and too well understood the state of feeling in England, to be easily overawed. By the time Charles reached Berwick, it was evident that they could not be reduced that summer. The first English force that saw the face of an enemy, made a precipitate retreat. The courtiers who longed for a return to their pleasures, the nobles and gentlemen who desired a redress of their wrongs, all urged the necessity of coming to an agreement with the Covenanters. Charles found himself obliged to sign a Pacification at Berwick, in which it was agreed that both a Parliament and a Church Assembly should be summoned in Scotland, for the settlement of all grievances, religious and civil (18th June, 1639).

<small>Pacification of Berwick.</small>

The king, however, signed the agreement merely as a temporary measure, and with the full intention of raising a larger force and renewing the war next summer. The Scots had plenty of friends in England to warn them of the policy pursued; how Wentworth had been summoned from Ireland, and created Earl of Strafford; how the Irish army was being increased in size; how a new army was being raised in England, and every nerve strained to get money.

In foreign policy meantime Charles had been inconsistent and wavering. At one time he had entered into negotiations with France, at another with Spain, for the restoration of the palatinate to his nephew. Now, therefore, that he was involved in difficulties with his subjects, governments which had received cause of offence assumed an unfriendly attitude. The pope forbade the Catholics to be so ready in lending money and offering to serve in the army, for after all, Laud's religion, which did not acknowledge the pope as head of the Church, was no more the Catholic religion than that of the Puritans. The Dutch grew so insolent that they destroyed a Spanish fleet which was riding in the Downs under Charles' own protection, while the English ambassador wrote from Spain that the Spaniards were instigating the Irish to rebel. Richelieu, bearing in mind the expeditions in aid of Rochelle, now took the opportunity to repay his injuries by sending supplies of money and arms to the Covenanters. A copy of a letter written by the Scots to Louis XIII. was intercepted by Charles, who thought that with this proof of treason in his hand, he might venture on meeting a Parliament. But indeed, the neces-

<small>Foreign governments unfriendly to Charles.</small>

sity of calling a Parliament if the war were to be continued, was daily becoming more and more manifest. 'Men's consciences awoke,' and forbade them to pay ship money. Even in Yorkshire, where Strafford possessed so much influence, gentlemen refused to equip soldiers without receiving some security for repayment of the money. Strafford advised the lords of the council to send for them to London, and "lay them up by the heels."* "What," he asked, "should become of the levy of 30,000 men in case the other counties should return the like answer?" A pregnant question, for everywhere the same spirit was manifested; London refused loans, country gentlemen made excuses, and the king was at last driven to that resource, which last year he would not hear mentioned. He summoned his fourth Parliament on the 13th April, 1640.

Illegal demands opposed.

Charles asked for an immediate grant of money. Pym rose, and in a speech of two hours, while speaking respectfully of the king, laid bare the offences of the government against religion, justice, and the power and privilege of Parliament. The House, with deep attention, heard him out, and then voted that they would find a remedy for their grievances before granting the king a supply. The letter of the Scots to Louis XIII. did not trouble the Commons at all, and was no fair proof of treason, as it was dated before the Pacification of Berwick. "The people," it was said, "would sooner pay subsidies to prevent the unhappy war than to carry it on." Grievances formed such an ample subject of debate, that Charles, growing impatient, sent a message saying, if the Parliament would grant him twelve subsidies, to be paid in three years, he would never levy ship money without consent of Parliament (4th May, 1640). Though the Commons felt indignant that they should be asked to purchase immunity from an illegal tax, they were about, after a long debate, to put the question to the vote, whether a supply should be given to the king, without, for the present, specifying any particular sum, when Sir Henry Vane, Charles' secretary, rose and said it was of no use to put that question, for the king would not accept less than he had asked. In disgust the House broke up; and the next morning, Charles having lost patience, dissolved the Parliament (5th May, 1640).

Charles' fourth Parliament.

* *I.e.*, to fetter, or put in gyves. See Shaks. Henry VIII. v. 3.

Arbitrary measures were now again employed to raise money for the war; and refusers of loans were imprisoned. But no severity was able to suppress the spirit of opposition. The gentry of Yorkshire sent a petition to the king, complaining of the billeting of unruly soldiers, "to whose violence and insolence we are so daily subject, as we cannot say we possess our wives and children in security. Wherefore," continues the petition, "we are emboldened to present these our complaints, beseeching your Majesty that, as the billeting of soldiers in any of your subjects' houses is contrary to the ancient laws of this kingdom confirmed by your Majesty in the Petition of Right, this insupportable charge may be taken off."* Riots broke out in London; the militia refused to serve; officers and soldiers said they would not fight 'to support the power and pride of bishops.' Soldiers had to be pressed, and artisans were daily dragged from the shops and forced on board the fleet. A disorderly army was at length formed; when formed it would not fight. Some regiments dispersed of themselves; others killed officers who were Catholics; others broke open the prisons, and made havoc of the country through which they passed. Before Strafford, the general of the army, reached the camp, his soldiers fled before the enemy; this was at Newburn Ford, on the borders of the two kingdoms (28th Aug., 1640). The Scots, having by this easy success gained possession of the passage of the Tyne, entered Newcastle without opposition, and continued to advance in the direction of York.

<small>Soldiers mutinous; refuse to fight.</small>

Charles' weakness was now proved. Doubtful and despondent, he knew not what to do or whither to turn for counsel. The Irish army, though in good training, was only about 5000 strong, and was required in Ireland to overawe the people. The Scots were in the kingdom, masters of the four northern counties, while his own army refused to fight. Yet a Parliament seemed a terribly caustic remedy to apply to his difficulties, and he bethought himself of calling an assembly, composed solely of peers, as had occasionally been the custom of English kings four centuries before, when the House of Commons was hardly recognized as an integral part of the government. Perhaps, thought some credulous courtier, this assembly of peers might even vote

<small>Assembly of peers at York.</small>

* Petition of Yorkshire gentry, 28th July, 1640, MSS. Clar. Pap. and Rushworth.

the king money. But the nation thought otherwise. "If," said two lords consulted by the king's council, "it be intended to raise money by any other way than a Parliament, it will give no satisfaction."* Charles was left in no doubt of his subjects' wishes; counties sent petitions for a Parliament; twelve of the chief peers of the realm signed a petition for a Parliament; the City of London petitioned for a Parliament; the Scots sent a petition: 'they were loyal subjects, their grievances were the cause of their being in arms; they begged their king to settle a firm and durable peace by advice of a Parliament.' So at last, forced by necessity, Charles yielded. When the peers met at York (24th Sept., 1640), he informed them that he had already sent out writs for a Parliament, and asked their advice for treating with the Scots. "They were so taken," writes the king's secretary, "with his Majesty's speech and with his Majesty's offer of a Parliament that whatever was afterwards proposed they yielded to. . . . There is no doubt but this black storm will be dispersed."† Charles summons his fifth Parliament.

Sixteen peers, none of them favourable to arbitrary government, negotiated with eight Scottish commissioners at Ripon. It was agreed that a cessation of arms should be made for two months; that both armies should remain where they were; that the northern counties should support the Scottish army by paying it £5600 a week, until a peace should be concluded in London (23rd Oct., 1640). Then king, lords, and Scottish commissioners hastened to the capital, where Charles met his fifth and last Parliament (3rd Nov., 1640).

* Clar. State Papers, 1—112.
† Windebank to Sir A. Hopton, 1st Oct., 1640, MSS. Clar. Papers in Bodleian.

CHAPTER IV.

MEETING OF LONG PARLIAMENT AND TRIAL OF STRAFFORD.
1640—1641.

> Had I but served my God with half the zeal
> I served my king, he would not in mine age
> Have left me naked to mine enemies.—HENRY VIII., iii. 2.

WESTMINSTER HALL, in the year 1640, was just the same building that we see to-day : but the house in which the Commons sat was utterly different. At right angles to the hall, between it and the river, stood a building which was once a chapel of the old palace of Westminster, but was now fitted with tiers of horse-shoe benches for the members of the Commons. The building itself was small, somewhat dingy and gloomy ; though sittings were generally by day, on winter afternoons candles were placed on a table in the centre. The appearance of the members, however, belied the meanness of their meeting-house; for these were peers' sons, country gentlemen, merchants, lawyers, distinguished in their towns or counties for birth or wealth, or both ; their dress displayed their quality—the sword by the side, the velvet coat, the large frilled linen collar to protect the lace and gold or silver trimming from the long hair falling in curls upon the shoulders, were sure signs that the House did not count among its members any of the fanatics from the lower orders, who cut their hair close and prided themselves upon the especial plainness of their attire.

<small>House of Commons.</small>

<small>Leading members.</small> Chief amongst the many notables of that assembly were John Pym, John Hampden, Lord Falkland,* Edward Hyde, Oliver Cromwell. Pym, the old opposer of tyranny in the previous reign ; Hampden, the ship-money hero, gentle and affable to all, and now the most popular man in the House ; Lord Falkland, whose truthful, generous nature made him the declared enemy of injustice in high places; Hyde, afterwards Earl of Clarendon, and

---

* He had succeeded his father (Sir H. Cary, Deputy of Ireland), as second Viscount of Falkland, in the county of Fife, in Scotland. He sat as burgess for Newport, Scotch peers being eligible before the Act of Union (1707).

the Royalist historian of the Rebellion, now carried along with the stream, and as eager as his friend Falkland to restore the old government of England by Parliaments; Cromwell, member for the town of Cambridge, a country gentleman, dressed in a plain cloth suit, and as yet little remarked, save for his activity in defending the poor of his own neighbourhood from oppression.

The members of both Houses of Parliament, urged by a hundred different motives, were almost unanimous in their determination to make the agents of the government answer for their conduct, and above all, the chief offender, Strafford. The noble ruinously fined in the Star Chamber; the courtier of whom Strafford had used sharp words, as 'that the king would do well to cut off his head;' the merchant, forced to pay illegal customs; the patriot, indignant at the judges' verdict that ship-money was a just and legal tax; the Presbyterian fined and insulted by the Court of High Commission, were all alike eager to gratify, as the case might be, their desires for reform, or justice, or revenge.

<small>Grievances, delinquents.</small>

The House proceeded to business at once. Votes were passed that all monopolists should be deprived of their seats (9th Nov.), that ship-money was against the laws of the realm (7th Dec.),* that all agents of the crown who had taken part in the collection of ship-money, or had shared in any other acts condemned by the

* Lord Falkland felt and spoke strongly on the extra-judicial opinion the judges had given at Charles' request, on the king's right to ship-money. "No meal undigested," he said, "can lie heavier upon the stomach than that unsaid would have lain upon my conscience." He complained that the judges, "the persons who should have been as dogs to defend the flock, have become the wolves to devour it;" that they had exceeded their functions, "being judges of law and not of necessity, that is, being judges and not philosophers or politicians;" that to justify the plea of necessity, they have "supposed mighty and eminent dangers in the most quiet and halcyon days, but a few contemptible pirates being our most formidable enemies;" they also "supposing the supposed doings to be so sudden that it could not stay for a Parliament which required but a forty days' stay, allowed to the king the sole power in necessity, the sole judgment of necessity, and by that enabled him to take from us what he would, when he would, and how he would." He especially declaimed against the Chief Justice (at this time Lord Keeper) Finch, who importuned the other judges "as a most admirable solicitor, but a most abominable judge." . . . "He it was who gave away with his breath what our ancestors have purchased with so long expense of their time, their care, their treasures, and their bloods, and strove to make our grievances mortal and our slavery irreparable," . . . "he who hath already undone us by wholesale [and now as chancellor] hath the power of undoing us by retail."—MSS. Clarendon Papers, No. 1464, and Rushworth.

House, were 'delinquents,' and might be proceeded against at any moment. This made offenders of all ranks tremble, lords of the Council and Star Chamber, lords-lieutenant of counties, sheriffs, judges, besides a host of inferior officers. It was not so much the intention of the Commons to proceed against all these delinquents, as to terrify them into submission. The chief criminals alone had real cause to fear.

Strafford* had seen the storm gathering and was anxious to return to Ireland, but Charles wrote him a positive command to come to London, assuring him, 'as he was King of England, he was able to secure him from any danger, and the Parliament should not touch one hair of his head.' The king was in fact afraid of meeting his enraged Parliament unsupported. Accordingly Strafford came prepared with charges of treason against some of the leading members, for having encouraged the Scots in rebellion. They were aware of his intention and determined to strike first. No time was lost. Their feelings at this crisis are analyzed in Browning's lines:

Strafford trusts in Charles.

"Now, by Heaven,
They may be cool who can, silent who will—
Some have a gift that way! Wentworth is here;
Here, and the king's safe closeted with him
Ere this. And when I think on all that's past—
. . . . how all this while
That man has set himself to one dear task,
The bringing Charles to relish more and more
Power—power without law, power and blood too—
Can I be still?"

Strafford had only been one day in London when, on the 11th of November, Pym proposed in the House of Commons to impeach of high treason the man who, "according to the nature of apostates, had become the greatest enemy to the liberties of his country, and the greatest promoter of tyranny that any age had produced."

Impeachment of Strafford.

The process by impeachment has been described in Buckingham's case,† it is still more familiar to us from the trial of Warren Hastings in the following century (1788). The king having no part in an impeachment, and the House of Lords being judge, the only preliminary required is a resolution of the Commons to pro-

---

* Wentworth created Earl of Strafford, 12 Jan. 1640.   † See page 34.

secute. The Commons now agreed to the proposal without a dissenting voice, and Pym, followed by a train of three hundred members, went up straight to the Lords' house, and there accused the earl of high treason, desiring that he might be lodged a prisoner in the Tower, until the time of his trial came on.

Thus, at one blow, was the king deprived of his ablest adviser, and Strafford himself of the awe with which power had previously invested him. Strafford was in consultation with the king when the news came. Hastening to the Lords' house with a "proud, glooming countenance, he makes towards his place at the board-head. But at once many bid him void the house. After consultation, being called in, he stands, but is commanded to kneel, and on his knees, is delivered to the keeper of the black rod, to be prisoner until he was cleared of those crimes the House of Commons had charged him with. As he passed through the gazing crowd outside to find his coach, no man capped to him, before whom that morning the greatest of England would have stood discovered, all crying, 'What is the matter?' He said, 'A small matter, I warrant you.' They replied, 'Yes, indeed, high treason is a small matter.'" *Strafford sent to Tower.*

The next month Laud was impeached too (18th Dec.), and followed his friend to the Tower, amid the curses and howlings of the populace. Windebank, the king's secretary, wise in time, jumped into an open boat, and, steering through the mist, succeeded in putting the Channel between him and his foes. Finch, though known as the first adviser of imposing ship-money on the inland counties, hoped much from the graceful defence he made before the Commons. But the temper of his hearers was too stern; "There be birds," said one, "that in the summer of Parliament will sing sweetly, that in winter turn into birds of prey!" The most he could effect was to be allowed, like others, to escape into exile. *Other 'delinquents.'*

Judge Berkeley, the principal supporter of ship-money, was also a marked man. The messenger of the Lords entered Westminster Hall, while the courts of justice were sitting, and then and there carried him off to the Tower, impeached by the Commons of high treason. The gazing crowd felt awe-struck, while the consciences of some of Berkeley's brethren gave them uneasy qualms.

Reparation to sufferers. Hand in hand with justice went reparation. The prison doors were opened to men shut up for five or eight or ten years, as the case might be. Chambers, the merchant, came out ruined; Leighton, a minister, unable to walk or stand or see; Lilburne, with a tale to tell of starvation, irons, and the scourge. Prynne, Burton, and Bastwick came from their distant prisons in Jersey, Guernsey, and Scilly, to forget the shame of the pillory and the loss of their ears, in the triumph of the day when they were welcomed back to London by thousands of men and women decked with white rosemary and bay and filling the air with their acclamations.* Large numbers of sufferers brought their cases before committees of Parliament, and had the satisfaction of hearing their sentences declared illegal, while many received compensation in money for their losses.

But the event which above all others excited men's minds, was the trial of Strafford. Until March, a committee of Parliament was engaged in examining witnesses and preparing the case. The Scots joined in the prosecution, accusing Strafford of having been the cause of the war, and even the Irish, lately so submissive, now sent over charges against the deputy. On the 22nd of March the trial began. In the cold spring morning, **Scene of trial.** as early as five o'clock, crowds might be seen gathering about Westminster. A stage was erected, reaching right across the end of the hall. Here sat the judges, the members of the House of Lords, about eighty in number, 'wearing their red robes lined with white ermine.' The lawn of the bishops was not seen at trials for life. At one end of the stage sat the committee of the Commons who conducted the impeachment, at the other Strafford's secretaries and counsel. Behind the lords' seats was the empty throne; the king and queen, though present, sat in a gallery concealed by curtains. On both sides of the hall, east and west, the forms rising one above another to the roof were occupied by the members of the Commons, with the Scottish commissioners, and some favoured friends. Ladies paid high prices for seats in galleries, and diligently took notes of the proceedings.

About eight Strafford was brought from the Tower by water. All were struck with his appearance. Clad in black, his coun-

---

* May, Long Parl., 54; Baillie, i. 222.

tenance pale through suffering, his body bent by illness, he bore himself with a proud humility, implying excess of courtesy, and not defect of confidence. Having first bowed to the court, he took his place in a small desk in front of his judges, where he stood or sat at pleasure.

Precedents of harsh procedure too often return to plague the inventors. The difficulties put in the way of state criminals whom kings attacked, were now all cast in the way of Strafford, whose life the people were seeking. He had himself to examine witnesses brought against him, and to speak as to the truth of the facts of which he was accused. His counsel were only allowed at the close of the trial to argue that the facts did not fall within the legal definition of high treason. Course of state trials in seventeenth century. Though most of his witnesses were in Ireland, he had not been allowed to summon them to attend, until three days before the trial. He did not know from day to day what charges would be brought against him, but after his accusers had spoken, was allowed half an hour to sit down with his secretaries and prepare his answer. The time given was not favourable for quiet thought. During these intervals the whole hall rose to its feet, judges, prosecutors, spectators, talking and laughing; bread and meat were handed about, bottles of beer and wine 'went thick from mouth to mouth,' and all this in the king's eyes, who, in the excitement of the trial, with his own hands tore down the curtains in front of his gallery, and there sat visible to all, but as unregarded as if he had not been present.*

Thus unaided for seventeen days, from eight in the morning until three or four in the afternoon, Strafford had to hear and answer his accusers and their witnesses.

The crime of high treason was defined by a statute of Edward III. (1351), to consist of seven offences. Law of high treason. Five of these did not touch Strafford. The two under which he was prosecuted were those of 'levying war upon the king,' and 'compassing the king's death.' Of all legal procedure, prosecutions for high treason are the most unintelligible to the ordinary mind. The interpretations of the judges had extended the meaning of 'levying war,' to mean any overt act which was considered objectionable; that 'of Forced interpretation of judges.

* Baillie, i. 259, 265.

compassing or imagining the king's death,' to mean any objectionable purpose which was not carried into act. To understand this process it is necessary to recall the origin of the act, and the fact of the dependence of the judges upon the crown. The act was brought forward by the nobles as a safeguard to themselves, by defining more clearly in what treason consisted. They had found before that if the crown wished to confiscate their lands, it could make out anything to be treason; but though they hoped much from a clearer definition, they gained little; first, because the judges extended the meaning of the words of the law; secondly, because untrustworthy evidence was admitted as to the facts. As an instance of the first, a rioter who had joined in an attack upon Laud's palace at Lambeth, was convicted of high treason for 'having levied war upon the king.' Of the second, Sir Walter Raleigh's case may serve as an epitome.* The evidence on which he was convicted of having intrigued with Spanish emissaries to set Arabella Stuart on the throne, was the written accusation of one witness, who retracted, and then retracted his retractation, and was never confronted with the prisoner. A correspondent of the time wrote of Raleigh's trial thus: "The evidence was no more to be weighed than the barking of a dog. I would not for much have been of the jury to have found him guilty."†

<small>Laxity of evidence.</small>

These forced interpretations of the judges and their laxity about evidence, were unjustifiable enough, but there was another process at work, of a perfectly legitimate character, which had enlarged the meaning of laws containing the king's name. In England the constitution has continually changed in fact, without changing in form, and the fictions of the constitutional lawyers have been the regular means by which, as liberty has advanced, new facts have been brought under old forms. It is on this principle, that from the doctrine of the irresponsibility of the king, the constitutional lawyers have justly treated the name of king as meaning not the mere fallible being who wears the crown for the moment, but the true king who acts in accordance with the constitution he represents. The obvious plea, that Strafford had acted according to Charles' wishes and therefore could not have levied war upon the king, no lawyer would have thought of urging in the earl's defence. The king, the ideal king of English

<small>Ideal king of English law.</small>

* See page 23. † Jardine: Criminal Trials.

law, 'can do no wrong,' and under all circumstances is the maintainer of the rights and liberties of his subjects. Though illegal acts are done by a king's command, a court of justice is bound to set this fact aside, and regard them as committed contrary to his wishes. The minister, therefore, who attacks the liberties of the subject, is also in the eye of the law attacking the authority of the king.

Yet the managers of the prosecution had a difficult task in trying to bring Strafford's acts within the definition of treason. As to the question of law, there were two main charges, which must be kept clearly distinct. The first and finally successful charge was the billeting of soldiers upon the people of Ireland, *in order to make them submit to illegal commands*, which was said to amount to 'levying war upon the king,' as it was really reducing the country by conquest. It must be allowed that technically Strafford had broken the law, and that what he had done amounted to treason within the meaning of the statute. But his counsel could argue that like arbitrary acts of power had been committed by previous deputies, and that he had not committed the offence in a manner systematic enough to be found guilty upon a liberal interpretation of the law. *'Levying war upon the king.'*

The second and unsuccessful point was the 'compassing the death of the king,' which they interpreted as meaning an endeavour to subvert the laws of the realm represented by the king. This accusation rested on Strafford's having advised Charles in council to bring over the Irish army to reduce 'this kingdom,' meaning England, to subjection. They had to prove both the question of fact and the question of law. *'Compassing the king's death.'*

As to the facts, Strafford could point to a straining of evidence, and could show up some charges as absurd in themselves, others as breaking down in proof. The prosecutors could retort, they were sufficiently proved, the sufficiency being in the custom of the time, and the usage of the courts which Strafford had administered. The fact that was most stoutly contested was 'the advising Charles to use the Irish army to reduce this kingdom.' The witness to this was no less than Sir Henry Vane, the king's secretary. Strafford's answer was that 'this kingdom' meant not England, but Scotland, which was then in rebellion, and he brought other members of the council to swear that they had no recollection of his advising Charles to use an army against English liberty. The importance which the Commons attached to the proof of this fact will be shown in the sequel.

<small>Cumulative treason.</small> As to the question of law, the Commons argued that it did not depend on this single article, but that the whole of the charges, twenty-eight in all, mounted up to a sort of accumulative treason, proving that Strafford had formed a scheme to subvert the laws of the realm, and govern by means of a standing army. This design of enforcing submission by means of an armed force was what moved the Commons most deeply. If that was not high treason, the constitution was a mockery indeed. If the law of high treason was to protect the sovereign power of the State, and if this sovereign power was not the king only, but the king acting through his Parliament, then to destroy Parliament was to destroy the vitality of the king. Was it 'compassing the king's death?' Well, would it not have been the death of the constitution? It would, no doubt, and should certainly have been included in a good law defining high treason against the State. But it was not. Pym felt this himself when he made the following grand rhetorical appeal to the earl's judges. "Shall it be treason to embase the king's coin, though but a piece of twelvepence or sixpence? and must it not needs be the effect of a greater treason to embase the spirit of his subjects, and to set up a stamp and character of servitude upon them, whereby they shall be disabled to do anything for the service of the king and the commonwealth?" The king can indeed have no interest but the good of his subjects, and Pym's view was here as ever that of the true constitutional statesman, but it lacked the support of precedents to commend it to judges. Strafford's plea of moderation on the other hand was easily met. "His moderation! when you find so many imprisoned of the nobility! so many men, some adjudged to death, some executed without law! when you find so many public rapines on the state, soldiers sent to make good his decrees, so many whippings in defence of monopolies, so many gentlemen that were jurors, because they would not apply themselves to give verdicts on his side, to be fined in the Star Chamber, men of quality to be disgraced, set in the pillory, and wearing papers and such things—can you, my lords, think there was any moderation?"

On the 10th of April, additional evidence, hitherto kept back, was read in the House of Commons, in support of the charge of advising the king to use the Irish army against English liberty. Before the meeting of the present Parliament, young Sir Henry Vane had found in his father's despatch box some notes made in council of the very debate in which Strafford advised the king to use the Irish army to reduce 'this kingdom.' He had shown them to Pym, who had made a copy, now produced. The double evidence upon the same article was considered conclusive of Strafford's guilt, and Sir Arthur Haslerig proposed to proceed against him by Bill of Attainder,* in other words to vote him guilty by act of Parliament. The motive for this change in procedure was "to avoid delay, which was now of extreme dangerous consequence." The known faithlessness of the king, and the peril impending from it, justified much informality. When a prisoner's friends threaten violence, they can hardly complain if his foes quicken the slow processes of law.

<small>Bill of Attainder.</small>

It has generally been supposed that this measure was brought in by the extreme patriots; but a member's notes, made in Parliament at the time, have revealed the fact that whereas it was warmly supported by the moderates, such as Hyde,† Falkland, Culpepper, and others, who took the Royalist side in the war; it was opposed by both Pym and Hampden, who preferred to ask the Lords to give judgment on the trial by impeachment. They had a quiet confidence in the goodness of their case, and were anxious to avoid even the appearance of differing from the Lords. However, on finding those who supported them were bent on the measure, they acquiesced, sharing, as they did, the universal conviction that, if Strafford escaped with his life, the king would restore him to power. But others gave utterance to the criticism to which such measures are undoubtedly open.

"I do not say," said the Royalist, Lord Digby, "but the charges may represent him as a man worthy to die, and perhaps worthier than many a traitor.

---

* Bills of Attainder were first introduced by Henry VIII. The last instance of the legislature's passing a Bill of Attainder, was in the case of Sir John Fenwick, in the reign of William III. See a remarkably clear statement of the character of such bills in Macaulay's Hist., c. 22 and 23.

† It is a significant fact that, among the Clarendon State Papers at Oxford, none are to be found relating to Strafford's trial. As there must have been such, it is presumed that Hyde destroyed them, wishing to conceal that he had acted on the popular side. His name is not in the list of 'Straffordians.'

I do not say but they may justly direct us to enact that they shall be treason for the future. But God keep me from giving judgment of death on any man upon a law made *à posteriori*. Let the mark be set on the door where the plague is, and then let him that will enter, die. I believe his practices in themselves as high, as tyrannical, as any subject ever ventured on; and the malignity of them largely aggravated by those rare abilities of his, whereof God has given him the use, but the devil the application. In one word, I believe him to be still that grand apostate to the commonwealth, who must not expect to be pardoned in this world till he be despatched to the other. And yet let me tell you, Mr. Speaker, my hand must not be to that despatch."

The bill, however, easily passed the Commons (21st April); only fifty-nine members voted against it, whose names were posted up in the streets of London, as 'Straffordians, enemies to their country.' The trial by impeachment in Westminster Hall still continued. Strafford made a brilliant defence, in which he carefully turned the attention of his hearers away from the billeting or 'levying war upon the king,' the weak point of his case, to the weak point of the prosecution, the charge of 'compassing the king's death.' The highway, which brought him to the Tower, furnished a simple illustration which seemed to demolish their laboured construction.

Strafford's defence.
"My lords," he said, "I do not conceive that there is either statute law, or common law, that hath declared this—endeavouring to subvert the fundamental laws—to be high treason. Jesu! my lords, where hath this fire lain all this while, so many hundred years together that no smoke should appear till it burst out now, to consume me and my children? Hard it is, and extreme hard, in my opinion, that I should be punished by a law subsequent to the act done. . . . If I pass down the Thames in a boat, and run and split myself upon an anchor, if there be not a buoy to give me warning, the party shall give me damages; but if it be marked out, then it is at my own peril. Now, my lords, where is the mark set upon this crime? where is the token by which I should discover? if it be not marked, if it lie under water and not above, there is no human providence can prevent the destruction of a man instantly and presently. My lords, I have troubled your lordships a great deal longer than I would have done; were it not for the interest of those pledges, that a saint in heaven left me, I should be loath, my lords [here his weeping stopped him]—what I forfeit for myself is nothing; but I confess that my indiscretion should forfeit for them, it wounds me very deeply; you will be pleased to pardon my importunity, something I should have said, but I see I shall not be able, and therefore I will leave it. . . ."*

---

* Nalson, ii. 123.

And then lifting up his hands and eyes, he said, 'In te, Domine, confido ne confundar in æternum.' Strafford's defence had laid bare the real principle at issue, as far as the court was concerned. A law has a relation to the innocent as well as to the guilty. If the law of high treason meant that those guilty of such and such crimes should die, it meant just as much that those not guilty of them should have their lives safe, as far as the crime of treason was concerned. Such stretching of a law might be as dangerous to the liberty of the subject as the offences with which Strafford was charged. For if the words, 'compassing the king's death' should at one time be made to include a scheme of subverting the laws, they might, he argued, at another be made to include some other offence equally far from their literal meaning, and thus men's lives, finding no protection in the law, would lie at the mercy of any party in power. Strafford carried his judges with him in thus repelling the charge of compassing the king's death. Peers indeed had no wish to extend the responsibility of ministers too far. The prosecutors, however, felt that the extension of this principle was the only security for their lives; they considered that the simple meaning of the words could not be trusted as a complete exponent of the cases included, without implying a perfection of form in English law which did not exist, and that the gist of his argument was, that a malefactor who found a new way to break the principle of a law should get the benefit of his ability at the expense of their liberties, while, as to the possibility of future consequences from such straining of law, they felt that their chief fear in that respect was from Strafford himself. It had fallen to Pym to reply to the earl's defence. As he ended his speech, he caught the eye of his old friend earnestly fixed upon him: he faltered, turned over his papers, and, with difficulty recovering himself, asked their lordships to close the proceedings for the day. Strafford's friends, meanwhile, were not idle. The queen, fond of exercising power, and anxious to avert this blow to royalty, now exerted herself in his behalf. Torch in hand, she was nightly to be found holding conferences with popular lords, offering them, as she thought, all they could desire, if only they would save Strafford's life.* A compromise was proposed: Charles offered to form a ministry out of the opposition leaders both in Opposition refuse office.

* De Motteville, i.

Lords and Commons; the Earl of Bedford was to be treasurer; St. John, a member of the Commons, had already been made solicitor-general; places were to be found for the Earl of Essex, for Hampden, Pym, Hollis, and others. The new ministry, on their side, were to allow Strafford to escape with his life, and to ward off any attack made against the bishops by the Presbyterians. The compromise, however, was never effected. Bedford died, Essex was not to be persuaded: "Stone dead," said the blunt, plain-spoken earl, "hath no fellow;* if he be fined or imprisoned, the king will grant him his pardon as soon as the Parliament is ended." Pym and Hampden were not less far-sighted than Essex, and had even better reasons for distrusting any advances from the king.

Army plot. The Scottish and English armies were still in the northern counties, awaiting the ratification of the treaty, after which the one was to be disbanded and the other to return to Scotland. The Parliament, looking upon the Scots as friends, who would, in case of need, render assistance against the king, had voted them £300,000 as a free gift. But the English army had no love for the Parliament, which had no wish to do anything for them. The soldiers had become discontented because their pay was in arrear, while of the officers, many were Catholics, almost all devoted partizans of the king. Ill-feeling towards the Parliament was so general, that some of the leading officers in London ventured on talking over with the queen an ill-matured plan of bringing up the army to coerce the Parliament. Charles gave his assent, though at the very time he was negotiating with the leaders of the Parliament. Naturally he would sooner have seen Hampden, Pym, and Essex changing places with Strafford and Laud in the Tower, than have had them sitting by his side in the council chamber. Still, such a double-dealing game was a hazardous one to play, and Pym was not an easy man to overreach: he had his spies abroad to tell him the tavern discourse of too sanguine officers; he had his friends even in the court circle; in fact, the whole plan had been betrayed by Lord Goring, one of the conspirators, and Pym was only holding back his knowledge from the Parliament until he should find the fittest moment for revealing it. While these

* Clar. Hist., i. 395.

negotiations and army plots were going on behind the scenes, the nation still had its attention fixed on the Bill of Attainder, which did not easily make its way through the Lords. Charles tried to intimidate by threatening to refuse his assent. He summoned the two Houses, and told them that he did not consider the earl fit to serve him even in the position of a constable, but that no fear, no respect whatsoever should make him act against his conscience in consenting to his death (1st May). But if the king threatened on the one side, the people threatened on the other. The next day was Sunday; the London pulpits preached the duty of justice upon a great delinquent. By the Monday London was roused; some thousands of apprentices and others, armed with swords and cudgels, gathered around Westminster Hall, crying, 'Justice on Strafford, justice on traitors,' and demanding from every lord as he went into the house, 'that they might have speedy execution on the earl, or they were all undone, their wives and children.' The Lords, dismayed at their violence, spoke them fair, and sent word to the Commons to demand aid in suppressing the tumult. But the messenger could gain no admittance; the doors of the Commons' house had been locked since seven o'clock in the morning, and remained locked until eight o'clock that evening. Within, fear, horror, and amazement sat on the faces of the members, for Pym was revealing to them, not only that grand idea of bringing up the army to crush the Parliament, but various other desperate designs formed by the friends of Strafford; how there was a plan of sending a hundred picked men into the Tower, where Strafford was confined, under the name of a guard; how bribery had been attempted on the governor to let his prisoner escape; how, lastly, there was some dark design of bringing over a French force into Portsmouth.

A protestation was drawn up on Pym's motion, to defend the privileges of Parliament and the lawful rights of the people, and signed by every member present. Hyde, who had written his name second on the list, took it up to the Lords himself to receive their signatures.* Great was the panic in London when the doors of the Commons were unbarred. To think of an army led by Royalist and Papist officers, marching into their city, the strong-

* Forster: Lives of British Statesmen, iii. 185. Grand Remonstrance.

hold of Presbyterian faith! Rumours of plots, true and false, were in every man's mouth, and easily found credence. The Lords began to think their own lives in danger from the populace, if they delayed the trial any longer. Having already voted the facts of some of the articles of impeachment proved, they now appealed to the judges on the question of law. The judges unanimously declared 'that upon all their lordships had voted to be proved, the earl was guilty of high treason.' On this the Lords passed the Bill of Attainder, voting the earl guilty, not upon all the articles, but only upon the fifteenth, the quartering of troops upon the people of Ireland, and the nineteenth, the imposing an unlawful oath upon the Scots in Ireland. In voting on the bill, it is important to observe, that they acted as nearly as possible as if they had been giving judgment on the impeachment, for they used the forms in which they were accustomed to vote as judges, not as legislators.* Thirty-four lords stayed away; twenty-six voted for the bill, nineteen against it (7th May).

<small>Lords pass Bill of Attainder.</small>

Strafford's warning that the precedent of the case might be used against others no doubt had weight with many who had supported the king in unconstitutional acts, but these only succeeded in protecting themselves so far as to insert a clause in the bill, to the effect that the judges should count nothing as treason in consequence of this bill which was not treason before. As the judges had pronounced the acts were treason, the clause was unmeaning. But now Charles' turn was come. If he had in him the courage to resist, if not to resent, intimidation, in these desperate circumstances he had still the opportunity of securing one of two triumphs, either of saving the life of the earl, or of throwing on Parliament the reproach of executing him against law, for that he possessed the legal right to refuse his consent to any bill was at that time undisputed. It might have been thought, therefore, that the king would have been glad of the substitution

---

* The difference between voting on a Bill of Attainder and an impeachment is, that in giving judgment on the latter a peer professed to be bound by the letter of the law and of the rules of evidence; in voting for the former, though bound by the spirit, he professedly held himself emancipated from the letter. Further, there was a great difference in form. In voting for a bill a peer says 'aye' in his seat, and if a division is called, walks in silence past the teller of his side; in voting on an impeachment each peer stands up in his place, puts his hand on his breast, and says, 'Guilty (or not) on my honour.'

of the bill for the impeachment, since the change gave him an opportunity of making good his promises to Strafford. But these were not Charles' feelings. His chief misery lay not in the fact that Strafford must die, but that his own hand must consent to his death. The angry rabble followed him to Whitehall, with their shouts of "justice, justice, we will have justice." The queen wept bitterly, in fear, it seems, for her own safety, as she began to make preparations to leave the country. In anguish of soul Charles asked his councillors how the rioters were to be suppressed; they bade him please his Parliament and pass the Bill of Attainder: he asked five bishops how he was to remove his scruples of conscience; all but one told him he had both a public and a private conscience, and that the duty of saving the life of a friend or servant was as nothing compared with that of preserving his kingdom. The same day a letter was handed him from the earl bidding him pass the bill—"Sire, my consent shall more acquit you herein to God than all the world can do besides; to a willing man there is no injury done."

Charles passes Bill of Attainder.

"My Lord of Strafford's condition," said Charles, "is more happy than mine."* He shed tears, but sent a commission for others to sign the bill, a mode of relieving his conscience suggested to him by his council. 'Put not your trust in princes, nor in the sons of men, for in them there is no salvation,' Strafford exclaimed when told that the king had consented to his death. After passing the bill, Charles sent a letter to the House of Lords by the hands of the Prince of Wales, requesting the Parliament to commute the punishment of death into that of perpetual imprisonment; the letter, however, had a postscript: 'If he must die, it were charity to reprieve him till Saturday.' But the discovery of the plot for Strafford's release had made longer imprisonment impossible, and the House ordered the execution for the next day (12th May).

In forming a judgment on the justice of the conviction upon which Strafford suffered, we must recall the various points—that the lawyers and judges in serving the interests of the crown, had really enlarged the statute; that undoubtedly the earl had technically offended against the

Question of justice of Strafford's conviction.

---

* Radcliffe's Life in Straff. Despatches.

law, by quartering troops to coerce the people; that the Commons heard the points of law argued at length in their house, and decided that his acts fell within the provision of the statute, before they passed the third reading of the bill ; that after this the judges declared that the facts voted to be proved amounted to high treason by law; that the Lords, by voting judicially upon the bill, were acting as supreme judges when they also declared that in their view the offences came within the statute ; and lastly, that proceeding by bill only gave the king a chance of exercising his prerogative of mercy, which he would not otherwise have had. Briefly put, the case would amount to this, that the judicial competence of the House of Lords was unquestioned, but in this case Strafford's peers, acting simply as a jury, declared certain facts proved, the judges of the land declared the law on these facts against him, and the peers then pronounced the verdict ; and though the fact that the conviction itself was on small and technical grounds might well be pleaded as an extenuating circumstance to reprieve him from the full punishment of death, yet his own conduct towards others deprived him of any such claim to exceptional mercy. It has hardly been sufficiently observed that, whatever the contemplated object of the bill, its actual effect was not to enlarge the statute retrospectively, but only to alter the procedure. If we apply the standard of the nineteenth century to judge of the procedure of the seventeenth, we shall say that this conviction of treason was not just, though it was far more just than any other of that day.

So far as to the technical issue. At the bar of history, Strafford is arraigned as a traitor to the constitution. He is proved guilty by the undoubted evidence of his own correspondence. The two restraints on the executive are, the freedom of Parliament and the independence of the judges. According to Strafford's scheme, judges were to receive percentages on verdicts for the crown, and dismissal for verdicts against it. Parliament was only to vote subsidies, and not inquire into grievances. Discontent at grievances unredressed was to be quelled by a standing army. This standing army was to be supported by taxes levied, like ship-money, on the sole authority of the crown. If we turn now to Pym's ideal, since realized, and look upon this picture and on that, we shall with Hallam 'distrust any one's attachment to the English constitution, who reveres the name of the Earl of Strafford.'

CHAPTER V.
GRAND REMONSTRANCE.—IMPEACHMENT OF FIVE MEMBERS.
1641—1642.

* * It is not so, thou hast misspoke, misheard ;
Be well advised, tell o'er thy tale again :
It cannot be ; thou dost but say 'tis so :
I trust I may not trust thee ; for thy word
Is but the vain breath of a common man:
Believe me, I do not believe thee, man ;
I have a king's oath to the contrary.—KING JOHN, iii. 1.

DURING Strafford's trial, the Commons had not been unmindful of reform. Early in the year Charles had given his consent to a bill which required that a Parliament should be elected once every three years, and that no future Parliament should be dissolved or adjourned, without its own consent, in less than fifty days from the opening of the session (16th Feb.). In order that the act might not remain a dead letter, it provided that if the king failed in his duty, various officers employed in the Government should send out writs for elections in his stead ; and that if these failed in their duty, the electors should meet of themselves and choose their representatives.

The too long continuance of the same Parliament changes the character of the House of Commons from that of a popular assembly to that of an oligarchical senate, by making the members heedless of the wishes of their constituents, and apt to sacrifice their duties to their interests. The too frequent election of new Parliaments renders members subservient to their electors, so that instead of following some settled course of action according to their own convictions, they act merely as delegates apt to reflect every prejudice that obtains amongst the multitude. There is no universal rule of right in this matter. In the seventeenth century, new Parliaments might, without injury to their character, have been elected every year, so slight was the control constituents possessed over their representatives. The House of Commons was subject to the influence of the court; the county members were gentlemen by birth, often connected by blood or marriage with peers and ministers; while the members for small boroughs were returned according to the directions of neighbouring peers and gentlemen. No public meetings were held for the debate of political questions. No petitions of a political character had been presented to any previous Parliament. No newspaper press existed before the commencement of the civil war. The votes of members were unrecorded. Parliamentary debates were never published. The privilege of excluding strangers from the House was constantly exerted by the Commons. London, however, in stirring times, knew much and judged freely; but at duller periods there was a want of the coffee-houses of a later date to bring public opinion to a focus. The knowledge of events in London took months in circulating through the country. The action, therefore, of a Triennial Bill would have been beneficial in itself, and the experience of the last eleven years had shown the absolute necessity of a guarantee for the meeting of Parliaments. The measure which followed was of a different character.

At the same time that he gave his consent to the Bill of Attainder, Charles, sick at heart, without heeding its contents, passed a second bill, depriving him of the right to dissolve the Parliament without its own consent (10th May). This bill had been introduced into the Commons upon the disclosure of the Army Plot, which gave Pym and Hampden good cause to doubt, whether their own lives or the liberties of the people would be safe, were the Parliament once dissolved.

Parliament cannot be dissolved without its own consent.

If too long Parliaments become oligarchical, much more will a Parliament which is indissoluble. It may now, in fact, be taken as an axiom that a Parliament which can only dissolve of its own consent, will never dissolve unless forced to do so by some power external to itself. Either it is in accordance with the popular feeling, in which case there is no reason it should dissolve as it is still representative; or, again, if the pulse of popular opinion beats feebly, it feels it can go on governing as it likes; or, lastly, public opinion is strongly against it, and under these circumstances it feels that dissolution is suicide, so it is then most determined to ride over the storm and wait for a time when sympathy is restored. But in a moment of terror like this such far-sighted calculations would have seemed

Danger of assembly which cannot be dissolved.

but mistrust of the patriotism of fellow-members.* It is not the only occasion on which the disregard of future dangers, induced by the terrors of the present, has brought countries into a constitutional dead-lock.

Statutes were passed to abolish those great engines of tyranny, the courts of Star Chamber, of High Commission, and of the North, and deprive the king's council of all jurisdiction, criminal or civil, and of the power of imprisoning without showing legal cause† (July); as also to prevent the recurrence of what was practically confiscation, by fixing the extent of the royal forests; and, lastly, to declare the illegality of all customs levied without consent of Parliament. *Illegal courts abolished.*

In the Church, reform was also carried on. The times were likened to 'a little Doomsday;' ministers who frequented taverns instead of teaching and preaching, those who burned three hundred wax candles in honour of our Lady, who called the communion table, altar, who taught the people that all they had belonged to the king, or in other ways had the character of being popishly or slavishly inclined, were now all alike turned out of their livings, fined, and imprisoned. *Reform in Church.*

All over the country the Presbyterians and sectarians rose again to the surface. The Presbyterians looked forward to overthrowing the Episcopal Church; the aspirations of the sectarians, or Independents, as they were often called, from the name of their most influential sect, looked rather to securing liberty to worship as they pleased. Men who had lain hid in corners, or migrated to New England, re-appeared to spread their special doctrines. Conventicles were filled, preachings held, by the poorest of the people. No wonder, it was said, "that chandlers, salters, and such like preached, when the Archbishop of Canterbury, instead of preaching, had busied himself in projects about leather, salt, soap, and the like. They had but reciprocally invaded each other's calling."‡ Nevertheless there *Presbyterians and Independents.*

---

* According to an act passed in the first year of George I. (1717), Parliaments now sit for seven years, unless previously dissolved by the crown.

† The statute abolishing the arbitrary courts contained a clause, that any person imprisoned by the command or warrant of the king, or any of his council, should be entitled to a writ of *Habeas Corpus* from the Courts of King's Bench or Common Pleas, without delay on any pretence whatsoever. —See p. 16.)

‡ May, L. P., 75.

were numbers both in the Parliament and the country unwilling to see strange forms of Church government, free preaching, and the growth of schism uncontrolled by the authority of the bishops. Hence when religious matters were debated, the House was far from being at unity. 'Let us keep the Church as it is,' said Hyde and his Church party. 'Let us allow bishops to keep their office, but shut them out of all share in State government, and lessen their power over the clergy,' said Pym and Hampden and the political reformers. 'Let us bring them down, root and branch,' said a third, the Presbyterians. The Independents joined their votes to the Presbyterians, for although they did not wish the Presbyterian Church to be established by law, they knew there was little hope of escaping persecution, until the old rule of Episcopacy was overthrown. "I can tell you, sir, what I would not have, though I cannot tell you what I would," said Cromwell, their leader, one day when pressed to declare his views.* The country was as divided in its wishes as the House. The abolition of Episcopal government was demanded by a petition of 15,000 Londoners (11th Dec., 1640), its maintenance by nineteen petitions from different counties.

Episcopalians and political reformers.

Different religious parties.

After the discovery of the Army Plot, the force of the Presbyterians in the Commons was much increased, for Pym and Hampden, with the political reformers, though not ill disposed to the Church, found it necessary to form an alliance with the Presbyterians. Hence for the present, in religious or political questions alike, these two sections voted as one. The results of this powerful coalition were soon shown in the introduction into the Lower House of a bill called the 'Root and Branch Bill,' which required, not simply that the clergy should be deprived of all civil power, and the bishops consequently of their seats in the House of Lords, as one did that had already passed the Commons (1st May), but that the very order of bishops should be abolished, their titles, their power over the clergy, their revenues, all taken from them (27th May). On this parties plainly declared themselves, and the previous unanimity gave way to a fierce division, which crushed the bill. Men such as Hyde and Falkland drew back from further change whether in Church or State. The work of reform and justice, they argued, had now been completed;

'Root and Branch Bill' thrown out.

* Warwick, Memoirs, 177.

ROYALISTS DRAW APART.

Strafford had paid the full penalty of his tyranny; **Royalist party**
Laud was in the Tower, a prisoner for life; other **formed.**
culprits had been punished by fine, imprisonment, or banishment; to ensure liberty, new statutes had been made, and the illegal courts abolished. If more was demanded of the king, the Commons would be trespassing on his just rights, and altering the ancient form of government as it had existed before Charles first encroached on the liberties of the people. On the other hand to Pym, Hampden, and their followers, the **Political**
Army Plot, and other intrigues in Strafford's behalf, **reformers.**
were convincing proofs that Charles was not to be trusted. Granted he had consented to many bills, how had he given this consent? His deep reluctance was not subdued, it was only biding its time till he could use force to recover what he had lost? Even now the queen was talking of going to Spa, nominally to recover her health, really to try and gain some foreign aid to help her husband in crushing the Parliament; Charles, of a journey to Scotland, no doubt to strengthen his party there, and maybe to foster the discontent of the English army he would pass through. And what then? So old friends parted company. The party of Hyde and Falkland, now become royalist, went one way; that of Pym and Hampden, followed by all the Presbyterians and Independents, another.

Charles, on his way to Scotland, visited the English army, at the time disbanding (Aug.), and readily obtained promises of assistance from Papist officers and soldiers of for- **Tampering**
tune. But his opponents were generals enough to **with army.**
have organized their intelligence department well: they numbered friends among the king's friends, and one wrote to the Earl of Essex, that strange attempts had been made to pervert and corrupt the army.

Arrived in Scotland, Charles granted the Scottish Parliament the establishment of the Presbyterian Church and triennial Parliaments, and bestowed honours and pensions upon the leading Covenanters, hoping by such means to win the favour of nobles and people, and prevent them from befriending **King in**
his enemies in England. At the same time he sought **Scotland.**
to obtain proofs against the leaders of the Parliament of having been in communication with the Covenanters in 1640, and on these he intended impeaching them of high treason on his return.

"I believe after all be done," he wrote to his secretary, who reported Pym's apparent cheerfulness, "that they will not have such great cause of joy." While his conduct, narrowly scanned as it was, was making Parliament more and more doubtful of his good faith, an act fell out that cast upon him the suspicion of all his Protestant subjects. On the 1st November, the Commons, holding their breaths through horror, heard that on the 23rd of October, the Irish of Ulster had risen in arms, and nearly surprised Dublin, and all over their own province were driving the Scotch and English from their homes with robbery, plunder, murder, while they displayed a commission, stamped, as they said, with the king's great seal, authorizing them to take up arms. Every week with fresh despatches the tale increased in horror. Ulster was the province where the settlers were most thickly planted, but the rebellion and its attendant massacre spread fast from county to county, from province to province. The scattered remains of Strafford's army, still some 3000 in number, joined the insurgents, the 'degenerate English,' also Papists, uniting with the Irish. It was a fearful time, a whole people in rebellion to avenge years of oppression and wrong, a people, moreover, brutal through ignorance, burning with fanaticism. Heartrending were the accounts that came to England, how men, women, and children were mercilessly butchered; how people of all conditions, spoiled and stripped, with only rags for coverings, some wounded to death, others frozen with cold, came crowding into Dublin, now almost their only asylum, until barns, stables, and outhouses were over-filled with dying wretches; how the Irish boldly declared their purpose to extirpate English Protestants, and not to lay down arms until the Romish religion was established, the government settled in the hands of natives, and the Irish restored to the lands of their ancestors.*

Though Charles declared that the commission published in his name was a forgery, and offered to commit the care of the war entirely to the Parliament, he did not succeed in counteracting the prevailing and persistent opinion that both he and the queen had been concerned in the rebellion.

* Lingard, vii. 283, from Nalson.

History has revealed that there was grave cause of suspicion. Charles, when the Parliament had insisted on his disbanding Strafford's army, had sent private instructions to the Earl of Antrim, in Ireland, to get the same forces together again, and to engage the lords of the Pale to seize possession of Dublin castle, and declare for himself against the English Parliament. But it is ill playing with edged tools. The native Irish, who had planned an insurrection on their own account, possibly with the knowledge and consent of the queen,* seized the occasion to wreak vengeance for the seizure of their lands, and rising before the English Catholics were ready to join them, began the rebellion with the inhuman massacre of the Protestant settlers.† The king seems now to have cherished the strangely mistaken idea that the horrors of the rebellion might make his English subjects more inclined to support his own authority. "I hope," he wrote to his secretary, "this ill news in Ireland will hinder some of these follies in England."

It had, of course, quite the opposite effect. Before Charles returned from Scotland, Pym and Hampden caused a Remonstrance to be drawn up, which it was intended afterwards to print and disperse throughout the country. This Remonstrance began by indicting the king's government for all its past errors, the voyage to Cadiz, the loss of Rochelle, the long imprisonments and cruel sentences of the Star Chamber, and the death of one whose "blood still cries for vengeance, or repentance of those ministers of State who at once obstructed the course both of his Majesty's justice and mercy."‡ Next followed a statement of the reforms effected by the Parliament, the abolition of the illegal courts, the beneficial laws passed, the justice meted to evil councillors. After this came a complaint against the enemies of the Parliament, who had tampered with the army, and whose "designs defeated in England and Scotland, had succeeded in Ireland," and this led up to the final demand that for the future the king should select councillors in whom Parliament could confide. To understand the motives which led a body of country gentle-

_{Grand Remonstrance.}

---

* The suspicion against the queen was revived at the Restoration by the extraordinary exertions she then made to procure for Antrim the restoration of the estates forfeited by his treasonable help to Cromwell. It was supposed he knew some dark secret; and the only other motive her apologist suggests was certainly inadequate. See Carte's Ormond, 277—293.
† Godwin, ii.   ‡ See p. 58.

men to propose what was in fact the first step to a revolution, we must imagine ourselves environed with the dangers that they saw around them on every side.

In England, Pym's life had been attempted, not only by a loathsome attempt to inoculate him with the plague, but in Westminster Hall another man had been stabbed by mistake for him. From Scotland accounts came of a plot to assassinate both Hamilton and Argyle; there were suspicions, which history has confirmed, that the would-be murderer was Montrose. The popular leaders had strong reasons for believing that there was a second Army Plot brewing in Scotland, by which Parliament was to be crushed. Meantime, within the House the union which had been strength was gone; the Lords were inclined to retrace their steps; in the Commons, the longer Parliament lasted the more court influence increased. The secession of Hyde had carried with it even Falkland, though noted as a lover of justice, and of Parliament as the fountain of justice. Outside there was one of the reactions which ensue on revolutionary legislation, however salutary. The weak are alarmed; the violent remain dissatisfied; while the masses, on finding their wild and unreasonable hopes have met with an inevitable disappointment, are apt to echo the cries of the privileged classes who resent or dread interference. The people in such a mood will sacrifice their friends, and let slip all they have gained, unless some leader appears to restore confidence by showing clearly what is yet to be done, and how. The Remonstrance was Pym's manifesto. In its pages the good of government by Parliament was contrasted with the well-known evils of government by Prerogative; the remedy was shown; the old method of electing the king's council must give way to a new and more constitutional one; and the country must be governed by ministers in whom the Parliament had confidence, whether the king had confidence in them or not. After a debate which lasted for more than fifteen hours, the House divided on the question whether the Remonstrance should be passed. It was passed. The yeas numbered 159, the noes 148. Whereupon a member moved that it should be printed at once. To print it was to appeal from the king to the people. Hyde and Colepepper said, if the motion were persisted in, they should ask leave to enter their protest in the journals of the House, a custom occasionally adopted in the Upper House, but unknown in the Lower. Pym and Hollis referred to the usage of the House. An opponent then, putting aside the question of leave, called out that he did then and there protest for himself and for all the rest of his party. 'All! all!' shouted the enemies of the Remonstrance, waving their hats over their heads and snatching their swords from their belts. In the passion of the moment, blood might have been shed within the walls of the Commons' House itself, had not Hampden, ever ready, calmed the turbulent spirits by a few well-timed words. Debates were then by day and not by night, but though no final vote was taken, it was not until two o'clock in the morning that the wearied members, depressed or elated by that majority of eleven, left their gloomy chamber for their homes* (Nov. 22).

So far the political reformers had gained a victory, but they were still far from carrying the whole sense of the House or the nation with them. Even in London, among the wealthier citizens a royalist party appeared, and celebrated the king's return from Scotland by a great demonstration. A royalist Lord Mayor was elected, who, attended by the city aldermen in their scarlet robes, by troops of horsemen, by gentlemen richly clad in velvet coats and chains of gold, went out to meet the king and queen, and entertained them royally in the city.

Royalist party.

Charles, elated by the rise of a royalist party, and with the lightly-given promises of Scotch nobles and army officers fresh in his mind, felt confident that he should yet be able to get the better of his enemies in the Parliament. But his acts gave warning of danger. A proclamation for the enforcement of laws against Puritans was published; the trainband that formed the guard of the two Houses, was dismissed by his orders; Balfour, a friend of the Parliament, was removed from the command of the Tower; and Lunsford, a cavalier of bad reputation, appointed in his place (22nd Dec.). On the news of this appointment, tumults arose in the city, where there was already excitement enough to warn Charles that his friends were not so many as he thought. But though he consented to cancel it within twenty-four hours at the representation of his friend the Lord Mayor, he could not allay the suspicion to which such peculiar measures had given rise.

The Remonstrance, printed by order of the House (15th Dec.), was

* Forster's Grand Remonstrance; Warwick's Mem.

already in the hands of the citizens. Reports were abroad that a charge of treason was intended against some members of Parlia-

Bill for depriving bishops of seats.
ment. At this critical time, a bill to deprive the bishops of their seats in the House of Lords, was rejected for the second time, owing, as was said, to the opposition of papist peers. It was the Christmas holidays; and apprentices, watermen, workmen, crowds of all sorts, came flooding out of the city to Westminster, threatening the lords opposed to the bill, and insulting the bishops.

Meanwhile, there had gathered round Charles at Whitehall, officers from the late disbanded army, young students from the inns of court, gentlemen from the country, eager for a fight with the Parliament. "What!" said one, in actual hearing of some members, "shall we suffer these base fellows at Westminster to domineer thus? Let us go into the country and bring up our tenants to pull them out?"* These reckless men, spreading themselves between Whitehall and Westminster, soon drew their swords upon the citizens, who were often armed only with clubs. In Westminster Hall, in Westminster Abbey, frays took place; citizens were wounded, and a knight, who supported the Parliament, was slain. The names of Roundheads and Cava-

Frays between 'Cavaliers' and 'Roundheads.'
liers were now first heard, bandied as epithets of reproach. The spiritual peers, as the cause of the quarrel, suffered most from the insolence of the mob; one day the Archbishop of York nearly had his robes torn off his back; on another, in real or pretended fear, the bishops slipped out of the House by back ways, or went home in the coaches of the popular lords.

After this last adventure, eleven bishops, following the lead of

Protest of bishops.
Williams, Archbishop of York, who, as some think, had arranged the whole matter with Charles, drew up a protestation declaring that all that should be done during their compelled absence from the Parliament was null and void. The protestation was presented to the king, who ordered it without delay to be read to the Lords (30th Dec.) fancying that now any bill passed by them during the bishops' absence would be recognized as void in law. The Lords, deeply offended at the conduct of the absentees, sent the protestation down to the Commons, who

* Ludlow, i. 19.

immediately impeached the bishops of high treason, for endeavouring to subvert the fundamental laws of the realm (30th Dec.). The violence offered in no case seems to have been great, in fact three prelates still continued to frequent the House; and, if a bishop had met with injuries while attending his post in the House of Lords, the question might have entered the minds of those not unfriendly to the Parliament, whether, after all, the tyranny of a king was not more tolerable than the tyranny of a mob. But, at the very time when his friends might have won golden opinions as the victims of violence, he laid himself open to the suspicion of double dealing. Straws show which way the wind blows; and his message only made the House think that he intended hereafter to declare acts of Parliament null and void, because the bishops had been too timid to face the menaces of a crowd. The suspicion in Pym's mind was not removed by a secret offer now made him of the chancellorship of the exchequer. At a previous crisis, such an offer had tempted one of the ablest leaders of the opposition to forsake the principles he professed. But Pym was not Strafford. The Remonstrance was not a bid for office, but a demand for a constitutional ministry. This demand could be satisfied not by a secret concession to one of its subscribers, but by the public resignation of a point of prerogative. The secrecy was itself a proof that there was no concession of the principle. Failing Pym, Charles sought new ministers out of the party of his friends.

Lord Falkland, with reluctance, became secretary of state. "I choose to serve the king," he said to his friend Hyde, "because honesty obliges me to it, but I foresee my own ruin." Charles, who had made him his minister only because of his influence in the Parliament, felt no gratitude; a man who objected to the opening of letters, or the employment of spies, was of little use for the measures he contemplated. Sir John Colepepper, another member belonging to the same party, was made chancellor of the exchequer (1st Jan., 1642). Hyde refused office, only to serve the king's interests in the House with less suspicion of his honesty. Charles, however, had framed his policy before he appointed his ministers; for he now determined on carrying into execution a deep-laid plot, which he had been discussing with the queen and his confidants ever since he went to Scotland. Among patriots, vague rumours of impending danger thickened. The Commons, growing more and more suspicious, petitioned the king to allow the restoration of their proper guard (31st Dec.). Charles took three days in replying, and then sent a refusal, concluding thus: "WE DO ENGAGE UNTO YOU SOLEMNLY, ON THE WORD OF A KING, THAT THE SECURITY OF ALL AND EVERY ONE OF YOU FROM VIOLENCE IS, AND SHALL EVER BE, AS MUCH OUR CARE AS THE PRESERVATION OF US AND OUR CHILDREN" (3rd Jan.). Upon the same day that this message was received, the king's attorney impeached of high treason, in the king's name, at the bar of the House of Lords, Lord Kimbolton, and five members of the Commons, Pym, Hampden, Hollis, Haslerig, and Strode; and desired immediate possession of the persons of the accused. He read seven articles of accusation, but the real charge, which Charles hoped hereafter to substantiate by proof, was the fourth, that of having invited a foreign foe to invade England. This referred to secret encouragement that had been given by some of the popular leaders to the invading Covenanters of 1640, the very men on whom the king had just been conferring honours in Scotland; and though such a charge could not be fairly made after the Scotch Act of Oblivion, passed in 1641, it was quite possible that, the members once in his power, he could find means to ensure their suffering the penalty of high treason. Shortly after the articles of impeachment had been read in the Upper House, a sergeant-at-arms entered the Lower and said, "In the name of the king, my master, I am come to require Mr. Speaker to place in my custody five gentlemen, members of this House, whom his Majesty hath commanded me to arrest for high treason." The Lords had refused to deliver up Lord Kimbolton; the Commons replied by sending a committee to the king, in which were both Falkland and Colepepper, to inform him that their members should be forthcoming as soon as a legal charge was preferred against them (3rd Jan.). The answer of the Commons meant more than it said, for the king's whole method of proceeding was illegal: 1st, a commoner cannot be called to answer at the suit of the crown to a criminal charge, unless the articles contained in the bill of accusation are first declared by a grand jury not to be groundless; 2nd, a commoner, unless impeached by the Commons before the House of Lords, can only be tried for treason before

Impeachment of five members.

Illegality of king's proceedings.

the common law judges by a petty jury, after the bill of accusation has been 'found' by a grand jury ; 3rd, the king cannot arrest in person or by a messenger, but only by a warrant drawn up and signed by a magistrate or councillor ; and for this reason, that, if the arrest is illegal, an action may be brought against a fellow-subject, but not against the king, who, in the eye of the law, is himself the fountain of justice.

Though the members, who should have been prisoners, were the heroes of the hour, Charles was far as yet from doubting his triumph. The next morning the queen at Whitehall was urging him not to hesitate in playing out the second act of his plan. "*Allez, poltron,*" said she, as he seemed to hesitate, " go, pull those rogues out by the ears, *ou ne me revoyez jamais.*" " In an hour," said the king, as he kissed her, " I will return master of my kingdom ;" and, followed by a train of some three hundred armed men, proceeded to Westminster to arrest his enemies in person.

The Commons had received intimations from various quarters that some violence was intended, and were sitting, foreboding evil, when a friendly officer, who had climbed over the roofs of some neighbouring houses to be in time, entered the House with the information that, from this vantage point, he had seen the king set out from Whitehall, attended by his guards and a long train of cavaliers. The five members slipped out through the Speaker's garden, and thence took boat for the city, not a moment too soon, as they were hardly out of the House before Charles was entering Palace Yard, outside Westminster Hall. He came to the door of the Commons' House, and taking his nephew, now elector palatine,* in with him, commanded all others upon their lives to stay without. " So the doors were kept open, and the Earl of Roxburgh stood within the door leaning upon it. Then the king came upwards towards the chair with his hat off, and the Speaker stepped out to meet him ; then the king stepped up to his place, and stood upon the steps, but sat not down in the chair. And after he had looked a great while, he told us he would not break our privileges, but treason had no privilege ; he came for those five gentlemen, for he expected obedience yesterday, and not an answer. Then

* Charles Louis, p. 14.

he called Mr. Pym and Mr. Hollis by name, but no answer was made. Then he asked the Speaker if they were here, or where they were. Upon this, the Speaker fell on his knees, and said, 'May it please your Majesty, I have neither eyes to see nor tongue to speak in this place, but as the House is pleased to direct me, whose servant I am here, and humbly beg your Majesty's pardon, that I cannot give any other answer than this, to what your Majesty is pleased to demand of me.' 'Well,' replied the king, 'since I see all the birds are flown, I do expect from you that you shall send them unto me as soon as they return hither, otherwise, I must take my own course to find them. But I assure you, on the word of a king, I never did intend any force, but shall proceed against them in a fair and legal way.' He then left the House, amid cries of 'Privilege! privilege!'" (4th Jan.).

Notwithstanding his protest, the House felt that bloodshed had only been averted by the narrow escape of the five members. The next morning, still adhering to his resolution of obtaining the persons of the accused, Charles, unattended by any guards, drove from Whitehall into the city. As he passed through the streets, cries were raised of 'Privilege of Parliament,' and some daring hand flung into his coach a paper inscribed, 'To your tents, O Israel!' a menace of revolt like that of the ten tribes to Rehoboam. Arrived at Guildhall, he addressed the lord mayor, aldermen, and common councilmen, demanding them not to shelter in the city those whom he had accused of high treason, and saying repeatedly he must have those traitors. But he had come on a bootless errand. Even among the city dignitaries his friends were few, while his foes were many, and cries of 'God bless the King,' were drowned by those of 'Privilege of Parliament.'* "I have," said Charles, "and will observe all privileges of Parliament, but no privileges can protect a traitor from a trial" (5th Jan.). Westminster being regarded as no longer safe, the Commons were installed in the Guildhall, where the city set a guard to defend them. There was no chance of Charles getting the members into his power, unless by force. The citizens were completely alienated. Even those who had doubted the reports of previous plots against the Parliament, now believed in them all,

* Forster, Five Members.

and recognized the foresight of Pym and Hampden, whom they had thought alarmists. All that had been whispered of Ireland was now talked aloud and printed, while the shops of the city were shut, as if an enemy were at the gates. "Our late troubles have been attended with one benefit," said Hampden to Hyde, "that we know who are our friends. I know well you have a mind we should be all in prison." Whether Hyde and the two new ministers did know or not, is still a moot point. Every one disclaims complicity in a plot that has failed. In Hyde's case even a knowledge of the intended impeachment involved treachery to friends he had long worked with. According to Hyde's own account, Charles had promised nothing should be done without their knowledge, and then concealed this from them. The best solution is to suppose that Hyde knew he was not to know.

City alienated.

There was now no hope of reconciliation between the two parties, short of Charles submitting to rule through a ministry responsible to Parliament. The march of those 300 on Westminster was in fact looked on as the declaration of war, or rather as war without a declaration. Men who remembered Eliot's fate, could not renounce self-defence after such a hair-breadth escape. Charles' hope had been, Periander like, to cut off the ears that overtopped. History has shown that a country can be unmanned by such a policy for a time. But by failure he had rather given the party heads than taken them away.

War inevitable.

The 11th of January was a gala day, a day of triumph for Presbyterians and reformers. While the London train-bands marched along the banks of the Thames, to the sound of drum and trumpet, as a guard, the five heroes of the day went by water from London Bridge to Westminster, followed by hundreds of boats and barges thronged with people and adorned with flags and streamers. Whitehall was silent as they passed. Charles had retired the day before to Hampton Court with his family to avoid the spectacle. "Where now are the king and his cavaliers? What has become of them?" cried the people, as with shouts of triumph they rowed on to reseat the members at Westminster. On landing the members were met by 4000 gentlemen and freeholders, who had come on horseback from Buckinghamshire, Hampden's native county, as a guard of honour for their insulted

8

representative, bringing with them a petition to the Parliament against the king's evil councillors.

The king had made a great mistake. A momentary triumph, if won, is not a final victory; and no successes won by violence or chicanery can make up for the lost vantage ground of clean hands and frank conduct. Charles was especially unfortunate; his secret plots were always revealed, always failed, and always precipitated the discussion of vital questions. It was now necessary to raise forces to send against the Irish rebels. To whom was the right of commanding and calling out the county militia to belong? By the statute of Winchester, passed in the thirteenth year of Edward I., every man was required to possess arms in quantity and value according to the value of his lands and goods, so that each county was provided with a sort of feudal militia, which was called out in lieu of police by the lord-lieutenant of the county, in case of any tumult or riot. Two rights with regard to this militia the king of England had always exercised; first, that of nominating the lords-lieutenant and other officers in command;* secondly, when invasion was threatened, that of sending so-called commissions of array to the lords-lieutenant, bidding them call out the militia and train them for service. But whether in time of peace the king could summon his subjects to service outside their respective counties, was a question that had never yet been determined, or if at all in the negative, as Charles had just passed a bill which deprived him of the power of pressing troops into his service.

<small>County militia.</small>

Both sides were equally keen on the question. The failure that rankled in Charles' breast was due, he thought, to the fact that his volunteers were enough to overawe the Commons, but not enough to overawe the capital. The Parliament had seen to what use Charles intended to put the sword, if he got it. Accordingly the Commons sent a petition to the king, asking that Parliament should nominate the commanders of fortified places, and the lords-lieutenant and other officers of the militia forces. The people beset the Upper House, demanding that the lords should both join in petitioning for the militia, which they had refused to do, and pass the bill removing ecclesiastics from all civil offices.

<small>Command of militia.</small>

Between the 20th of January, and 5th of February, numbers of

* Hallam, Const. Hist. i. p. 552.

petitions to this effect flowed in from town and country, from young men, apprentices, seamen, tradesmen, porters, women. Many lords left the House in disgust at the noise and violence of their petitioners. Those that remained yielded in both the points required, and an ordinance was at once prepared to transfer the command of the militia from the king to the Parliament (Feb.). Since his departure from London, Charles had been preparing for war. The queen was to cross to Holland to procure arms and ammunition by the sale of the crown jewels. He intended himself to fix his residence at York, where it was expected his friends would gather round him, and the people be found more devoted to their king than in the immediate neighbourhood of London. When the bill to deprive the bishops of their seats in the House of Lords was presented to Charles, Colepepper urged him to yield, hoping that he might save the command of the militia. 'It is better,' he said, 'to satisfy them in one or other of these bills; this one can easily be repealed, and while the sword remains in your hands, there will be no attempts to make further alterations.'* 'Is Ned Hyde of this mind?' asked the king. 'No, he does not wish that either of the bills should be passed; a very unreasonable judgment, as times go.' 'It is mine too, though,' replied Charles, 'and I will run the hazard.' Finding the king obstinate, Colepepper went to the queen, and assured her that in consequence of this refusal, the Parliament would stop her journey abroad. Henrietta, eager to get out of a country in which she felt herself always hated and now defenceless, never ceased importuning her husband with tears till he gave his consent to this bill.

Lords pass Bishops' Exclusion Bill.

Charles consents to Bishops' Exclusion Bill,

At Newmarket, on his way to York, Charles gave his final answer to the commissioners sent by the Parliament to ask his consent to the Militia Ordinance. 'Talk of your fears and jealousies,' he said indignantly, after hearing a bitterly worded declaration read, 'what would you have? Have I violated your laws? Have I declined to pass one bill for the ease and security of my subjects? I do not ask you what you have done for me. God so deal with me and mine as all my thoughts and intentions are upright for the observance of the laws of the land.' 'I wish,' said one of the commissioners, 'your

but refuses Militia Bill.

* Clar. Mem. 114.

Majesty would reside nearer your Parliament.' 'I would you had given me cause; but I am sure this declaration is not the way to it.' 'Might not the militia be granted for a time?' 'By God, not for an hour. You have asked that of me in this, was never asked of a king, and with which I will not trust my wife and children' (9th March).

At York, Charles found himself again in possession of power. The Cavaliers followed in eager crowds; friends, who had been forced into exile, returned to his side, and many gentlemen from the neighbouring counties came to offer their support to his cause. His first step was to demand admittance to Hull, at that time the arsenal of the north. On his approach he found the gates shut, the bridges drawn, the walls manned, as though an enemy were expected : and Sir John Hotham, who had been lately sent down as governor by the Commons, came upon the walls and, kneeling down, said he durst not open the gates, being placed in trust by the Parliament (April). When the Commons were attacked as endangering the foundations of private property by thus denying the king access to his own arsenal, Pym replied by attacking as unconstitutional the principle, "that his Majesty hath the same right and title to his towns and magazines that every particular man hath to his house, lands, and goods. . . . This erroneous maxim, being infused into princes, that their kingdoms are their own, and that they may do with them what they will (as if their kingdoms were for them, and not they for their kingdoms) is the root of all the subjects' misery, and of all the invading of their just rights and liberties. Whereas, they are only intrusted with their kingdoms. . . . By the known law of this kingdom, the very jewels of the crown are not the king's proper goods, but are only intrusted to him for the use and ornament thereof; as the towns, forts, treasures, magazines, offices, and people of the kingdom, and the whole kingdom itself, are intrusted unto him for the good, and safety, and best advantage thereof; and as this trust is for the use of the kingdom, so it ought to be managed by the advice of the Houses of Parliament, whom the kingdom hath trusted for that purpose; it being their duty to see it be discharged according to the condition and true intent thereof."

Charles refused admittance into Hull.

Even the pretence of peace could hardly be maintained much

longer; and events were hurried on by the gentlemen of Yorkshire, who held a meeting in which it was proposed to raise a guard for the king's person (14th May). On the other side, after a century and a half of civil peace, the great body of the nation, whatever the injuries they suffered, were not willing to see the flames of civil war re-lighted; and now, while the gentlemen were assembling, the freeholders of the county came crowding into York, declaring that they also ought to have been summoned, for the knights and gentlemen had no right to act in their names. To satisfy them, a second meeting was held on the 3rd of June, at Heyworth Moor, where some 40,000 men assembled to meet the king. The freeholders had prepared a petition, begging him to dismiss the Cavaliers and be at accord with his Parliament. The Cavaliers, indignant at its contents, tore the petition out of the hands of those who were reading it to approving groups. Yet the freeholders had their wish, for young Thomas Fairfax, a Yorkshire gentleman, who sympathized with them, forced his way right up to the king, and falling upon one knee, fixed a copy of the petition upon the pommel of the royal saddle. *Meeting at Heyworth Moor.*

The Parliament, on its side, was making active preparations. First it formed itself into a war-council, eliminating obstructives. The House had made up its mind on the end to be pursued, and freedom of discussion was confined henceforward to the means. Open supporters of the royal enemy were put in confinement for a time or expelled the House.* One by one, as occasion or excuse offered, the king's friends fled to York; the House of Peers, in which, when the Parliament first met, had sat above eighty, now dwindled down to twenty members;† of the House of Commons sixty-five departed, amongst them Hyde and Falkland. An order was passed for raising troops and money (10th June); the money lent was to receive eight per cent. interest, the Parliament promising repayment on the nation's credit. Within a few days, such an amount of money and plate was brought to the treasurer at Guildhall, that there was hardly room to stow it; the wealthy bringing their large bags and goblets, the poor women their very wedding-rings, and their gold and silver hair-pins, thimble and bodkin money,‡ as the royalists contemptuously called it. The city was treated as a *Parliament becomes a war-council.*

* Clar. Mem. 134.　　† Hallam, i. 537.　　‡ May, 139.

camp; one who called the leaders traitors as a spy. In the artillery grounds in Finsbury fields, the muster ground of the volunteer troops, citizens were nearly all day at drill. The Presbyterians, who had formerly looked on the grounds with disfavour, as the resort of courtiers and gentlemen, now hastened thither to practise themselves in arms, and enlist in the London trained bands. Major-General Skippon soon commanded eight regiments, above 8000 soldiers. The militia ordinance was put in force without further care for the king's consent. In the same counties, in the same towns, sometimes on the very same day, appeared the officer appointed by the Parliament, and the officer appointed by the crown, the one summoning the people to arms in the name of the ordinance, the other in that of the king's commission of array.

Without slackening their preparations, the Parliament sent to the king at York nineteen propositions, for the first time formally tabulating their demands. Their hope was not so much that the king would grant them, as that the blame of the war would fall upon him for his refusal. They asked, that he should resign to Parliament (1) the nomination of his privy councillors and other officers of state, (2) the command of the militia and all fortified places; (3) that he should suffer the Church to be reformed by the advice of Parliament, and (4) not marry his children without asking its consent. Though securities practically equivalent to these are now incorporated in the constitution, the king of the seventeenth century was indignant at their bare proposal. "These being passed," he said, "we may be waited on bare-headed, have swords and maces carried before us, and please ourselves with the sight of a crown and sceptre, but as to true and real power, we should remain but the picture, but the sign of a king." The Commons fixed on the Earl of Essex as the general for their army. He had fought in his youth for the Protestant cause in the Low Countries. Charles had appointed him lieutenant-general in the first Scotch campaign, and after it had dismissed him with studied discourtesy. In earlier times he had suffered a deeper wrong from the Stuart court, for James the First had caused him to be divorced from his wife, in order to marry her to his own profligate favourite, Robert Carr, afterwards Earl of Somerset. Thus experience and personal antecedents seemed alike to fit him for the post. His nomination was acceptable to the Pres-

Charles refuses propositions of York.

byterians, who sympathized with his creed; to gentlemen, who would have scorned to serve under a general of inferior rank; to the people at large, who loved his honest, straightforward nature. On being voted general (4th July), he proved at once his honesty and courage, by accepting the dangerous honour, defeat meaning death to the leader of a rebel army. Several members of the Parliament received commands; St. John, Hampden, Hollis, were named colonels of regiments of foot; Cromwell, Haslerig, Fiennes, of regiments of horse. Great excitement prevailed in London; everybody went about decorated with orange ribands, the colour of Essex' house, the shops were closed, and civil business was almost at a standstill. *[sidenote: Essex appointed general.]*

The king was not idle; the queen sent arms and money from Holland, and, as soon as a small force was collected, he raised his standard on a hill near Nottingham (23rd August). Thence he marched into the west, making many friendly speeches to the people on his way, declaring his good intentions towards the laws and liberties of the kingdom.* His nephews, Rupert and Maurice, sons of his sister Elizabeth, came over from Germany to fight for him; the Catholics lent him money, and by the middle of October he mustered at Shrewsbury an army of about 12,000 men. *[sidenote: King raises his standard.]*

And now the people had to choose between King and Commons. Declarations and pamphlets were eagerly devoured. Though half a year had passed, the Grand Remonstrance still served as the chief manifesto of the Parliament. In that document the king had been depicted as the tyrant, imprisoning without law, and taxing without right; as the friend of Rome and the persecutor, cruelly maiming his subjects' bodies, and more cruelly maiming their souls' health; while the Parliament stood forth as the upholder of true and tempered liberty, who kept the property of the rich safe from the grasping hand of confiscation, the hard-won earnings of the poor from being wasted by monopolies and illegal customs; who enabled peer and peasant to walk again on English soil, free of all constraint but the well-known laws; and above all as the protector of tender consciences, godly itself, and *[sidenote: Charles depicted by Parliament as tyrant and persecutor.]*

* May, 134.

a shield to the godly against the courts which formed the new English Inquisition.

<small>Commons depicted by Royalists as rebels and fanatics.</small> In the royalist pamphlets the king was God's anointed, ruling by divine right, a pillar of the Church, the preserver of order, the upholder of the ancient constitution, yet giving up his right at his subjects' desire, and passing every law that conduced to his people's good; while the Commons were rebels, bent on encroaching alike on the king's prerogative and the rightful authority of the peers, friends of anarchy and misrule, ready to plunge the country in civil war to gratify their inordinate ambition, with a sullen and fanatical religion, which could neither take enjoyment itself, nor tolerate it in others; in fact, with that in them which might make a tyranny of many, far worse than any tyranny of one.

<small>Charles the deceiver.</small> But since the Remonstrance the king had unfortunately added to the reckoning his enemies kept against him. Not only had the tyranny received a new illustration in their eyes from the attempted arrest of the five members; the friendship with Rome by the muster of Catholics, and the persecution from a proclamation against Puritans; but a new count of crime was added. The solemn assurance to the Commons, that their preservation was as much his care as that of his wife and children, had been used to lull them into a false security; the oath that, on the honour of a king, he had never intended force, stood blankly contradicted by his armed retinue at the door. The untruthfulness of character suspected from his answer to the Petition of Right, and more than suspected from the army plots, now seemed a certainty. To the Parliament the king was not only the tyrant and the persecutor, but the deceiver. This count was really the cause of the war. Charles was not incapable of the position of a constitutional governor. He had ability above the average, dignity of manners, and a higher dignity, raising him above all low tastes; and he had not that unbending obstinacy, which would amount to incapacity, as a governor. But he was believed to have admitted an unfortunate distinction between a public and private conscience, which dispensed him from the necessity of keeping faith with political opponents. Measures past, concessions obtained, promises to observe the law; all these the cherished victories of peaceful patriots, seemed as unavailing as bands to bind a Proteus. The very awe of majesty

requires a king's truthfulness to be above suspicion. But the leaders of the Commons had to work with a vision of the Tower ever before their eyes: the fairer the offers made to them the more the dread of foul play. This prevented the due action of that safety-valve of the State, a constitutional opposition. Even in foreign diplomacy, where bad faith is not uncommon, the discoverer of fraud is held justified in laying arbitration aside and drawing the sword at once: at home the interests of king and subjects being really identical, deceit has still less occasion for practice.

Devoted partisans on either side were not very many in number. Those of the king were mostly to be found in the soldiers of fortune from Germany, and the more reckless of the country gentlemen, who looked forward to the excitement of war. On the Parliament's side the Presbyterians and sectarians, seeing in their own cause the cause of God, strove for the overthrow of the Established Church with all the ardour of religious enthusiasts. But between the views of these two extreme parties opinion generally fluctuated, and men took sides doubtingly as their natures or circumstances prompted.

The greater part of the nobility and gentry either openly joined the king, or tried to remain neutral, and generally had sufficient influence over their tenantry to cause them to embrace the same side as themselves. To many it seemed absurd to hazard wealth and a secured position to avoid paying a few shillings arbitrarily raised; an upheaval from below was more dangerous to them than pressure from above; others, again, who recognized the importance of the principle at stake, were still inclined to their king by the instincts of chivalry, or the abhorrence of fanaticism. On the other hand, the inhabitants of manufacturing towns, independent county freeholders, merchants, and others, who had made fortunes in trade, and afterwards bought land in the country, showed themselves, as a rule, friendly to Parliament. Besides being influenced by religion and a sense of independence, these classes had especially suffered from the monopolies and extortions which had raised the price of necessaries and shackled the enterprise of trade. There were exceptions, however, on both sides. Many gentlemen felt that the cause of the Parliament was so good, they were bound to take up arms in its defence; many yeomen and burghers adhered to their

Gentry with king.

Towns and freeholders with Commons.

county magnates and their king. As a general rule, where the contagion of neighbourhood or the necessities of religion did not decide the question, the king was preferred to the Parliament. It was only the men of strong convictions, of unusual foresight, who would coolly and deliberately embark on an unknown sea, without chart or compass of guidance, and risk all for the sake of liberty, and the doubtful gratitude of posterity. So with unwilling hearts did men array themselves. One Royalist wrote to his wife, that though he loved not his side, 'grinning honour' compelled him to stay by it, for he could not bring himself to fight for the Parliament, and if he remained neutral he should be called a coward.* "You," said Sir Edmund Verney, the king's standard-bearer, to Hyde, who reproved him for looking melancholy, "are satisfied in conscience that the king ought not to grant what they desire. I have eaten my master's bread, and served him near these thirty years, and will not do so base a thing as to forsake him, but for my part I do not like the quarrel, and wish he would yield."†

Sir William Waller, one of the Parliament's commanders, wrote to Sir Ralph Hopton, a Royalist officer : "The great God, who is the searcher of my heart, knows with what reluctance I go upon this service, and with what perfect hatred I look upon a war without an enemy. The God of peace in His good time send us peace, and in the meantime fit us to receive it! We are both on the stage, and we must act the parts that are assigned us in this tragedy; let us do it in a way of honour, and without personal animosities."

At any rate, thought these unwilling enemies, one battle will decide everything, so that, whatever the consequences to the vanquished, our country will soon rest again on 'the gentle bosom of civil peace.'

* Forster, B. S. iii. 50. † Clar. Mem. 160.

CHAPTER VI.

FIRST YEARS OF THE WAR.—BATTLES OF EDGEHILL AND NEWBURY.—1642—1643.

> They stood aloof, the scars remaining,
> Like cliffs which had been rent asunder,
> A dreary sea now flows between,—
> But neither heat, nor frost, nor thunder,
> Shall wholly do away, I ween,
> The marks of that which once hath been.
> COLERIDGE.

IT must not be supposed that the Commons declared war against the king. The popular leaders were most careful to maintain a quasi-legal ground for their resistance. Novel and subtle as their principles seemed at the time, they have since been largely accepted. Pym's speeches in fact may be said to have laid down the lines of the theory on which modern constitutional government is based. Thus the Remonstrance was framed as an attack, not on the king, but on his councillors; and when the king objected that actions which he avowed as his own were 'censured under that common style,' Pym's answer was, "How often and undutifully soever these wicked counsellors fix their dishonour upon the king, by making his Majesty the author of those evil actions which are the effects of their own evil counsels, we, his Majesty's loyal and dutiful subjects, can use no other style, according to that maxim in the law, 'the king can do no wrong,' but if any ill be committed in matter of State, the council must answer for it: if in matters of justice, the judges."* So now the Commons went to war with the actual king to protect the ideal king of the constitution from evil counsellors. This appears in their declaration "that, whereas the king was seduced by wicked counsel to make war against the Parliament, who proposed no other end unto themselves than the

Constitutional attitude of Commons.

* Forster, British Statesmen. Pym, p. 269.

care of his kingdom and the performance of all loyalty to his person, it was a breach of the trust reposed in him by his people, and tending to the dissolution of his government." The legal maxims of the royal lawyers of the past had received a new reading from the popular lawyers of the present. The new wine seemed bursting the old bottles, but the bottles have since expanded to the strain. That these ideas were genuine beliefs of the time, is shown as well by the cherished clause of the covenant, "to preserve the king's person and authority," as by the real horror felt when Republicans first broke through this reserve, or when Cromwell averred that his pistol would be no respecter of persons. The patriots were not, however, wanting in readiness to chastise their 'poor, semi-divine, misguided father, fallen insane.'*

Essex marched from London into the west (9th Sept., 1642), and took up his head-quarters at Worcester, where he remained without venturing to offer the Royalists battle. Charles, wishing to fight before the rebel army could be reinforced, broke up his camp at Shrewsbury (12th Oct.), and marched across the country in the direction of London, feeling certain that Essex would follow him to protect the city. He went by way of Wolverhampton, Birmingham, Kenilworth, and passing Southam, on the road to Banbury and Buckingham, arrived at Edgecote, without having any knowledge of his enemies' movements (22nd Oct.).† Here, however, Rupert, who was encamped with the rear at Wormleighton, learnt from his scouts that fires were to be seen from the Dassett hills, and that Essex had his head-quarters that night at the village of Kineton, half way between Warwick and Banbury, and only ten miles to the north-west of Edgecote. The king, aroused from sleep at three in the morning, on hearing this news, at once summoned a council of war, in which it was agreed to hold without delay a general rendezvous of the army on the top of Edgehill.

To appreciate the tactics of the time it is necessary to remember the nature of the weapons. The soldiers on either side were armed after the same fashion. The introduction of fire-arms had caused the defensive armour of the ordinary horse and foot soldiers to be reduced to a back and breast piece and a broad iron hat, commonly called a pot; calves'-leather boots reaching up to the knees, and a long buff coat worn under the armour,

<small>Armour of foot soldiers.</small>

* Carl. i. 160. † See Map, p. 127.

completed their equipment. Officers often wore open helmets, arm and shoulder pieces, and tassets or skirts to protect the thighs.

The cavalry was divided into three classes—the cuirassiers, the carabineers, and the dragoons.* The cuirassiers being almost without exception gentlemen, arming themselves at their own expense, came to battle magnificently appointed, with silver-hilted swords, plumes of feathers waving above open helmets, and buff coats gay with gold and silver trimmings. Their usual weapons were the sword and pistol. The carabineers were so called from the name of their carbine or musket. The dragoons were light armed, having only the buff coat and iron hat, and were like mounted riflemen, fighting as much on foot as on horse, but with swords for cavalry work. *Cavalry,—three classes.*

The infantry was divided into bodies of pikemen and musketeers, the use of musket and bayonet not yet being combined in the same weapons. The pike, made of ash, was fifteen or sixteen feet long, and headed with steel. *Musket and pike.*

The musket or matchlock was not advanced beyond the first stage of invention. The spark to fire the gunpowder was applied from the outside, instead of being produced by the concussion of flint and steel. The match consisted of little ropes of tow, boiled in spirit; these, when lighted at one end, smouldered on until the whole was consumed. The musket was still such a heavy and cumbersome weapon that it had to be fixed on a rest. This rest was made of ash-wood, headed at one end with iron to fix in the ground, and having at the other a half hoop of iron. Before the end of the war the musketeer was relieved of this additional burden. Rests were disused owing to the introduction of lighter and more portable muskets. To a belt, fastened round the musketeer's left shoulder, hung a bullet bag, some twists of spare match, a flask of touch powder, and a bandeleer, with twelve little cases, made of leather or tin, each of which contained a separate charge of powder. As loading and firing were both long operations, only one rank fired at a time, and the

---

* The dragoons are said to have received their name from the locks of the first muskets in use amongst them, on which was represented a *dragon's* head with a lighted match in its jaws, a natural image of a death-dealing engine. Both weapon and name came from France. The cuirassiers were so called from the original name of the back and breast piece, a cuirasse. Like other pieces of defensive arms the cuirasse was made of leather (cuir) before it was made of iron. Buff was leather like buffalo-hide; it would often turn a sword-cut.

musket was by no means so great an advance in the art of destruction as we might suppose from our experience of the modern rifle. Field guns were also cumbersome, and seem to have done little execution. It was when the ranks had come to push of pike, or when the victors mercilessly cut down the flying foe with the sword, that the dead fell thickest. There were no regular uniforms. Different regiments of infantry on either side often wore buff coats dyed the colour belonging to the house of their colonel. Thus Hampden's men wore green coats; Lord Grey's blue; others, red, purple, and gray. All the officers of the Parliament wore orange scarfs, the colour of the house of Essex. But in the confusion of the battle, a twig of green, a sprig of broom, or a bit of coloured riband, fastened to the hat, with the help of the word for the day, was the chief guide by which to distinguish friend from foe.

Edgehill, which forms 'the face or edge of the tableland of the north of Oxfordshire,' looks abruptly down on the Warwickshire level below, and as it is approached from Kineton, stands out a long bold line of hill against the horizon. The eastern slopes rise more gently, and hither on Sunday morning, the 23rd of October, came the Royalist regiments from their scattered quarters on the Southam and Banbury road, many of them having to march eight miles or more before they reached the summit. The side of the hill, which faces Kineton, is now covered with large trees, wearing on an October day all the varied tints of autumn, but then only a few bushes were scattered over it. The undulating plain below, lying between Kineton and Radway, now all brought under cultivation and crossed by innumerable hedgerows, was then an open desolate-looking pasture ground; one long hedge alone, which survives to the present day and probably marked the enclosure of an old homestead there, struck across it about midway between the two villages.

Battle of Edgehill.

Essex saw the Royalist horse moving on the top of Edgehill before eight o'clock, and at once formed his army in front of Kineton, facing south-east, ready to fight if the king should come down and offer battle on equal terms. Several causes induced Charles to gratify the wishes of his enemies, and abandon his unassailable position on the summit of Edgehill. Extreme confidence prevailed amongst the Cavaliers. Rupert made no doubt of victory, and urged immediate battle. It was known

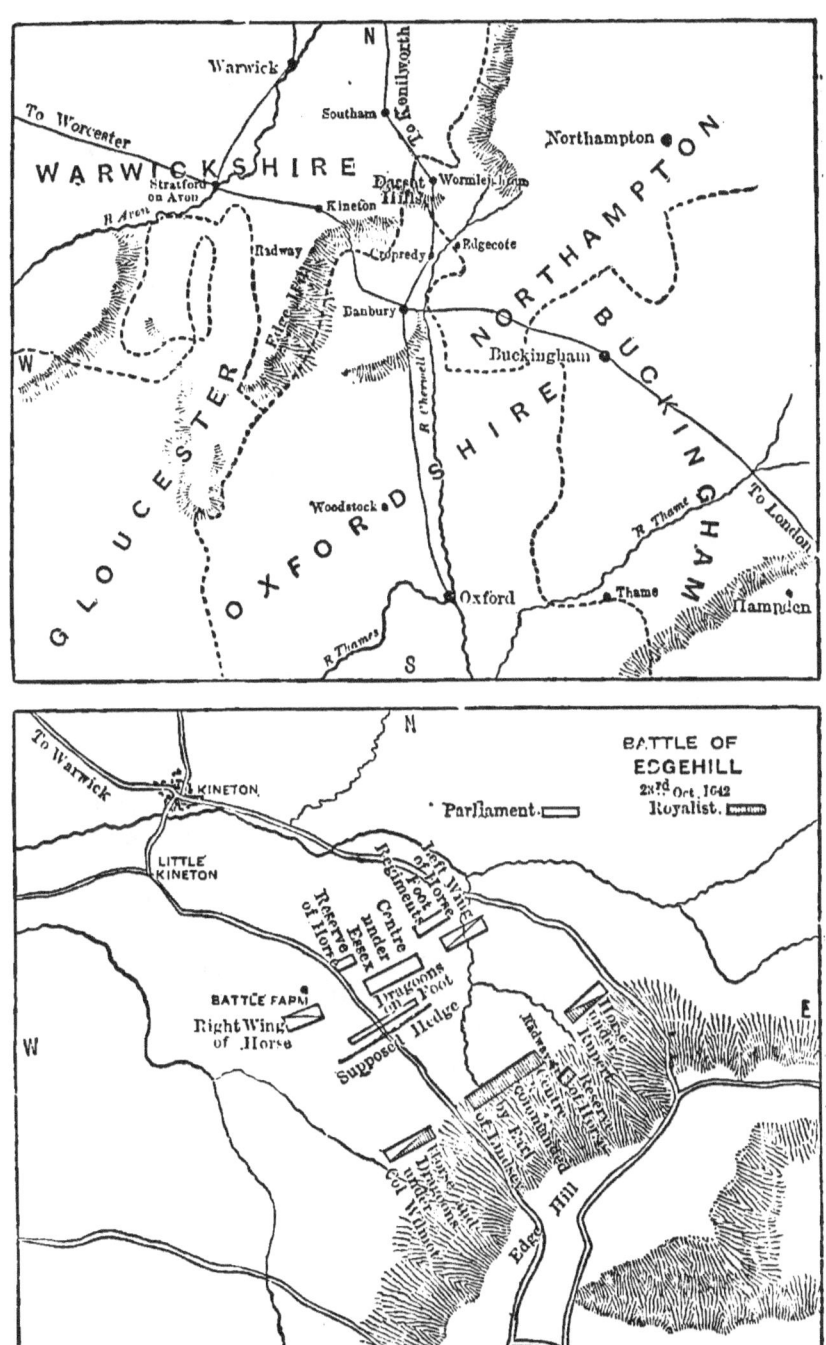

that two regiments of horse and one of foot under Colonel Hampden were a day's march behind the rest of Essex' army, engaged in bringing up some artillery, which it was hard to drag through the heavy clayey soil. Lastly, ever since the army had reached Kenilworth, there was no food to be got. The country people, in these Midland counties more inclined to the Parliament than to the king, and frightened by reports of the cruel and plundering habits of the Cavaliers, had hidden their provisions, so that some of the common soldiers were half starved, and had hardly eaten bread for forty-eight hours. The prince thought no better remedy could be found to bring the people to their reason than a victory gained over the rebels. Accordingly the Royalists formed on the top of Edgehill, fronting the north-west, ready to march down the hill and give the enemy battle on the level between Radway and Kineton. The king's army was about 12,000 strong; that of Essex about 10,000. Both were disposed according to the tactics of the time. The main body of foot held the centre. Every corps of infantry consisted of pikemen and musketeers, the pikemen drawn up in the centre, the musketeers in the flanks. The lines were rarely less than ten deep, in order that when the front rank of musketeers had fired, they might have time to retire to the rear, form and reload, while the other nine ranks were severally performing the same motions. In either wing was placed the horse, generally supported by regiments of infantry or dragoons. A body of horse was kept in reserve, ready at any critical moment to assist friends or press hard upon foes. Essex commanded his centre in person. On his left wing, he placed his principal body of horse, and part of five regiments of infantry; on his right, three regiments of horse, his artillery on some slightly rising ground near where Battle Farm now stands, and dragoons on foot to line the long hedge that ran across the ground. The king's centre was commanded by his general-in-chief, the Earl of Lindsey. Rupert was half a mile off to the right; Colonel Wilmot, who commanded the left wing, as far off on the left.

Disposition of armies.

Rupert, though far more distinguished for courage than judgment, and only twenty-three years old, had been made by Charles lieutenant-general of the horse. His temper was imperious, his manners overbearing, and now, refusing to obey any commands, except those received directly from the king's lips, he acted as though he was entirely independent of the Earl of Lindsey.

About one o'clock, the Royalists, having a front of two miles, streamed down the hill in three lines, their two wings gradually converging towards their centre as they approached the enemy. It was already three o'clock, and the October day on its decline, before the battle commenced. "Come life or death," said Charles to his principal officers, as he left his tent, "your king will bear you company," and with his own hand fired the first piece of artillery.

As Rupert was advancing upon the enemy's left wing, Sir Faithful Fortescue, a major in Essex' army, and his whole troop of horse, rode forward and joined the ranks of the prince. Thus encouraged, the Cavaliers charged impetuously, while the Parliament's horse, inexperienced, and panic-stricken by the base desertion of their comrades, having once fired their pistols into the air, turned their horses' heads and fled, throwing into confusion several regiments of infantry behind them, which also took to flight, in spite of all the efforts of their officers. *Essex' left wing routed.* "The Lord Mandeville's* men would not stand the field, though his lordship beseeched, nay cudgelled, them ; no nor yet the Lord Wharton's men ; Sir William Fairfax his regiment, except some eighty of them, used their heels." Horse and foot fled in one confusion together towards Kineton, whither they were closely pursued by Rupert, who was intent on plundering the baggage carts, which could be seen standing unguarded in the village streets.

Meanwhile, on the king's left wing, the Royalists had been equally successful in clearing the field of the larger part of the Parliamentary horse. But whatever advantage *Essex' right wing routed.* these mounted gentlemen gained over the raw recruits of the Parliament, who had but just learnt to sit a horse or fire a pistol, was all lost through want of subordination to their general. For what folly in Rupert to be plundering at Kineton, instead of seeing how the battle went under Edgehill ! What rashness in the king's reserve of horse, whose special function it was to decide the day by a charge at the critical moment on the critical point, and as a reserve never to follow up an advantage till the whole field was theirs. to clap spurs into their horses, and without orders join in this idiotic pursuit of one wing of the enemy, while his centre was still unbroken ! These heedless acts lost the king his victory. In the absence of all the Royalist horse from the field,

---

* Lord Kimbolton (p. 111), afterwards Earl of Manchester (p. 155).

the Parliament's reserve, after charging through the enemy's lines, and spiking several pieces of cannon, fell upon the rear of his centre. At the same time Essex, supported by the officers from his broken wings, who, scorning to fly with their men, had rallied around their own main battle, put himself at the head of his infantry, and fiercely charged the Royalist ranks in front. And now came the real struggle of the day. Charles, conspicuous in his steel armour and black velvet mantle, on which glittered his Star and George, rode into the leading ranks, encouraging his troops to hold their ground. But no valour could resist the odds against which his men were fighting, attacked at once in front and rear, and outflanked through the absence of their own wings and the superior numbers of the enemy. What slope of the ground there was favoured the troops of the Parliament; the slain and wounded fell by scores in the space of a few yards; the Earl of Lindsey, badly shot, was carried off the field by the enemy; the king's standard-bearer was slain, and his standard placed in the hands of Essex. But a gallant Royalist captain, by the simple artifice of fastening an orange scarf to his person, and riding boldly up to the earl's secretary, to whose keeping the prize had been entrusted, succeeded in quietly taking it from him, saying it was not fit for a penman to have the honour of carrying that standard; then bearing it back in triumph to the king, he was knighted beneath its shadow.

<small>Meeting of centres.</small>

Charles, though he had only a hundred horse about him, and was within half a musket-shot of the enemy, refused to retire. He ordered Charles and James, his two boys of twelve and nine years old, who were by his side, to be taken out of danger. His physician, the great Harvey, the discoverer of the circulation of the blood, having retired with the princes to the shelter of some bushes, took a book out of his pocket, and read, quite regardless of the turmoil round him, until a bullet grazed the ground close by, and warned him to remove his charges out of range.

Meanwhile Rupert and the Cavaliers, after plundering the baggage, were following up the pursuit of the Parliament's horse, when they were stopped at a hill a little beyond Kineton, which is still known as Rupert's headland, by the approach of Hampden's three regiments with the artillery. Rupert retreated hastily, but only to find the Royal infantry forced up under the foot of the hill, and the ground he had occupied in the morning now held by the troops of the Parlia-

<small>Rupert retires before Hampden.</small>

ment. "I can give a good account of the enemy's horse," he said, when he saw the confusion of his party. "Ay!" exclaimed a Cavalier, with an oath, "and of their carts too." As it was now half-past five, it was quite impossible to distinguish friends from foes, and the two armies drew apart. The Royalists passed the night at the foot and on the side of the hill, where, pinched with cold and hunger, they made what fires they might out of the few bushes growing about. Essex' troops also spent that Sunday night on the field, in little better plight than their enemies. "I had tasted no meat," says one, "since the Saturday before, and having nothing to keep me warm but a suit of iron, I was obliged to walk about all night, which proved very cold by reason of a sharp frost." Large numbers on both sides deserted during the night, and the next morning there was, in either army, a general unwillingness to renew the battle. The king retired, over Edgehill into Oxfordshire; Essex to Warwick, whence he had come.*

Though the Parliamentarians laid claim to a victory, the results of the battle seemed to favour the king. Banbury, Abingdon, Henley, opened their gates without a show of resistance; and soon Rupert and the Cavaliers were plundering the country in the very neighbourhood of London. *Results of battle.*

The disposition of London was most important. Not only did the opinions and acts of the Londoners exercise weight all over the kingdom, but on the readiness of the city merchants to lend money was likely for some time to depend the pay and maintenance of the Parliament's army. Though often terrified, the city never failed in its support to the Parliament, nor was it unfairly called by Charles "the nursery of the rebellion." It opened wide its coffers; sent out apprentices by thousands to enlist in the army; organized a formidable force of its own under the name of the city trained bands; and, in fact, was always ready to give the nation some striking, if not turbulent, proof of its zeal. *Disposition of Londoners.*

The principal motive that urged the citizens to support the war was their eager longing to be allowed to worship according to the forms of the Presbyterian Church. Had Charles at this time granted toleration to Presbyterians, he would have deprived the Parliament of some half of its most zealous supporters. The day

* Clar. Hist., iii.; Ludlow, i.; Ellis, Orig. Letters, 2nd series, iii. 300; May, 23; Warwick Mem., 231; Beesley, Hist. of Banbury, 303, 320; Grose, Hist. of Ancient Armour.

after Essex' arrival in London, Lord Brook,* who had fought at Edgehill, addressed a crowded audience at the Guildhall (8th Nov.). "Gentlemen, citizens of London," he said, "you must not think to fight in the sighs and tears of your wives and children. Therefore, when you hear the drums beat, say not, I beseech you, I am not of the trained band, nor this, nor that, nor the other, but doubt not to go out to the work, and this shall be the day of your deliverance. What is it we fight for? It is for our religion, and for our God, and for our liberty and all. And what is it they fight for? For their lust, for their wills, and for their tyranny; to make us slaves, and to overthrow all. Gentlemen, methinks I see your courage in your faces. I spy you ready to do anything, and the general's resolution is to go out to-morrow, and do as a man of courage and resolution, and never man did like him."†

In spite, however, of the exhortations of the leaders of the Parliament, and the presence of Essex and his army, fear was so prevalent in the city that the Commons sent a petition to the king, *Proposed Treaty. Attack on Brentford.* proposing a treaty. Charles, after returning a gracious answer, in which he called God to witness his great desire for peace and offered to treat at Windsor or wherever else he might be (12th Nov.), took advantage of a thick mist to advance unperceived from Colnbrook, and fall upon a few regiments of foot and a small party of horse, that garrisoned Brentford and protected the road to London (13th Nov.).‡ For this action he was accused by his enemies of treachery. Since no ces-

* Heir to Sir Fulke Greville, to whom James I. granted the barony, with Warwick Castle. † Parl. Hist., ii.
‡ On this occasion Milton fixed this sonnet on his door, claiming the reverence Lysander showed to the city of Euripides, and Alexander to the poet of Thebes:

    Captain or colonel, or knight in arms,
    Whose chance on these defenceless doors may seize,
    If deed of honour did thee ever please,
    Guard them, and him within protect from harms.
    He can requite thee, for he knows the charms
    That call fame on such gentle acts as these,
    And he can spread thy name o'er lands and seas,
    Whatever clime the sun's bright circle warms.
    Lift not thy spear against the muses' bower:
    The great Emathian conqueror bid spare
    The house of Pindarus, when temple and tower
    Went to the ground: and the repeated air
    Of sad Electra's poet had the power
    To save the Athenian walls from ruin bare.

sation of arms had been made, he was justified, by the rules of war, in seizing any advantage that offered him an opportunity of treating from a more favourable position. Still he had been trusted as a king rather than as an enemy, and the citizens were exasperated on finding that his gracious answer to their petition had been intended as a mere blind, and that his hope, when he gave it, had been to enter London at the sword's point. Not a word was any longer heard of a treaty. All the night after the action at Brentford, the indignant city was pouring out men, encouraging its apprentices to en- list, and reinforcing the army of Essex out of its own trainbands. "Come, my boys, my brave boys," said their commander, Skippon, to these new troops, "I will run the same fortunes and hazards with you. Remember, the cause is for God, and for the defence of yourselves, your wives and children. Come, my honest and brave boys, pray heartily, and fight heartily, and God will bless us." Two days after the fight, 24,000 men were reviewed on Turnham Green, midway between London and Brentford; yet Essex, habitually cautious, refused to risk a battle, so that the king was allowed to withdraw his troops, without opposition, to the neighbourhood of Oxford, a town devoted to his cause, which he intended making his headquarters for the winter.

<small>Indignation in London.</small>

The whole country now began to take part in the war. Leaders on either side appeared in nearly every county, and maintained a desultory warfare. Towns, castles, houses, were fortified, garrisoned, and besieged. The number of the troops on each side depended on the inclinations of the people. Those counties alone enjoyed peace within their borders, in which one party far outnumbered the other.

<small>Whole country engaged in struggle.</small>

In the east, where there were many towns engaged in the staple manufacture of England—woollen cloth—as Norwich, Sudbury, Colchester, Yarmouth, and Lynn, the king's enemies so far outnumbered his friends, that all opposition to the Parliament was quickly crushed by the energy of Colonel Cromwell, who associated the seven counties of Norfolk, Essex, Suffolk, Cambridge, Huntingdon, Lincoln, and Hertford together into a confederacy against the king. In Kent and the other south-eastern counties, though many of the gentry were Royalists, the Parliament's friends were so far the stronger, that little opposition could be offered them.

Berkshire went with Oxford for the king, while Hampshire and Wiltshire were battle-grounds between the two. In the west, where there were fewer freeholders than in the east, the king's friends predominated, though even here many important trading, manufacturing, or fishing towns were held for the Parliament, as Bristol, the second town in the kingdom for size and wealth, Gloucester, Weymouth, Plymouth, and Lyme. The backward district of Wales, and the Cornish, like their Breton brethren in later time, went wholly with their king and feudal lords : but elsewhere in the west, the king's enemies were generally to be found in numbers sufficient to keep the country in a state of constant warfare. In the midland counties, the partisans of the Parliament again predominated, though here the Royalists made head against their enemies, and held a strong garrison at Newark, in Nottinghamshire, by which communication was kept up between Oxford and York. North of the Humber, the two parties were about equally matched. The Earl of Newcastle and his numerous tenantry declared for the king; but many of the county freeholders joined the inhabitants of Bradford, Leeds, Wakefield, Halifax, Manchester, and the other seats of the woollen manufacture, in adhering to the Parliament. Thus, as generally happens in times of movement, the towns favoured progress, the country reaction.

The queen, who had been successful in Holland, through the interest of the Prince of Orange, her son-in-law, returned to England in the spring, accompanied by four ships, laden with arms and ammunition, soldiers and officers (22nd February.) She escaped the fleet of the Parliament in her passage, but about two days after her landing at Bridlington, in Yorkshire, the town was bombarded by Admiral Batten with such effect, that she was forced to fly from her lodging, and seek shelter in a ditch in the open fields, where balls scoured over her head. She escaped however without injury, and by the union of her resources with those of the Earl of Newcastle, a formidable army was soon raised, which was called by the friends of the Parliament 'the Northern Papist Army,' being regarded with special aversion.

Newcastle's army of 'Papists.' Papists there were in plenty amongst its ranks, for Charles, though in his printed delarations he constantly denied the fact, had ordered Newcastle to let any serve who would. "You see," said the joking earl, one day as he pointed out the weakness of some fortifications, "though they call us the army of Papists, we cannot trust in our good works."

The increasing power and success of the Royalist forces now caused discouragement to many friends of the Parliament, who had thought to bring the king to terms within a few months. In the Parliament and in the city, a peace party appeared, composed in large part of men who observed with annoyance the influence into which the war was raising both sectarians and people of inferior rank. It was not pleasant to the lord to hear himself spoken of as on an equality with a plain country gentleman ; the Presbyterian did not like to hear the sectarian demanding toleration for all creeds ; indignation burnt in more breasts than those of Royalists, when the tale was told how Admiral Batten had done such an ungracious, unchivalrous act as to fire on the very house the queen was in. Some began to think it time to change sides. The governor of Scarborough betrayed his trust, and surrendered the town to the queen. Sir John Hotham, governor of Hull, would now have followed this example, had not the Parliament discovered his intention in time to prevent its execution. Many Presbyterians would gladly have made peace, if only they could have obtained the king's consent to the establishment of their own Church: while the evils of the hour made those who were no friends to arbitrary power overlook the many proofs they had experienced of Charles' ill faith, and forget the importance of the cause for which they were engaged. But the leaders of the Commons, Pym, Hampden, and their close followers, never wavered for an instant ; they had taken the resolution of continuing the war until the king was really conquered and forced to submit to terms that would deprive him of power to injure his subjects' liberties, and from this resolution they never swerved. These firmer spirits found their warmest supporters in the sectarians, to whom peace and a consequent triumph of Presbyterians or Episcopalians offered nothing but a prospect of bitter persecution. At Oxford councils were as divided as at Westminster. There also two parties appeared ; the one desired to restore Charles to the exercise of absolute power at the sword's point ; the other to obtain by negotiations a peace restoring him to the exercise of power bounded by law. The war party was led by the king's nephews, Rupert and Maurice, two imperious young foreigners. "Tush," Rupert would say, when any objection was made to his commands, as contrary to law, "we will have no more law in England but the

Peace party formed in London.

Parties in Oxford.

sword." This party was supported by the professional soldiers from the continent, the Papists, many of the country gentlemen, and by courtiers and self-seekers generally, who thought that if a peace were effected by negotiation, the rebels at Westminster would get too good terms for themselves, and the king be unable to reward his friends sufficiently for their services. The peace party, on the other hand, was composed of men of less selfish and less violent dispositions, who, though fighting under Charles' banner, loved their country's liberties, and grieved over its sufferings. The people, indeed, endured much, and the war was raising up a bitter spirit even between members of the same families. The nearest relations constantly fought in opposite ranks, and it was no uncommon tale to hear of the dying soldier who took his death the more heavily because he had seen the fatal shot fired by a brother's hand. The courteous and affable Lord Falkland was so altered by grief, that to his friends he seemed hardly the same man. He became pale, morose, short in his answers, untidy in his dress; and sitting among his friends would after a long silence cry out passionately, "Peace, peace," and say, "that the very agony of the war, and the view of the calamities and desolation the kingdom did and must endure, took his sleep from him, and would shortly break his heart." So loud was the cry for peace raised, both in London and at Oxford, that the extreme party on either side was obliged to yield and allow negotiations to be held (March). The propositions now drawn up for the king's acceptance, like those before offered at York, required him to abolish Episcopacy, and to resign the command of the militia and other executive powers to Parliament.

<small>Peace propositions offered at Oxford.</small>

Charles, having been proved a match for his opponents in arms, of course refused these terms. Though he pretended to be exceedingly desirous for peace, he belonged at heart to the war party, and looked forward to being restored to an arbitrary throne by the force of his friends' swords. Angrily interrupting the Earl of Northumberland, when reading as one of the Parliament's propositions, 'A bill to vindicate the five members,' he proposed as his final answer that the Parliament should deliver into his hands forts, towns, magazines, ships, and revenue, and adjourn to some place twenty miles from the capital, in which case he would consent to the disbanding of the armies, and speedily return to London. By this, negotiations were at once broken off (15th April). Soon after a plot was discovered, which had been formed by some of the disappointed peace party. Their design was to seize the leaders of the Parliament, occupy the military posts, and then admit the royal forces into the city (May). *Waller's plot.*

The intercepted letters by which the plot was discovered implicated Waller, the poet, a cousin of Hampden, and a member of Parliament; and by his confessions, several others were involved. But though it was startling to discover the presence of traitors within the very walls of the Commons' House, Pym, acting with his accustomed moderation, did not increase the irritation of the friends of peace by pressing uncertain evidence. Out of five persons condemned by court-martial, only two were executed. Waller, who had made a most abject submission, was allowed to escape with no greater punishment than a fine and a short imprisonment.

Meanwhile, both parties made ready for a second summer's campaign. The Parliament's officers were divided in counsel. Hampden advised an immediate advance upon Oxford, but Essex persisted in first laying siege to Reading. The war party began to be doubtful of the zeal of their general, and took little trouble to see that his troops were well supplied with pay and clothing. His conduct led men to think that he wished, not to reduce the king to the Parliament's mercy, but only to keep up a balance of parties and so bring about a peace by negotiation. After Edgehill, he had retreated to Warwick, leaving the road to London open to the enemy—a movement several of his officers failed to understand. After the action at Brentford, he had refused to risk a battle, saying he dared not trust his young and raw recruits. Men who wished to conquer would gladly have seen Colonel Hampden command in Essex' place. Hampden's regiment of green-coats, raised and trained by himself, was known as one of the best in the army; his military genius he had proved unmistakably in many minor actions; his daring was more likely to lead to victory than Essex' caution. But no one ventured to propose to displace the earl. All the peace party, all the Presbyterians, were warmly attached to him, while many noblemen and gentlemen would have been averse to serving under any one his inferior in rank. *Distrust of Essex.*

But the first and last duty of a general is to win, and he must be chosen for no other object. A half-hearted policy ruins an army, and either ruins a cause or prolongs the miseries of war. Through the hesitation of their aristocratic leader, a series of disasters now befell the Parliament's forces. Essex' head-quarters were at Thame, a few miles east of Oxford. His army, through disease and desertion, had gradually dwindled down to a force of about 5000 men. Though long urged by Hampden to act boldly on the offensive, or at least to concentrate his troops, now too scattered to be safe, he persisted in maintaining a defensive attitude on a weak and extended line. His troops, thus dotted about in detachments, were hardly able to defend their own outposts, much less the neighbouring counties, against the Cavaliers, who weekly, almost nightly, crept out of Oxford to burn and plunder villages and manor houses. It was on one of these occasions that the Parliament experienced the loss of a leader who was not to be replaced. A body of Royalists, commanded by Rupert himself, had surprised a troop at Chinnor on the Chilterns, and were bearing off booty and prisoners in triumph to Oxford. Colonel Hampden started in pursuit from Watlington, and overtook them at Chalgrove Common on their way to the bridge over the Thame at Chiselhampton. A sharp skirmish followed. At the first charge two balls entered Hampden's shoulder and broke the bone. A prisoner brought the news to Oxford. "I saw him," he said, "ride off the field before the action was done, which he never used to do, and with his head hanging down, and resting his hands upon the neck of his horse" (18th June). Hampden only lived for a week more. After receiving the sacrament, he prayed with his last breath that the God of hosts would 'have 'these realms in His special keeping: that He would level in the 'dust those who would rob the people of their liberty, and would 'let the king see his error and turn the hearts of his wicked 'counsellors from the malice of their designs.' "O Lord, save my bleeding country," were almost the last words he spoke. His body, carried from Thame to be buried at his native village of Hampden, was followed as a hero's to the grave by soldiers with heads uncovered, drums and ensigns muffled, arms reversed. The grief of soldier and citizen was real enough. As general and as statesman Hampden had the true leader's spirit, whose presence inspires:

followers with confidence and commands their sympathy by mere contact. " The memory of the deceased colonel," says a newspaper of the day, " is such that in no age to come but it will more and more be had in honour and esteem ; a man so religious, and of that prudence, judgment, temper, valour, and integrity, that he hath left few his like behind." After two hundred and thirty years we can but endorse the verdict.

It seemed as though all the forces of the Parliament were dispirited by Hampden's death. In the north Fairfax, defeated by Newcastle at Atherton Moor near Bradford (30th June), was shut up in Hull, so that the eastern counties lay open to the approach of the northern 'Papist' army. In the west their successful general, Sir William Waller, suffered two severe defeats ; in fact, the king's commanders there, Prince Maurice and Sir Ralph Hopton, 'the soldier's darling,' gained one success on another, until the Parliament lost all its hold over the three counties of Devon, Somerset, and Wilts. The Cornish peasants and the Cavaliers united overcame all enemies. The former would ask their commander's leave to fetch off cannon from hills surmounted with breastworks, and dauntlessly perform what they proposed—a feat repeated by their Breton brethren at La Vendée—the latter would think it play-work to storm defences, on which the soldiers of the Parliament would have looked askance. Stories went about amongst the terrified garrisons " that the king's soldiers made nothing of running up walls twenty feet high, and that no works could keep them out." One town after another surrendered during the summer and autumn months ; Taunton, Bridgewater, Bath (July), Dorchester, Weymouth, Portland, Barnstaple, Bideford (August), Exeter (September 4). Prince Rupert took Bristol by storm. The governor, Nathaniel Fiennes, capitulated without disputing his entrance by a hand to hand fight in the streets, though Rupert's losses had been heavy enough to warrant the attempt (25th July). It was agreed that the garrison should march off with arms and baggage, and the townspeople be preserved from plunder and violence. But the Cavaliers, without regard to the terms they had made, plundered the waggons belonging to the garrison and sacked the city ; and so mercenary was the spirit of some of the Parliament's troops, that they took service in Rupert's army, and pointed out to their new friends the houses

<small>Royalist successes in north and west.</small>

<small>Bristol stormed by Cavaliers.</small>

where the most valuable plunder might be found. By the middle of the summer, Gloucester was the only important city still held for the Parliament in the west.

The news of the surrender of Bristol, the second town in the kingdom, caused extreme depression in London. The House of Lords drew up propositions for peace, the most moderate yet brought forward. Both armies were to be disbanded; the militia question was to be settled by a future Parliament, the Church by a future synod. After a long and fierce debate, the propositions were carried in the Commons by a majority of twenty-nine votes (5th Aug.). The vote was an act of political suicide, and the war party appealed from Parliament to the people, knowing that if Charles returned to London on these terms, his word would be no guarantee for the performance of his promises. The result was that two days after the propositions were passed, the Lord Mayor and Common Council came to the door of the Commons to present a petition against peace, followed by a tumultuous rabble of several thousands. The demonstration succeeded, and the House agreed by a majority of seven to lay aside the peace propositions (7th Aug.).

Peace propositions of Lords.

Tumults in London.

Two days after this scene had occurred, some hundreds of women, wearing white silk ribands in their hats, as an emblem of their mission, came to the Commons' House, bearing a counter-petition for peace. Four or five members went to the door, and telling them that the House was no enemy to peace, ordered them to return to their homes. But dissatisfied with this answer, they stayed on, and by noon there were some 5000 women, with men amongst them dressed in women's clothes, pressing round about the house, allowing none to pass in or out, and crying, "Peace, peace," "Give us those traitors that are against peace," "Give us that dog, Pym."

The Parliament's guards, after firing powder without dispersing the mob, loaded with ball and shot a ballad-singer dead at the moment she was urging her companions on with her songs. A troop of cavalry at the same time coming up, charged in upon the crowd, slashing with their swords at hands and faces, until the women fled on all sides, leaving some seven or eight of their number lying wounded or dead upon the ground (9th Aug.). The friends of peace, disgusted with such scenes and with their own defeat, tried to persuade Essex to make use of his army in forcing the Parliament to offer propositions to the king. But Essex, though he had himself advised the Parliament to treat, was too honourable to think of betraying his trust, and felt indignant that such a proposal should have been made to him. In consequence of his refusal, seven lords and several members of the Commons changed sides and went to Oxford.*

Extreme danger now threatened the Parliament. There was no force between Oxford and London to oppose the king's approach, except Essex' wretched army, whose thinned ranks had not yet been refilled. The Parliament, says May, its own historian, "was then in a low ebb; and before the end of that July, they had no forces at all to keep the field, their main armies being quite ruined. Thus seemed the Parliament to be quite sunk beyond any hope of recovery, and was so believed by many men. The king was possessed of all the western counties from the farthest part of Cornwall, and from thence northward as far as the borders of Scotland. His armies were full and flourishing, free to march wherever they pleased, and numerous enough to be divided for several exploits." Charles judged rightly that the time had come, when one bold stroke might finish the war. His plan was conceived with unusual force and spirit. His own and Newcastle's army were to converge on the capital and form a junction within sight of it. But his generals were jealous of one another, and slow to obey even royal commands. Newcastle was not inclined to give up the independent authority he had in the north, merely to be domineered over by Prince Rupert; so he sent word to Charles, that he could not carry out his orders and march through the associated counties upon London, because he was sure the gentlemen in his army would refuse to leave Yorkshire unless Hull were first reduced. Meanwhile, the desertion of many of the peace party had united the friends of the Parliament, while the extremity of the danger itself inspired them. The Londoners were hard at work raising fortifications for the protection of their threatened city. Thousands were to be seen, men and women of every "profession, trade, and occupation," marching out daily in a body to dig at their appointed place of labour, with colours flying and drums beating before

<small>Ill success of Parliament.</small>

<small>Charles' proposed march on London.</small>

<small>London fortified.</small>

* Clar., iv. 175; May, 214.

them. The tailors went out 8000 strong, the watchmen 7000, the shoemakers numbered 5000; the very oyster women from Billingsgate 1000. It was one of those stirring moments when all feel proud to labour, and knights, ladies, and gentlemen might be seen marching out with the crowd, spade and mattock in hand, so that within a few weeks a breastwork was raised all round the city for a circuit of twelve miles, strengthened by twenty-four forts and carrying 212 pieces of cannon.* Before, however, these fortifications were fully completed, the citizens breathed more freely. Newcastle's aversion to leave Yorkshire brought them a respite when their doom seemed fixed. His dislike of the plan, falling in, as it did, with the feeling of many of the officers, induced Charles to try and make the conquest of the west complete by besieging Gloucester, before marching east. The town was known to be badly provided with stores; everybody said it could not hold out long; and Massey, the governor, was suspected of an inclination to desert the side of the Parliament. The king summoned the town, fully expecting it would surrender at once, but a stern defiance was brought from 'the godly city of Gloucester' by two citizens, whose plain garb, close cut hair, Scripture phrases, and quiet yet assured demeanour marked them out as undoubted Puritans. "Waller is extinct, and Essex cannot come," replied Charles, quietly, more surprised than disconcerted at the confidence they displayed, so sure was he that the town would be compelled to surrender before the Parliament could find an army for its relief (10th Aug.).†

March on London deferred.

Much hung on the resolution of this garrison of 1500 men, who possessed but forty barrels of gunpowder and a slender artillery. If they yielded, Charles would turn immediately upon the disheartened and defenceless capital; if they resisted, the Parliament would obtain a breathing time in which to recruit its forces. Neither soldiers nor citizens showed any lack of resolution. They set on fire the suburbs of the town, in order to deprive the Royalists of shelter while forming their entrenchments. They made constant sallies, and met the besiegers' mines by counter mines. The women and children daily laboured at repairing the breaches, and sallied out under the eyes of the king's horse to fetch in the turf. There was little

Siege of Gloucester, 10th Aug.— 5th Sept.

---

* Somers, Tracts, iv.; May, 311.

† May, 218; Somers, Tracts, v.; Clar. Hist., iv. 167.

complaining heard in the streets, and no disaffection took place amongst the garrison. Though constant opportunities were offered by the sallies, only three soldiers deserted. Though the country people, whose cattle the Royalists were killing by thousands through mere wantonness, implored the town to surrender, soldiers and citizens endured on, trusting that relief would come to them in time.

"Waller is extinct, and Essex cannot come," Charles, in his confidence, had said. But he was wrong. With wonderful speed the thinned ranks of the Parliament's army were filled up; four regiments of the London train-bands volunteered for the service, and Essex left London on the 24th of August at the head of 14,000 men. He conducted his march with speed and dexterity, driving before him a body of horse sent by the king to oppose him; but the besieged had no knowledge of the succour which was coming, still less of its whereabouts, until, on the 4th of September, they heard the sound of guns fired from the Presbury hills. The next morning they saw the royal forces withdraw from their trenches, fire their huts, and depart. Relief had come but just in time, for the garrison had only three barrels of gunpowder left.* _{Essex relieves Gloucester.}

Essex, after re-supplying Gloucester with provisions and ammunition, returned eastwards for the protection of London. The Royalists at first did not know what road he had taken, and he succeeded in surprising their garrison at Cirencester and securing their supplies for himself before pursuit commenced. He had nearly crossed the Wiltshire Downs between Swindon and Hungerford, when Rupert and the Cavaliers attacked his rear while embarrassed in some deep lanes, near Aldbourn Chase, and a sharp skirmish took place, in which the Parliamentarians suffered considerable loss. Charles, while Rupert delayed the enemy, had pressed on with the infantry by forced marches on a more direct road to Newbury, which he entered the following day, so that Essex, on approaching it from the Hungerford side, found the road to London barred (19th Sept.). _{March to Newbury.}

South of Newbury, which lies low on the banks of the Kennet, the ground gradually rises, until, at the distance of about a mile from the town, it reaches the level of a long line of hill, running east and west, and dividing the beds of the two rivers, the Kennet and the Emborne. This high ground was then open common;

* Somers, Tracts, v.; May, 222.

MAP OF NEWBURY.

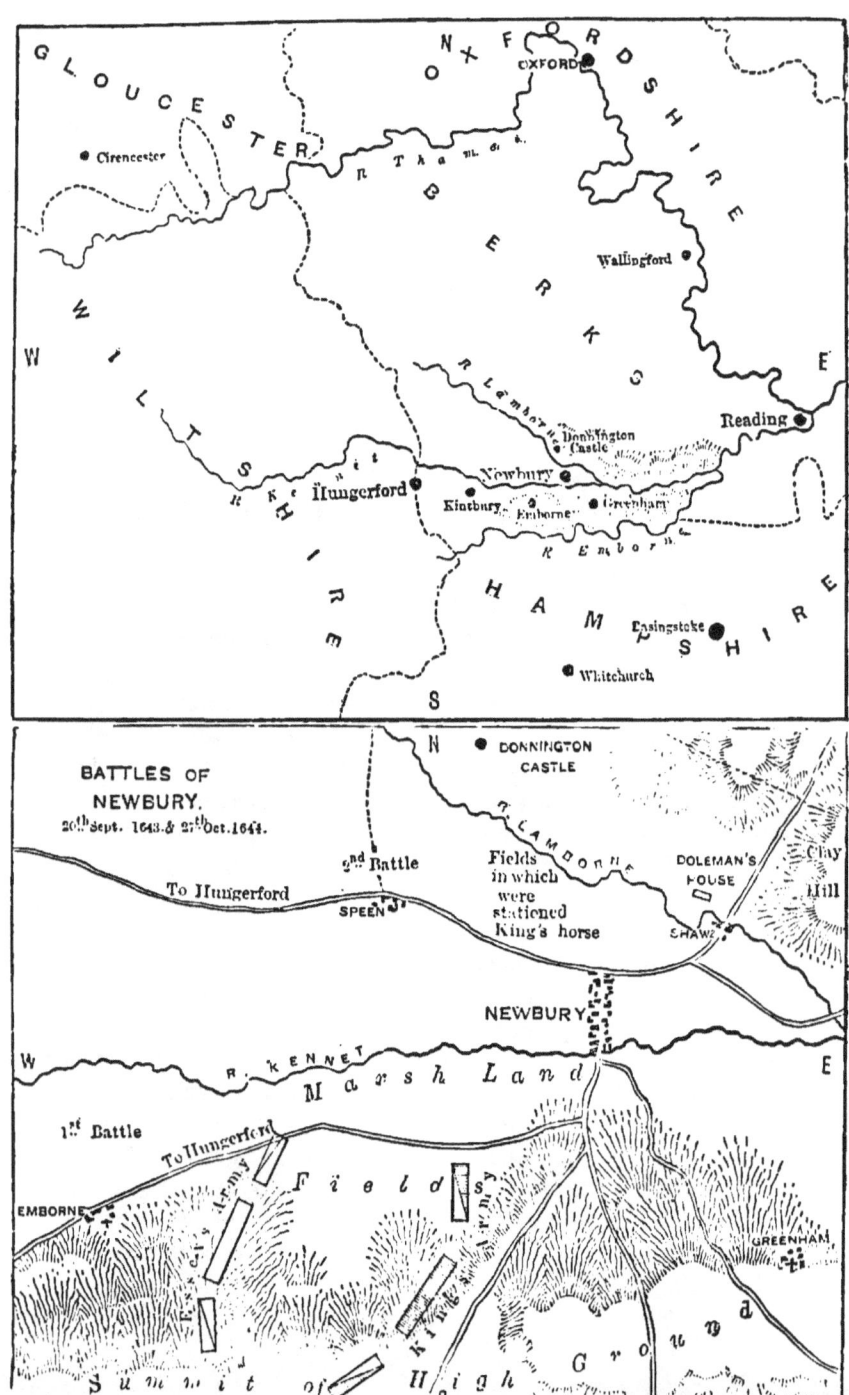

FIRST BATTLE OF NEWBURY.

but the side of the spur sloping down to Newbury, as well as much of the low ground lying nearer the Kennet, was under cultivation and crossed by hedgerows. Charles stationed his left wing, centre, and artillery upon the brow of the hill, facing west towards Emborne and Hungerford, his right wing only on the lower ground in front of Newbury, protected by hedges and resting on the Kennet. Aware of the strength of this position, he determined, with the advice of his chief officers, to maintain a defensive attitude there, and not advance to meet the enemy as the more hot-headed subordinates would have liked. The Parliamentarians, on the other hand, could have no choice but to attack, as the enemy lay between them and their supplies, and to attack meant forcing their way up a hillside in the face of an artillery fire before they could come to close quarters.

On seeing the king's tactics, Essex drew up his army upon some open ground in front of Emborne. Two causes compelled him to fight at all hazards. The first, that, for the protection of London, it was necessary he should make his way through the enemy; the second, that, while delay mattered nothing to the king, who could refresh his troops in Newbury, and draw provisions, if necessary, from his garrisons at Wallingford and Oxford, it was fatal to himself, lying in the open fields and in an unfriendly country. The king, on the other hand, failed to reap the advantages of his position; for he could not secure the obedience of his own followers any more than of his Parliament. His own wise resolution was broken by the rashness and insubordination of his officers, some of whom, despising the London militia, and making sure of victory, became so excited at the sight of an enemy drawn up for action that they charged impetuously and, the battle soon becoming general, obliged their friends to advance for their support, leaving much of the artillery behind them on the hill. Many of the officers flung off their doublets in bravado, and led on their men in their shirts, as if armour was a useless encumbrance in dealing with the base-born apprentices, whom they came rather to triumph over than to fight.

Essex' left and the king's right were so impeded by the hedges that they could only engage in small parties. The horse, however, on the king's left found a free passage down a lane by which Essex had intended to advance his right. Essex' horse, though at first thrown into

Hedges prevent horse from deciding the day.

some disorder, soon rallied, and returned the charge of the impetuous Cavaliers. But in an enclosed country as this was the cavalry could not have much effect in deciding the day. It was the daring and skill of Essex, and the valour of the troops he led —the very train-bands the Royalists despised—that were destined to win the laurels of the field. The general, " being foremost in person, did lead up the city regiments, and when a vast body of the enemy's horse had given so violent a charge, that they had broken quite through, he quickly rallied his men together, and with undaunted courage did lead them up the hill. In this way he did beat the infantry of the king from hedge to hedge, and after six hours' long fight planted his ordnance upon the brow of the hill. The train-bands of the City of London endured the chiefest heat of the day, for being now upon the brow of the hill, they lay not only open to the horse but to the cannon of the enemy; yet they stood undaunted and conquerors against all, and like a grove of pines, in a day of wind and tempest, they only moved their heads, but kept their footing sure." It was on this hard-fought day that Lord Falkland met his death. In the morning he seemed to have recovered a little of his old cheerfulness, and dressed himself with unusual care, saying, "he was weary of his country's misery, and believed he should be out of it before night." Though his duties as the king's secretary gave him no position in the field, he fought as a volunteer at the head of Lord Byron's regiment of horse. This was on the right wing, where the ground was cut up by enclosures. Byron found his approach to a body of the enemy's infantry impeded by a high quick hedge. A single gap offered a passage through, which was so narrow that only one horse could pass at a time. The enemy stationed on the other side of the hedge were keeping up a hot fire, and as Byron viewed the place his horse was shot under him. While he retired to remount, Lord Falkland, "more gallantly than advisedly," clapped spurs into his horse, and charged through the gap. In an instant horse and rider fell dead together.* His end gives us a painful insight into the misery the more delicate minds endured during such a time. There was no doubt his life had been a burden to him for months.

Death of Lord Falkland.

* Lord Byron's account of battle of Newbury, in a letter to Hyde, in MSS. Clar. State Papers in Bodleian, No. 1738.

A patriot at heart, he had chosen his side from chivalry rather than from insight; and, though he followed his king, had no sympathy for that policy of 'thorough' which lay at the root of the civil war.

Darkness at last caused the two armies to separate. Both spent the night on the hill, the Royalists retiring to the further side of it, towards Greenham, and leaving the ground they had held in the morning in the hands of the Parliament's infantry. Essex fully expected the battle to be renewed the next day, and determined to force his way through the enemy or die. But the Royalists were dispirited. Though the loss of life was not so great as might have been expected, it had fallen heavily upon men of rank. More than twenty officers, distinguished for birth or merit, were among the dead. Such a catastrophe seemed to the king's friends in no way compensated by the loss of an equal number of obscure Parliamentary colonels. With these feelings the Royalists withdrew during the night into Newbury. Essex, finding the way by Greenham open before him, continued his march to Reading and London.* Charles, after leaving Newbury, retired to Oxford for the winter.† *Royalists withdraw into Newbury. Essex marches to London.*

* Byron's letter to Hyde leaves no doubt that Essex, instead of marching through Newbury (as is often stated), kept south of the Kennet. "The next morning early, Essex, finding the ground quitted by us, drew his army upon it, and there made a bravado in sight of ours, which was then drawn into the town of Newbury. Prince Rupert marched with such horse as were nearest to him, and fell on the enemy's rear as they marched off. But the country being full of enclosures secured them so that no great execution could be done upon them before they recovered Reading, and thus concluded the battle."

† May, Long Parl.; Clar. Hist.; Rush, Abr., v.; Account in Harl. Miscellany; Lord Byron's letter to Hyde in Clar. Papers in Bodleian, 1738.

CHAPTER VII.

RISE OF INDEPENDENTS.—BATTLE OF MARSTON MOOR.—
SELF-DENYING ORDINANCE.—1643—1645.

'Επέπεσι πολλὰ καὶ χαλεπὰ κατὰ στάσιν ταῖς πόλεσι, γιγνόμενα
μὲν καὶ ἀεὶ ἐσόμενα ἕως ἂν ἡ αὐτὴ φύσις ἀνθρώπων ᾖ, μᾶλλον δὲ καὶ
ἡσυχαίτερα καὶ τοῖς εἴδεσι διηλλαγμένα ὡς ἂν ἕκασται αἱ μεταβολαὶ τῶν
ξυντυχιῶν ἐφιστῶνται. ἐν μὲν γὰρ εἰρήνῃ καὶ ἀγαθοῖς πράγμασιν αἵ
τε πόλεις καὶ οἱ ἰδιῶται ἀμείνους τὰς γνώμας ἔχουσι, διὰ τὸ μὴ ἐς ἀκου-
σίους ἀνάγκας πίπτειν. ὁ δὲ πόλεμος, ἀφελὼν τὴν εὐπορίαν τοῦ καθ᾽
ἡμέραν βίαιος διδάσκαλος καὶ πρὸς τὰ παρόντα τὰς ὀργὰς τῶν πολλῶν
ὁμοιοῖ.—THUC. iii. 82.

The communities of Greece suffered all the embittering results of civil strife that visit men, and always will visit them, so long as human nature remains the same, though with more or less intensity, and varying in form, according to the special circumstances that arise in each case. The fact is, that, in times of peace and prosperity, states alike and individuals form their judgments in a better spirit from the absence of constraining necessities, while war, by besetting daily life with difficulties, teaches violence, and frames men's temper to suit their surroundings.

THOUGH the Parliament was saved, the Royalists might fairly boast that the balance of success was on their side. In the west they had driven their enemies out of every important town but Gloucester. In the north, the reduction of Hull would leave them masters of the whole of Yorkshire. It might well seem that the current of their success would remain unchecked, or that if there was a check, they could at any moment win a favourable peace by negotiation; but there were causes at work which made either of these results impossible.

Success did not improve the character of the king's troops. The cavaliers and officers were becoming cruel and rapacious in their habits of warfare; while the common soldiers, often in want of pay, and retained in little discipline, followed the example of their leaders, and plundered the country people without distinction of friend or foe. Though

Character of king's troops.

feelings of honour still caused generals and officers to treat prisoners, their own equals in rank, with courtesy if not with generosity, the common soldier was too often ruthlessly handed over to the care of some inhuman gaoler. Rupert, on one occasion, marched prisoners from Cirencester to Oxford, half-clad, bareheaded, barefooted, bound together by cords, with gaping wounds still undressed, though there was a cutting wind and snow on the ground : the king, the two princes, and several lords, rode about a mile out of Oxford on purpose to see Rupert's prisoners come in ; Charles was observed to smile : no words of pity, no order for their relief, passed his lips. If a tender-hearted Lord Falkland were by, what wonder he grew weary of his life, when such were the acts of his party? For the captives such marches were but the beginning of misery. Prisoners were kept crowded together for months in noisome dungeons, and sometimes left two days together without food. "I was so hungry," said one prisoner, after making a vain attempt to cut his throat, "the devil tempted me to cut it and be out of my misery."* This cruel usage of prisoners was not confined to the Royalists. The governor of Windsor Castle so starved the common soldiers committed to his keeping, that three men, it was said, fell down dead in the street on their release. Some hypocrites went so far as to parade their brutality as a proof of godliness. "My soul abhors to see this favour done to the enemies of God," said a turn-coat captain, addressing the wife of the governor of Nottingham Castle, as she bound up the wounds of her Royalist prisoners. Tales such as these, sayings ascribed to Puritans or Cavaliers, not to mention the harrowing details of battles and sieges—all these were published weekly, almost daily, in papers and pamphlets, and spread broadcast over the kingdom. No story was too foul or false to be refused a place in these publications. For instance, the *Mercurius Aulicus*, the chief Oxford paper, selecting domestic grief as an instance of God's judgments, after relating in a tone of exultation that death had deprived Hampden of his two eldest children, added gratuitously the lie that of his two remaining sons, the one was a cripple, the other a lunatic.† Slander thus did its part with violence and cruelty in embittering the feelings of men who, in

---

* Somers, Tracts, iv. 510, 532. † Forster, ii. 358.

the outset of the war, had felt almost as friends. Religious animosity helped to broaden the gulf. Ministers especially suffered. If they refused to read out the king's declarations, where the king had power, or the Parliament's declarations, where it had power, they had to fly their parishes to escape imprisonment. Thus deprived of home and livelihood, Puritans and Episcopalians had no choice but to take refuge with the nearest friendly garrison or come to regiments as chaplains. As they suffered most, they hated most. It was not bad usage only; as wars go on, the questions which touch men's hearts most deeply come more and more to the front. The church question was one of these, and one on which the ministers could not but feel deeply. So it was that the religious influence which should have tempered the bitterness of faction, gave its sanction to acts breathing more of the Old Testament than the New; and those who should have been the mediators taught that any parleying with the foe was treason against God. Thus the demands of the Parliamentarians increased, and there was no basis for negotiation, unless Charles would consent not simply to lessen the power of bishops, but to establish a non-Episcopal church. Through Scottish influence, Parliament had already summoned to London an assembly of divines to settle uniformity of worship for the two countries. This, of course, simply meant to discuss the means for the establishment of the Presbyterian Church in England (1st July). The bishops had completely lost all influence in the country, and as far as that went, Episcopacy was already dead. London was quite changed from the time when a gay court was held at Whitehall, when Laud lived at Lambeth, when cavaliers daily visited the artillery gardens, when crowds frequented the theatres. The grass was already growing in the courts of Whitehall;* Lambeth Palace was deserted, and was soon to be used as a prison. In the artillery gardens, once so gay, grave citizens now learnt the use of pike and musket; the theatres were all closed by order of Parliament (September 2nd, 1642). Services, preachings, and fasts had taken the place of the old bonfires, dances, and feasts. The book of sports had been burnt by the common hangman by another order of Parliament (5th May, 1643).

* Scotsman's letter in Somers Tracts, v.

Services were no more conducted with vestments and postures, lighted candles, and choirs. The wearing of any vestment was become a matter of indifference; the liturgy was read or prayers extemporized as minister and congregation pleased; organs, images, altars, were gone from churches. The beautiful old crosses, remains of Catholic times, and still left standing in the streets, were removed by order of Parliament. Presbyterians rejoiced to see bonfires made of "fine pictures of Christ and the saints, of relics, beads, and the like remains of Catholic superstition."*

The gaming houses were put down, and laws and ordinances for the punishment of vice† so strictly enforced, that no swearing was to be heard, no drunken man to be seen in the streets. Everybody led, or affected to lead, a life of strictness; for he who failed to attend some place of worship, or in public swore or drank, was looked upon as a reprobate, and could not hope to exercise any influence amongst his fellows. Sundays were no longer holidays of pleasure, but were strictly spent in religious services. In the evening men might pass through the town, and hear nothing but the voice of prayer and praise, from private houses as from churches.‡ No fruiterer or herb woman dared stand about and sell in the streets; no milk-woman cry her milk on that day, but at stated hours; no one but travellers by necessity might be received in taverns. Even if a child danced round a maypole, its parents were fined twelvepence for the offence. Fast days were observed after each success or failure, and, soon after the breaking out of the Irish rebellion, an order of Parliament was issued, enacting that the last Wednesday in every month should be kept regularly as a solemn fast and day of humiliation (8th January, 1642).

The Presbyterians, who now ruled, regarding as they did their own as the true church coeval with the early ages of Christianity, were unwilling to tolerate any other worship, and had they possessed the power would have been as despotic as the bishops. As it was, they persecuted as far as they dared. They hunted out Catholic priests, and put to death on an average about three a year;§ others they sent into banishment or left to die in prison. To keep under the

Presbyterian intolerance.

* Birch, ii. 355; Baillie, i. 425. † Neal, ii. 506.
‡ Neal, ii. 508; iii. 37. § Lingard, viii. 35, 323.

sectarians, they tried to restrain the liberty of the press by passing an ordinance for the suppression of slanderous papers and pamphlets (11th June). But the sectarians were now too numerous to be crushed, and could disobey the ordinance with impunity.

Ideas grow rapidly in times of revolution. The habit of private judgment grows still more rapidly. The very means by which the popular leaders have carried the mass to their point of view, soon carry it beyond them. The pamphlets of the Presbyterians and Episcopalians had made the people controversialists; and in many cases undermined the authority of the teachers who had converted them. The same phenomenon occurred in the region of political strife. The war of words, bandied between patriots and Royalists, discussing the rights of King and Parliament, had familiarized the people with the discussion of constitutional questions. When such questions are left to popular discussion moderation is soon lost; violent opinions grow apace, and the claims of custom and prescription evaporate, like subtler elements, in that rough crucible. Out of the ranks of the sectarians arose a new set of political reformers, who no longer ascribed the divisions existing between King and Parliament to evil counsellors, but spoke of Charles as personally in fault. Some went further. A pamphlet was published, saying that if the king did not yield to what was demanded of him, he and his race ought to be destroyed. Henry Marten, one of the Independent party, defended the writer in the Lower House. "I see no reason," he said, "to condemn him; it is better one family should be destroyed than many." "I move," said another member, "that Mr. Marten be ordered to explain what one family he means." "The king and his children," replied the Republican boldly. The use of such language horrified the Presbyterians, and Marten was for some time expelled the House.

New political reformers.

It was evident that there was an advanced party with whom the Presbyterians were as much at issue as they were with the Royalists. But the presence of a common danger checked a schism for the time. The Presbyterians still far outnumbered all other sections on their side, and the misfortunes that befell the arms of the Parliament in this summer of 1643, made the Independents not merely rally to them, but agree to call in the aid of Scotland on terms which would require the establishment of the national church of the north. The interest of the Scots was really identical with that of the English Presbyterians, for if Charles and Episcopacy were restored together, Scotland would not long be allowed to retain her own form of worship. They tried, therefore, to bind their allies down by prescribing a solemn league and covenant (August). Subscribers to this document bound themselves: (1.) To endeavour to reform religion in England and Ireland according to the Word of God, Solemn league and covenant. and practice of the best reformed churches, and to bring the three churches in the three kngdoms to uniformity in confession of faith, form of church government, and directory or prayer-book for worship; (2.) To extirpate Popery, prelacy, schism; (3.) To preserve the liberties of the kingdom, the king's person and authority, and to bring malignants to punishment; (4.) To assist and defend all such as should enter into the covenant. All civil and military officers, all ministers holding livings, and all members of Parliament were required to take the covenant. Thus Episcopalian representatives were obliged to leave the Assembly of Divines, and over 1500 ministers resigned their livings.

Union in a State must of course necessitate many sacrifices of the individual. A subject must often be required to give a passive submission, and sometimes an active co-operation, to acts of which he does not approve. There are two limits to such interference. Firstly, it should be confined, as far as possible, to political as distinguished from religious duties, since it is only when religious questions have taken a political form that they can lead to the disruption of the State; and further, in political matters the duty of bowing to the majority is more clear, and Covenant a test. the conscience less tender, than in cases which seem to touch the intercourse of man with his Maker. Secondly, the interference should be limited to overt acts as distinguished from opinions; if a man does what is required by the law, he should not be required to make a declaration of his feelings. Such a requirement is simply inquisitorial, and generally defeats its own ends, by encouraging either open defiance, or a disregard of the sanctity of oaths. The Presbyterian system recognized no such limits to interference. Some of the Independents, indeed, had learnt the lesson of a higher duty, and strove earnestly to make the league with Scotland a political league only, and not a religious covenant; in fact, Sir Henry Vane, had power been in his hands, would have been ready to grant toleration even to Catholics. The Scots, however, were impracticable, and all Vane could do was to procure the insertion of the ambiguous words "to endeavour the reformation of religion according to the Word of God and the best reformed churches." These words, though, when taken in connection with their context, they obviously referred to the Presbyterian Church, yet served as a loophole for the Independents in the army, the Parliament, and the Assembly of Divines, who subscribed in numbers to a test which was intended to eliminate them. The 2nd clause left the Episcopalians no such opening, yet many followed the example of the Independents, putting some forced meaning on the words to suit their own consciences. Such laxity of conscience must not be too severely censured. In these cases the real guilt lies rather on those who induce hypocrisy than on those who practise it. The determination of successive governments to exact oaths of fidelity to themselves resulted finally in a general relaxation of the moral fibre of the nation.

<small>Failure of test. Covenant subscribed to by Independents.</small>

For the time, however, the power of the Presbyterians seemed to have overwhelmed the Independents. Four Scotch ministers were admitted into the Assembly of Divines; a Scotch army was engaged to enter England early in the ensuing spring; and Scotch commissioners were joined with a committee of the two Houses, who sat in the capital at Derby House to direct the operations of the war.

<small>Causes of decline of Presbyterian ascendancy.</small>

In spite, however, of Scotch support, the ascendancy of the Presbyterians was already on the decline; for though superior in position and in numbers, their leaders were no match for the Independents in ability. Hampden's death had been a blow to the moderate party. Pym, like Hampden, had possessed the trust of both parties, of Independents, because of the vigour with which he had prosecuted the war, and of Presbyterians because he seemed to acquiesce in their views of church matters, and had agreed with them politically in advocating a limited monarchy. Himself sincere, yet no bigot, he had long kept the peace between the intolerant Presbyterians and Independents. His death now came after a short illness, in which he preserved his usual calmness of temper, telling his chaplain "that it was a most indifferent thing to him to live or die; if he lived, he would do what service

<small>Death of Pym (8th Dec.).</small>

he could ; if he died, he would go to God whom he had served, and who would carry on his work by others " (8th Dec.).

In Oxford bonfires were lighted the night the news came that Pym was dead, and the Cavaliers "drank deeper healths than usual to the confusion of the Roundheads." In London there was real sorrow among all parties. The Commons paid off a sum of £10,000, the amount of debts their great leader had incurred in his country's service, and erected a monument in his honour in Westminster Abbey.

The political reformers, who hitherto had implicitly followed Pym, now drifted to the right or the left, and either became absorbed in the ranks of the Presbyterians, or passed over to the new men who were now rising into influence. Thus after Pym's death the breach with the Independents widened rapidly, and the Presbyterians were soon in a false position. Obliged to continue the war, because the king refused to grant them the establishment of their Church, they were, at the same time, afraid of winning a decisive victory, which they saw would only encourage the sectarians and men of new ideas in politics. *False position of Presbyterians.*

On the other hand, the Independents desired nothing more than to crush the king's forces, and so bring the war to a speedy end. They were already in possession of a force fitted, if any, for the accomplishment of the task. Cromwell, lieutenant-general of the horse to the Earl of Manchester, had been very active in forming a new army, raised by order of Parliament in the eastern counties. He had long seen that Essex and Waller's half-hearted soldiers were not the men to gain great victories. "Your troops," he said one day to Hampden, "are most of them old decayed serving men, and tapsters, and such kind of fellows ; their troops are gentlemen's sons, younger sons, and persons of quality ; do you think that the spirits of such base and mean fellows will ever be able to encounter gentlemen, that have honour and courage and resolution in them ; you must get men of a spirit ; and take it not ill what I say—I know you will not—of a spirit that is likely to go as far as gentlemen will go— or else you will be beaten still." Hampden thought the notion good, but impracticable. Cromwell undertook to put it into practice. He sought out soldiers amongst the more independent classes, the sons of freeholders and artisans, sectarians, who fought not for pay and plunder, but with the *Eastern counties' army.* *Cromwell's Ironsides.*

higher motive of winning liberty to worship God according to their own fashion. From the very first, when Cromwell only commanded a troop of horse in Essex' army, it was observed that his men were of a different stamp to their fellow-soldiers. They did not plunder or drink; he who swore paid his twelvepence; he who drank was put in the stocks. And now Cromwell was forming a whole army on the same principles, not heeding to what despised sect his recruits belonged, so long as they proved good soldiers. "I raised such men," he boasted long afterwards, "as had the fear of God before them, as made some conscience of what they did, and from that time forward, I must say, they were never beaten, and wherever they were engaged against the enemy, they beat continually." The valour of the troops thus raised was early attested by their popular name of "The Ironsides."

The rise of the Independents created no alarm at Oxford, as Charles expected to reap a new advantage from the divisions of his enemies. He exulted, moreover, in having found a fresh means of increasing the strength of his own armies.

Since the rebellion broke out in 1641, the war in Ireland had *Cessation of arms with Irish.* been carried on with great success on the part of the Catholics, and a Catholic council of twenty-four persons established at Kilkenny now ruled the larger part of the kingdom. The old English settlers at the head of this party were, however, now eager to make peace with the king, and caused numerous petitions to be sent to Oxford, begging for the free exercise of the Catholic worship, and the calling of a Parliament. Charles, making no absolute promises, agreed to a cessation of arms for a year, and then ordered the Duke of Ormond, his general in Ireland, a devoted and able Royalist, to send over to England ten regiments of the troops that had hitherto been engaged in fighting Irish rebels.

This truce with the Irish Catholics excited indignation not only amongst Charles' enemies, but also amongst his Protestant friends. It was believed that many rebels were to be found among the regiments sent over by Ormond. "The queen's army," it was commonly said, "of French and Walloon Papists, the king's army of English Papists, together with the Irish rebels, are to settle the Protestant religion, and the liberties of England."*

* May, Brev.; Whitelock.

Hyde suggested to the king that, in order to make his cause more popular with the nation, which reverenced the very word 'Parliament,' he should summon to sit at Oxford those members whom fear had driven from Westminster. Charles unwillingly consented; he feared the proposed assembly would force peace on him, and so mar the success he hoped from the new accession to his forces. His fears proved correct. This body, though it was Royalist, showed a strong dislike to certain of the council, as Papists, and as having been the old instruments of tyranny. They even showed some suspicion of the king's own intentions; and, in fact, this half Parliament was evidently inclined to make peace with its other half at Westminster. All overtures, however, proved nugatory, for "the Lords and Commons" of the Long Parliament refused to hold any communication with the king while he spoke of the Oxford assembly as on an equality with themselves. After a three months' session, Charles gladly adjourned the Parliament of his friends (16th April), which he described, in writing to his wife, as "this mongrel assembly, the haunt of cowardly and seditious motions."

Oxford Parliament.

When hostilities re-commenced, the Parliament had no less than five armies afoot; the army of Lord Fairfax, now moving freely in Yorkshire, as the siege of Hull had been raised by the advance of the Scots; that of Essex, now being recruited in London after its successes at Gloucester and Newbury; that of Waller, now reinforced after its expulsion from the west; the eastern counties' army, under the command of Cromwell and Manchester; and, lastly, the army of the Scots, 21,000 strong, commanded by a Scotchman, Leslie, Earl of Leven.

Armies of the Parliament.

Charles had two large armies—his own, at Oxford, of 10,000 men; that of Newcastle, in Yorkshire, of 14,000 men; besides several considerable forces scattered over the country, and regiments of English and Irish troops landing from time to time in Wales, and at Chester and Bristol.

Armies of the king.

The Parliament had laid on the country heavy taxes for the maintenance of its armies. Custom duties were levied on various articles of export and import. An ordinance had been passed for a weekly assessment of £10,000 on London, and of £24,000 on the rest of the kingdom. This tax, like the subsidy, was levied on lands and goods, but not after the same

Taxes.

fashion. The subsidies had been levied after an old rate, and by commissioners appointed by the Chancellor from amongst the inhabitants of the county or borough. Through the laxity of these commissioners the receipts had steadily decreased. Now a specific sum was laid upon each county, and raised by commissioners named by Parliament. By further ordinances, the excise duty, a tax hitherto unknown in England, was introduced, which consisted of a tax on the manufacture of commodities as distinct from the custom duties on their importation, and as touching home rather than foreign produce. The ignorant always prefer customs to excise, because the incidence of the former is less visible; but the objection to customs is that they take much more out of the pocket of the consumer than they bring to the exchequer. Customs, being mainly levied on raw produce, have to be paid by the merchant; his payment has to be recouped by the manufacturer and the dealers, besides other intermediaries, all of whom require a profit on the money sunk in the payment of the tax. Excise, being levied on the last stage before sale, is, therefore, a more economical tax. The Dutch had employed it before this, but its introduction into England was due to the genius of Pym.

Such excise was now laid upon many articles of every-day use and consumption; upon ale, cider, perry, wine, oil, sugar, pepper, salt, silk, soap, and even meat (May, 1643—July, 1644). Counties under the power of the Royalists were no better off than those under the power of the Parliament. The Oxford Parliament copied that of Westminster, and laid on an excise; irregular contributions were constantly levied by the king's troops, and his whole army, when unpaid, as it now often was, lived at free quarters.

The committee of the two nations, sitting at Derby House, directed the movements of the generals. Fairfax, Manchester, and Lesley received instructions to attack Newcastle's army, and lay siege to York; Essex and Waller to invest Oxford. When it was known within Oxford that a siege was impending, Discontent in Oxford. faction and discontent broke all bonds of control. Money was getting scarce, and everybody was out of humour. The queen took fright, and departed for Exeter, bidding Charles her last farewell. Courtiers grumbled, and considered themselves neglected. The officers wanted to govern everything, and quarrelled with the civilians in the council. The number of Papists in the town annoyed many of the king's Protestant friends. Charles was incapable of silencing discontent and making men work together. He had no faculty for putting the right man into the right place. Promotion went by caprice or importunity. His officers quarrelled with one another for command. In fact it was a reign of jealousy before ; and now, to gratify his nephews Rupert and Maurice, he displaced and offended some of the best and most trustworthy of his servants.

Oxford was already nearly invested, when Charles, by a skilful manœuvre, saved both his army and the town. At the dead of night, accompanied by his cavalry and 2500 foot, he passed undiscovered between the two armies of Essex and Waller (3rd June), and proceeded by quick marches to Worcester, and thence across the Severn to Bewdley. Rupert, in command of his Cavaliers and some of the troops which had been sent over from Ireland, was now in Lancashire, engaged in reducing the fortified places which were held for the Parliament. But Charles, hearing that Newcastle—who was closely besieged in York—could not hold out for six weeks longer unless relieved, sent orders to Rupert to march straight to York and relieve it by engaging the Scots.

Meanwhile, the Parliamentary leaders, as soon as they became aware of Charles' escape, agreed that Waller and his army should pursue the royal forces, while Essex and his army reduced the towns in the west. Waller thought the king was making for Lancashire to join Rupert, and so kept ahead of him on the eastern bank of the Severn. But Charles' plan was much bolder; on hearing the Parliament's forces were divided, his aim was to regain his head-quarters immediately and attack before his enemies could re-unite. With this view he crossed the river behind Waller, and on the 20th June was again in Oxford. Without giving any time for Essex to reappear, he marched out at once at the head of his whole army, and soon fell in with Waller, who, on hearing of his movements, had returned in haste to cover the road to London. The two armies were in sight of one another as they marched northwards from Banbury, Charles being on the eastern, Waller on the western, bank of the Cherwell.

About midday, Waller, observing that the rear of the king's army was some distance behind the main body, forced a passage across Cropredy Bridge, and fell upon it in front, while at the same time he sent a body of

Battle of Cropredy Bridge. (Map, p. 127.)

horse to make their way over a ford about a mile lower down the river. Charles, seeing his rear about to be attacked on two sides, at once recalled his advanced troops, and a succession of skirmishes followed, in which the Royalists were generally victorious, taking several pieces of cannon, and beating the enemy back both over the ford and the bridge. Fighting lasted until night caused the two armies to separate. The action in itself might have been called indecisive, but the king gained all the advantages of a victory, for death and desertion soon reduced Waller's army to half its numbers.

Three days after the battle of Cropredy Bridge, the eastern counties' army was brought into action in Yorkshire. It was supporting the Scots in besieging York; but the generals of the Parliament, on hearing that Rupert was marching from Lancashire with 20,000 men to raise the siege, withdrew from their entrenchments to Hessay Moor in order to oppose his approach (30th June). The prince, however, disappointed their expectations, for instead of following the high road from Knaresborough, over Skip Bridge, he crossed the Ouse with his army above its junction with the Nidd, and entered York the same evening without opposition (1st July).

As Rupert had already effected his object in relieving the town, Newcastle wished to avoid, or at least delay a battle; urging in the first place that divisions would probably break out in the enemy's army, composed as it was of Scots and English, Presbyterians and Independents, in the second, that he was expecting a reinforcement of 3000 men, and that no battle ought to be fought until after their arrival. But Rupert, confident of victory, put forward the king's letter: "I have his Majesty's commands," he said; "I am bound to fight." "I am ready to obey your Highness," replied Newcastle, "as if the king himself were here." The prince's army was encamped a few miles to the north of York, and it was agreed that Newcastle's foot should be ready by two o'clock at night to march out and unite with it. Their sudden and unlooked-for deliverance seemed, however, for the time to have demoralized the York forces. Some of the soldiers were out seeking for booty in the deserted trenches of the enemy; others were already drawn together, when a report spread that before marching they were to receive their pay; at once the men broke from their ranks and dispersed, and some hours elapsed before they could be gathered together again.* Rupert rode out of the town at daybreak, without waiting for Newcastle,† and proceeded to lead his army across the Ouse at Poppelton, where the Scots had left standing a bridge of boats (2nd July).

The counsels of the Parliament's generals were, like those of the Royalists, divided. The English were for seeking out the enemy and fighting, but the Scots proposed to retreat to Cawood, where, by forming a *tête-de-pont* to defend the bridge at the junction of the branches of the Ouse, they might oppose Rupert's further advance south. The Scots' counsel prevailed, and the army drew off from Hessay Moor southwards, in the direction of Tadcaster: those in the van had already advanced some miles, when it was attacked in the rear by Rupert's horse at Marston village and forced hastily to turn and form in order of battle.

Both Hessay and Marston Moors form part of a low plain, watered by the Ouse and the Nidd. Drainage and tillage have now changed the character of a tract that was then in the main really moor, open and unenclosed. Immediately south of the road that joins Tockwith and Marston, the dead level ends, and an easy ascent of ten minutes leads to the summit of a line of higher ground, running from one village to the other. The Parliamentarians on the first attack promptly faced about to the north, and formed upon the brow of this hill, on Marston Field, a large enclosure with crops of rye then dotted over it. Their right wing, consisting of Sir Thomas Fairfax' regiments of horse and foot, together with the larger part of the Scotch horse, and a reserve of Scottish infantry, occupied a position immediately west of Marston village, where the elevation is highest. Their main battle was composed of Scotch and English infantry, commanded by Lords Leven and Manchester and Sir Thomas's father, Lord Fairfax. Still farther west, resting on the village of Tockwith, where the hill is much lower than at Marston, was the left wing, comprised of three regiments of Scottish cavalry and the eastern counties' horse, under the command respectively of David Leslie

---

* There is a curious account of the 'battle of York' (*i.e.*, Marston Moor) in the Clarendon State Papers at Oxford. The writing is in the same hand as a paper printed in the Clar. State Papers, ii. p. 181, which is endorsed by Hyde, 'Sir Hugh Cholmeley's Memorials.' The writer, whoever he is, tells us he received his account 'from a gentleman of quality of that country who was a colonel and had a command there and present all the time.' The other accounts of the battle given by eye-witnesses are nearly all written by Parliamentarians.

† William Cavendish, Earl of Newcastle (p. 134), now Marquis.

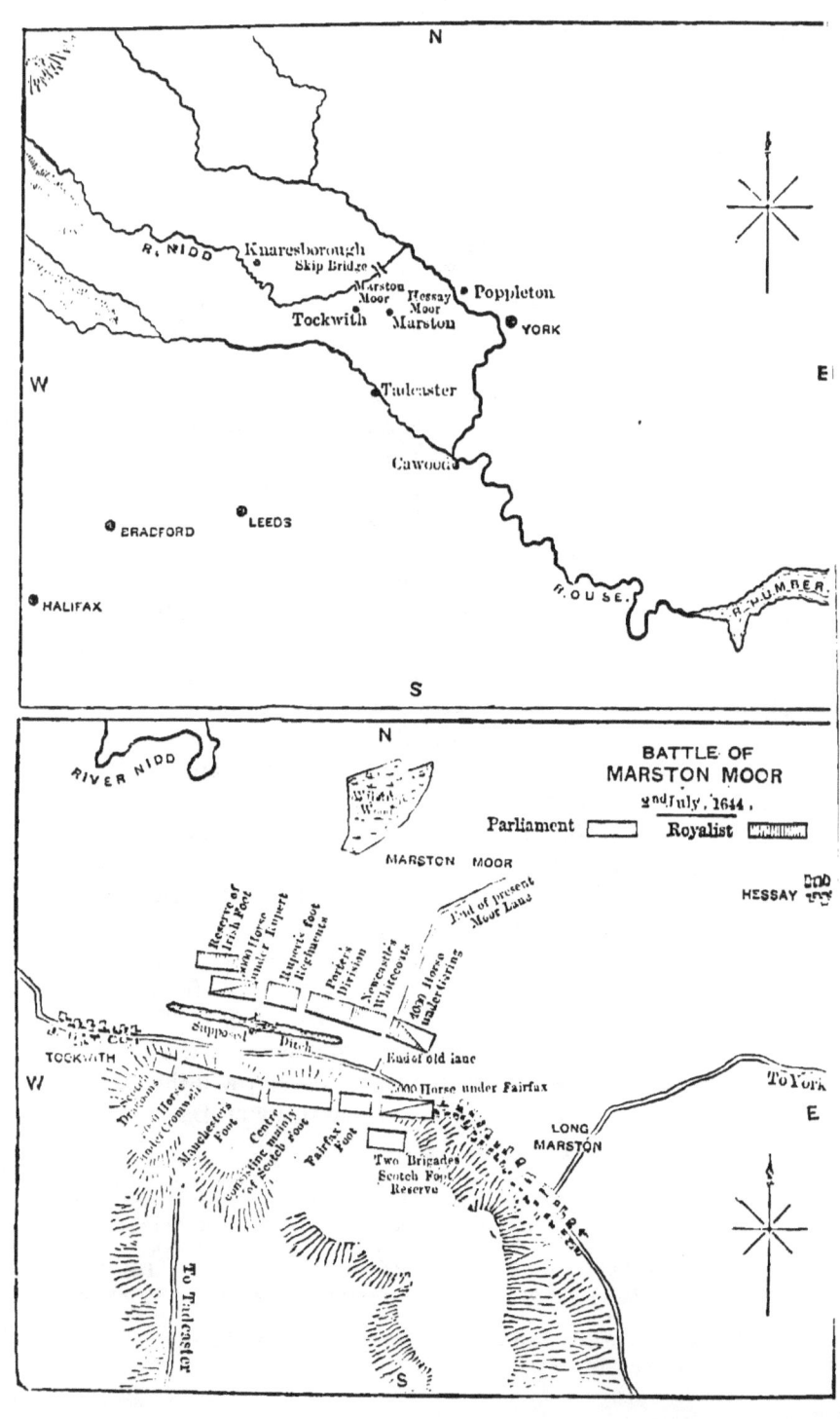

and Lieutenant-General Cromwell. Its outer flank was supported by a body of Scotch dragoons.

Rupert, who was following from the north-east, finding that his enemies were facing about to accept battle, formed his army upon Marston Moor, awaiting meanwhile impatiently the arrival of the York forces. After some delay the marquis, "accompanied with all the gentlemen of quality which were in York, came to the prince, who said, ' My lord, I wish you had come sooner with your forces, but I hope we shall yet have a glorious day.' The marquis informed him how his foot had been a-plundering in the trenches, and that it was impossible to have got together all at the time fixed, but that he had left General King about the work, who would bring them up with all the expedition that might be. The prince, seeing the marquis' foot were not come up, would with his own forces have been falling upon the enemy, but the marquis dissuaded him, telling him that he had 4000 good foot as were in the world coming. About four o'clock in the afternoon General King brought up the marquis' foot, of which yet many were wanting, for there was not above 3000. The prince demanded of King how he liked the marshalling of his army, who replied, he did not approve of it, being drawn too near the enemy and in a place of disadvantage. Then said the prince, ' They may be drawn a further distance.' 'No, sire,' said King, 'it is too late.'"

The two armies were drawn up so close together that "their foot," says a Parliamentarian, "was close to our noses." Rupert had been beforehand in gaining possession of a deep ditch that ran in a straight line between them. In this he placed four bodies of musketeers opposite the eastern counties' army. His right wing he led in person. Newcastle's foot fell into position on the extreme left of the main body, which was placed under the command of General King; the left wing was commanded by Colonel Goring. A few fields cut up the moor on this side, so that the only approach for the horse on the enemy's right lay up a narrow lane with a hedge on one side and a ditch on the other, both lined with dismounted dragoons. All along the line waved banners magnificent with gold and silver fringes. Here a red pennon with a white cross, and motto, 'Pro rege et regno ;' there a black coronet and sword reaching from the clouds, 'Terribilis ut acies ordinata ;' while far on the right the presence of the prince was marked by a standard nearly five yards long and broad, with a red cross in the centre. Each army was nearly 23,000 strong, so that never before in the course of the war had such large forces met face to face. The Parliamentarians wore as their mark a white paper or handkerchief in their hats; their word for the day was 'God with us.' The Royalist mark was to be without bands or scarfs; their word 'God and the king.'

Since two o'clock the cannon had been booming, but still the two armies delayed to join battle. The Parliament's generals, trusting in Rupert's proverbial daring, waited for him to disorder his lines by being the first to charge across the ditch. Their soldiers meanwhile 'fell to singing psalms,' a sign that they at least were nerved and ready for any odds.

When the forces from York had at last arrived, Rupert's impetuosity was restrained by the representations of Newcastle and King, both of whom were averse to fighting because of the lateness of the hour. He declared accordingly his intention of delaying the battle till the next day, ordered provisions to be brought for his army from York, and with most culpable neglect suffered many of his horsemen to dismount and lie on the ground, with their horses' bridles in their hands.

But that long summer's day was not so to end. It was already seven o'clock when Leven, who acted as commander-in-chief, finding that the enemy would not charge him, determined to charge them, and ordered the whole line of his army to advance. "We came down the hill," says Oliver's scout-master, "in the bravest order, and with the greatest resolution—I mean the left wing of our horse, led by Cromwell, which was to charge their right wing, led by Rupert, in which was all their gallant men." At the sound of the enemy's alarums, the prince in hot haste sprung to horse and galloped up to the front of the field. He found his own regiment taken by surprise, and in some disorder. "'Swounds!" he cried, "do you run—follow me!" and fiercely led the way to meet the enemy's charge. Meanwhile Manchester's foot, in the face of a fierce fire, dashed down the hill at a bit of level, where there was a break in the ditch, and thus taking the Royalist musketeers in flank, drove them out of their shelter. A desperate struggle ensued. The horsemen discharged their pistols, and then, flinging them at one another's heads, fell to with their swords. A company of Cavaliers, led by Rupert in person, charged Cromwell's own division of three hundred horse in front and flank. A shot grazed the lieutenant's-general's neck. "A miss is as good as a mile," he exclaimed, and, scattering his assailants before him "like a little dust," pressed onwards till he broke through the lines of the enemy. "Manchester's foot, on the right hand, went on by our side," says Oliver's scout-master again, "dispersing the enemy's foot almost as fast as they charged them, still going by our side, cutting them down that we carried the whole field before us, thinking the victory wholly ours, and nothing to be done but to kill and take prisoners." Soon Rupert's whole wing, horse and foot, was in full flight, and the Cavaliers were swept off the field, flying northwards "along by Wilstrop woodside as fast and thick as could be."

Meanwhile the Parliament's troops on the right wing found their advance impeded by the hedge and ditch which protected the enemy's left. They could only march up the lane three or four abreast, and were exposed all the while to a hot fire from the musketeers stationed by Rupert on either side. After forcing their way to the open ground at the end of the lane, they were received by large bodies of the enemy, who fell upon each party as it emerged. Fairfax, indeed, in face of all difficulties, charged right through Goring's squadrons, at the head of four hundred horse. But finding himself left unsupported, he was fain to take the white handkerchief out of his hat, and pass for a Royalist commander while he rode hastily back to his own side.

Meantime his van, composed of newly-levied regiments, had wheeled round before the enemy, and disordered his own infantry and the Scots' reserve, so that on his return, he found his whole wing broken and already in flight. Some of the Cavaliers, with their usual impetuosity, pursued the flying enemy over the hill which shut out their view of the field, and miles on to the south in the direction of Cawood and Tadcaster; others tarried to plunder the carriages and baggage left by the Parliamentarians on the top of the hill; others under the command of Goring joined Newcastle's regiment of Whitecoats, and wheeled round on the unprotected right flank of the enemy's centre. Thus attacked in front and flank, the Scots' infantry on this side gave way. In vain Leven exhorted his men to stand. "Though you run from your enemies," he cried, "yet leave not your general." Believing the battle to be lost, he joined the stream of fugitives, and never drew rein until he came to Leeds.

The general confusion -- account of an eye-witness.   The confusion was not confined to the Parliament side. "I knew not for my soul," says one who was there looking for Rupert, "whither to incline: runaways on both sides, so many, so breathless, so speechless, not a man of them able to give me the least hope where the prince was to be found, both armies being mingled, horse and foot. In this terrible distraction did I scour the country, here meeting with a shoal of Scots crying out, 'Wae's us, we're a' undone!' then with a ragged troop, reduced to four and a cornet, by-and-by with a little foot-officer, without hat, band, or anything but feet."

It is a time of confusion such as this that gives an opening for the calm and collected officer who has his men well in hand. Half the Royalist left wing were far away, triumphantly driving the blow home, as they thought, by a hot pursuit. Goring had only Newcastle's Whitecoats and a sprinkling of his own Cavaliers, when the fading light revealed to him a new enemy occupying the very ground he had himself held in the morning.

Cromwell redeems the day.   It was the Parliament's left wing, led by Cromwell and Leslie; who, after dispersing the Royalist right, had relinquished pursuit and crossed the battle-field to support their less fortunate friends. Once again Cavaliers and Ironsides fiercely charged, and once again victory remained with the Ironsides. The Cavaliers fled the field, while Newcastle's regiment of Whitecoats, a thousand brave Northumbrians raised out of his own tenantry, scorning to receive quarter or to fly, were all, save some thirty, cut down to a man, in the same order and rank in which they stood. Major-General Porter, who had forced back part of the Parliament's main battle, now, in the moment of success, found foes in his own rear, and had to surrender with his men.

Broken and routed, the Royalists on all sides fled, and were chased with terrible slaughter to within a mile of York. By ten o'clock, the battle was over, and after scarce three hours' fighting, more than 3000 Royalists lay dead upon the field. The Parliamentarians lost, it was said, only some 300 men; they made 1500 prisoners, and took all the enemy's artillery, ammunition, and baggage. "The Earl of Manchester," says his chaplain, "about eleven o'clock that night, did ride about to the soldiers both horse and foot, giving them many thanks for the exceeding good service they had done for the kingdom; and he often earnestly entreated them to give the honour of the victory unto God alone. The soldiers unanimously gave God the glory of their great deliverance and victory, and told his lordship with much cheerfulness that, though they had long fasted and were faint, yet they would willingly want three days longer, rather than to give up the service or leave his lordship." It was not, however, till noon the next day, that the joyful news reached Leven, who had fled in the belief that the battle was irrecoverably lost. Upon hearing of this, he knocks upon his breast, and says, " I would to God I had died upon the plain."* Leven bewails his flight.

Newcastle, in disgust at seeing his army destroyed and power gone through Rupert's rashness, went beyond seas, accompanied by more than eighty gentlemen. The prince returned to Chester, with the remnants of a broken army. York surrendered to the Parliament, and the king lost all hold in the north. Such was one result of the battle; but there was a second hardly less momentous. The Independents had triumphed not only over the Royalists, but over the Presbyterians. In London, it was told how "Cromwell, with his unspeakable valorous regiments, had done all the service; the Presbyterians, the Scots, had fled."† As though to render the triumph of the Ironsides the more complete, a terrible misfortune befell the army in which the Presbyterians placed their trust. Results of battle.

The Royalist leader, Sir Richard Grenville, on hearing of the presence of Essex in the west, raised the siege of Plymouth, and marched for refuge into Cornwall. Essex had already advanced as far as Exeter, when the news reached him that the king had defeated Waller, and was now following in pursuit of himself. Some of his officers, who had estates in Cornwall which they wished to visit, persuaded him to march after Grenville, instead of turning at once to meet the royal forces. He soon found that he had taken a fatal step. The country people were Royalists, and gave him no support. The country itself is enough to embarrass a general, with its bare back-bone of mountain, moor, or marsh, while the southern coast, which is the least desolate, is split up into a succession of deep valleys running to the sea.

* Rushworth; Ormond Pap., i. 56; Fairfax' Mem.; Cromwelliana; Sir H. Slingsby's Mem.; Letters and Accounts of Ash, Watson, and Steward, in King's Pamphlets, 164, 166; Memorials touching the battle of York, in Clarendon Papers in Bodleian. † Baillie, ii. 40.

Essex had his head-quarters at Lostwithiel, in the valley of the Fowey, then spelt, as it is still pronounced, Foy, when the king, advancing from Liskeard, pitched his camp and standard on Broadoak or Braddoc Downs, near Boconnoc. Hoping to profit by the enmity existing between the Presbyterian and Independent commanders, he wrote Essex a letter, calling on him to end the war by uniting the two armies, and promising on the word of a king that he would ever prove a faithful friend to both him and his army. The Royalist officers afterwards set their names to a letter, in which they undertook to see carried out all that his Majesty might promise. But Essex' honesty stood the test. In answer to their overtures he declared his inability to treat, and referred the king to the Parliament. His generalship, however, did not prove equal to his honesty. Though he was in possession of the valley of the Foy, from the haven itself to Lanhydrock, a house belonging to the Parliamentarian Lord Robartes, so that supplies could be brought into his army, both by sea and land, from all sides, excepting the east; yet with little opposition, he suffered the king to draw the toils so closely round him, that starvation or surrender were the only alternatives left. Grenville, at the head of 1400 men, advanced from Bodmin, gained possession of Lanhydrock, and thus opened communication with Charles on Broadoak Downs, and shut in the army of the enemy on the north (12th August). Essex had neglected to occupy View Hall, a house on the east bank of the river opposite Foy, and Pernon Fort, standing on the same side and commanding the entrance of the harbour. These important positions were now seized and occupied by the Royalists, so that the Parliamentarians were prevented any longer from bringing provisions into Fowey by sea (13th August). Their position at Lostwithiel soon became still more circumscribed. Sir Richard Grenville advanced from Lanhydrock and drove Essex out of Lestormel Castle, which commands the Fowey valley scarce a mile above Lostwithiel (21st August). The same day the king, advancing from enclosures which bounded the south side of Boconnoc Park, forced the Parliamentarians to quit their quarters on a beacon hill, which stands about a mile east of Lostwithiel. Here the following night, he raised a battery, whence he shot right into their camp. The west was now the only side still open to

Surrender at Lostwithiel.

ESSEX' ARMY SURRENDERS.

Essex, and even from this he was shortly to be cut off. Goring and the horse seized possession of St. Austell, and thus commanded all the country round Tywardreath Bay, whence provisions had still reached Lostwithiel by sea (25th August). Essex had now no choice left but to surrender.

The horse escaped by riding off about three o'clock one misty morning, between the armies of the king and Prince Maurice, which were encamped a small distance apart (31st August).

Essex and the foot marched from Lostwithiel for Foy, hoping as a last resource to escape across the river and sail from Lanteglos to Plymouth. Before leaving Lostwithiel, they tried to break down the bridge over the river, but were prevented by the enemy's infantry, who followed them through the town and down the valley, forcing them to a hasty retreat. On the march they came to some high ground and enclosures, which they occupied, and succeeded for the time in making a successful stand and driving the enemy back. The next day, Essex sailed from

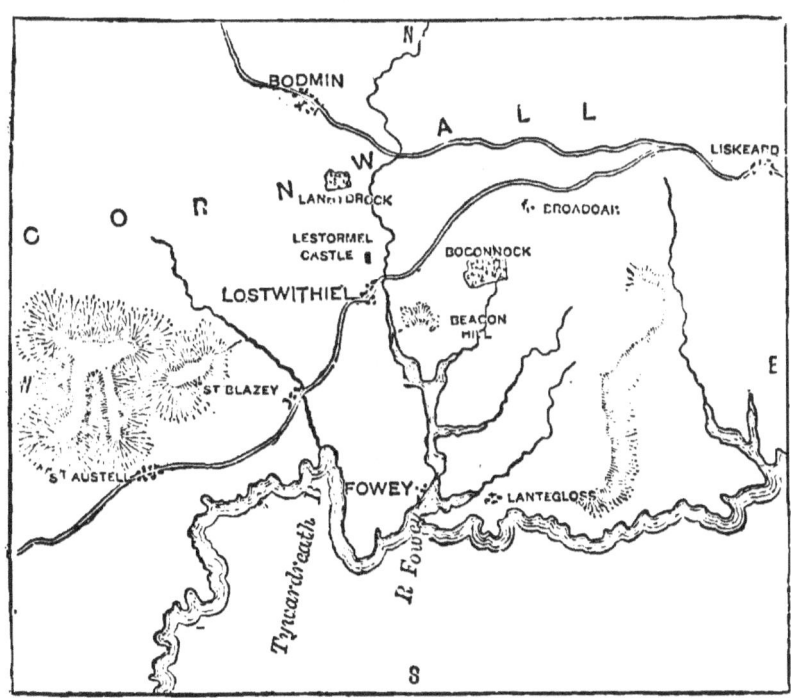

Foy, in company with his principal officers. As he left the harbour, he narrowly escaped being taken prisoner by the garrison of Pernon Fort. The infantry, about 6000 in number, surrendered their ammunition, artillery, and arms, on condition that they should be allowed their liberty and conducted to the nearest quarters of their friends. The terms, however, were not kept; the men were maltreated and plundered all the way on their march through the enemy's country, and so many were the deaths and desertions, that only some 1000 arrived at Poole in safety. Thus the two Presbyterian generals in the west were crushed in a single campaign. "Mr. Sheriff," said Charles, on his departure from Cornwall, "I leave the country entirely at peace in your hands."*

At this time the flames of civil war had spread from England into Scotland. Before the cessation of arms had been concluded with the Irish, and before the Scots had declared themselves for the Parliament, the Marquis of Montrose had formed with Charles a secret plan of raising the Highlanders and uniting them with a body of troops to be transported from Ireland, and thus beginning a second civil war in Scotland. An attempt was made to carry this plan into execution during the present summer; and Montrose, coming down from the Highlands at the head of a brave, but savage and undisciplined, army of Highlanders and Irishmen, twice defeated such forces as the Covenanters were able to bring together during the absence of their best troops in England.†

<small>Civil war in Scotland.</small>

Hostilities were carried on in a more and more brutal spirit. This was especially the case after the introduction of Irish troops into England. The introduction of troops of a lower order of civilization is always looked upon with horror. If not savages as Indians in America, or 'Turcos' in France, both Highlanders and Irish were looked upon as such. They both fought without regard to the ordinary rules of war. Montrose's Highland 'hell hounds,' as they were called, were allowed to plunder and butcher at will; while the Irish came stained with the blood of massacred Protestants. An ordi-

<small>Irish and Highlanders</small>

---

* Letter of Sir F. Basset; Hals' Parochial History (both *apud* Davies Gilbert's History of Cornwall); Clar. Hist.; Sir E. Walker's Historical Discourses.

† At Tipper Muir, 1st September, 1644. At Bridge of Dee, 14th September, 1644.

nance passed by the Parliament forbidding quarter to be given to any Irishmen or Papists taken in arms (Oct. 3rd), was in their case literally enforced. Irish soldiers seized on their way to English ports were tied back to back and cast into the sea; those made prisoners in England were shot by hundreds. The more moderate of the Royalists had objected to the introduction of the Irish; but the less scrupulous, not to be behind in acts of cruelty, would retaliate by hanging English prisoners, taken in arms, twelve at a time, on a tree, or by putting members of garrisons to death on slight excuses, contrary to articles of capitulation. Thus the war was more and more embittered as it went on.

Charles, on hearing of Montrose's victories, regarded the disastrous day of Marston Moor as already retrieved. He expected either that the Scotch army would return to defend their homes, or else that Montrose would march into England, fight the Scots, and recover his lost ascendancy in the north. But his wishes made him overlook the character of Montrose's army. After a raid on the Lowlands, the Highlanders' custom was to return to the mountains, and enjoy their spoil. The present expedition was nothing to them but a raid on a larger scale than usual; and no sooner did the winter set in, than they melted away from their leader, who found his Irish troops insufficient to protect him, and was fain to follow his Highlanders and take refuge in their mountains.

Charles, meantime, was marching back from Cornwall to Oxfordshire. He had passed through Wiltshire, and reached Newbury, when he heard that the armies of Waller, Essex, and Manchester were advancing from London to meet him. The Independents, content with the proved superiority of their army, had not pressed their victory over the fallen Essex and Waller. Waller's army had been recruited once more; and Essex' men had been re-furnished with arms on returning from their catastrophe in the west. Essex himself pleaded sickness, and remained absent from his army, feeling that since the relief of Gloucester, the day of his triumphs was over.

As the united armies of the enemy were 16,000 strong, and his own forces not above 8000, Charles, not venturing to risk a battle in the open field, took up a strong defensive position in Newbury, between the rivers Kennet and Lamborne. On the south the town was protected by the Kennet. On the north-east troops were quartered in Shaw village, which was strengthened with a breastwork, and in a large house, called Doleman's, still standing, as the map shows (p. 144), a little in advance of the village on the northern bank of the Lamborne. Bodies of horse occupied a gentle eminence rising immediately east of Doleman's House, and a few neighbouring hedges were lined with musketeers. On the west Prince Maurice's infantry was quartered in the village of Speen; and in two large fields, lying north of Newbury, between the rivers Kennet and Lamborne, was stationed a large body of horse together with a train of artillery. Approach to this quarter was rendered the more difficult by the neighbourhood of Donnington Castle, which was held by a strong garrison for the king.

The Parliament's generals took possession of Clay Hill, lying to the north-east of Newbury, and agreed to make a combined attack upon Shaw and Speen. For this purpose, the greater part of Manchester's horse, all Essex' horse and foot, and almost all the forces under Waller, separated from Manchester, and making a detour beyond Donnington Castle, surprised the Royalists in their quarters on the north-west. Many of the king's guards being absent from their posts, the Lamborne was crossed without opposition, and Prince Maurice's infantry quickly dislodged from Speen. A fierce three-hours' contest followed in the fields lying between Donnington and Newbury. The king, who was present in person, could not prevent some of his troops from flying under the walls of the castle for protection. Essex' men, crying out "that they would be revenged for the business of Cornwall," carried off in triumph the very cannon they had before surrendered. The Royalists, however, succeeded in retaining possession of the field, and when night caused the battle to end, Waller retired into Speen. Meanwhile, on the other side of the town, a still fiercer struggle had been maintained. Manchester had agreed with Waller that as soon as the sound of cannon should be heard from Speen, he would advance with his forces upon the Royalist quarters at Shaw. During the morning he "rode about from regiment to regiment to encourage the soldiers, and to keep them in due order fit for that service which every hour almost was expected." It was about four o'clock in the afternoon when, says an eye-witness, "we saw the firing of the muskets in Speen, which discovered the service to be very hot, and with joy and thankfulness beheld the hasty disorderly retreat of the enemy towards Newbury." On this encouraging sight 3000 of Manchester's foot burst down Clay Hill singing a psalm as they came, intending to storm the defences of the Royalists, and meet their friends in the fields lying between Newbury and Donnington. Charging furiously, the Parliamentarians forced the king's horse back into the garden of Doleman's House, and made their way right up to the breastworks. Here, however, they were exposed to a murderous fire, and fell in numbers, while they were able to do little execution upon enemies sheltered by walls and earthworks. As was not seldom the case in this war, with the approach of night, friends were mistaken for foes; so that after one company of Manchester's foot had possessed themselves of one of the enemy's outworks, a second beat them out again with great loss of life to both. After four hours' hard fighting, the Parliamentarians gave up the attack and drew off, while sheltered from pursuit by their own horse, which had stayed all the time barely beyond range of the enemy's pistols. It was now ten o'clock, and a clear, moonlight night. Charles, seeing that he had lost ground upon the western side of the town, forsook his quarters, and, without meeting any opposition, withdrew by Donnington Castle to Wallingford, passing between Waller's and Manchester's armies.*

It was a victory, but not a victory to break the king's power in the south, as Marston Moor had broken it in the north. When the generals returned to London, Cromwell laid a heavy charge against the Presbyterian earl in the House of Commons; how Manchester had always been for such a peace as a victory would be a disadvantage to; how he had often acted as if he thought the king too low and the Parliament too high, but especially at Donnington Castle : "Though," said Cromwell, "I showed him evidently how this success might be obtained, and only desired leave with my own brigade of horse, to charge the king's army in their retreat, leaving it to the earl's choice, if he thought proper to remain neutral with the rest of his forces. But he positively refused his consent, and gave no other reason but that, if we met with a defeat, there was an end of our pretensions—we should all be rebels and traitors, and be executed and forfeited by law." Dissensions in London.

* Ludlow Mem.; Clar. Hist.; E. Walker's Hist. Discourses; A true relation of the most chief occurrences at and since the Battle at Newbury, (by Simeon Ash, chaplain to Manchester) in King's Tracts.

Manchester, in turn, retorted on his lieutenant-general charges of insubordination, and of deep dark designs; of having said, "that it would never be well in England till I were plain Mr. Montague, and there was never a peer nor a lord in the land." Indeed, it was reported that Cromwell said to his soldiers, "if he met the king in battle, he would fire his pistol at the king as at another." The charges were not pressed on either side, and no judgment was passed. But the Presbyterians from this time feared Cromwell as the ablest and most determined of their opponents. Pym was dead nearly a year now, and there had risen up in his place a man they owned to be "of a very wise and active head, universally well-beloved as religious and stout, being a known Independent, and loved by the soldiers." Their fears made them the more eager to effect a peace, which would secure their own ascendancy, and crush the hated Independents. Peace propositions were accordingly brought forward, and passed both Houses of Parliament after meeting much opposition from the Independent party (9th Nov.). Charles agreed to send seventeen commissioners to Uxbridge, to discuss the terms proposed, with thirty-five members of Parliament and the Scottish commissioners.

But while the Presbyterians were intending peace, the Independents were preparing to re-model the army, and place it in the hands of men who knew how to conquer; for it was evident that the war would never be brought to a successful close while the command of the forces of the Parliament was divided between rival generals of different principles, some of whom did not wish to push matters to an extreme. To effect their purpose, they proposed to deprive of office, civil and military, all members of Parliament. The House was considering the sad condition of the kingdom, when Cromwell rose and spoke to the following effect: "It is now time to speak, or for ever hold the tongue. The important occasion now is no less than to save a nation out of a bleeding, nay almost out of a dying condition. . . . For what do the enemy say? Nay, what do men say that were friends at the beginning of the Parliament? Even this, that the members of both Houses have got great places, and commands, and the sword into their hands, and will not permit the war speedily to end, lest their own power should determine with it." "Whatever is the matter," continued another member; "two summers are passed over, and we are not

Self-denying ordinance.

saved. A summer's victory has proved but a winter's story; the game has shut up with autumn, to be new played again next spring, as if the blood that has been shed were only to manure the field of war I determine nothing, but it is apparent that the forces being under several great commanders has oftentimes hindered the public service." "There is but one way of ending so many evils," said a third member. "I move that no member of either house shall, during this war, execute any office or command, civil or military" (9th Dec.).

The motion was acted upon, and a 'self-denying ordinance' to the effect proposed was ordered to be brought into the House. Since the Presbyterians fully understood that this measure was intended to place the army under the sole control of the Independents, they were not inclined to relax in their opposition. But they had now been three years at the head of affairs and not yet brought the war to an end. Public opinion was strong against them and turned the waverers, so that the ordinance was carried by a small majority of seven votes (19th Dec.).

In the Upper House, the opposition was even stronger than in the Commons. The peers of England had always held the highest command in the state, and were now unwilling to make way for the rise of their inferiors in rank, by yielding up honours that they regarded as their hereditary right. They accordingly rejected the ordinance, saying, that they did not know what shape the army would take (15th Jan., 1645). The Independents answered the objection by introducing into the Commons a second ordinance for the re-modelling of the army. There was only to be one army, to consist of 21,000 men. Sir Thomas Fairfax was named commander-in-chief; Skippon, major-general; and a blank was left for the name of the new lieutenant-general. This ordinance also passed the Commons, and was sent up to the Lords (28th Jan.). *Ordinance for re-modelling army.*

Meanwhile, commissioners from king and Parliament met, as agreed, at Uxbridge. The question of religion was first discussed. The Parliament demanded that Episcopacy should be abolished, the Presbyterian Church established, and the king himself take the covenant. The king's commissioners offered so far to reduce the power of bishops that, in most points, they should be incapable of acting without the consent of the ministers of their respective dioceses. *Uxbridge negotiations.*

This concession might have been accepted at the beginning of the war, before the hopes of the Presbyterians had soared so high. But the two nations were now bound together by their solemn league and covenant, and nothing would satisfy Scotch or English Presbyterians but the entire abolition of the order of bishops. Next came the question of the militia. The king offered to resign the command to Parliament for seven years, on condition it should then revert to the crown. Two years ago, this concession also might have given satisfaction, but the strength of the Independent party was now far too great to allow of its acceptance by the Commons. Thirdly it was required that the cessation of arms, made by Charles with the Irish, should be declared void, and, hardest of all, that all his friends, even his very nephews, should be excepted from receiving the benefit of the royal prerogative of pardon. It was through the Independents that the stringency of the terms had been increased. The offer of peace was genuine on the part of the Presbyterians, who were most anxious that the king should accept terms before the army passed out of their hands. It was certainly a time for Charles to consider the question seriously. If he accepted, the Presbyterians would restore him—at least, in a manner—to his throne; the army of the Scots, the armies of Essex and Waller, united with the Cavaliers, would present a force more than enough to meet any opposition the Independents might offer. On the other hand, if he refused, the Independents would gain the sole control of the forces of the Parliament, and the result was sure to be some crushing defeat to himself.

This was the sober truth; but Charles' eyes were dazzled by a far more brilliant prospect, as he sat over letters and despatches in his rooms at Oxford. The queen, who had fled from Exeter to France, when Essex marched into the west, constantly sent her husband advice, much in the shape of command, bidding him be careful of making any peace that should not restore him to his full rights, and ensure her own safety. Montrose, who had gained a third victory in Scotland, at Inverlochy (2nd Feb.), wrote to implore him not to make himself 'a king of straw,' promising, before the end of the next summer, to be in England at the head of a gallant army. Charles, however, did not need to be dissuaded from accepting the terms offered by the Parliament, for he still believed in the final success of his arms.

Charles opposed to peace.

He was soliciting both France and Denmark for assistance, and, through the queen, was carrying on a negotiation with the Duke of Lorraine for the transportation of 10,000 soldiers into England. He was writing to Ormond that if the Irish Catholics should assist him, and he be restored to his throne by their means, he would consent to repeal all the penal statutes made against them.* He was trusting for success to the divisions of his enemies, and believed that, if he failed in the field, he could still play off one against the other, and that either section must be glad to bid high for his support against the other. Buoyed up by such hopes, Charles wrote to the queen, that he would never quit Episcopacy, nor the sword which God had put into his hands, and that she need not doubt the issue of the negotiations, for there was "no probability of a peace." He forbade the commissioners to make any further concessions, and the negotiations at Uxbridge were accordingly broken off (21st Feb.).

The king's rejection of the propositions was a terrible blow to the Presbyterians. The Lords, of whom only five or six had any sympathy with the Independents, had now to pass the ordinance for the re-modelling of the army (15th Feb.), and a second self-denying ordinance, depriving members of any office conferred on them since the election of the Parliament (3rd April). Any further opposition on their part would only have accelerated the speed of the revolution, by causing the Commons to declare their ordinance good at law without the consent of the House of Lords. For, in times of revolution, when the real powers in the State are the sword and the people, an upper chamber is useless and weak. The Commons, now acting as the executive, commanded the sword, the people supported the Commons, and the Lords were powerless to guide or stay the march of events.

Lords pass self-denying ordinance.

The self-denying ordinance, which now passed the Upper House, differed in an important point from the one before rejected. By this, members were not precluded from taking office on any future occasion. Its only effect was, in fact, to make, as it were, a fresh start. The existing Presbyterian generals were practically cashiered, but new nominees could be generals as well as members. But the Presbyterians, though foiled in these matters through their political half-heartedness, could still console them-

* Ludlow, iii. 232, Letter to Ormond.

selves with their ecclesiastical supremacy. In that sphere they never pretended to be tolerant. Their victim now was Laud. He had been impeached of high treason at the same time as Strafford, but the charge in his case was not pressed to an issue, and Pym and his party had contented themselves with leaving him to die a natural death in the Tower. Now, however, through the bigotry of Scotch and English Presbyterians, these proceedings were revived against the old man, already a four years' prisoner. His innovations in religion, the cruel sentences of the Star Chamber, and his interference with the judges, were charged against him, as an endeavour to subvert the laws and overthrow the Protestant religion. The judges, on being asked their opinion by the Lords, replied that the charges did not fall within the legal definition of high treason. The Lords would doubtless have followed the opinions of the judges. The Presbyterians, however, being determined on his death, voted him guilty by an ordinance of Parliament, which the House of Lords wanted spirit to reject. The verdict of the judges marked this as far more unjustifiable than Strafford's case. The fact that the chief prosecutor was Prynne, whose body showed the marks of the cruel judgments of the Star Chamber, roused, no doubt, a strong feeling against the archbishop. But a Parliament cannot plead the excuses of a mob, and cruelty did not constitute high treason. The conviction shows how little the securities that fence justice round are likely to be regarded when a popular assembly usurps the functions of the judicature. It shows, also, the evil of the precedent which was set when Strafford's conviction was secured by a Bill of Attainder instead of the legal process of an impeachment. The ordinance was simply a Bill of Attainder without the king's consent. The Presbyterians desired the blood of their former persecutor; and the Independents, in return for the passing of the self-denying ordinance, refrained from offering opposition to the gratification of their rivals' vengeance.

CHAPTER VIII.

NASEBY.—END OF WAR (1645—1646).

Fellows in arms, and my most loving friends,
Bruised underneath the yoke of tyranny,
  *   *   *   *
In God's name cheerly on, courageous friends,
To reap the harvest of perpetual peace
By this one bloody trial of sharp war.—RICH. III., v. 2, 1—10.

THE army, re-modelled at Windsor, was reduced, according to the ordinance, to a body of 21,000 men—14,000 foot, 6000 horse, 1000 dragoons. Though a smaller, it was a far more formidable force than it had ever been before, its ranks being now almost entirely composed of sectarians, and these either freeholders' sons or artisans. A clause introduced into the self-denying ordinance allowed religious men to serve without first taking the covenant, so that the new army was in no way bound to the Presbyterians.

These men had taken up arms, not to earn pay, but to win the victory of liberty of conscience. They proved no ordi- nary soldiers. A severe but popular discipline banished profane language and drunkenness from their camp. They would pass hours with their officers reading and expounding the Bible, and were able and ready to win converts for their doctrine by argument. A Presbyterian, appointed chaplain to one of these regiments, found his life a 'daily misery,' from abhorrence of the new views of these zealots. One soldier would argue against set forms of prayer; another against the baptism of infants; a third would maintain the thesis that there was no need of ordained ministers at all, since any man might be moved by the Spirit of God to preach and pray—a doctrine as horrible to the Presbyterian as making priests of the lowest of the people to the Levite; while all alike would contend for liberty of conscience, including the right of every sect to worship with its own forms, and promulgate its own doctrines.

[margin: Re-modelled army.]

In Oxford the new army was rather despised than feared. The Cavaliers scoffed at "Noll Cromwell" going forth "in the might of his spirit, with his swords and his Bibles, and all the train of his disciples, every one of whom is as David, a man of war and a prophet." Yet such confidence was singularly ill founded. It was Cromwell's men who had overthrown the Cavaliers on Marston Moor, and now a whole army was coming against them, fired by the same fierce enthusiasm as the Ironsides. Fanatical as these might be in their zeal, their courage was undoubtedly steeled by the conviction that, like the Israelites of old, they were fighting in God's cause, and that in such a cause victory must come, and death was better than delaying it.*

Obedience—the first step to victory—was rigidly enforced. Soon after the army left Windsor, a council of war was held upon several soldiers for disobeying regulations, and the body of one was left hanging upon a tree, as a warning to his comrades. The following day a proclamation was made that it was 'death for any to plunder.' The man whom Charles described as the "rebels' new brutish general," was Fairfax. He had been the chief framer of the new model army. He was no self-seeker, but a simple and straightforward patriot. Too refined to be a fanatic, he was deeply religious. His family had fought for the Protestant cause in the Low Countries, and he had himself seen service there as a lad. Fearless as a lion, fire and daring were his chief characteristics at first, but he soon showed power as an organizer, and was as vigilant as he was collected in the field. His wife was a general's daughter, and cheered his soldiers by her presence in the camp. Though of delicate health, he was as ready to face discomfort and hardships as peril. Once, when his own regiment grumbled at being ordered to bring up the rear instead of leading the column, he dismounted from his horse, and himself marched on foot that whole day at its head. Lessons like these have not to be read twice. By the self-denying ordinance Crom-

* The spirit of the Ironsides is not wholly extinct. In 1856 the question whether Kansas was to be a free or slave state gave rise to a border war. John Brown, a descendant of one of the English pilgrims who sailed to America in the "Mayflower" in 1620, formed a camp of God-fearing Puritans, who were "earnestness incarnate." Six of them were his own sons. Twenty-eight of these defeated fifty-six pro-slave borderers, and once 2000 Missourians retreated before 250 of his men. John Brown was taken and hanged in 1859, but his story became the marching-song in the great war of abolition (1861—1865).

well had been displaced. But Cromwell's name had become a talisman of victory, and instructions were soon sent him by the committee of the two nations to take command of a body of horse in the west (23rd April). Fairfax and his officers not long afterwards petitioned the Lower House for Cromwell's appointment as lieutenant-general of the horse (6th June); and though the appointment was nominally temporary, it was always renewed, and his position, both as officer and member, soon became unassailable. *Cromwell lieutenant-general of new army.*

On the other hand some of the best of the king's officers had been killed, others displaced to make way for worse men than themselves. Goring and Grenville, two unprincipled adventurers, commanded in the west, and were ruining the king's cause by their conduct towards one another and the people. Hyde and Colepepper were sent with the Prince of Wales, now a boy of fourteen, to bring them to obedience; but the prince's presence only added new fuel to the fire, and between the jealousy of the generals, the insubordination of the officers, and the marauding habits of the soldiers, the king's interest declined rapidly in those parts. *Royalist decline in west.*

Early in May the king himself left Oxford for the north, and joined Rupert near Chester, intending to take the enemy in detail, and attack the Scots before he met the re-modelled army of Fairfax. This plan was changed on the news that the re-modelled army was itself investing Oxford. He now determined to march east towards the associated counties, expecting that Fairfax would draw off his forces from Oxford for their protection. The line of march led the army by Leicester, which was held for the Parliament. Rupert erected a battery, and sent a summons to the garrison to surrender. Not receiving an answer at once, he opened fire. For some hours "both sides plied each other with cannon and musket-shot as fast as they could charge and discharge, and so continued all day" till midnight, when a great breach was made, and on the morning of the fourth day a general assault was ordered on six or seven different points, and, after a terrible struggle, the Cavaliers forced their way into the town, falling three to one, according to their own calculation. The garrison, about 1000 in number, threw down their arms and became prisoners of war; but the townspeople suffered dreadfully, the Royalists at their first entrance putting many to the sword, and *Storming of Leicester.*

plundering churches, hospitals, Royalists and Roundheads indiscriminately.* Charles was so much elated by this success that, a few days after the storming of Leicester, he wrote to the queen: "I may, without being too much sanguine, affirm that since the rebellion my affairs were never in so fair and hopeful a way."

Rupert was still in favour of one of the bolder courses, of marching either east against the associated counties, or northwards on the Scots; but Charles was persuaded to turn south and relieve Oxford, which he believed was still closely invested. He was grievously misinformed. On hearing of the fate of Leicester, Fairfax had raised the siege, and was now marching north to offer the king battle. On reaching Kislingbury, within five miles of the Royalist quarters, which were on Borough Hill, outside Daventry (12th June), he learnt from some stragglers that the enemy were in complete ignorance of his movements, the king out hunting, the soldiers in no order, the horses at grass. Yet all that night the careful general rode round his outposts in the rain, half expecting the Royalists would attempt a surprise on hearing of his presence. But at three in the morning he saw a blaze on Borough Hill; the Royalists had fired the huts they had made of the furze then covering the hill, and could be seen riding fast away to the north. The unexpected arrival of the enemy had, in fact, determined Charles to return to Leicester, and there recruit his army before risking a battle. Fairfax was holding a council of war at six in the morning, when Cromwell, just made lieutenant-general of the horse, came in from the associated counties, bringing with him a troop of six hundred horse and dragoons. The soldiers greeted Cromwell's arrival with huzzas; the generals soon settled their plans; the king was pursued; and that same evening (13th June) a body of horse under Ireton beat up the Royalist rear at Naseby, taking several prisoners. The fugitives carried the news that night to the main body, who had advanced some seven miles to Harborough. The king himself was lodged at Lubenham Hall, a mile or two west of Harborough, to which town he rode at once, and summoned a council of war, 'resting in a chair in a low room,' till his officers were roused from their beds, and collected from their various quarters. Of the council, some proposed

Charles holds a council of war.

* Sprigge (but see p. 392); King's Tracts, 212.

to wait for reinforcements expected from the west, but the majority agreed with Rupert that the insult was too much to be endured; that, as the Roundheads pleased to follow, they would turn and fight, not doubting they would defeat the psalm-singing saints, who had cast off their natural leaders.

Between Sibbertoft and Naseby the country rises and falls in a succession of rounded undulating hills. Both villages stand high; the lowest depression between the two is a piece of marshy land, now called Broad Moor. From Broad Moor the ground rises rapidly at first to the south; it is then broken by smaller hollows, and then continues to rise more gradually to the village of Naseby. This country, now covered with trees, hedges, cornfields, and meadows, on that morning of the 14th of June lay still in nature's keeping, for the most part an open pasture-ground, scattered over with furze-bushes. Patches of corn-land were discernible here and there, but the ground was mainly unenclosed, as in fact it remained till within the last half-century.

Fairfax, who early in the morning saw large bodies of horse moving on a hill a little south of Harborough, drew up his army on the brow of Mill Hill, which immediately slopes down into Broad Moor. Cromwell and the Ironsides occupied the ground on the right, flanked by Naseby rabbit-warren. Fairfax himself commanded the main body. The left wing, led by Ireton, was composed of horse, with some dragoons on foot, who were set to line the one hedge on the field which then, as now, marked the boundary line of the parishes of Naseby and Sulby. The baggage was left behind at Naseby, nearly two miles in the rear. The word for the day was passed along the ranks as "God is our strength."

About ten o'clock the Royalists were seen advancing over the Sibbertoft Hills in order of battle. The two armies were both between 10,000 and 11,000 strong, there not being "five hundred odds in number." The king's force consisted of about 5520 horse and 5300 foot. The Parliamentarians were stronger in infantry than in horse. Fairfax, wishing to conceal from the advancing enemy the exact form of his battle, ordered his soldiers to fall back a hundred paces in a hollow behind the brow of Mill Hill. Rupert, who, as usual, commanded the Royalist right wing, gathered from this movement that the enemy was in full retreat, and thought the day already his own.

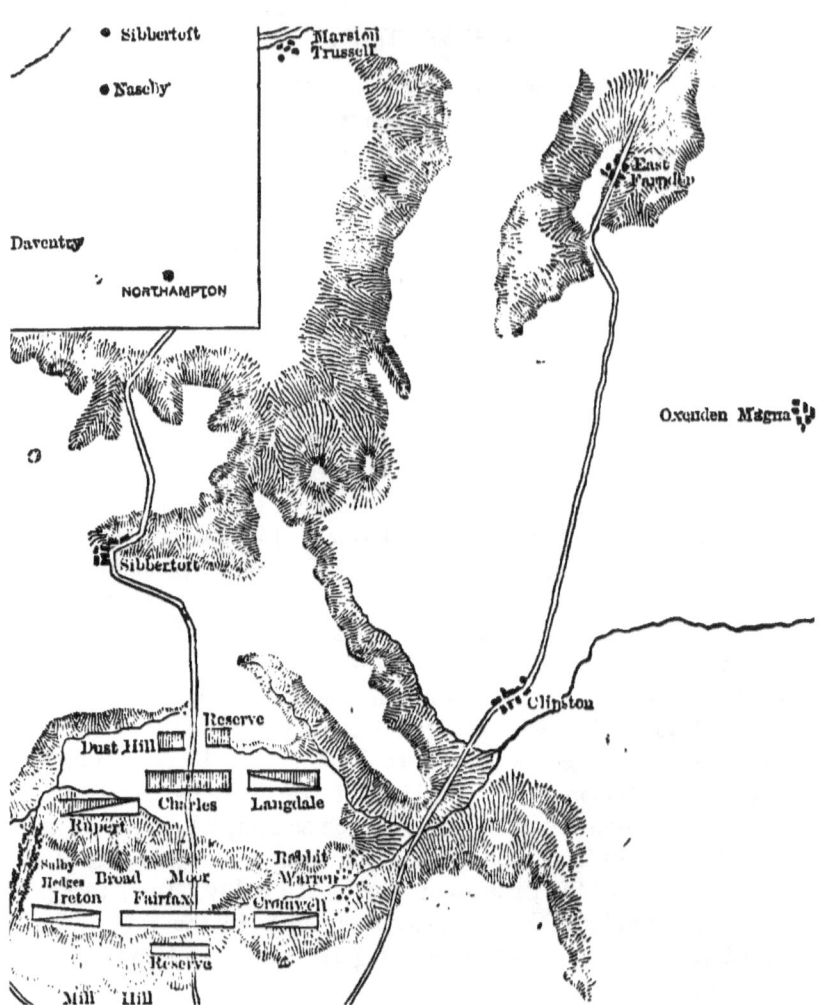

It was the work of a moment to send word back and bid Charles come on with all speed, and then he and his Cavaliers, shouting their word, "Queen Mary!" dashed down Dust Hill, over Broad Moor, and up Mill Hill. The dragoons who lined Sulby hedges on his right fired hotly on him as he passed, but he charged till he drove into Ireton's horse, sent them flying before him, and in headlong course galloped away hard up to Naseby hamlet. There he spied the baggage-train, and made for it; the commander, hardly thinking the Cavaliers could be there already, seeing, as he thought, his own general officer approaching, asked, hat in hand, "How goes the day?" "Will you have quarter?" was Rupert's curt rejoinder, for it was he. The commander declined, and Rupert, still nothing doubting his friends were as successful as himself, wasted much precious time in an attack on the baggage, which the guard successfully repelled. <small>Charge of Rupert.</small>

The other divisions of the king's army hurried on after the right wing, in slight disorder and too quickly to bring up all their artillery with them. Their left wing was ordered to charge up the hill against Cromwell, who commanded the Parliament's right wing. But before they had time to charge home, the Ironsides came on over rabbit-burrows and furze-bushes, swinging down upon Broad Moor with all the impetus of the hill, broke the Royalist horse, and sent them flying fast and far behind their foot. Leaving some horse to prevent their rallying again, Cromwell turned round with the remaining troops to assist his friends. The infantry in the Parliament's centre was in difficulties; on the first charge of the king's foot all, except Fairfax' own regiment, "gave back in disorder," but their officers snatched the colours, and, with the help of the reserve, soon rallied and brought them on again. Fairfax, with animation in voice and eye, looking even taller than his wont, rode about in the thick of the danger, cheering on his troops. His helmet was beaten off by a sword, and the colonel of his guards, seeing him riding bareheaded amid showering bullets, begged him to take his own in its place. "'Tis well enough," shortly replied the general. Skippon behaved as bravely; though dangerously shot in the side, he refused to leave the field—"As long as one man will stand, I will not stir." It was at this critical moment, when the Royalist left wing was broken, Rupert and the right wing nowhere to be seen, that Cromwell's horse rode up and charged the king's main <small>Ironsides break Royalist left.</small>

body in flank. This decided the day. The Royalist lines turned and fled. One regiment of Bluecoats, indeed, rivalled the gallantry of Newcastle's Whitecoats on Marston Moor in resisting the efforts of the enemy to break them. Leaving their greater number lying wounded or dead upon the ground, they too at last were scattered before the combined charge of Cromwell and Fairfax. The Royalist reserves of horse and foot now alone remained undisordered. Rupert, as usual, brought back some of his Cavaliers to the field in time to see the battle lost. His return awoke a gleam of hope in Charles' breast, who, placing himself at the head of his horse-guards, prepared for a last desperate charge upon the Ironsides. "Face about once!" he cried, "give one charge more, and recover the day!" But a Scotchman, the Earl of Carnwath, seized his bridle and turned his horse's head, swearing and saying, "Will you go upon your death?" Some one at the same moment cried out, "March to the right!" an order which caused the whole troop to turn their backs on the enemy, thinking they were intended to shift for themselves. In an instant all were in full flight, and had ridden a quarter of a mile before they could be rallied again. And then, indeed, the day was lost, for the Royalist foot were flying, hopelessly broken by the final charge of Cromwell and Fairfax. "They ran away," says a Parliamentarian, "both fronts and reserves, without standing one stroke more." Off went the beaten Cavaliers after the foot, leaving for the enemy their cannon, carriages, arms, jewels, clothes, and a cabinet of letters belonging to the king, "supposed to be of great consequence." The battle had lasted only three hours when the day was won. The chase was carried for twenty miles, through Harborough, to within sight of Leicester; 5000 prisoners were taken; 2000 Royalists said to be left dead on the ground.*

<small>King's letters taken.</small>

The victory was complete, but it was not the Royalists only who were depressed by it. The Presbyterians felt their sun had set to the Independents, and became more desirous than ever to conclude a peace with the king. This was the king's chance, but the cabinet of letters foiled it. The Independents agreed the Presbyterians should have their way if this prize proved the king was not the deceiver they had painted him. A trial of the

---

* Rushworth; Whitelock; Clar. Hist. v., 175; Sprigge, Anglia Rediviva; King's Tracts, 212; Markham, Life of Lord Fairfax; Carlyle, Letters and Speeches of Cromwell.

king's capacity for keeping treaties was then held before a crowd of citizens at Guildhall. The letters were read, and amongst other passages the following, addressed to the queen :—" I give thee power to promise in my name, to whom thou thinkest most fit, that I will take away all the Penal Laws against Roman Catholics in England, as soon as God shall make me able to do it ; so as by their means I have so powerful assistance as may deserve so great a favour, and enable me to do it" (5th March, 1645).— " I must again tell thee that most assuredly France will be the best way for transporting the Duke of Lorraine's army, there being divers fit and safe places of landing for them upon the western coasts" (Oxford, 30th March, 1645). These letters were then published by order of Parliament, who were bound to make known to the nation the dangers that menaced it. A cry of indignation rose on all sides against the king. Men said there could be no doubt of his bad faith. Though he had so often declared his intention of maintaining the Protestant religion, he was allowing his wife to make promises to the Catholics in his name ; and then, while his commissioners were negotiating peace at Uxbridge, he had been intriguing to bring over foreign soldiers into England. The questions of peace, war, and religion were all to be settled by the Catholic queen ; she was to have the disposal of the destinies of England, and the concessions at Uxbridge had been only a blind—no peace was ever intended. To offer the repeal of the law as a price for the aid of the English Papists was either a mockery, or a proof of the intention to rule without Parliaments.

The war now entered on its last stage. Charles' army was gone ; all that was left were small forces, scattered about in the west, or engaged in garrison duty. The Scots, who had been besieging the towns near the Border, now marched right down through the country and laid siege to Hereford, while Fairfax and Cromwell marched west, driving before them Goring and Grenville's beggarly troops, with their knavish leaders—as Clarendon himself described them—and forcing the garrison of one town to surrender after another. The king, meanwhile, with a body of 1000 horse, was in Wales and the western counties, flitting about from place to place in a purposeless way, and sometimes hardly knowing where to betake himself for safety. "Whatever you do," writes Colepepper, still with the

Last stage of war.

Prince of Wales, to Lord Digby, "take care of the king's person. I assure you these skipping jaunts make my heart ache."

Though the war had now reached its lowest ebb, the country suffered more than ever. The adherents of the Parliament, whose estates lay in districts hitherto Royalist, now came down upon their tenants for rents already paid to the king's friends. Excisemen, sent by the Parliament into the country, compelled the people to pay taxes for sheep, money, or provisions of which they had been robbed by the plundering Royalists. In some cases so much suffering ensued, that the very soldiers said "they would starve before they would be employed in forcing the tax, or take any of it for their pay." In the north the Scots lived at free quarters, and their conduct made the people look on them as freebooters rather than as friends. In the west the king's soldiers became mere marauders; men were captured with as much as £20 in their pockets; while their leaders cast innocent men into prison, merely to exact a ransom.

When Fairfax and Cromwell marched into the west, they found *Clubmen in west.* that in these counties the country-people had begun to assemble in bodies, sometimes 5000 strong, to resist their oppressors, whether they fought in the name of King or Parliament. They were called clubmen from their arms, and carried banners, with the motto—

> "If you offer to plunder our cattle,
> Be assured we will give you battle.'

The clubmen, however, could not hope to control the movements of the disciplined troops who now appeared against them. After a few fruitless attempts at resistance they dispersed, leaving the new army to do their work more effectually by completely suppressing the Royalists.

Charles himself, in the midst of his wanderings and reverses, was too proud to think of leaving England or deserting his throne, or even as yet of humbling himself to purchase peace from Presbyterians or Independents. But his friends began to despair. *Rupert surrenders Bristol.* Rupert himself wrote to counsel peace, and soon afterwards surrendered Bristol, the most important town in the west. The defences had been stormed and partially carried by Cromwell and Fairfax; and though Rupert was severely criticized by men who believed the town might still have held out, there seems no just ground for attributing the capture to any pusillanimity in the prince. Charles, however, who had understood from Rupert that, if no mutiny happened in the garrison, he would keep the place for four months, felt deeply wounded at this apparent desertion of his cause. He sent the prince an indignant letter, with a pass to take him beyond seas.

The surrender of Bristol was soon followed by a second blow. Montrose had come down from the Highlands for another summer's raid, in which he gained three victories over the Covenanters (Aulderne, 4th May; Alford, 2nd July; Kilsyth, 15th August); gentlemen of the Lowlands had been induced by his success to declare for the king; Edinburgh had opened its gates; and the army of the Covenanters in England had been obliged to raise the siege of Hereford, and march back northwards to meet this new enemy. Charles, on hearing of the surrender of Bristol, started to join Montrose, now, as he believed, about to fulfil his promises, and enter England at the head of a Royalist army. But at Chester his own troops were defeated and dispersed by Poyntz, a commander of the Parliament, and, after he had escaped himself to Wales, he heard the disastrous news that the army he sought to join no longer existed. Montrose, surprised by Leslie at Philiphaugh, on the border, not far north of Carlisle, had been entirely routed, and had again become a fugitive in the Highlands. *Montrose defeated at Philiphaugh (13th Sept., 1645).* The king with difficulty now made his way first to Newark, and afterwards to Oxford, where he was thankful to find himself once again in safety for a time (6th Nov.). But it was evident that Oxford would not be safe for long. Fairfax was completing his victorious career in the west; that over, the siege of Oxford would follow at once, and then it would not be long before the king was a prisoner of war. Overtures of peace were the only hope, and Charles sent one message upon the heels of another, offering to come to London and treat in person with the Parliament (Dec. and Jan., 1645-6). But his messages met with no friendly reception at Westminster. The Presbyterians, no doubt, would before have been glad to treat, preferring even the Royalists to the Independents; but they had now lost alike the power and the will to treat. Two causes had weakened their power. During the autumn months 130 new members were elected to fill the vacancies five years had caused by death, desertion, or expulsion. Though Presbyterians were returned in larger numbers, *Presbyterian decline. —Causes: I. New elections.*

yet through want of experience, or want of ability, they did not carry half so much weight with them as the new Independent members, many of whom had already won distinction in politics or in war. Such were Hutchinson, Ludlow, Blake the admiral of the future, Fleetwood, Ireton who soon afterwards became Cromwell's son-in-law,* and Algernon Sidney son of the Earl of Leicester. The officers who got their seats by these new elections did not come under the provisions of the self-denying ordinance, so that, while the Presbyterians had lost their commissions, the newer party won their seats and kept their commissions as well.

The second cause that weakened the influence of the Presbyterians was the oppressive conduct of their friends the Scots while quartered in the northern counties. But, supposing the Presbyterian party had had the power to make peace of themselves, at this time they had no longer the will. This was in consequence of a new disclosure. A year before this Charles had authorized Ormond to make promises to the Irish Catholics in his name.† The Catholics, however, were wary, and refused to hear of a peace, or of rendering the king any assistance, without first obtaining his consent to the establishment of their own religion in Ireland. If Charles granted these conditions, he knew the affection of his own party in England would be cooled, while the hate of the Puritans would be increased ten-thousand-fold against him. The problem that had been occupying his mind for the last twelve months was how to obtain aid from the Irish, and yet keep concealed from the English the terms on which it was granted, until victory should enable him to set public opinion at defiance. He had solved it by entrusting to Lord Herbert, Earl of Glamorgan, the most loyal of Catholics, a secret warrant, signed by his own hand, and sealed with his private seal, giving him power to make terms with the Council of Kilkenny, without the privity of the Earl of Ormond. Accordingly Glamorgan concluded a secret treaty, in which it was agreed that, all penal laws being repealed, the Roman Catholics were to be allowed the public exercise of their religion, and to hold the revenues of all churches of which they had gained possession since the war first broke out. As they held far more than half the churches, this amounted to the establishment of their religion. They, on their side, were to send 20,000 men to assist his Majesty in England (12th Aug., 1645). After the defeat

* Married Bridget Cromwell, 15th June, 1646. † See p. 176.

at Naseby, Charles also wrote to the pope, engaging his royal word to fulfil whatever conditions should be agreed upon by Glamorgan. But this treaty came to light, like Charles' other secret plots. In a skirmish fought in Ireland, duplicates of the whole transaction were taken in the carriage of a Catholic archbishop, and sent to London to the committee of the two nations (Oct., 1645). After having reserved this secret for three months, the Independents caused the papers to be read in Parliament and published, at the very time when Charles was sending one message after another for a treaty of peace (Jan.). The country was in a ferment of indignation. The establishment of the Roman Catholic religion in a Catholic country seems an innocent proposition, if not a just concession. To understand the ferment it raised, it is necessary to recall the circumstances of the time. The Thirty Years' War was still in progress. The fire of the Reformation was still burning in men's hearts. They had come out of a great struggle, in which Europe had been split into two camps. Protestant nations had preserved their religious independence only by resisting the armed assaults of Catholicism. The gain was worth the struggle, but there is no struggle without some bitterness remaining, and the Catholics were the victims of this bitterness. The hate felt by Protestants towards Catholics was, in fact, one of the characteristics of the age. The Protestants regarded the Catholic religion as at once idolatrous and subversive of all good government. The gorgeous and imposing ceremonies, standing in such striking contrast to the simplicity of Puritan worship; the blind obedience to the pope; the doctrine that the end justifies the means, illustrated as this had been by the massacre of St. Bartholomew, the Gunpowder Plot, and the late butchery in Ireland—all this had raised up in the nation's mind such a wall of prejudice that the Catholics, regarded as a class, were shut out of all sympathy whatsoever. For a people with these feelings to see, as it seemed, the fruits of the victory over Spain bartered away by the king in return for the loan of savage and Popish troops, to be used against the liberty of Protestant subjects, was more than could be borne. The Royalist Hyde, in the history he wrote of the rebellion, omitted all mention of this business with Glamorgan, which he could not palliate. In his private correspondence he calls it "inexcusable to justice, piety, and prudence."

While Charles' friends were disgusted with the treaty, his enemies looked upon it as another proof of the unfathomable deceitfulness of his nature: for, "while he was protesting before God to the Parliament, saying, 'I will never abrogate the laws against the Papists,' he was underhand dealing with the Irish rebels, and promising to repeal the laws against them; and while he said, 'I abhor to think of bringing foreign soldiers into the kingdom,' he was soliciting the Duke of Lorraine, the French, the Danes, the very Irish, for assistance." The newspapers had their scathing criticisms. "We are experienced," wrote a weekly Intelligencer, "that kings often deal like watermen: look one way and row another. What else mean those overtures of a treaty with us, when those bloodthirsty rebels are proffered the enjoyment of Popery! Now judge whether the king hath any real intention of peace, when he labours to bring over 10,000 of the Irish rebels to cut our throats here, as they have done to divers of our brethren there!" Meantime, to save the king's character, the Earl of Ormond put Glamorgan at once into prison, as though he had acted without authority. Charles again offered to come to London for a personal treaty, declaring to the Parliament that, until Glamorgan's arrest, he had never heard of the negotiations (January 29th). His words, however, found no credit at Westminster, and his warrant to Glamorgan still remains to give the lie to his statement. Glamorgan, who had been devoted enough not to reveal his secret instructions, was released after a month's imprisonment (February 1st), and continued the negotiation. The landing of a body of Irish troops was, it seems, only prevented by the war coming to an end before they were ready to sail.

<small>Indignation felt in the country.</small>

Whether or no such a treaty would have been politic at any time in the war, it was certainly impolitic now. The one chance now was to divide the two parties; the arrival of Irish soldiers on such terms would have thrown Presbyterians and Independents into one another's arms as brothers, while the troops themselves would have been taken at sea, or crushed on landing, where there would have been no force to join them.

By the end of March, the royal forces, scattered over the west, were all defeated and dispersed, or forced to take refuge in garrison towns. Hyde and the Prince of Wales were driven down to the very extremity of Cornwall, and had to sail from the coast (March 1st). Sir Jacob Astley, an old gray-headed Cavalier, was the last to resist in the open field. "Now, gentlemen," he said, to the officers of the Parliament, on surrendering, " you have done your work, and may go play, unless you choose to fall out amongst yourselves " (March 22nd).

It was on the belief that his enemies would still fall out among themselves, that Charles now grounded his hopes of restoration to his throne. At the same time that he was courting the Presbyterians, and proposing to come to London and treat with them in person, he was making secret offers to the Independents to root out the Presbyterians, offering them freedom of conscience, if they would ensure the same to the Royalists. " I am not without hope," he wrote about this time, " that I shall be able to draw either the Presbyterians or Independents to side with me for extirpating the other—that I shall be really king again."* But the distrust he had engendered was too deep : his advances were not met, and he soon found that, unless he made haste to get out of Oxford before it was invested, he should fall into his enemies' hands, without having bound them to any conditions at all.

After much consultation, it was agreed that his best plan would be to seek a refuge in the Scottish army. M. de Montreuil, the French ambassador, had been authorized by Cardinal Mazarin, the chief minister of Louis XIV., to negotiate an agreement between Charles and the Scots, and engage the faith of France for the performance of whatever promises either side should make. Though Charles refused to agree to take the covenant, Montreuil at first obtained some civil speeches from the Scots' commissioners in London, to the effect that if the king came to them, they would receive him as their natural king, offer no violence to his person or conscience, and endeavour to procure a happy and well-grounded peace. But the London commissioners soon drew back, thinking they had gone too far ; while the commissioners at the Scottish camp refused to make any such agreement, only promising to receive the king, and demanding that he should give them satisfaction in the question of religion, by which they meant, take the covenant, as soon as possible. Upon this poor security, Charles, accompanied by two companions, left Charles with Oxford in the guise of a servant (27th April), and after Scots. nine days' wanderings, arrived in safety at Kelham, near Newark, the head-quarters of the Scots. Montreuil brought him some

13

verbal promise of safety and introduced him into the camp (5th May). The chief officers affected extreme surprise at his appearance, but at the same time great gratitude for the trust he had placed in them. "I shall be well satisfied," replied the king, "if you perform the conditions upon which I have come to you." But they corrected him when he used the word "conditions," saying, 'they had never been privy to anything of that nature; and if the king had made any treaty, it must be with the Scottish commissioners in London, which was no concern of theirs.' Charles' spirits fell, and he already wished himself out of their power.

When the news reached London, the Independents were furious. They thought the king would never have taken the step without having made up his mind to consent to the covenant, establish the Presbyterian Church, and in return be allowed to rule subject to Presbyterian guidance; while they, the true conquerors, would be persecuted by Presbyterians and Royalists, their noble army be disbanded, their noble cause—freedom of conscience—be stifled at its birth. To stave off such an end as this, they might, no doubt, have used their army, and appealed to force. But the Independents still aimed at a victory within the lines of the constitution. Parliament, and not the army, was the supreme authority; it was in the sacred name of Parliament that they had won their victories, and they still wished to lead the Parliament, and not to fight it. Although, therefore, inclined in the first flush of anger to have followed the Scots and taken possession of the king's person by force, they contented themselves with doing all in their power to produce a rupture between the two nations, in order that the Commons might vote war, and they, in obedience to the supreme authority of the nation, might lead the Ironsides to fight the hated allies. In the newspapers, in pamphlets, in Parliament, at all times, in all places, the Independents attacked the Scots as traitors, the cruel oppressors of the northern counties, who designed to betray and ruin England. The national hatred was readily excited, and, after many debates, the Commons voted that the Scotch army was no longer required, that it should be asked what was owing to it, and be requested to withdraw (11th June).

But the Scots, who had already retreated in fear as far as Newcastle, were willing to bear any amount of reproach rather than draw down upon themselves the Independent army. On their side, the English Presbyterians, still the majority in the Commons, were far more anxious to disband the dangerous sectarian army, than to batten it on the blood of their own northern allies. The Independents could not bring about a war, when so many were determined not to quarrel. Charles outwardly did what he could to effect an agreement. He sent messages to the two Houses, urging them to draw up peace propositions; ordered the commanders of all towns and castles still held for him to surrender (10th June); bade Montrose, who was then a wanderer in the Highlands, to lay down his arms; and made a parade of sending orders to Ormond to make no peace with the Irish rebels—orders which Ormond had secret instructions to disobey (11th June).

Charles' outward submission aided the efforts of the Presbyterians, and he finally received peace propositions from Newcastle Parliament (23rd July). By these, he was required propositions. to take the covenant, to establish the Presbyterian Church, to surrender to Parliament, for twenty years, the command of the army, navy, and militia; to consent that seventy-seven of his friends should be excluded from amnesty, and that all his party should be shut out from public employment during the pleasure of Parliament. Anxiously was Charles' answer looked for on both sides. If he consented, the Independents would either be obliged to submit to Presbyterian tyranny, or begin a second civil war against Scots, English Presbyterians, and Royalists united. If he refused, the Presbyterians were checkmated; they could make no concession on the Church question; on the militia question they could not get easier terms for him against the opposition of the Independents, and dared not offer easier terms if they got them, because they had no confidence in his word. The possible prospect of his refusal revealed darkly looming before them a thousand difficulties in retaining their own supremacy over the sectarians. "The great God," was their prayer, "soften that man's heart, or else he will fall in tragic miseries, and bring ruin upon himself and us together."

The king endured a bitter trial for the next six months. He would have made some concessions about the militia, had not his wife forbidden him; but he could not bring himself to establish a new Presbyterian Church in England. Some trace his reluctance on this point to a belief that the support of the Church was even more essential to monarchical power than the command of the militia ; but this view seems to do injustice both to his sense and his sincerity. He had too much ability to believe the pen of the bishop could guard his throne as well as the sword of the army. The 'command of the militia' had been the stake of the war, and there was now not a militia, but an army, to command. Secondly, a careful study of his letters induces the belief that his religious convictions were deeper and stronger than his political views. His political views may have been taught to him by his father and his ministers ; his religious views were taught by his father, his ministers, and his heart. Yet it was on this very point that his friends, both at home and abroad, most urgently pressed him to yield. They thought that if this concession by itself did not win over the Parliament, it would certainly win over the Scots. To keep the militia, to yield the Church, was the command, rather than the advice, of his wife. "By granting the militia," she wrote, "you cut your own throat, for then there is nothing you can refuse, no not my life even, if they ask it ; but I will take care not to fall into their hands."* Her letters were always written in the same heartless tone. She was far less tender of her husband's happiness, conscience, or life, than she was of his power. If he regained his old authority, she was ready to return and share it with him ; if he lost it, she would sooner he stayed a prisoner in England than trouble her with the presence of a crownless fugitive. Charles, however, wrote doleful letters, pointing out that if he did not quit the kingdom now, he might lose his last chance of escape. These she only answered by forbidding him to think of escape, until the Scots should have declared in plain language they would not protect him. Poor Charles ! there were two acts for which he felt real regret, and to both of which he had been urged by his queen ; the first was, in his own words, " that base, unworthy concession about Strafford ;" the second, " that great wrong and injustice to the Church, of taking away bishops' votes in Parliament." Though he sacrificed his personal safety to her wishes, he refused to load his conscience a third time for her

* " Vous vous êtes coupé la gorge ; car vous ne leur pouvez rien refuser, pas même ma vie, s'ils vous la demandent. Mais je ne me mettrai pas entre leurs mains."

satisfaction. He did, indeed, endeavour to meet her wishes by a compromise. He proposed to her that he should let the Presbyterian Church remain as the established Church of England for three years, on condition that the question should then be referred to Parliament for an ultimate decision after previous discussion by an Assembly of Divines. This compromise was approved by Juxon, to whom Charles submitted it as at once the keeper of his conscience and the maintainer of the Church. But the queen treated the compromise with scorn ; she taunted him with the folly of having a conscience which would give up a point for three years, when nothing was to be got by it, and yet scrupled to give up the point for life to save his kingdom. " Permettez moi de vous dire, que je crois, si je me pouvais dispenser d'une chose que je croyais contre ma conscience pour trois ans et pour rien, j'irais plus loin pour sauver mon royaume. Mais pour toutes autres choses n'accordez plus rien." Thus brow-beaten out of all concession on the militia question, and heartlessly ridiculed out of his attempt to meet his wife's wishes on the Church question, Charles in despair returned to his original intention, and sent messages to Parliament, making no concessions, but only proposing to come to London and treat in person (Aug., Dec.).

Though the Presbyterians were disappointed with his answer, which was tantamount to a refusal, they still believed that, once in their hands, they could wring the concessions from him, and then disband the Independent army. After some haggling, the Scots secured a written promise for £400,000, as the charge to which they had been put by the war. A treaty was signed accordingly (Dec.). Though no mention was made of the king, it was fully understood that the Scots were to deliver him up, when their army evacuated Newcastle. As Charles had come to his enemies' camp, uninvited, after refusing the covenant, the only terms on which they offered to protect him, they were not bound to let him go, still less to fight for him ; though they would have done even that, if he would now have agreed to their offer. It was understood that if he was given up, the English Presbyterians would restore him to the throne, on their own terms, and disband the 'evil army'* of the Independents. It would have been perfectly justifiable in the Scots to give him up

<small>Scots surrender king.</small>

* Baillie.

on these terms. Not content with this they made a canny bargain. No doubt, had they given him up without a money treaty, they would never have been paid their arrears, and this was much to poor men. As it was, they got their money, but more than their money's worth of abuse. They earned the abuse by making the terms of surrender mercenary, and not political. The distinction may seem fine, and the judgment hard. But there are cases where a high sense of honour can alone save men from deep dishonour. They were now called 'the traitor Scots,' 'the Jews who sold their king,' and as they marched out of Newcastle, which was always Royalist in feeling, the very women were all but stoning them (30th Jan.). Meantime, the Presbyterian commissioners escorted the king from Newcastle to the residence assigned him at Holmby House in Northamptonshire. On the road crowds flocked to see him. The country people everywhere hoped that their troubles were over, that an agreement would be made on which the army would be disbanded, and the king return to London with honour and safety.* Near Nottingham Charles met Sir Thomas Fairfax, who dismounted to kiss his hand, and afterwards rode through the town by his side. At Holmby he received a hearty welcome from a large concourse of gentlemen, ladies, and yeomen (Feb. 13th). Well content with his reception, his spirits rose, and he made no doubt he should yet get either Presbyterians or Independents to unite with him, "to extirpate the other and make him really a king again !"

* Ludlow, i. 162.

CHAPTER IX.

PRESBYTERIANS, INDEPENDENTS, ERASTIANS, AND THEIR THEORIES.

> O wad some pow'r the giftie gie us
> To see oursel's as others see us!
> It wad frae monie a blunder free us
>   An' foolish notion;
> What airs in dress an' gait wad lea'e us,
>   An' e'en devotion.—BURNS.

FOR the last three years the Assembly of Divines had been sitting almost daily in the Jerusalem Chamber of Westminster Abbey. The assembly consisted of a hundred and twenty ministers, all Presbyterians but ten or twelve Inde- Presbytependents; twenty members of the Commons and ten rians. peers; besides four ministers and three laymen from Scotland. They were preparing a new Prayer-book, a form of Church Government, a Confession of Faith, and a Catechism; but the real questions at issue were the establishment of the Presbyterian Church and the toleration of sectarians.

The Presbyterians, as we know, desired to establish their own form of Church government by assemblies and synods, without any toleration for nonconformists, whether Catholics, Episcopalians, or sectarians. But though they formed a large majority in the assembly, there was a well-organized opposition of Independents and Erastians, whose union made it no easy matter for the Presbyterians to carry every vote their own way.

The Independents agreed with the Presbyterians in freeing the Church from the control of the State, but the essential requirements of their theory of Church government were—1st, the independence of each separate congregation, including the Church election of its own ministers; 2nd, that penalties for Government spiritual offences should be spiritual and not temporal; dents. inflicted, not by the civil magistrate, nor by assemblies, but by the congregation. Their theory on this second point was expressed by Milton in a pamphlet in which he wrote, "It is not to be expected all in a church to be gold and silver and precious stones; it is not possible for man to sever the wheat from the tares, the good fish from the other fry; that must be the angels' ministry, at the end of mortal things. Yet, if all cannot be of one mind, as who looks they should be? this, doubtless, is more wholesome, more prudent, and more Christian, that many be tolerated rather than all compelled." This noble theory of toleration naturally, but illogically, they confined to all sects who taught the fundamental doctrines of Christianity.

The name of the Erastian party was derived from a German of the sixteenth century, called Erastus. These were at the opposite pole to their allies. The Independents made each congregation independent of both Church and State; the Presbyterians made the congregation dependent on an independent Church; while the Erastians made the Church itself dependent on the State. Their wish being to reduce the power of the Church, they were as strongly opposed as the Independents to the strong Church government of the Presbyterians, and were quite willing to agree with them in making the congregation independent of any such central authority as the Scotch assembly. They also agreed with the Independents in their objection to civil penalties for spiritual offences. In fact they went further, and objected to spiritual offences being punished by the spiritual weapon of excommunication. Their party mainly consisted of lay members from the Parliament, who had the intuitive dislike of lawyers to courts administered by ecclesiastics. Episcopacy many of them would have been willing to restore, if shorn of the moral and social jurisdiction it enforced under civil penalties. The English Church, as administered at the present day, would have nearly come up to their ideal.

The Presbyterian Church could be seen in full work in Scotland. There toleration was unknown. Those who conformed held their goods and chattels at the mercy of ministers and elders sitting in kirk session; while those who did not conform were imprisoned till they did; neighbours and servants acted as informers, and the edifice was crowned by a great Church Assembly, in power more than a match for the Scotch Parliament. Bad as it is to have Church and State acting in antagonism to one another, in Scotland the establishment of the Presbyterian system kept political liberty alive among the people. The Scotch Parliament was corrupt, and did not represent the country. The Church assemblies, on the contrary, were really popular in constitution; conscious that their power was based on the affections of the people, the ministers and elders who sat in them dared to uphold the cause of liberty, when their Parliament was suffering itself to be made a tool in the hands of the executive. Thus, however contentious they showed themselves, however unreasonable the claims they put forward, the assemblies none the less played the same part as the English House of Commons in preventing the establishment of an arbitrary monarchy. Further, the excessive influence which the Presbyterian Church exercised in Scotland was itself due to the fact that a very large proportion of the nation was Presbyterian, so that even where tyranny was exercised the sufferers as a rule themselves approved of the discipline. In England neither of these conditions existed; the Parliament was far better fitted than an assembly of churchmen to defend the nation's liberties, while the Presbyterians themselves were in a minority. It was impossible, however, that in the warmth of their zeal the Presbyterian party should be brought to recognize the force of the different conditions prevailing in the two countries. In fact, the arguments used in the assembly did not regard these points. The question was debated from the theological point of view, whether the Presbyterian Church had been originally established by the will of God. When the Presbyterians were opposed by Erastians and Independents, the ignorance which accompanied their dogmatism was often exposed. When they quoted a telling text, Selden, the Erastian lawyer, would say, "Perhaps in your little pocket Bibles with gilt leaves" (which they would often pull out and read) "the translation may be thus or thus, but in the Greek or Hebrew it signifies the other." His opponents had to bow to his superior knowledge. Thus the Opposition went on for months, battling every point; and "besides all this," says a Presbyterian, plaintively, "we have to answer the pamphlets of our many opponents, often very plausibly written, demanding liberty for all religions." The Commons, moreover, in summoning the divines, meant to hear their advice, not to abide by their votes. As soon as a debate ended in the assembly it began again in the House. There the Presbyterians found it more difficult to command a majority, for the ranks of their opponents were swelled by a new contingent, the "worldly profane men," who, though impartial as Gallio as to creeds, evinced a desperate antagonism to any 'kirk-sessional' discipline.

At last, however, after the assembly had sat a year and a half, the Parliament passed an ordinance for putting a directory, prepared by the divines, into force, and taking away the Common Prayer-book (3rd Jan., 1645). The sign of the cross in baptism, the ring in marriage, the wearing of vestments, the keeping of saints' days, were discontinued. The communion table was ordered to be set in the body of the church, about which the people were to stand or sit; the passages of Scripture to be read were left to the minister's choice; no forms of prayer were prescribed. The same year a new directory for ordination of ministers was passed into an ordinance. The Presbyterian assemblies, called presbyteries, were empowered to ordain, and none were allowed to enter the ministry without first taking the covenant (8th Nov., 1645). This was followed by a third ordinance for establishing the Presbyterian system of Church government in England by way of trial for three years. As originally introduced into the House, this ordinance met with great opposition, because it gave power to ministers of refusing the sacrament and turning men out of the Church for scandalous offences. Now, in what, argued the Erastians, did scandalous offences consist? Were 10,000 little courts of justice to be set up over the kingdom, searching into men's lives, and punishing any fault they pleased to call a scandalous offence? A modified ordinance accordingly was passed; scandalous offences, for which ministers might refuse the sacrament and excommunicate, were specified; assemblies were declared subject to Parliament, and leave was granted to those who thought themselves unjustly sentenced, to appeal right up from one Church assembly after another to the civil power—the Parliament (16th March, 1646).

Presbyterians, both in England and Scotland, felt deeply mortified. After all these years' contending, then, just when they thought they were entering on the fruits of their labours, to see the Church still left under the power of the State—the disappointment was intense to a degree we cannot estimate. They looked on the Independents as the enemies of God; this 'lame Erastian Presbytery' as hardly worth the having.

Through Presbyterian influence, a severe ordinance passed the Parliament for the suppression of blasphemies and heresies (2nd May, 1648). Those who denied the doctrines of the Trinity, the Atonement, or the inspiration of the Scriptures, were to be punished with death as felons. Anabaptists and those who denied the lawfulness of the Presbyterian government to be imprisoned until they should recant. But, happily, these terrible persecutors failed in power. It seemed, indeed, as if all their force was spent in the process of getting their ordinances through Parliament. Thus, to the very last, their Church government was only set up in London and Lancashire, while their ordinance to suppress heresies entirely failed in its object. To get the ordinance passed the assembly had sent petition after petition to the Commons, showing the daily growth of heresies and schisms; the city of London had complained that private meetings multiplied, that eleven were held in one parish alone, that women and ignorant persons preached.* But, after all, the passing of the ordinance did not abate the evil. The Presbyterian party in Parliament dared not attempt strong measures for the suppression of sectarians, while the fatal Independent army remained undisbanded, while the king obstinately rejected the terms offered him, and the Royalists stood by mocking and exulting over the feuds and heart-burnings of their opponents. Milton with bold bitterness appealed to Parliament against these new forcers of conscience :

marginal note: Ordinance for the suppression of blasphemies and heresies.

> "Men whose life, learning, faith, and pure intent,
> Would have been held in high esteem with Paul,
> Must now be named and printed Heretics,
> By shallow Edwards and Scotch what-d'ye-call;
> But we do hope to find out all your tricks,
> Your plots and packing, worse than those of Trent,
>   That so the Parliament
> May with their wholesome and preventive shears
> Clip your phylacteries, though balk your ears,†
>   And succour our just fears,
> When they shall read this clearly in your charge
> New Presbyter is but Old Priest writ large."

Colonel Hutchinson, governor of Nottingham Castle, and Cromwell's friend, was not a man who could be imprisoned because he refused to have his child baptized, nor yet one likely to fail in protecting poorer brethren of his own persuasion. Persecution to any extent was only possible against Catholics and

* Weekly Account, Jan., 1646.   † *I.e.*, leave untouched.

Episcopalians, who were regarded as Royalists by Independents and Presbyterians alike. An ordinance was passed, forbidding the Prayer-book to be publicly or privately read, on payment of a fine of £5 for the first offence, £10 for the second, a year's imprisonment for the third. Catholic priests taken in the country were remorselessly imprisoned, banished, or executed. Meanwhile new sects sprung up on all sides, and obtained safe shelter under the shadow of the army and its leaders. Any man, however ignorant and untaught, might obtain his little band of followers, for the people's minds were restless and willing to give ear to every new doctrine. A book written at this time asserted that there were 176 heresies which found believers in the nation. Amongst many other sects, appeared the Brownists, who would have had the laws of England modelled upon those of the Old Testament, and even blasphemers and Sabbath-breakers punished by the magistrates with death; the Anabaptists, who rejected the baptism of infants, and went about rebaptizing their converts in the rivers by a hundred at a time: the Quakers, who lived lives of extreme austerity, refusing to take oaths, declaring all war sinful, and teaching that the light within man is his sufficient rule of conduct:* and lastly the Fifth Monarchists, who held that the world's history was comprised under four monarchies,—the Assyrian, the Persian, the Greek, and the Roman; that the Roman was soon, like its predecessors, to pass away, and the Fifth Monarchy—the reign of Christ upon earth—to begin. In every country town and village, an Anabaptist, or some other sectarian, would appear, and it was well for the Presbyterian minister, if, by holding a public disputation in his church,† he could convince his parishioners of the stranger's error, and drive schism from their doors.‡

Leading sects.

The mental excitement, the questioning, revolving, doubting, was not confined to one side or to one question. Not only did sectarians increase in numbers, but also men of new political ideas, demanding reforms in the law, the Church, the constitution of the State; some called for a reform of the law, observing

* Baxter's Life; Neal; Baillie.   † Baxter's Life, 30, 76.
‡ The Assembly of Divines practically came to an end in 1649, when it was changed into a committee for examining candidates for the Presbyterian ministry. It finally broke up without any formal dismissal on the dispersion of the Rump Parliament in March, 1653.

that lawyers pocketed enormous fees, and that suitors were often kept waiting years before they could get a cause decided in Westminster Hall; others, with feeling for poor debtors, shut up for life within a prison's walls, demanded the abolition of imprisonment for debt; Republicans, disgusted with Charles' perfidy, openly avowed their opinion, that a republic, in which a House of Commons, or some other representative assembly, exercised supreme authority by itself, was a far superior form of government to a monarchy, and the only one under which liberty could be secured; whilst boldest of all, sectarian soldiers, who had read in the Old Testament that blood defiles a land, and that a land cannot be cleansed of the blood that is shed therein, but by the blood of him that shed it, talked of the duty of bringing the king to justice, as guilty of the blood of the thousands who had lost their lives in the war. Amid the general confusion, the Presbyterians made their voices heard plainly enough. Though they could not produce a Milton to write, or a Cromwell to act, they at least endeavoured to make up for quality by quantity, and gave to the world thousands of pamphlets extolling their own form of Church government. Yet all their efforts to keep down their opponents were unavailing. Sectarians, Republicans, law reformers, though they did not necessarily share one another's special views, all agreed in opposing the Presbyterians, whose ideas of reform were rapidly narrowing to the establishment of their own Church in place of the Episcopal. The Presbyterians gazed in dismay upon the increasing numbers of their enemies, the birth of the war they had themselves begun. Nor was their fear groundless; for, either on the side of Independents or of Royalists, the greater part of the intellect of England was engaged against them.

Ever since Pym's death, the young Sir Henry Vane had stood at the head of civil leaders. This English stoic at the age of twenty sacrificed his brilliant prospects at court and emigrated to America for conscience' sake. Chosen governor of the little colony of Massachusetts at twenty-three, after exciting enthusiastic admiration for a time, he soon displeased the colonists by his advocacy of toleration. He thus returned to England in time to take an active part in the discussions preceding the meeting of the Long Parliament, of which he was elected a member. Though he was hated by the Presbyterians, Sir Henry Vane.

the troublous war times necessarily brought to the helm of the State the men, whatever their opinions, whose judgment and skill were greatest in directing immediate operations. Vane's sagacity in practical matters even his enemies did not dispute. Clarendon describes him as a man of extraordinary parts, with a wonderful insight into character, and in fact as "all in any business where others were joined with him." It had chiefly been through his exertions that the Parliament secured the aid of the Scots in 1643, at the critical juncture when the triumph of the king's arms made many regard the cause of the Parliament as lost. Milton recognized his greatness, and thus at a later date described his administration in the perilous times of the Dutch war:

> "Vane, young in years, but in sage counsel old,
> Than whom a better senator ne'er held
> The helm of Rome, when gowns not arms repelled
> The fierce Epirot and the African bold,
> Whether to settle peace, or to unfold
> The drift of hollow States, hard to be spelled,
> Then to advise how war may, best upheld,
> Move by her two main nerves, iron and gold,
> In all her equipage; besides to know
> Both spiritual power and civil, what each means,
> What severs each, thou hast learn'd, which few have done:
> The bounds of either sword to thee we owe:
> Therefore, on thy firm hand Religion leans
> In peace, and reckons thee her eldest son."

His abstract theories of government, however, for Church and State, were generally ill understood, and laid him open to much misrepresentation. Though called an Independent, he in fact belonged to no particular sect, being, as some said, 'above ordinances;' for he held that there was no true church established by Divine Right—neither Episcopalian, Presbyterian, nor Independent; but that they, whatever their creed, who acted in the spirit of Christ, best deserved to be called members of the true Church of Christ. Thus he lost caste with each sect by his enthusiastic advocacy of toleration of all; he braved the denunciations of Baxter in supporting Catholics, and stood by the Unitarian on trial; and, while himself spending much of most days in prayer, he claimed to be at one with Paul in accounting the Sabbath as now a mere "magisterial institution." With an infinite belief in the perfectibility of human nature he aimed at attaining this object, not through weakening the will by repression, but through strengthening it by freedom. In the government of the State, as in that of the Church, he desired that, as far as possible, men should be left free to think and act for themselves. While at one with his age in earnestness, his ideas were tinged with mysticism, and his theories were too far in advance of his age to be understood. By his friends he was regarded as an impracticable enthusiast; by the Presbyterians as a dreamer of dreams, a man of obscure doctrines; by the Royalists as a fanatic who was expecting the saints to govern the earth, and himself to reign as their king.

Milton's name had already emerged among the Independents. In 1644 he published a tract, maintaining that non-suitability of temper between man and wife is a sufficient ground for divorce; a doctrine so objectionable to the Presbyterians, that they caused the author to be called to account before the House of Lords. But Milton's pen was soon engaged in a nobler cause, the freedom of the press (1644). Since the Reformation, the crown had assumed the power before exercised by the Church, of maintaining a censorship over the publication of books; and authors, printers, and importers of prohibited works had been prosecuted in the Star Chamber, and often barbarously punished. The Presbyterians, copying the example of the tyranny they had overthrown, framed an ordinance, forbidding the publication of books, that had not been first perused and licensed by officers appointed by Parliament (June, 1643). The ordinance was evaded by all parties, but Milton wrote to show the falseness of the principles on which it rested. He addressed his tract to the Lords and Commons, and told them that their ordinance could do no good, because evil manners are learnt in a thousand other ways than by books; that if it answered its purpose it must do harm, because it would stop the search for truth and expel as much of virtue as of sin. "Truth, indeed," he wrote, "came once into the world with her Divine Master, and was a perfect shape, most glorious to look on; but when He ascended, and His apostles after Him were laid asleep, there straight arose a wicked race of deceivers, who, as that story goes of the Egyptian Typhon, with his conspirators took the virgin Truth, hewed her lovely form into a thousand pieces, and scattered them to the four

John Milton Areopagitica or liberty of unlicensed printing (1644).

winds. From that time ever since, the sad friends of truth, such as durst appear, imitating the careful search that Isis made for the mangled body of Osiris, went up and down gathering up limb by limb still as they could find them. We have not yet found them all, Lords and Commons, nor ever shall do, till her Master's second coming; He shall bring together every joint and member, and shall mould them into an immortal feature of loveliness and perfection. Suffer not these licensing prohibitions to stand at every place of opportunity forbidding and disturbing them that continue seeking, that continue to do our obsequies to the torn body of our martyred saint." "Opinion in good men," he said, "is but knowledge in the making." That the greater part of the people should be taken up with the study of the highest and most important matters; that there should be a disputing, reasoning, reading, inventing, discoursing, he told them, betokened, not that the nation was degenerated or "drooping to a fatal decay, but casting off the old and wrinkled skin of corruption, to outlive these pangs and wax young again, entering the glorious ways of truth and prosperous virtue, destined to become great and honourable in these later ages. Methinks I see in my mind," he continued, "a noble and puissant nation rousing herself like a strong man after sleep, and shaking her invincible locks; methinks I see her as an eagle, muing* her mighty youth, and kindling her undazzled eyes at the full midday beam; purging and unscaling her long-abused sight at the fountain itself of heavenly radiance; while the whole noise of timorous and flocking birds, with those also that love the twilight, flutter about, amazed at what she means, and in their envious gabble would prognosticate a year of sects and schisms."† The Parliament, however, far from being influenced by Milton's noble appeal, passed several further ordinances for restraining unlicensed printing‡ (Ord. 1647—1649—1652).

On the military side there were Ludlow and Hutchinson, both

* The *mew* was the dark cage where falcons were *mewed up* while they *mewed* or moulted their feathers. See Spenser's 'darksome *mew*' and Hastings' exclamation on Clarence's imprisonment:
    'More pity that the eagle should be *mew'd*,
    While kites and buzzards prey at liberty.'—Richard III., i. 132.

† Areopagitica, or speech for the liberty of unlicensed printing. Published 1644.

‡ The press was set free in 1693, when the Commons refused to renew the Licensing Act passed soon after the Restoration (1662).

of them officers in the army and members of the Commons, open-hearted men, who made no concealment of their desire to effect a revolution in the government of the State. Distrust of the king had gradually ripened into distrust of monarchy, and a belief that England could never enjoy true liberty or freedom of conscience under any but a republican form of government. Ireton, Cromwell's son-in-law, was abler and more reserved than these brother-officers of his. Though devoted to the cause of freedom, he had not, as they, attached himself blindly to republicanism as the only security for England's liberties. [Ludlow and Hutchinson.]

It was Cromwell, however, whom all adherents of the party that now found itself standing in such fierce opposition to the Presbyterians, regarded as their chief; whom the enthusiastic Vane, the cautious Ireton, the generous Hutchinson, the sincere Ludlow, as well as the sectarian, whatever his denomination, Independent, Brownist, or Anabaptist, all alike looked upon as the one man able to understand their wants, and to lead them to the accomplishment of their aims. For above others he possessed a power of sympathy, talking to each in the language of the hearer's heart, until one and all found it impossible to doubt that his obvious sympathy with their feelings must spring from a sympathy with their views; with Ludlow and Hutchinson he would discuss republican government; with Vane he could look forward to the time when men, instead of being governed by self-interest, should strive to act as Christ would act did He reign upon earth; with his soldiers he could pray and humble himself before the Lord, feeling that he and they were but as weak worms, and that it was God in His mercy who bestowed victory upon His saints; with the more worldly-minded he could unbend and be a pleasant companion, using the language of the ordinary English gentleman, while in debate he could either attest his sincerity with the fervid words and tears of a more demonstrative age, or rein in his feelings and battle with the calm arguments of reason. Freedom with the various forms of vigorous life that spring from freedom—this was his ideal, and it was one that had room within itself for all the others. A man whose nature is based on a principle so wide and deep, when dealing with those whose aims converge in different lines on the same point as his own, is not to be considered false-hearted because his conversation seems to accord with his companion's character; it is rather that his mind is more capacious, able to entertain more ideas and feelings than those of his fellows; he sees the many sides to a question, they but one. Sympathy is, in fact, the first quality of a leader. To move men he must be moved by them; thus alone will they follow while he leads. It was thus through his being able to obtain the confidence of all that Cromwell took his natural position as chief of a coalition, united by common hatred of Presbyterian ascendancy, and including fanatical Anabaptists and Fifth-Monarchists, aristocratical Republicans and Independents, democratical law reformers and Church reformers, with lawyers and Erastians who were Monarchists at heart.

The features of this man who, having begun life as a farmer, was rapidly rising to become the director of a great nation, rough as they were to look upon, could not fail to bear upon them the expression of his true worth. A big head, which was covered with light brown hair curling down upon his neck; a forehead broad and high; shaggy eyebrows, with stern, deep-set eyes looking out from beneath them; a nose that stood well out from the face, rather broad and red; a chin and mouth expressive of firmness; a skin tanned brown with exposure to wind and weather; a rough-looking face, with a big wart over the right eyebrow; the whole, bearing the expression of dignity though not of grace, showing a man of strong feelings with stronger self-control, of spirit stern and just. One of his household, writing to a friend in America, thus describes him: "His body was well compact and strong, his stature under six foot about two inches; his head so shaped, as you might see it a store-house and shop both of a vast treasury of natural parts; his temper exceeding fiery (as I have known), but the flame of it kept down for the most part, or soon allayed with those moral endowments he had. He was naturally compassionate towards objects in distress, even to an effeminate measure. Though God had made him a heart wherein was little room for any fear, but what was due to Himself, of which there was a large proportion, yet he did exceed in tenderness towards sufferers. A larger soul, I think, hath seldom dwelt in a house of clay than his was."*

* Thurloe, i. 766.

The thorough Presbyterians boasted no great names, but there were those among the king's friends who have won fame for their theories on Church and State. The philosopher Hobbes published the 'Leviathan' in 1651 : in this he proposed to give the sovereign absolute power, both in Church and State, with the right to make laws, impose taxes, and decide what creeds should be tolerated in his kingdom, arguing that whatever dangers attended this form of government were none of them so bad as that anarchy which attends civil war. In short, Hobbes' ideal was a wise and just despotism, a form of government almost impossible to get, and quite impossible to keep.

There were others among the Royalists who could plead for religious toleration in words as noble as those of the Independents themselves. Jeremy Taylor, an Episcopalian minister, driven from his living during the war, but drawing a noble lesson from his own and others' sufferings, was teaching in his 'Liberty of Prophesying, (1647), that no matters of mere opinion, no errors that are not sins, ought to be persecuted or punished. Chillingworth, also, who fought in the royal armies, had written before the war broke out a book called the "Religion of Protestants," in which he maintains that the Bible is the sole religion of Protestants, and each man's reason its interpreter. Protestants, he says, are inexcusable, if they offer violence to other men's consciences, and if faulty in the matter of claiming authority, " it is for doing it too much and not too little. This presumptuous imposing of the senses of men upon the words of God, the special senses of men upon the general words of God, and laying them upon men's conscience together, under the equal penalty of death and damnation .... this restraining of the word of God from that latitude and generality, and the understandings of men from that liberty wherein Christ and the apostles left them, is and hath been the only fountain of all the schisms of the Church, and that which makes them immortal. . . . Take away these walls of separation, and all will quickly be one. Take away this persecuting, burning, cursing, damning of men for not subscribing the words of men as the words of God ; require of Christians only to believe Christ and to call no man master but Him only ; let those leave claiming infallibility that have no title to it, and let them that in their words disclaim it, disclaim it also in their actions."

CHAPTER X.
TRIUMPH OF THE ARMY OVER PARLIAMENT.
DEATH OF THE KING.
1647—1649.

Men must reap the things they sow;
Force from force must ever flow.
SHELLEY.

The ablest men that ever were, have had all an openness and frankness of dealing, and a name of certainty and veracity. Dissimulation is but a faint kind of policy or wisdom; it commonly carries with it a show of fearfulness which in any business doth spoil the feathers of sound flying up to the mark; it depriveth a man of one of the most principal instruments for action, which is trust and belief.—BACON, ESSAY, vi.

THE war was now at an end. Harlech Castle, in Wales, the last place to hold out for the king, surrendered in April (1647). A committee of Parliament sat daily at Goldsmith's Hall, whither came Royalists in numbers to compound for their estates; compounding being the resignation of a part to avert the confiscation of the whole. Yet the Presbyterians could have little pleasure in the submission of the Royalists; what they yearned for was a triumph over the Independents. In the Commons the Presbyterian majority was but small; and the hopes they had built on the king had fallen through. The Earl of Essex, their most respected leader, had been some months in the grave (ob. 14th Sept., 1646). The Scotch army had left the kingdom, and it was hazardous for unarmed politicians to irritate an armed body of some thirty thousand men. They had to rely on themselves, and they had no genius for policy. The pay of the army was ten months in arrear. The Presbyterians proposed to pay a sixth of this sum and disband these dangerous allies. Their

Presbyterians pass votes for disbanding army. proposal was carried by a bare majority of ten. Of the few regiments who were excepted, some were to be despatched to Ireland, others employed upon garrison duty at home (Feb. 19th). They then passed a new self-denying ordinance to eliminate from the army the Independent officers who were in the Commons, while they required subscription of the covenant to eliminate those who were not (8th March). A bare majority saved Fairfax from being cashiered (5th March). In passing these votes, the Presbyterians had at once attacked the soldier by an attempt to deprive him of his arrears; the officer, by threatening to remove him from command; the sectarian, by the imposition of the covenant, the first step to persecution. A petition was drawn up by officers and soldiers, to be presented to Fairfax, demanding that all arrears should be paid; that none should be required to go to Ireland against their will; that provision should be made for orphans and wounded; that an Act of Indemnity should be passed to protect the soldiers from being called to account for any past acts—crimes, perhaps, in the eye of the common law, but justified by the necessities of war. The Presbyterians, still thinking themselves masters of the situation, sent orders to Fairfax to suppress the petition, and published a declaration, that whoever joined in it "was an enemy to the State, and a disturber of the public peace" (20th March). The army was in a ferment. "Have we," said the soldiers, "who have been the instruments to recover the lost liberties of the nation, fought ourselves into slavery? Hard it is that we should be denied the subject's liberty to petition."* Two councils were formed, in communication with one another; the first of officers, the second of 'adjutators' or representatives of the regiments. The officers addressed to Parliament a vindication of their conduct, complaining of the treatment they had received, and asserting that, by being soldiers, they had not lost the subject's capacity of petitioning (30th April). No sooner had the Commons heard this paper read, than Skippon produced a second, given him by three troopers, which declared the service in Ireland "a perfidious design to separate the soldiers from the officers they loved, and to conceal the ambition of a few men, who had long been servants, but having lately tasted of sovereign power, were degenerating into tyrants." The Presbyterians fully understood at whom these bold expressions were aimed. The three troopers were called in and questioned. "Were your

<small>Army petitions Parliament.</small>

* Rushworth, Abr., vi. 99, 100.

officers engaged in this letter, or not?" "No; it was drawn up by the agents of eight regiments, and few of the officers knew of it." "Were you ever Cavaliers; for none but Cavaliers would have been concerned in such a letter?" "No; we have been engaged in the Parliament's cause ever since Edgehill fight, and have been wounded in several battles." "What does that expression mean—'certain men aiming at sovereignty'?" "The letter being a joint act, we cannot answer; but if you will put your question in writing, we will bring you back the replies of the regiments."* The Presbyterians were at first inclined to pass some violent votes, but fear soon got the better of anger, and they agreed to send down to head-quarters four of the Independent officers, Cromwell, Ireton, Fleetwood, and Skippon, with instructions to pacify the soldiers before disbanding, inquire into grievances, and promise redress (7th May). They afterwards increased their offer of pay by a miserable pittance (14th May), drew up an ordinance for an amnesty (21st May), voted funds for widows and orphans, and then, thinking they had granted enough to carry their point, sent down Presbyterian commissioners to see the army disbanded (22nd May). The soldiers, however, mutinied instead of disbanding, seized money intended for their pay, expelled officers they mistrusted, and then demanded of Fairfax a general meeting of the army.

Army refuses to disband.

A dangerous crisis had now arrived, when it was natural that both army and Parliament should turn their thoughts upon the king as a possible makeweight to one side or the other. At two o'clock in the morning of the 3rd of June, a body of horse was discovered before the gates of Holmby Castle. "Who commands?" anxiously inquired the Presbyterian commissioners, entrusted by Parliament with the care of Charles. "All command," replied the strange troops; "we come from the army to secure the king's person, there being a plot to steal him away and raise another army to suppress this, which is under Sir Thomas Fairfax." No attempt was made at resistance, for the soldiers of the garrison were at one with the troopers.

Charles carried off from Holmby.

The following evening, about ten o'clock, Cornet Joyce, the leader of the party, holding a cocked pistol in his hand, went to

* Rushworth, Abr., vi 113.

the door of the king's chamber. "I am sorry," he said, "to disquiet the king, but cannot help it, for speak with him I will." The gentlemen of the bedchamber, not liking the look of the pistol, disputed his entrance, until Charles, awakened by the noise, bade them let the intruder in. After a long conversation, the king half promised to leave the castle in his company. "Come, Mr. Joyce," he said, the next morning, standing on the castle steps. "deal ingenuously with me, and tell me what commission you have." "Here," said the cornet, pointing with his hand behind him to his mounted soldiers drawn up in the court below. "As fair a commission," replied the king, smiling, "as I ever saw in my life; such a company of proper handsome men as I have not seen a great while." The king made a pretence of unwillingness to blind the Presbyterian commissioners, but soon rode off with his new escort to Cambridge, the merriest of the party.* It was clear that the value of his support was rising; he might yet get his terms. Fairfax, who was perfectly sincere, wishing neither to disband the army, nor to quarrel with the Parliament, was displeased when he heard the news.† "I don't like it," he said; "who gave the orders?" But none of the officers owned to them. Ireton said he had ordered that the king should be secured at Holmby, but not that he should be carried away. Cromwell, who was much suspected by his Presbyterian fellow-members, left London quietly one day, and joined the army in the eastern counties. The Presbyterians, thoroughly depressed at the loss of their prize, now passed a Bill of Indemnity, voted that some instalments of the arrears should be paid down on disbanding, and once again sent down commissioners to see the army disbanded. At a rendezvous, held at Triploe Heath, near Cambridge, the votes of the Parliament were read to the assembled regiments. It was not likely they would disband now. The commissioners received their answer in loud shouts of 'Justice, justice!' and that same afternoon Cromwell and Fairfax set the army in motion for London (10th June). Both Parliament and city had for some time past been taking measures to oppose force by force. The command of the city militia was taken from the Independents and given to a committee of Presbyterians (4th May). Strong

Rendezvous at Triploe Heath.

---

* Herb. Mem.; Rush. Abr., vi. 140, 144.
† Huntingdon in Masères Tracts, 398.

guards were set, the shops were shut, and Presbyterian officers of Waller's and Essex' old armies crowded to serve in the trainbands, which were largely recruited. But no one really believed the city forces could stand an attack for a day. The army meanwhile was approaching, and sent in its demands. The House was required to give a month's pay to the troops, without conditions, to raise no new forces, and to suspend eleven of the leading Presbyterian members, against whom an impeachment of treason was preferred, for having caused a misunderstanding between the Parliament and the army (16th, 17th June). The Commons granted a month's pay, and reversed an ordinance passed for raising new forces, but could not bring themselves to turn out their own members. The army, however, still advanced. It was at Uxbridge and Kingston-upon-Thames, within twenty miles of the city, when the eleven members saved the pride of their friends by asking leave to absent themselves for six months from the House (26th June). The army, so far satisfied, withdrew from the immediate neighbourhood of the city.

At this time, 'settlement of the kingdom' were the only words in men's mouths, the only hope in their hearts. No one perceived more clearly than Cromwell how much a settlement was needed, nor how difficult it would be to effect. Royalists, Republicans, Presbyterians, sectarians, soldiers, reformers—what possible form of government was to harmonize all these? The Royalists beaten, but numerous; the Republicans speaking with calm contempt of the rule of kings; the Presbyterians regarding the sectarians " as the most wicked men that breathed;" the army filled with fanatics and revolutionists, demanding reform in the law, the Church, and society. On one point alone was Cromwell's mind at this time fixed, that, as far as in his power lay, he would prevent any settlement that did not provide for civil liberty and freedom of conscience. And now the clouds seemed to break, and the sun again to shine upon Charles; for the officers decided that the best way of making a settlement, satisfactory to at least the larger part of the nation, would be by restoring the king to some shadow of his former power. At Holmby under the care of the Presbyterians, Charles, though always civilly treated, had been deprived of the attendance of his chaplains, forced to dismiss his favourite servants, and not allowed to see his friends and children, or to correspond with his wife. But, from the time of his arrival in the army's quarters, he met with far more liberal treatment. Four chaplains were permitted to attend him, and perform the old Church of England service ; the officers were his frequent and respectful visitors ; and his friends found ready access to his presence. At the request of Fairfax, the Parliament allowed the Duke of York, the Lady Elizabeth, and the Duke of Gloucester to visit their father for two days. The meeting took place at Maidenhead ; people strewed flowers on the road, and the Republicans remembered afterwards with horror that Cromwell, their hoped-for leader, came away shedding tears, and saying that the interview between the king and his children was one of the tenderest sights that ever his eyes beheld.

The propositions now drawn up for the king's acceptance by commissioners from the Parliament and the army demanded that a period should be put to the present Parliament within a year at most ; that new Parliaments should be elected every two years, and should appoint standing committees to continue during the intervals ; that the command of the militia by sea and land should reside in Parliament for ten years, and should not even then return to the crown, without the consent of both Houses ; that Parliament and its committees should dispose of all great offices of State, and that peace and war should not be made without their consent. Thus far these demands aimed at transferring the executive power from king to Parliament in much the same way as previous propositions, with the one exception of the dissolution of the existing assembly, a measure specially dreaded by the Presbyterians, because they had lost the confidence of the country. But the propositions on religion and reform, which now emanated from the Independents, were conceived in a very different spirit from those which had been proposed by the Presbyterians. Instead of requiring the king to abolish Episcopacy, establish the Presbyterian Church, and take the covenant, they asked that an Act of Parliament should be passed, repealing all laws which inflicted civil penalties for spiritual offences. There was to be no privilege for covenant any more than for Prayer-book ; the sword of the persecutor was to be changed into the harmless crook of the pastor. To the king's friends they were as merciful as they were to his conscience : with the exception of seven persons, Royalists were to be allowed to compound for their estates at easier rates, and their incapacity for office was to be limited to five years. "There must," said Ireton "be some distinction made between the conquerors and the conquered." Lastly, there were additional reforms proposed, in which the popular instinct of the army showed to advantage beside Presbyterians and Republicans, who cared more to gratify their theories than to relieve the wants of the people. No man's life was to be taken away by less than two witnesses. The course of law was to be reformed, so that suits might be more certain in their issues, and costs not so great. Poor debtors were not to be kept in perpetual imprisonment. The excise was to be taken off the necessaries of life. Lastly, there was to be a redistribution of seats, giving more weight in the Commons to the chief centres of population.

These propositions, with which Ireton was chiefly credited, were by far the most liberal towards all parties that had yet been brought forward. But we must not suppose that the officers intended to trust themselves or their friends to the generosity of Presbyterians and Royalists. Not a word was said about disbanding the army. Had these offers been accepted, Cromwell, as privy councillor, member of Parliament, and general of a devoted army, would have stood by the side of the throne, the controller of the king's actions, and with a sword to repel attacks on religious toleration or civil liberty. Such a position was not what Charles held before the war; but it was a tolerable position. The loss of the power of the sword was a great loss; but Charles had put this question to the arbitrament of war, and had been beaten. He could not hope to be trusted with the sword by either Presbyterians or Independents. But the Independents offered him great advantages. His religious convictions would be respected, and if he could not resuscitate the glories of the Laudian hierarchy, he at least escaped the establishment of the Presbyterian Church and the subscription of the covenant. The treatment of himself and his friends was liberal. Further, the Independents had the power to perform what they promised, which the Presbyterians had not. They had not only the army with them, but the country. Moreover, had Charles understood the country which he ruled, he would have seen that two or three years of real constitutional government, enforced or not, would have cleared off the remains of his unpopularity, so that when the inevitable reaction set in, the current would have carried him on the flood of popular favour into much of his former dignity and power. But this was not to be. Charles was, unfortunately, too astute to be wise. While outwardly treating with the officers, he was secretly dealing with their enemies, and as he wrote to his friends, "he was engaged either to Presbyterians or Independents, and whichever bid most for him should have him."* He was, in fact, hoping for a new civil war, which might end in his own restoration to absolute power.

The impeachment of the eleven members not only cowed the Presbyterians, but put them in an actual minority. But though they lost command of the House, the city was still at their back, and when the Commons passed an ordinance, giving the command of the train-bands to Independents, London rose in tumult, and the citizens, flocking in crowds to Skinners' Hall, put their hands to an engagement to 'endeavour the king's return to his Parliament with safety, honour, and freedom.' Parliament passed a vote that all who joined in the engagement were traitors. On this, a mob of apprentices, watermen, and officers invaded the House with petitions for the restoration of the city militia to its Presbyterian officers, and for the return of the eleven members to their seats. Though the terrified Parliament yielded to both these demands, their petitioners still barred the doors. "What question," said Lenthall, the speaker, "do you further desire to be put?" "That the king be invited to come to London with safety, honour, and freedom," shouted the rabble. "No!" cried the Republican Ludlow, at the top of his voice. The question, however, being put to the vote, was carried, in the midst of general noise and confusion, and Lenthall, at last released from his chair and hustled downstairs by the mob, was thankful to escape into the first coach he could find (26th July). On hearing of this adverse vote, the indignation of both officers and soldiers turned upon the king. They knew, or believed, that he had been at the bottom of the rising. "Sire," said Ireton, "you intend to be arbitrator between the Parliament and us, and we intend to be so between your Majesty and the Parliament." The Army Propositions were presented to him notwithstanding. To these Charles' refusal was so defiant, that it made his own friends stand aghast when they

King rejects army propositions.

* Clar. State Papers, ii. appendix.

heard it. First alluding to the exclusion of seven Royalists from the amnesty, "I will have no man suffer for my sake," he said. "I repent of nothing so much as that I passed the bill against the Earl of Strafford." He then added, that he wished Episcopacy to be established by law; and repeated several times over, "You cannot be without me; you will fall to ruin if I do not sustain you." Enraged with king and Presbyterians alike, the officers and soldiers marched on the capital, to teach the citizens to recognize their masters; on the way, at Hounslow Heath, they met the speaker, accompanied by a hundred members of the Lower House and fourteen of the Upper, who in disgust at the violence offered them, sought refuge with the army (30th July). Meanwhile in London the shops were again shut, the drums beat, and new troops enlisted in the train-bands. But the hearts of the citizens began to fail them when they heard the army had already reached Hounslow Heath, and was still continuing its advance, after receiving the fugitive members with shouts of joy (3rd Aug.). If a scout reported a halt of the army, the word in London was, "One and all; live and die;" if an advance, the cry was, "Treat, treat, treat." The Borough of Southwark refused to fight, and the Lord Mayor and City Council finally wrote to Fairfax that they quite concurred with him in wishing to restore the fugitive members. Thus the king's hopes were disappointed: all passed over without a blow; the eleven Presbyterian members fled a second time; the fugitive Republicans and Independents retook their seats (6th Aug.), and the whole army marched in triumph through London (8th Aug.).

Cromwell, however, was aware that at least two-thirds of the nation still desired the king's restoration. He, therefore, continued to treat with Charles. It was doubtful, however, whether it was any longer in his power to conclude a treaty, even if Charles would have made the required concessions. The distrust that had always prevailed of the king's good faith, had deepened into an absolute certainty. Republicans and sectarians had from the first disliked holding dealings with a man they regarded as the "chief delinquent, guilty of all the blood shed in the war," and now finding themselves absolute masters of city, Parliament, and king, they were far from thinking of allowing Charles any shadow of power. On seeing that Cromwell continued to treat, they openly talked of the "baseness of those who would for the sake of honours and office desert a noble cause, and a second time enslave the people." A report was soon credited in the army that Cromwell had been promised the command-in-chief of the king's armies with the title of Earl of Essex, and Ireton the government of Ireland, as the price of betraying their cause and their friends. *Republicans, sectarians, Levellers, refuse to treat any longer with king.* The army had, in fact, been leavened by a new class of reformers, who had won over to their opinions a majority of both soldiers and officers. These reformers were nicknamed Levellers, being rather pure Democrats than Republicans. They disliked the House of Lords as much as the king, and their aim was equality of ranks and abolition of all class privileges before the law. Their leader, John Lilburne, who began life by defying the Court of Star Chamber,* tried to stir the soldiers to mutiny against the generals. Cromwell knew that divisions in the army would only pave the way for the triumph of Presbyterians and Royalists. In that event his cherished cause, ' Liberty of conscience,' would be lost. He therefore determined on making his peace with his old friends, and giving up the attempt to effect a settlement by restoring Charles to the throne. In this he was perfectly justified, for there was no doubt that the king was acting insincerely towards the officers. " I shall play my game as well as I can," Charles said, in one of his sanguine moments. " If your Majesty have a game to play," replied Ireton, " you must give us also liberty to play ours." All this time Charles was placing his faith in the Scots, who, finding that the Independent army was not, after all, disbanded, nor the king restored to his throne, began to use menacing language, and to threaten an invasion of England. So well was Cromwell aware of the whole thread of the king's policy, that he told the royalist, Berkley, "he had in his own possession letters which showed that the king had commanded all his party to serve under the Parliament and the city, and that he had at that instant, when he made greatest profession to close with the army, a treaty with the Scots, which did very much justify the general misfortune he lived under of having the reputation of little faith in his dealings."†

Charles, who was residing at Hampton Court, found his position altered ; his movements were more restrained ; his friends

---

* See p. 73.   † Ashburnham's Narrative, 94.

were shut out from his presence, and anonymous letters reached his hands, warning him that his life was in danger. Accompanied only by a servant and two friends, Berkley and Ashburnham, he fled from Hampton Court one dark stormy evening, and after riding hard all night arrived early the next morning at the coast opposite the Isle of Wight (12th Nov.). Here, taking refuge the while in a neighbouring house, he sent Berkley and Ashburnham over to the island with instructions to extract from the governor, Hammond, a promise to grant his Majesty means of conduct to a place of safety. Hammond turned pale, and at first, in terror at the news, begged that the king might not be brought to the island, for "what between his duty to the king and his trust to the army, he should be confounded." But he soon changed his mind, and became anxious to know where the king was to be found. "I will promise to perform," he said, "whatever can be expected of a person of honour and honesty." Though little confidence could be placed in such a vague expression of good-will, Ashburnham and Berkley, not knowing how to rid themselves of the governor's company, undertook to conduct him and one other man, Captain Basket, to the royal presence. "Oh, you have undone me!" exclaimed Charles, when he heard that they had brought Hammond with them, "for I am by this means made fast from stirring." "Since what has been done does not please your Majesty," replied Ashburnham in tears, "I will kill the governor and the captain with my own hands." Charles took two or three turns up and down the room. "No," he replied; "it would be said that he ventured his life for me, and I took it away from him. We must go through with it now." Arrived at Carisbrooke, Charles felt in better spirits. Hammond treated him courteously; gentlemen came to visit him, and being left at liberty to ride over the island he did not doubt of being able at any time to escape across the Channel.

Cromwell has been accused of having purposely frightened Charles away from Hampton Court, with the intention of getting him more completely into the power of the army. He certainly wrote a note to Colonel Whalley, bidding him have a care of his guards, for "if any attempt should be made upon his Majesty's person, it would be accounted a most horrid act." He was also the first to hear from Whalley of the king's escape, and reported the news to Parliament. But this evidence does not seem strong enough to support the conclusion drawn from it. Many of the Levellers were so unscrupulous that the rumours of an intended assassination were not likely to be without foundation. Cromwell's note, therefore, may have been intended simply as a caution to Whalley. Further, Cromwell could not have foreseen that the fugitives would seek refuge in the Isle of Wight; in fact, when there the king was not more but less in the power of the army than before. At Hampton Court, his keeper was Whalley, who was throughout on the side of the army, and was afterwards one of his judges; whereas in the Isle of Wight he was under Hammond, who disapproved of the dealings of the army with the Parliament, and was afterwards removed from his post to make place for a surer man. Had he, on the other hand, escaped into Scotland, he would undoubtedly have soon been again in England at the head of an army, and Royalists by thousands been flocking to his standard. The obvious conclusion is that if Cromwell connived at the flight from Hampton Court, his desire can only have been to save Charles' life from the assassin's dagger, and to give him a chance of escape across the Channel.

Cromwell had incurred unpopularity with the army by being too favourable to the king, and now had to turn his mind to the suppression of the mutinous spirit that had appeared amongst the soldiers. Different regiments of the army were ordered to attend him at three several meetings. To the first meeting, held between Hertford and Ware, only three regiments were summoned. But when Fairfax and Cromwell arrived on the ground, they found that Robert Lilburne's regiment of infantry and Colonel Harrison's regiment of cavalry had come without orders. The soldiers, most of whom were Levellers, were in a state of great excitement, and had fixed to their hats copies of one of Lilburne's pamphlets, entitled 'The Agreement of the People.' Fairfax read a remonstrance to the quieter regiments, reminding them of the good faith their chiefs had always shown them, and promising that he would support the demands of the soldiers, if they would obey the orders of their officers. This appeal to the soldiers' feelings was answered by shouts of approval. Even Harrison's troopers, on hearing the address, tore the copies of the 'Agreement' from their hats, declaring that they had been deceived, and would live and die with their general. But Lilburne's regiment showed no signs of submission. "Take that paper from your hats!" cried Cromwell; and when none obeyed, riding with drawn sword into the ranks, he ordered fourteen of the leading mutineers to be arrested. Old habits of discipline in the soldier, the commanding voice and gesture of the officer, produced obedience. A court-martial was held on the spot, and, out of three condemned, one soldier was shot to death in front of the regiment (Nov. 15th). The two following meetings went off quietly.

Yet, though he had overawed them for the moment, Cromwell knew that these soldiers held the destinies of England in their hands, and that, if he would be their master and stay their hands from havoc, he must first regain their confidence. Several meetings were held between officers and adjutators, at which he and the officers admitted that the treaty with the king, entered into 'through the fear of man and want of a spirit of faith, had become a cause of division, to the danger of the blessed cause in which the army was engaged.' In thus speaking it is not to be supposed that Cromwell and his officers were acting the parts of knaves and hypocrites. It was an undeniable fact that, in treating with Charles, they had taken a wrong road to effect a settlement which would secure religious toleration and civil liberty. Charles had deceived them; he had not only stirred up the city against them, but now at his summons a Scotch army was about to invade the country, while Royalists were preparing to rise. In the divisions that had ensued amongst themselves, in the dangers that now threatened them, they recognized a judgment of God on their own backslidings. The conferences concluded with "a very clear and joint resolution, on many grounds at large there debated amongst us, that it was our duty, if ever the Lord brought us back again in peace, to call Charles Stuart, that man of blood, to an account for that blood he had shed and mischief he had done to his utmost against the Lord's cause and people in these poor nations." *

While this was the final resolution of the army, the Presbyterians in Parliament carried a vote that, if the king gave his consent to four bills, granting the command of the militia to the Parliament, and revoking his declarations of treason against the two Houses, he should be allowed to come to London and treat

* Somers, Tracts, vi.

in person (Dec. 14th). Charles, however, rejected the bills; for about the same time that they were presented, commissioners came from Scotland to Carisbrooke, and concluded a treaty with him on easier terms than had ever yet been proposed. It was agreed that a Scotch army should enter the kingdom in the ensuing spring; that the Cavaliers should rise at the same time; that the Presbyterian Church should be established in England for three years; and that the king should not be required to take the covenant or conform to the public worship (26th Dec.). The papers containing the terms were carefully closed up in lead, and concealed in a private house, for it would have been fatal to the king's character had their contents become known to the English Parliament. Charles, however, had, unfortunately, but little character for honesty left with either party. Both Parliament and army knew he had made a secret agreement with the Scots, and ascribed his rejection of the four bills to its true cause (27th Dec.). Having delayed to escape until he had concluded the treaty with the Scots, Charles found that the opportunity was gone; his guards were doubled, his friends dismissed, and his walks confined to a small garden. *Charles' secret treaty with Scots.*

The Republicans seized the advantage offered them by the rejection of the bills to venture on the boldest step they had yet taken; they openly proposed, in Parliament, to exclude the king from the throne. "Mr. Speaker," said Sir Thomas Wroth, "Bedlam was appointed for madmen, and Tophet for kings; but our kings of late have carried themselves as if they were fit for no place but Bedlam. I propose we lay the king by, and settle the kingdom without him. I care not what form of government you set up, so it be not by kings or devils." *Republicans propose dethronement.*

After a warm debate, the Presbyterians were beaten, and a resolution was carried by 141 votes against 92, that no more addresses should be made to the king by any person whatsoever, without consent of both Houses, under penalties of high treason (3rd Jan., 1648). Yet, in spite of this success within Parliament House, outside there were many signs of disaffection, which boded but a stormy birth for the young Republic. An invasion from Scotland was expected; the city was slow to lend money to pay the army, and hated the Parliament ever since the exclusion of the eleven Presbyterian members; the country people were clamouring against the taxes and calling for the restoration of the king. Cromwell, hoping at least to effect cordial co-operation between the friends of a common cause, brought together the 'Parliament grandees' and the 'army grandees' at a dinner at his own house. He there stated, as his own opinion, that either a monarchical, aristocratical, or democratical government might be good in themselves, or good for England, according to the directions of Providence. The Republicans disputed both points. God, they said, had charged upon the Israelites their choice of Saul as a rejection of Himself; therefore, monarchy could not be good in itself, any more than it could be good for England, to which it had been the main source of oppression. "It is our duty," they said, "to call the king to account for the blood that has been shed, and then to establish a commonwealth, founded upon the consent of the people, so that it may have their hearts and hands in its support." Cromwell, being pressed by Ludlow to declare himself plainly for or against a republic, flung a cushion at his questioner's head, and ran downstairs, to give some vent to the irritation he was obliged to suppress. Fools to talk of founding a republic, with the consent of the nation! when against it were not Royalists only, but Presbyterians and thousands of honest men who had taken arms against the king, not to abolish kingship, but to ensure their own liberties. "I see," he said to Ludlow the next day, "that it is desirable, but not that it is possible;" whereupon Ludlow angrily left him, suspicious of his intentions. For these Republicans had now become so deeply imbued with the idea that the only way to ensure England's liberties was by founding a commonwealth without king or House of Lords, that they disbelieved in the honesty of every one who doubted the efficacy of the nostrum.

But the storm, which Cromwell had foreseen, now burst, and the presence of a common foe made Levellers, Republicans, and army officers unite again. Great excitement had prevailed throughout the country since the vote passed against making further addresses to the king. Reverence for their country's past combined with pity for their fallen monarch. Bands of the City militia would patrol the streets, stop coaches, and force their occupants to drink the king's health. Some apprentices, playing at bowls in Moorfields one Sunday, drove off a body of soldiers who would have stopped their game, and then marched to the City, raising the cry of 'God and King Charles!' Joined on their way by thousands of sympathizers, they broke open an arsenal, placed chains across the streets, and remained masters of the City till the following morning (April 13th).

In the country similar scenes were witnessed. In defiance of the soldiers, tumultuous crowds of country people assembled to raise the forbidden maypole, and were seldom dispersed without bloodshed. Rebellion followed tumult. The knowledge that the Scots were coming to deliver the king from prison raised the drooping spirits of the Cavaliers. In Wales, in Kent, in Essex, in Hertfordshire, in Nottinghamshire, in Cornwall, in the western counties, the royal standard was unfurled. The same reaction extended to the navy. Seventeen ships of war sailed to Holland and offered their services to the Prince of Wales. But the army had generals who were not slow to act, and troops such as the raw levies of the Cavaliers could not long resist. Cromwell soon triumphed in the west, and forced the Royalists to take refuge in Pembroke Castle (May). In the counties round London, after a fortnight's fighting, little remained of the royal forces, and this little was besieged by Fairfax in Colchester (June).

There was serious danger, however, yet to come. Scotland, at this time, was a country divided against itself. The Covenanters had split into two parties. The first, headed by the Duke of Argyle, and supported by the Church Assembly, were indignant at the terms of the treaty their commissioners had made in the Isle of Wight. A war to replace a king who refused the Covenant seemed at once treason to their religion and a breach of their treaty with the English Parliament. The second, or moderate party, under the Duke of Hamilton, were ready to forgive any shortcomings of the king sooner than see Independents triumph over Presbyterians. In defence of the war they could argue, not without truth, that the purpose of their solemn league and covenant had been to establish the Presbyterian Church in England, and secure constitutional rule, and not to enable Republicans and sectarians to overthrow monarchy and secure liberty of conscience. The moderate party was strongest in the Scottish Parliament, and, in spite of the opposition of the Church Assembly, a vote had been passed to raise an army of 40,000 men to fight in defence of the Covenant and of the king. The service, however, was not popular. Under Hamilton's command some

20,000 came straggling into England, followed by the curses of the extreme Covenanters. Fairfax being before Colchester, Cromwell before Pembroke, the invaders marched loosely and confidently. On the 16th of August, Hamilton, with the main body of

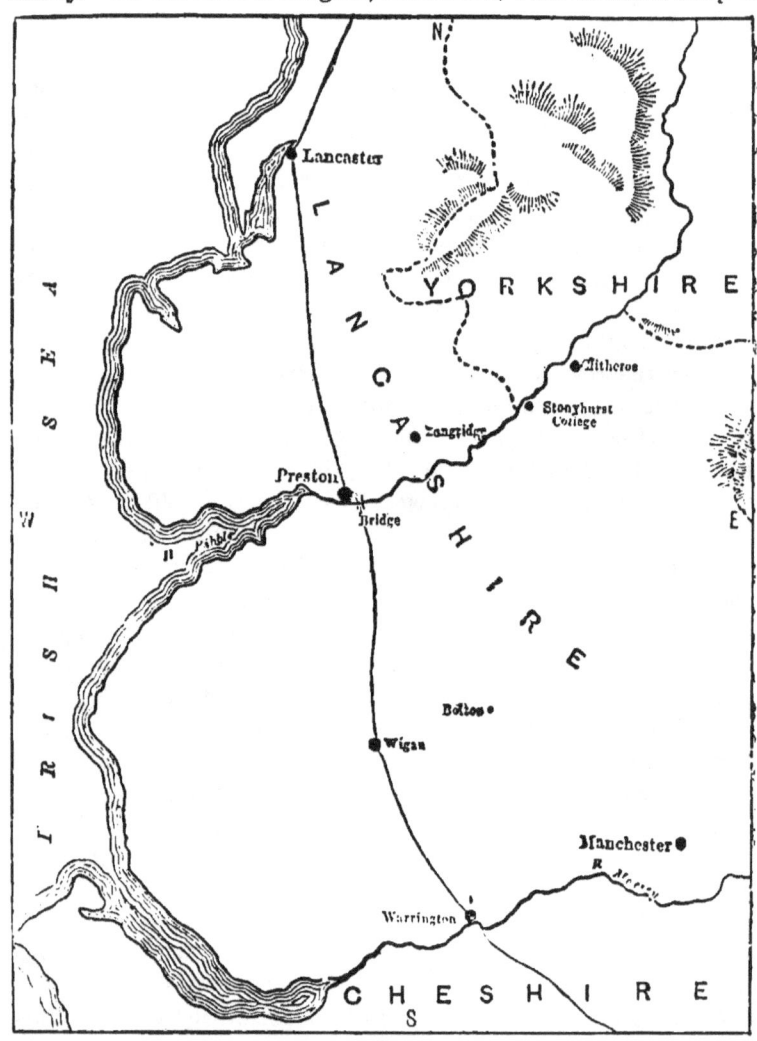

MAP OF LANCASHIRE.

his army, was at Preston; his horse at Wigan, more than ten miles in advance; his rear straggling another ten miles behind. At Langridge, about four miles to the east, up the northern bank of the Ribble, was Sir Marmaduke Langdale and a body of 3000 English Cavaliers. But security is not safety. Further east, another four or five miles up the same stream, at Stonyhurst and Clitheroe, was Cromwell, with an army of nearly 9000 men, a fact of which Duke Hamilton lay in complete ignorance. Pembroke had, in fact, surrendered just in time to allow the Ironsides to hasten north by forced marches, and meet the new enemy before he had advanced far into Lancashire. In the morning Cromwell descended the stream of the Ribble on the northern bank, and attacked the Cavaliers at Langridge. Hamilton, believing the enemy to be merely some small body of Yorkshiremen, sent no reinforcements to Langdale, who, after a gallant resistance and four hours' hard fighting, was driven back from hedge to hedge into Preston town, the enemy following close at his heels, and charging through the streets. While the Cavaliers were fighting, the main body of the Scots had been making their way in happy ignorance to the south side of the Ribble, intending to follow their horse. While in this plight, Cromwell fell upon them and drove them off Ribble bridge before their rear had crossed. The troops thus left on the north bank of the river were cut to pieces, and chased to Lancaster with terrible loss (Aug. 17th).

South of the Ribble, Hamilton held a council of war. Most of his officers were for pushing on the same night to Wigan, where they expected to find their horse. "But what," said others, "will become of our unfortunate ammunition, since forward with us we cannot get it?" "It shall be blown up by a train," said the duke. But, in the hurry and confusion of a retreat by night, it was not blown up, and the whole fell into the hands of Cromwell. The next morning (Aug. 18th), after this "drumless march," the Scots found themselves at Wigan Moor, weary in body and depressed in spirit, for weather was wet and ways were bad, and the twenty thousand had dwindled to ten. The officers agreed to push the retreat on to Warrington, another ten miles south, where they hoped to take up a strong defensive position, and dispute the passage of the enemy at the bridge over the Mersey. But before their rear, which did not begin its march until the evening, was through Wigan, Cromwell was upon them. In the market-place the moon cast dim light upon a scene of inextricable confusion. The Ironsides charged the Scots' rear; the Scots' horse dashed headlong onwards, and were received on the pikes of their own infantry, who cried out, "These are Cromwell's men!" They charged, however, so fiercely that the pikemen threw down their weapons and fled for refuge to the nearest houses. The same mistakes were repeated. "After this," says one who was present, "all the horse galloped away, and, as I was told afterwards, rode not through, but over our whole foot." Such were the scenes of the night. In the morning (Aug. 19th), at a place called Redbank, two miles outside Warrington, a body of pikemen took advantage of a favourable position to face about and dispute the ground with the enemy. After several hours' hard fighting, driven back at push of pike, they entered Warrington in company with their pursuers, and pressed on to the bridge over the Mersey, which was already held by their friends, and strongly barricaded. Here, however, the three days' battle ended. Hamilton and the horse had made off some time before, sending word to the lieutenant-general of the foot to make as good conditions for himself as he could. Officers and soldiers yielded themselves prisoners of war, being promised their lives and civil usage. Hamilton and his horse were caught in Staffordshire. Thus, as Cromwell wrote to the Parliament, did an army of 8600 men shatter and dissipate another of at least 21,000. Two thousand Scots were slain, and eight or nine thousand more made prisoners, without counting those destroyed or brought in by the country people * (August 17, 18, 19).

Cromwell, after his victory, marched with his army into Scotland, where the extreme Covenanters had risen in arms against the friends of Hamilton's invasion. A peace was effected by his influence (Sept. 28th). The Engagers, the name given to those who served under Hamilton, were disqualified from serving in any public employment, but were left in possession of their property, on condition of disbanding their forces and renewing their allegiance to the Covenant. The government was thus left entirely in the hands of Argyle and other opponents of the late war.

A few days after Cromwell's victory over the Scots in Lancashire, Fairfax brought the war to a close in the south. Subdued by famine, the gentlemen and officers shut up in Colchester surrendered at discretion, the soldiers upon promise of quarter (Aug. 27th). Three of the garrison were condemned by a council of war to be shot. "It is necessary," Ireton is reported to have said,

* Carl., i. 279—295; Hodgson and Slingsby, Mem.

"for the example of others, and to prevent the peace of the kingdom from being disturbed in this way again, that some should suffer." Fairfax, though always inclined to the side of mercy, agreed with Ireton. One, a foreigner, he reprieved; the other two, who had both broken their word of honour not to bear arms against the Parliament, were executed.

While the generals were engaged in fighting Royalists and Scots, the Presbyterians in London, taking advantage of the absence of many Independent members with the army, were doing their utmost to ruin the cause of civil and religious liberty. There were, without doubt, many members of the Parliament who would sooner have seen victory on the side of the Scots than of the Independents. In the Upper House this party was in a majority, so that when the Commons voted that all Englishmen who should abet the invaders were traitors, the Lords actually refused to concur in the vote (July 18th). A persecuting ordinance was fulminated against sectarians (p. 203). The eleven Presbyterian members were recalled to their seats (June). The Presbyterian major-general, Huntingdon, presented to Parliament a paper, modestly entitled, 'Sundry Reasons inducing him to lay down his Commission,' but really containing charges against his commander, which, in the event of the Scots' success, might have served to cost Cromwell his head. Even those Presbyterians whose feelings of nationality were too strong to suffer them to wish success to the invaders, were yet most eager to conclude a treaty with the king, and thereby sacrifice the cause for which the English armies were fighting. The vote of the 3rd of January, forbidding any addresses to be made to the king, under penalties of treason, was now rescinded (June 30th), and, after some time had passed in preliminaries, fifteen commissioners were sent to negotiate the terms of a treaty with Charles at Newport (Sept. 13th).

The Parliament had now exercised supreme power since the breaking out of the war in the year '41. Once looked upon as the saviour of the nation's liberties, it was now hated and despised. The causes of this were manifold. In the first place, however able and honest were some of its members, it had, as a body, been subjected to violence, and had sacrificed all consistency, voting one day to please the soldiers, another to please a City mob. A former Royalist member justly reproaches them with "voting of members in and out so often; voting there shall be no more addresses to the king, and then voting that there shall—a temper something like that of Henry VIII., who advanced men in a good humour he knew not why, and ruined them again in another he knew not why."*

A second cause that brought the Parliament into disfavour with the people, was that both Houses of Parliament constantly trespassed on the liberties of the people by fining and imprisoning political offenders, under the pretence of breach of privilege, without showing legal cause or bringing the victims to trial. Yet the House of Lords, except in cases of impeachment or appeals from inferior courts, possessed an undisputed jurisdiction only over peers; while the House of Commons possessed no judicial power at all, except in disputed elections and in cases of interference with the free action of members. Lilburne had already signalized himself by attacking the encroachments thus made upon the liberties of the people. He had been committed to prison by order of the Lords (July, 1646), and it was two years before he succeeded in obtaining from the judges of the King's Bench his writ of 'habeas corpus.' It was not to be expected that in time of war a troublesome agitator should meet with other than summary treatment. Lilburne had attacked one of the two Houses under which he served, and, when imprisoned for this, had been writing pamphlets exciting the soldiers to mutiny. In such a case, a temporary suspension of the subject's right to a 'habeas corpus' was necessary and justifiable. It probably, however, did the Parliament quite as much injury as if the man had been left at liberty. A revolutionary government, though surrounded by enemies, and with none of the prestige of an old-established régime to protect it, is none the less expected to show a far greater regard to the liberties of the subject than the government it has displaced. So now crowds of sympathizing spectators thronged the court when Lilburne demanded his liberty on the ground that the Lords acted illegally in calling any but peers to the bar of their House. The judges, however, supported the jurisdiction of the Lords, and refused to grant Lilburne his release, on the ground that he had been committed by a superior court. Notwithstanding the decision of the judges, abuse of privilege was a real

* " Letter of an Ejected Member " (printed 1648).

blot on the administration: so was also the subservience the Parliament had shown.

There can be no doubt, however, that what ruined the government in the opinion of the country at large was the bad financial administration. The other causes touched the men who thought and the men who felt; but this weighed with the average men who did not either think much or feel much. Such men are four out of five in any community. As a rule they follow their leaders, but in England, if their pockets are once touched, they take a course of their own. These men the Parliament had alienated by bad finance. Properly administered, the revenue would have been more than sufficient to meet the expenditure. Its sources were numerous—the excise, the customs, the monthly assessment on land and goods, the compositions made by Royalists, and the seizure and sale of bishops' lands, crown lands, and the estates of those who preferred poverty and exile to having any dealings with rebels. But the machinery for collection was both oppressive and expensive. There was a bureaucracy of the worst kind, for the counties were put in the hands of committees, who levied the taxes, looked after Royalists' estates, and secured obedience to the government. It was said, indeed, that one half of the revenue was devoured by these committees and their officials. Large sums of money were lavishly granted by the Parliament to its adherents, sometimes as rewards for services, sometimes as payments of loans, borrowed at a high interest during the war. Adventurers who had joined the side of the Parliament as a paying speculation, succeeded in their object, making large fortunes either as members of Parliament or as members of county committees. Colonel Birch, a merchant of Bristol, who had abandoned his business as unprofitable, and enlisted in the Parliament's army, was granted at different times the sums of £1500, £800, and £4900, and in the year 1650 had so much spare capital that he bought bishops' lands to the value of £2000. While these liberal gifts were made, the pay of the soldiers was left in arrear. To meet the deficit, heavy extra impositions were laid on the country. Thus, in 1647, the people in many parts of Radnor, though they had already paid their six months' contribution, were required to raise an additional rate of three shillings for each foot soldier quartered amongst them. During the war Fairfax exacted from the city of Bath £90,000 in six months, in addition to twelve months' pay, which had been previously granted. Thus, while men connected with the government grew rich, the tradespeople in garrison towns were being gradually reduced to beggary, and the country people in some places were almost starving. "Amazing," says Lilburne in one of his pamphlets, "that so many men in Parliament, and their associates elsewhere, who pride themselves as the only saints and godly men upon earth, and have large possessions of their own, can take yearly salaries of £1000, £3000, £6000."*

From these various causes the House of Commons was unpopular, It was also divided against itself. It contained three chief political parties. First, the Presbyterians, eager to recover their former ascendancy by making a treaty with the king; secondly, the Republicans, who aimed at getting rid of king and House of Lords; thirdly, Independents, still true to the cause of liberty of conscience: besides these were the lawyers and the waverers, who voted with the Republicans, either through dread of Presbyterian ascendancy, or because, after long enjoying the sweets of power, they were loath to see the present Parliament dissolved. Outside the Commons' House was an army of between 20,000 and 30,000 men, at this time the real power in the land. The officers' views of sett'ement differed from those of the Republicans principally in the following point, that while the Republicans wished the army to act as an obedient servant in establishing their Republican ideal, the officers cared little about the form of the civil power as long as it carried out their own views of reform. The two parties, however, were closely allied, and, in fact, intermingled. A standing army had never before been known in England, and was as little loved by the people as the perpetual Parliament itself. Thus the officers, unable to rule in their own names, hoped to rule by coalescing with the Republicans. The Republicans, in their anxiety to found their own form of government, mistook the character and aims of their only and necessary supporters. The ranks of the army were really filled with sectarians and Levellers. The reforms these demanded were not theoretical, but practical and popular—the abolition of imprisonment for debt, the lessening of lawyers' fees, an adjustment of seats to population, the meeting of new parliaments every year, and the reform of the Church.

* Memoirs of Col. Birch, 68, 96, 152, 236 ; Whitelock, Mem ; Hollis, Memoirs; 'Fundamental Liberties of England vindicated,' in King's Tracts.

A Leveller has given us a picture of a meeting of officers, Republicans, Independents, and some of his own party, held during the autumn months, while the Presbyterians were treating with the king. "We intend," said the officers, "to cut off the king's head, and purge, if not dissolve, the Parliament." "We know," replied Lilburne, as the spokesman of the Levellers, "that the king is a bad man, but the army deceived us last year, and is not to be trusted. It is our interest to keep up one tyrant against the other, until we can know which tyrant will give more freedom. For we do not wish the government to develop into the wills and swords of the army, and we [be] dealt with as the slavish peasants of France, who can call nothing their own. An agreement must be drawn up before anything else is done." "There is no time," objected an officer; "the treaty between the king and the Parliament will be concluded, and then you will be destroyed as well as we." "We must dissolve the Parliament," said Ireton for the officers, "for how else are we to get rid of it? It will never dissolve itself." On the other hand, Republican and Independent members of the House opposed a dissolution, thinking a purge of their Presbyterian companions a far more desirable remedy, and by no means objecting to concentrating all civil power in their own hands.

When such were the counsels of the men in power, the negotiations begun at Newport in September appear little better than a farce. There Charles was himself receiving, disputing, and answering the propositions of the Parliament, which were the same as those offered at Newcastle. Two of the commissioners on their knees implored him to waste no time, but to grant on the first day all that he could on the last. It probably mattered less than they thought whether he yielded on the first or last day, for where in either case was to be found the means to resist the will of the army, which was opposed to all compromise? At last, after protracting the negotiations over six weeks, Charles agreed to grant to Parliament the command of the militia and the government of Ireland for twenty years; to suspend the power of bishops for three years, until a form of Church government should be agreed upon by himself and the two Houses; and to allow seven of his friends to be excepted from pardon. How far, however, he was sincere in making these concessions may be judged from his own letters. "Be not startled," he wrote to Ormond, "at my great concessions about Ireland, for that they will come to nothing."

For some time past Charles' mind had been occupied with thoughts of escape. He was beginning at last to realize that it was possible for subjects to take the life of an anointed king. Still he hardly dared leave the country without first obtaining the consent of his wife. The Prince of Wales might have sailed from Holland with the revolted ships to attempt his father's release, but he made no effort. One day Charles told Sir John Bowring, who frequently pressed him to escape, that he had received a letter from beyond seas, advising him not to go out of the island, for it was not in the power of the army to touch a hair of his head. "So," he continued, "as I have made concessions, and the treaty has had a fair end, and especially since I have received this advice (you guess from whence it comes), I am resolved to stay here, and God's will be done." It was in fact his wife's will which was still to be done, till her fatal influence had finally ruined him. The will of the army was soon shown. Regiment after regiment presented petitions to Fairfax demanding 'that the same fault may have the same punishment in a king or lord as in the poorest commoner.' A united Army Remonstrance was read in Parliament, requiring the House to set aside the treaty and 'proceed against the king in a way of justice.' By a majority of ninety, the Commons decided not to take the Army Remonstrance into consideration.

On the 2nd of December they were debating whether the king's concessions were sufficient to serve as a basis of peace. Meanwhile the soldiers were taking up their quarters in the City, and Fairfax was establishing himself at Whitehall. "The debate ought to be laid aside," said Prynne, "until we are a free Parliament. Our debates cannot be with liberty now we are environed by the army." On Monday (Dec. 4th) the news came that Charles had been carried off by a party of soldiers from Carisbrooke to Hurst Castle, a gloomy fortress on the Hampshire coast. The Presbyterians, more indignant than alarmed, declared the honour of Parliament at stake, for it had voted that the king should treat in honour, safety, and freedom. Prynne appeared as the king's champion, so vastly had times changed within the last eight years. "Mr. Speaker," he said, "all the royal favour I ever yet received from his Majesty was the slitting off my ears in a most barbarous manner; the setting me upon three several pillories for two hours at a time; the burning of my books by the hand of the hangman; the imposing two fines upon me of £5000 a piece; expulsion from the University of Oxford; above eight years' imprisonment without pens, ink, paper, or books except my Bible. If any member envy me for such royal favour, I only wish him the same badges of favour, and then he will no more asperse me for a royal favourite or apostate from the public cause." For hours he continued speaking, showing that there was no danger to liberty in accepting the king's concessions, and calling on the House not to sacrifice its freedom to fear of the army. "If the king and we shall happily close upon this treaty, I hope we shall have not such great need of their future service; however, *fiat justitia, ruat cœlum*—let us do our duty and leave the issue to God."

It was five o'clock on Tuesday morning before the **House** divided, when a resolution was carried by 140 to 104, that the answers of the king were a sufficient ground to proceed upon for a settlement of the kingdom. The next day (6th Dec.) was memorable as that of Pride's Purge A party of officers, headed by Ireton, had determined to put an end to what they considered Presbyterian dictation. Cromwell was on his way from Scotland, and did not reach London till the next day; and Fairfax was in ignorance of the designs of his officers. But by seven o'clock in the morning every approach to the Commons' House was barred by soldiers. At the door stood their officer, Colonel Pride, with a list of the proscribed in his hand. When a leading Presbyterian came up the staircase, Lord Grey of Groby pointed him out to Pride, and if the member refused to go away of his own accord, the soldiers forced him down the staircase. Forty Presbyterians were thus excluded, while several others were frightened and kept away of themselves. As the House refused to proceed to business until its absent members should be restored, the next morning the same scene was repeated, and forty more members were excluded (Dec. 7). A minority of twenty-six withdrew of their own accord; the remainder, nicknamed the Rump, formed a House of fifty-three members, all bound to work in accordance with their friends in the army.

First, in order to have a law by which to convict Charles of treason, the Commons voted that it was treason in the King of

England to levy war against the Parliament and kingdom; next, in order to have a court by which to try him, they framed an ordinance for making a special or High Court of Justice, composed of men of their own party. As the House of Lords, though it had now dwindled down to twelve members, still had spirit enough to reject the ordinance unanimously, the Commons resolved, that whatever is enacted by the Commons has the force of law without the consent of king or House of Peers, and then passed the ordinance in their own name alone (Jan. 6th).

<small>Ordinance for High Court of Justice.</small>

The court first met in private in order to make preparations for the trial. 135 judges were named on the ordinance, but many refused to attend the sittings. Algernon Sidney came once, and interrupted the debate by saying, "The king can be tried by no court, and no man by this court." "I tell you," said Cromwell, "we will cut off his head with the crown upon it." "You may take your course, I cannot stop you," replied Algernon; "but I will keep myself clean from having any hand in the business."* He then left the room and never returned. Sir Henry Vane retired into the country; Fairfax attended the first meeting only.

Charles had already been removed from Hurst Castle to Windsor, and after a few days was taken on to London. The trial was held in Westminster Hall. The judges, about eighty in number, sat upon benches, which rose one above another at the upper end of the hall. Bradshaw, Cromwell's cousin, sat on a chair of state as Lord President of the Court. Below the President's chair was a table, on which lay the sword and mace of the House of Commons. Twenty-one gentlemen, bearing 'partisans,' were ranged on either side in front of the judges. At the other end of the table, opposite the President's seat, was placed a red velvet chair for the prisoner; within a bar on the right-hand side of the prisoner's chair stood the three solicitors for the Commonwealth. Ladies and others were seated in galleries. The body of the hall was filled with a tearful, expectant crowd, separated from the soldiers by scaffoldings. The king was conducted up the centre of the hall by a guard of soldiers. He did not raise his hat or show any sign of respect to the court, but after regarding his judges severely for some moments, turned round

* Blencowe, Sidney Papers, i. 237.

and inspected the crowds behind. Cook, the solicitor of the Commonwealth, read the charge, in which Charles Stuart was accused of having endeavoured to overturn the liberties of the people, and of being guilty of all the murders and spoils under which the nation had suffered, "wherefore the people of England impeached Charles Stuart as a tyrant, traitor, and murderer." The king smiled visibly when he heard the words, "tyrant, traitor, murderer." He persistently refused to answer to the charge, asserting that the court had no lawful authority derived from the people of England by which to try him, and that therefore in refusing to plead "he stood more for the liberties of the people than did his pretended judges." Cook accordingly demanded that sentence might be pronounced against the prisoner, in accordance with the rule of law, that if the accused refuses to plead guilty or not guilty, his silence be taken as a confession of guilt. The king was brought before the court for the fourth and last time to hear his sentence read. The President had changed his black for a scarlet gown. He spoke as follows : ' Gentlemen, it is well known to all, or most of you here present, that the prisoner at the bar hath been several times brought before the court to make answer to a charge of high treason, exhibited against him in the name of the people of England——'

'It's a lie ! not one half of them. Oliver Cromwell is a traitor !' shouted a voice from one of the galleries.

A violent commotion arose in the hall ; murmurs of indignation amongst the soldiers, of applause amongst the crowd. The speaker was found to be no less a person than Lady Fairfax, and order with some difficulty having been restored, Bradshaw offered the prisoner for the last time leave to answer to his charge, before sentence was pronounced. "I desire," said the king, "to make a proposal to the Lords and Commons in the Painted Chamber, touching the peace of the kingdom and the liberty of the subject." The judges withdrew for half an hour, and on their return Bradshaw first informed the king that his proposal was rejected, and then made a long speech to justify the conduct of the Parliament, charging the king with having ruled as a tyrant, and thereby rendered resistance both a duty and necessity. "A great necessity," he said, " occasioned the calling of the Parliament, and what your designs and plots and endeavours all along have been for the crushing and confounding of this Parliament hath been very notorious to the whole kingdom; it makes me call to mind that that we read of a great Roman emperor—by-the-way, let us call him a great Roman tyrant—Caligula, that wished that the people of Rome had had but one neck, that at one blow he might cut it off. And your proceedings have been somewhat like to this, for the body of the people of England hath been represented but in the Parliament, and could you but have confounded that, you had at one blow cut off the neck of England. But God hath reserved better things for us, and hath pleased for to confound your designs and to break your forces, and to bring your person into custody that you might be responsible to justice."

The whole court stood up in sign of assent, while the clerk read the sentence, that Charles Stuart, as a tyrant, traitor, and murderer, should be put to death by the severance of the head from the body.

The king appeared deeply agitated and now tried to speak, but as he had refused to plead before the sentence was given, he was not allowed to speak after, and the judges rose and retired. The king, in the midst of vain endeavours to make himself heard, was forced down the hall by the soldiers, who shouted in his ears, 'Justice! justice!' 'Execution!' As he passed in his chair from Westminster to Whitehall, the windows, the shops, the streets, were crowded with people weeping and praying 'God to bless the king'* (Jan. 27th).

On taking leave of his two youngest children, who were still in England, Charles bade the Lady Elizabeth, a girl of twelve years old, tell her brother James it was his father's last desire that he should no longer look on Charles as his eldest brother only, but be obedient to him as his sovereign. Then taking the little Duke of Gloucester on his knee, he said to him, "Sweet heart, now they'll cut off thy father's head; mark, child, what I say, they'll cut off my head, and perhaps make thee a king; but mark what I say, you must not be king so long as your brothers Charles and James live; for they'll cut off your brothers' heads when they can catch them, and cut off thy head too at last; and, therefore, I charge you not to be made a king by them.' 'I will be torn in pieces first,' said the child weeping.† Charles kissed

* Herb., Mem., 168.
† Rushworth, vi. 604; Herbert, 180.

them both, and bade Bishop Juxon have them taken away, while he turned to the window to hide his own emotion. The next morning the king walked from St. James's to Whitehall amidst a guard of soldiers, with Juxon on one side and Col. Tomlinson on the other, talking to them on the way calmly and cheerfully. About noon he was conducted through a passage, made in the wall of the Banqueting House at Whitehall, on to the scaffold, which had been erected in the open street. Men and women who had forced their way into the hall uttered prayers in his behalf as he passed by. The soldiers throughout the whole occasion kept a deep silence, awed by the solemnity of their own act. On the scaffold, which was hung with black, stood two executioners disguised in masks. Soldiers filled the space immediately below, so that the crowded spectators beyond could hear no word the king uttered. Charles died in the firm belief in which he had lived, that in the quarrel between himself and his subjects he had been always in the right, they always in the wrong. He addressed a short, cold speech to the few assembled on the scaffold, in which he asserted this belief, and then prepared calmly to die. "Hurt not the axe," he said to a gentlemen who touched its edge while he was speaking; "that may hurt me." In the words of Marvell:

> "He nothing common did or mean
> Upon that memorable scene,
>   But with his keener eye
>   The axe's edge did try;
> Nor call'd the gods with vulgar spite
> To vindicate his helpless right;
>   But bow'd his comely head
>   Down, as upon a bed."

"I go from a corruptible to an incorruptible crown," he said to the bishop, "where no disturbance can be, no disturbance in the world." Then putting his head upon the block, he said to the executioner, "When I put out my hands this way, then — ; stay for the sign." Within a few moments the sign was given, and the executioner, holding the head up in his hand, cried to the people, "Behold the head of a traitor."

By Charles' trial two issues were decided, the king's deposition and his execution. The two issues are distinct. That a king holds office for the good of his people, and, if he perverts his power to their injury, may justly be deprived of it by their representatives, is a constitutional principle, which has been acted on in the later as well as in the earlier years of our history. Forty years after the trial and execution of Charles I., Parliament resolved that his son, King James II., having endeavoured to subvert the constitution of the kingdom by breaking the original contract between king and people, and having violated the fundamental laws, and having withdrawn himself out of the kingdom, had abdicated the government, and that the throne had thereby become vacant. The crown which the House of Stuart thus for a second time forfeited, they proceeded to bestow upon William and Mary of Orange. For a hundred years, in fact till the death of Charles Edward in 1788, that the kings ruled by a Parliamentary title was not merely a theoretical principle, but the actual basis of the settlement of the crown. It was also one of the original principles of the nation. The Saxon kings were, in fact, elected, and the principle was partly recognized that what the nation gave, it could take away; Sigeberht, Æthelred, Harthacnut were all deposed by the Witenagemot, or great council of the nation. Hereditary succession was not established as the rule in practice till the accession of Edward I. The sanction of the nation was added in doubtful cases. Nor did the Great Council, when transformed into the two Houses of Parliament, forget the use of its ultimate power of deposition. In 1327 the moral sense of the nation revolted at the conduct of its king. A bill, charging him with immorality, incapacity, cruelty, and oppression was read and admitted as a sufficient ground of deposition. By this, Parliament declared that Edward II. had ceased to reign, and bestowed the crown on his son. In 1399 thirty-three charges were read in Parliament against Richard II. The king was declared guilty on every charge, and his deposition pronounced. The scene was one which the great dramatist had made familiar to the nation. When, therefore, the court told Charles that he was responsible to the Commons of England, and was tried in the name of the people of England, they were introducing no new principle into the constitution. In such cases, the fictions of lawyers, which in ordinary times may often be useful as preventives against revolutions, are cast aside like gossamer threads, and the king, "who can do no wrong," stands arraigned as a common criminal.

If Charles then had been merely deposed by Parliament, he

would never have gained the reputation he has had as a martyr. The justice and legality of the course taken to compass his death is, however, a distinct question. His trial and execution was the work, not of a full Parliament, but of a small minority which could make no pretence of representing the people of England. To carry out their end, this minority proceeded to violent measures which only circumstances of extreme necessity could justify. They excluded members by violence from the House of Commons;* they virtually abolished the House of Lords; they passed a retrospective ordinance; and, instead of exercising their function in Parliament according to precedent, they erected a new and arbitrary court of justice.

It must, indeed, be said that a great advance had been made in the treatment of deposed kings since the fourteenth century. An arbitrary court and an *ex post facto* law are better than the secret murder which was the lot of Edward and Richard. The light of day and the presence of the chief men of the nation gave the semblance of a fair trial. Even this semblance is less debasing to the morality of the community than the sanction of murder by government. Compared with this, informalities were but a slight evil; indeed it could scarcely be expected that a constitution could provide special legal forms for the trial of the

* This great blot on the proceedings was well hit by a remonstrance addressed to Ireton. "The godly and moral jealousy, I have over you and others related to the lieutenant-general, makes me present these few lines.......Surely of all others the change of laws and government had need to be done in full Parliament. But that it may be as near as possible the act of the whole people, as many as may be should be present, lest it fails of the *esse* of *magnum consilium*, or that the absence of many by a forced or legal impediment be not judged a just impediment to proceedings. And whether this Parliament be either a free or impartial one will abide disputed at least, and if ever time shall come in which examination may be of things and present transactions in reference to this Parliament, who can tell if it may not be judged beyond the Earl of Strafford's fault, which was but arbitrary government, which is but a slighting of laws—much of this a total abolition of them?......It may, perhaps, come to be said of your many dangerous ends and extraordinary actings, as the Romans of Pompey the Great, his daughter, it was a fair and happy daughter, brought forth of an ugly and odious mother; I wish it may be so—only thus much, if you save the people of this land in the way you are in, it must be both against their wills and prayers." "This I delivered to Ireton about a fortnight before the king's trial. Signed, John Clayton." See an unpublished pamphlet among Clarendon Papers in Bodleian, entitled, "State Colours and Complections, in which are reasons against the proceedings to try the king."

chief of the State, who could never be tried except after a revolution.

On the one hand it has been said that the people had been rent asunder into two great bodies, one engaged for the king, the other for the Parliament, and that, therefore, if Charles was to be put on trial for his life at all, he ought to have been tried, not by the rules of common or statute law, but by those of international law, which obtain between foreign nations. These forbid that the victors should take the lives of the vanquished. It was, in fact, on these principles that the struggle had been maintained. Prisoners on either side had rarely been put to death as traitors, the fellow-feeling of the combatants, as well as the fear of retaliation, having prevented such cruelty. The rules of international law applied as much to the leaders as to their followers. On the other hand, it was undoubtedly true that Charles was guilty in a sense in which no other leader was guilty, and no mere general could have been. For it was his deceptions, followed as they were by the refusal of the necessary Militia Bill, that caused the war. Had he read aright the history of the past, he would have seen that the great Edward's "pactum serva" contained the whole law for a constitutional king. Charles was not punished as a combatant, but as the cause of the combat, in other words, for his previous actions as a king. As for the rights of war, the Independent leaders could scarcely have doubted that, had the cases been reversed, he would have meted the same measure to them.

The voice of the nation, however, was for clemency in the hour of their king's fall; they did not think he had committed such sanguinary crimes as justified the violation of law to accomplish his death. Thousands had fought on his side; thousands who had fought against him wished to spare his life. His enemies might plead that they were acting in self-defence; but if they counted on the king's death stopping the reaction, they greatly miscalculated. When Charles was dead, they had his son to deal with, who had not, as his father, lost the confidence of the nation.

These objections were so strongly felt at the time, that several officers, and several Republicans, stood aloof from the whole proceeding. Fairfax, Skippon, Vane, Algernon Sidney, exerted all their influence to prevent a trial for life, wishing to see the king merely deposed. On the other hand, the mass of sectarians,

Republicans, and Levellers pressed for Charles' execution as a grand and signal display of justice; one that had not its record in history, and might serve as a warning to all crowned heads for the future. Charles, according to them, had broken his coronation oath, in which he swore to govern by the laws of the land, and had thereby been the author of the civil war, and the bloodshed attendant upon it. Any accommodation was alike unsafe and wicked; unsafe, because his duplicity had been proved over and over again; wicked, because of the express words to be found in God's law, that "blood defileth the land, and the land cannot be cleansed of the blood that is shed therein, but by the blood of him that shed it."* "As for Mr. Hutchinson," says his wife, "although he was very much confirmed in his judgment concerning the cause, yet being here called to an extraordinary action, whereof many were of several minds, he addressed himself to God by prayer, desiring the Lord, that, if through any human frailty he were led into any error, He would open his eyes and not suffer him to proceed—and finding no check, he proceeded to sign the sentence against the king. Although he did not then believe but it might one day come to be again disputed among men, yet both he and others thought they could not refuse it without giving up the people of God (whom they had led forth and engaged themselves unto by oath) into the hands of God and their enemies."

Cromwell and Ireton placed themselves at the head of the movement they were powerless to prevent. There is no doubt that they sympathized in it. Only once does Cromwell allude to the execution, at least in the letters and speeches that still remain. "They," he says, "that acted this great business have given a reason of their faith in the action, and some here are ready, further, to do it against all gainsayers."† Such a decision as the Independent leaders had to make in regard to the execution of Charles I., shows what is really terrible in revolutions. It is not that men carry their lives in their hands, the soldier thinks nothing of that. It is that crises come then, when men cannot choose the good, cannot stand aside, but must choose between two evils, and see the evil of what they choose. At such a time many a man would gladly oppose both and fall; but a leader is bound to the helm, though he may see no course but to run his ship on the rocks, and drown

* Numbers xxxv. 33. † Carl. ii. 210.

some to save many. This is what is most terrible in revolutions; after the fact it is terrible to all; it is terrible at the time only to the weaker or more delicate spirits. These birds of calm are caught by the storm and drowned while doubting. Not so the real leaders of revolutions. They ride upon the storm. They see but as the lightning flashes. To them the lesser evil seems a transcendent good. Charles had hoped by his intrigues to crush Cromwell; he failed; and Cromwell thenceforth looked upon him as hopelessly false; as one who was destitute of that sense of truth between man and man, which was a necessity of political life. Such a man, if a ruler, he held, must be dealt with by banishment or by death, as an incurable evil of the commonwealth. His was a stern mind, and a mind into which an idea of privilege did not enter. There was with him no respect of persons. If he had no mercy on Lilburne's misguided Leveller, who endangered the fidelity of a regiment, he was as severe to the prince, who endangered the liberty of the country. Such a mind, intensely confident of its own sense of justice, never recoiled from its conclusion. If it could not draw back, still less could it conceal its purpose. As it abhorred secret murder, so it abhorred that lingering murder, which, while it shrinks from taking away life, shrinks not from taking away the means of life. If Charles was to die, it could not be by the lingering death Charles himself had assigned to Eliot. There was no secrecy in Cromwell's dealing with prince or private; the one was given over to martial law before the eyes of his comrades; the other was given as openly to no less stern inquisitors of blood.

The world, however, has not judged as Cromwell did. And, though on grounds of abstract justice, it is hard to say why a king deserves a mercy which he has denied to his subjects, yet many faults will be forgiven to those who have had the difficult task of governing others. Among the causes which have won an excess of sympathy for Charles, we observe the natural pity for the greatness of the fall, a disinclination to judge hardly of the fallen, but, above all, the deep-rooted sentiment of loyalty, which the restriction of prerogative has itself attached to the king, by making his throne the ideal element of the constitution, and thus so raising him above parties, that when his ministers do well, he receives the honour, when ill, he can restore, or even increase, his own popularity by ridding himself of his advisers.

Besides these general considerations, it will be remembered that the interpreter of his times for all the generations before our own, has been one who wrote in the full tide of the reaction, and who, as is now known, has not shrunk on occasion from suppressing truth, in his endeavour to palliate the faults of one side or blacken those of the other. The historian has been seconded so ably by the painter and novelist, that a Cavalier has been held the type of all that is noble, and a patriot of all that is mean. It will be noticed that the two classes by whom Charles has been most admired, have been the clergy, who may have been unconsciously biassed by a not unnatural antipathy to the religious theories of his opponents; and those whose lives have brought them least in contact with public interests: these have judged him as one of their own society, and have been carried away by the many virtues of his private life, his courage in the field, his tender nature and his piety, as well as by the noble attitude in which these qualities sustained him at his death. Those, on the other hand, who have interested themselves deeply in the cause of the people, must perforce judge public men by what they have done for the nation. In their roll of martyrs will come not Charles, who died from reluctance to abandon boldly a prerogative which had been proved to be untenable and pernicious, but Eliot, who died in defence of the necessary rights of the Commons' house, and the ransacking of whose most secret papers has only proved more clearly what was clear before, that the only ends he aimed at were his country's, his God's, and truth's. Those who look to national interests will hold that the first intellectual virtue of a ruler is an insight into the spirit of his time and the first moral virtue, a sympathy with his people's hopes and fears. As men may be too good fathers, if they use patronage as a vehicle of nepotism, so kings are too good husbands, when they give or withhold their consent to the nation's wishes according to the tempers or caprices of their wives, and too good churchmen, when they put one half of their subjects without the pale of toleration. This is not the sense in which, with kings, as with others, "England expects every man to do his duty."

CHAPTER XI.

SOCIAL STATE OF ENGLAND.

Οἶσθ' οὖν ὅτι καὶ ἀνθρώπων εἴδη τοσαῦτα ἀνάγκη τρόπων εἶναι, ὅσαπερ καὶ πολιτειῶν; ἢ οἴει ἐκ δρυός ποθεν ἢ ἐκ πέτρας τὰς πολιτείας γίγνεσθαι, ἀλλ' οὐχὶ ἐκ τῶν ἠθῶν τῶν ἐν ταῖς πόλεσιν, ἃ ἂν ὥσπερ ῥέψαντα τἆλλα ἐφελκύσηται.

You are doubtless aware that the varieties of human character must involve a corresponding number of constitutions. Or do you think that the constitutions we see are foundlings from the woods and rocks, and not the legitimate offspring of the moral dispositions of the members of each State which, so to speak, turn the scale, carrying the whole balance with them?—PLATO, REP., vii. 2.

THE population of England, now over three and twenty millions, and increasing two more every decade, numbered, in the middle of the seventeenth century, but about five and a half millions. Commerce was too insufficiently extended, too little of the soil had been brought under cultivation, too little science introduced into the processes of manufacture and agriculture, for the country to provide food or employment for a large number of inhabitants.

The largest and most important trading towns were in the southern half of the kingdom. London contained about 500,000 inhabitants, a sixth of its present population. The population of Bristol, the next place to London in size, was not 30,000. The large manufacturing towns in the north were just beginning to rise into importance. Sheffield, where knives were made, contained between 2000 and 3000 inhabitants; Leeds, a great seat of the woollen manufacture, between 3000 and 4000; 5000 or 6000 formed the population of Manchester, where cotton, imported from Cyprus and Smyrna, had been manufactured for the last thirty or forty years.

It is now acknowledged that the result of granting to persons or classes special privileges for the conduct of any trade or manufacture can only be to destroy competition and so raise prices to the injury of the consumers, for the supposed or real advantage of a few. Nor is this the whole of the evil. Wages can only come out of capital, and when capital lies idle and is checked in its natural growth by a narrowing of the market and an artificial enhancement of price, then wages are checked as well. In the seventeenth century, however, these principles were not understood, and trade was shackled by restrictions, imposed sometimes by the Executive, sometimes by the Legislature. {Trade and commerce.} The monopolies granted by Elizabeth, James I., and Charles I. were especially injurious, because the owners of each patent were so few, that they were enabled, by combining together, to force upon the consumer a bad article, and at the same time to raise its price and tax the public for their own benefit. Though the granting of monopolies was forbidden by statute law in James' last Parliament (1623), the practice was continued until the Scotch war, when Charles recalled all patents, in the hope of regaining some of the popularity he had lost. Though, in this case, the evils of interference were very clearly felt and seen, yet there was no perception of the principle that trade flourishes most when left alone ; and the interference of Parliament was often invoked to protect both producers and traders against their own countrymen and against foreigners. For instance, indigo was brought from the Indies to Europe, and was soon largely employed in the place of woad for dyeing cloth, as the dye was richer, and the process cheaper ; but when farmers, merchants, and carriers, engaged in the woad trade, found their employment decreasing, they raised a loud outcry against the new dye, saying that it injured the material of the cloth : on this the governments in England, Germany, and France forbade the use of indigo, branding it with the name of the ' Devil's dye.' An act, passed in England to this effect, under Elizabeth, remained in force until the reign of Charles II., so that the price of cloth was artificially raised, for nearly a century, through the interference of the government.

Nations, like individuals, gain by being allowed to interchange their goods freely. Each can then expend its labour and capital upon those branches of industry for which it possesses special advantages, while it has its own wants supplied at the least possible cost, by taking from other nations those products which they can supply more cheaply than itself. For these imports the nation pays by exporting, in exchange, the superfluity of its own special products. Legislators of the seventeenth century believed, however in the mercantile system, which assumed that money was wealth, and that the more money a country contained, the more prosperous it would be. Money, however, is, of course, only one form of wealth, although the medium of exchange for all other wealth. If the amount of coin in a country was doubled, and none of it allowed to quit the country, its true wealth, its corn, stock, its mineral produce, and the like, would not be doubled also. A rise of prices would result. Where one shilling had been paid before, two shillings would now have to be paid. Everybody's pocket would be heavier, but nobody would be any the richer. Governments, however, from a belief in the mercantile system, tried to prevent the importation of goods, in order to stop money from going out of the country, and encouraged their exportation, in order to bring money into the country ; and the more exports and fewer imports of a people, the more prosperous they were supposed to be. Hence it followed that nations were jealous of one another's trade, and it was thought a happy thing for England, that while she was at peace, the Continent was devastated by war, because she was likely to find fewer rivals to compete with in foreign markets. Heavy duties were laid on articles of importation, in order that the country, instead of buying them of foreigners, might, if possible, produce them at home. Such duties could only be pernicious. They compelled consumers to pay high prices ; they did not provide extra employment for Englishmen, because the same amount of labour and capital, given to industries more suited to the climate, the soil, or the character of the people, would have served to buy the protected articles from foreigners, and left a surplus over, to be employed upon further production.

During the sixteenth century, merchants trading to foreign parts had generally obtained charters from the crown, incorporating them into companies with special privileges. Thus the *Foreign trade in hands of companies.* trade with Russia was monopolized by a 'Russian Company,' incorporated in 1554 ; that with the Low Countries and Germany by the 'Merchant Adventurers,' who were incorporated as early as 1407. One company traded with Norway, Sweden, and Denmark; while the 'Turkey Company' engrossed the trade with the Levant. The fact that the members of these companies were generally Londoners, helps to explain the great size and wealth of the capital compared with other ports. In the year 1604, the sum received in the port of London for customs and imposts amounted to £110,000, while that collected from the same sources in all the rest of the kingdom only to £17,000. At the accession of James I., the French trade alone was open to merchants not members of the companies. This monopoly of the foreign trade excited great discontent among the excluded, and, in 1604, a bill to throw open foreign commerce passed the Commons, but was rejected by the Lords. An act, however, was passed in 1606, granting liberty of trade with France, Spain, and Portugal; and the Turkey Company was formed on a new footing, so that all who paid a certain subscription were allowed to become members. Commerce grew, and the long peace that lasted from the beginning of the century until the breaking out of the civil war, was so favourable to its extension, that, if the accounts of writers of the time may be believed, the progress of the present century has hardly been in a greater ratio than that which prevailed in all but the war decade.*

In the year 1600, three years before James' accession, the first charter was granted to an East India Company, 'freely and solely to trade into countries and parts of Asia, Africa, and America, beyond the Cape of Good Hope to the Straits of Magellan.' Without the licence of this company, no merchant might trade in all this sea, upon pain of forfeiting ships and cargoes. The first trading stations or factories on the coasts of India, and in the West India islands, had been established by the Portuguese. Jealous of the appearance of strangers, the Portuguese starved and imprisoned Englishmen unfortunate enough to fall into their power, and, by blocking up the river mouths, prevented English vessels from approaching the trading town of Surat, which was then the emporium of the western coast of India (1606). English captains, however, by defeating the Portuguese with a smaller number of ships, greatly impressed the natives with an idea of English courage and seamanship. The enterprise of English merchants soon made its way inland to Agra, then the seat of government of the Great Mogul, and obtained from him a charter, granting their countrymen liberty to trade. English trading stations were established in Sumatra and Java, and

* Hallam, Lit. of Europe, iii. 457.

at last, in spite of the opposition of the Portuguese, an English factory was founded at Surat (1612). In 1616, there were nine factories in India alone, one in Japan, besides many in Celebes, Borneo, and other of the East India islands. About the same time as the English, the Dutch also opened a trade with the East. The Portuguese had made themselves so detested through their cruelties, that the natives willingly joined with the newcomers in driving them from their stations. But by the time that they had quitted the field, commercial jealousy arose between the English and the Dutch. The seven united provinces of Holland, ever since they had won their independence of Spain, had prospered to such an extent, that the number and activity of their inhabitants was the marvel of every traveller. The English merchant service could not cope in number with the vessels the Dutch sent annually to France, Spain, Norway, Russia, Germany, and the East. The herring fisheries off the English coasts were mostly carried on by Dutch fishing-boats, called busses. The most valuable export of England was wool in the raw or manufactured state; but the Dutch were so much the better workmen, that they imported large quantities of wool from England, and having worked it up into cloth, made their money by selling it again to foreigners, including the English themselves. They possessed further a large carrying trade; for, having the true instinct for business, and being content with a low rate of interest, when combined with security of payment and quickness of returns, they became the carriers of Europe, buying the produce of one country and selling it to another, requiring such a small profit in addition to the original cost of the goods, that merchants of other nations did not care to compete with them.*

<small>Commercial prosperity of Holland.</small>

As the English showed a more enterprising spirit, and an intention of extending their trade, they awoke the jealousy of their neighbours in Holland. The seamen of the two nations had already come into unfriendly contact off the coast of Spitzbergen, where whale fisheries were carried on. The English, the Dutch, and the Danes, each making a preposterous claim to the

* "It cometh many times to pass," says Bacon, 'that *materiam superabit opus*'—that the work and carriage is more worth than the material, and enricheth a State more; as is notably seen in the Low Countries, who have the best mines above ground in the world."—BACON'S ESSAYS, xv.

dominion of this island and the surrounding waters, used to demand toll of all foreign vessels in return for licence to fish. It was rare, however, for the demand to be enforced, as the merchants of each nation took the precaution of sending out a fleet sufficiently strong to resist the claims of all opponents. In the East Indies, the Dutch, relying on James' well-known dislike to war, made outrageous aggressions on English merchants and traders. They drove the English out of the Molucca islands, and would have massacred them in Japan but for the interference of the natives (1619). At Amboyna, one of the Moluccas, they murdered ten Englishmen on a groundless charge of conspiracy (1623). From this time, though the two countries continued nominally at peace, constant fighting took place upon these Eastern waters between the sailors of the Dutch and English East India Companies. Little law prevailed at sea, and a merchant vessel, if a safe opportunity occurred, felt no shame in taking up the calling of a pirate. The English were finally driven from several of their settlements, and the affairs of the East India Company languished in consequence.

The principal imports from the East were silk, indigo, and spices. From Turkey, besides gems, came silk, cotton, and yarn. Coffee was first brought to England by a merchant belonging to the Turkey Company, who set up a coffee-house in Cornhill (1652). From that time coffee-houses multiplied in London, and became favourite places of resort. Tea, though commonly drunk by Europeans in Surat, was not imported to England in any quantity before the end of the century. The principal exports which England exchanged for her imports were her wool and cloth, with tin and lead.

Imports.

Exports.

In 1606 James I. had incorporated by charter two companies for the colonization of America. The one called the South Virginian Company, or London Adventurers, was authorized to colonize the territory which now forms the States of Delaware, Maryland, and Virginia; the second, or Plymouth Company, the territory which forms the modern Pennsylvania, New Jersey, New York, and New England States. Neither company was to form any settlement within a hundred miles of land previously colonized by the other. The first, or London Adventurers, indeed, set to work at once, and colonized Virginia (1607). Maryland, however, was not colonized

Colonization of North American coast.

by them, but through the exertions of Lord Baltimore, who obtained from Charles I. a charter, granting him the country to hold of the crown for himself and his heirs (1634). The Plymouth Company was simply obstructive. The earliest colonists in New England were the Pilgrim Fathers, a body of persecuted sectarians. Having obtained leave from the London Adventurers, on hard terms, to settle in Virginia, they were carried by a treacherous captain in the bleak months of winter to the coast of Massachusetts, where, fighting hard with cold, hunger, and disease, they founded Plymouth (1620). But though their endurance had conquered nature, it had still to struggle with the 'laws in defence of trade.' The fact that the original Plymouth Company had never succeeded in founding a single colony did not impair its exclusive rights; and, without the consent of that company, "not a ship might sail into a harbour from Newfoundland to the latitude of Philadelphia; not a skin might be purchased in the interior; not a fish caught on the coast; not an emigrant tread the soil."* In 1624, the company was fiercely assailed in the House of Commons. "Your patent," said Coke, to one of its members, "is a monopoly; and the ends of private gain are concealed under colour of planting a colony. . . . Shall none visit the sea-coast for fishing? This is to make a monopoly upon the seas, which wont to be free. If you alone are to pack and dry fish, you attempt a monopoly of wind and sun." On the coast of Maine private adventurers were soon emboldened to plant fishing stations, which gradually ripened into colonies. The company, however, so far maintained its exclusive privileges, that it used to sell patents to individuals and companies, authorizing them to colonize vast tracts of country. Thus Charlestown was founded in 1628. A company bought Massachusetts and founded Salem (1629). Connecticut was colonized from Massachusetts (1636). By the middle of the century, the whole line of coast reaching from Newfoundland to Florida, and many of the West India islands, were studded with settlements. The principal imports from these colonies were tobacco, grain, and fish.

The influx of wealth from these extensions of trade was enormous; but though wealth, where it falls on worthy shoulders,

* Bancroft, Hist. Am. i.

brings refinement, in many it breeds mere luxury and ostentation. There was immense extravagance in dress and style of living; this was especially displayed in London, before the ascendancy of the Presbyterians. Ladies, while they followed the fashions in wearing paint and patches upon their faces, vied with one another in the amount of gold they could show broidered on their silks and satins. Gentlemen would

> 'Wear a farm in shoe-strings edged with gold,
> And spangled garters worth a copyhold;
> A hose and doublet which a lordship cost;
> A gaudy cloak, three manors' price almost;
> A beaver band and feather for the head,
> Prized at the Church's tithe—the poor man's bread.'*

The costume was picturesque enough. A broad-brimmed beaver hat, adorned with feathers; the long and curling hair shown off by a lace collar; a doublet of silk or satin, with slashed sleeves; a short cloak hanging over one shoulder; breeches reaching to the knee, and finished off with ribands; silk stockings and shoes adorned with rosettes; a sword-belt, with weapon attached; and the whole set off with jewels and gold lace.

In many the leisure which wealth gave was well employed. Intellectual activity, a love of music and of art, a spirit of enterprise and research, distinguished the upper and educated classes of society. Sir John Eliot's previous studies enabled him to employ his years of captivity in writing a philosophical treatise. At that 'college situated in purer air,' as Hyde called Lord Falkland's house near Oxford, men, who afterwards took different sides in the war, used to meet and discuss their different opinions, whether scientific or social, political or religious, with the happy freedom of friendly intercourse. Sir Robert Cotton formed an antiquarian and historical library, whence the popular leaders drew stores of precedents on which to base their defence of their country's liberties, in their struggle with the prerogative. On a trivial excuse, Sir Robert was imprisoned by order of the Council, and his library put under lock and key. "I went several times to visit and comfort him," wrote one of his friends in the year 1630. "He would tell me they had broken his heart that had locked up his

Upper classes cultivated.

* The Water Poet (temp. Charles I.)

library from him." He remained in prison for several months, and died in the spring of the following year (1631). Though men such as Falkland, Eliot, and Cotton were the élite of their class, they were also its representatives. Noblemen and gentlemen commonly made collections of pictures, antiquities, ancient armour, bronzes, and medals; and took interest in scientific discoveries. The barometer, the microscope, the telescope, were all instruments newly invented. Glamorgan, Charles' agent in Ireland, was renowned for his mechanical skill. In love of art, Charles was at one with some of the first of his enemies. He made a fine collection of pictures, medals, and curiosities of all kinds, and treated English and foreign artists liberally. Rubens, who was sent to Charles as the Spanish king's envoy, painted for him the ceiling of the Banqueting House at Whitehall, built by Inigo Jones for James I. Vandyke passed the best years of his life in England; and though Charles' weakness may be read in eyes and mouth on his canvas, yet the painter has done much to foster the ideal conception of the cavalier-king. Walker, an English painter, has left several portraits of Cromwell. But love of knowledge, of art, of antiquities, would never have created the greatness which shone out in the English character during the great rebellion. The enterprise and patriotism of the Elizabethan age remained unimpaired, and was spiritualized by religion. Except the courtiers, all classes, lettered and unlettered, seemed inspired by fulness of belief and earnestness of purpose. Men were unselfish and faithful, ready to risk fortune and life in their cause. Hence the first New England colonies struggled into existence through a terrible ordeal of cold and want. Hence the appearance of men with the heroic qualities of Eliot, Hampden, Pym, Vane, and Cromwell, rising up one after another, to lead the way in defence of liberty. Hence the devotion with which the perilous cause of the Parliament was embraced by thousands, while the result of the war was yet doubtful; and the unquenched hope with which Cavaliers met the ruin of themselves and their families, clinging to the cause of their master after all was lost.

Puritan tradesmen and yeomen had played a leading part in accomplishing the overthrow of the government of Church and State. These denounced the pursuit of pleasure as vanity, if not actual sin. Discarding jewels, lace, silks, and satins, they dressed themselves in plain black suits, long black cloaks, and high steeple-crowned hats. Many went so far as to exclaim against music, art, and profane learning, as temptations of the devil, that divert the thoughts from God. Yet their fanaticism, however exaggerated, had its apology in the exaggeration of the opposite principles, as well as in the grandeur of the religious movement from which their feelings sprang. The character of the stage had been deteriorating ever since the death of Elizabeth. The plays of Beaumont, Fletcher, and Massinger, were far coarser in language and spirit than those of the earlier dramatists, and, from their low moral tone and the character of their plots, were but too often calculated to make the theatre a school of vice. The courtiers of James I. and Charles I., amongst the most constant of play-goers, were not only absurdly extravagant in their dress, but often outrageously profligate in their lives. The latest historian of English literature observes how at this period of the stage, 'the noble chivalric paganism' of the sixteenth century had degenerated into 'a base and coarse sensuality.' Elizabeth's old courtiers, though by no means straitlaced, were astounded at the licence of James' court. Sir John Harrington thus describes an entertainment given by James in honour of the King of Denmark. "The ladies abandon their sobriety, and are seen to roll about in intoxication. . . . The lady who did play the queen's part (in the masque of the Queen of Sheba) did carry most precious gifts to both their majesties; but, forgetting the steps arising to the canopy, overset her caskets into his Danish Majesty's lap and fell at his feet, though I rather think it was in his face. Much was the hurry and confusion; cloths and napkins were at hand to make all clean. His Majesty then got up and would dance with the Queen of Sheba; but he fell down and humbled himself before her, and was carried to an inner chamber and laid on a bed of state, which was not a little defiled with the presents of the Queen, which had been bestowed on his garments; such as wine, cream, jelly, beverage, cakes, spices, and other good matters. . . . . Now did appear in rich dress Hope, Faith, and Charity; Hope did essay to speak, but wine rendered her endeavours so feeble that she withdrew and hoped the king would excuse her brevity; Faith left the court in a staggering condition. Next came Victory, who after much lamentable utterance, was led away like a silly captive, and laid to sleep on the outer steps of the ante-chamber. As for Peace, she most rudely made war with her olive branch, and laid on the pates of those who did oppose her coming. I ne'er did see such lack of good order, discretion, and sobriety in our queen's days."* Though Charles himself was not addicted to the coarser vices, and required the forms of propriety to be observed in his court, he had no such hatred of vice as to cause him to select his friends or companions from amongst men of pure lives. Neither Buckingham, the king's favourite, nor Lord Jermyn, the queen's favourite, made the least pretence to purity of morals.† The example of courtiers had its weight in influencing the conduct of the classes beneath them. Gentlemen from the country came up to London and ruined themselves in trying to keep pace with a fashionable life. Idlers of all ranks spent their days drinking, smoking, and gambling in taverns. When such was the order of the day amongst the pleasure-seeking classes of society, it was no matter of wonder that, by a revulsion of feeling, the more earnest amongst the uneducated should seek refuge from vice in austerity of life, and that amusements, constantly abused, should come to be regarded as wicked and demoralizing in themselves. It was a noble disgust at whatever was really lowering to human nature, that led the Puritans into the error of trying to suppress vice by discountenancing games and sports that had delighted many generations of Englishmen. Thus it was that theatrical exhibitions of all kinds were put down by ordinance of Parliament; spectators were ordered to be fined; actors to be whipped at the cart's tail. The dance round the maypole, the wrestling match on the village green, were proscribed. Christmas-day, kept from time immemorial as a feast, was turned into a solemn fast. Music and art had been taken into the service both of Laud's Church and of levity; they were therefore regarded as accessories to the spread of Popish superstitions and laxity of life, and against them a like war was waged. Paintings and sculptures were removed from churches, and organs were forbidden. Though, in

Margin notes: Immorality amongst upper classes generated fanatics amongst lower.

---

* Nugæ Antiquæ, i. 349, apud Taine, II. i. 3.
† Jermyn debauched Lord Grandison's sister, Miss Villiers; this incident was important, as it first led Hyde, a connection of the lady, into a correspondence with the king, whom Hyde tried to get to act firmly in the matter. Such misconduct, however, in no way impaired Jermyn's influence with the queen, who not only supported him against the king at home, but afterwards kept him by her as her constant companion abroad.—LISTER'S LIFE OF CLARENDON.

many cases, the ravages done by time. war, spoliation, and neglect have been unfairly put down to the Puritans, yet in others there is little doubt that works of art which had been spared for their beauty and antiquity at the Reformation, were now wantonly defaced and destroyed by the ignorant and fanatical soldiers who fought in the armies of the Commonwealth. It would be unfair, however, to class all Puritans together as holding upon these points the same opinions. Like other great religious movements, Puritanism, beginning with the people, spread upwards, and in its course became subject to the influences of education and class feeling. Hence there were numbers of Puritan gentlemen, whose minds knowledge had rendered too liberal, or in whom the pride of birth was too strong to allow them to adopt the habits, language, and ideas of their more ignorant and fanatical companions. Rembrandt's etching of the Dutch Anabaptist minister shows a face by no means wanting in intelligence, refinement, and capacity for enjoyment of life. Mrs. Hutchinson's description of her husband, an Anabaptist officer, presents us with a picture of the Puritan English gentleman, as he appeared at the time when Puritanism was most in repute :—" He could dance admirably well, but neither in youth nor riper years made any practice of it ; he had skill in fencing, such as became a gentleman ; he had a great love of music, and often diverted himself with a viol, on which he played masterly ; he shot excellently in bows and guns, and much used them for his exercise ; he had great judgment in paintings, gravings, sculpture, and all liberal arts, and had many curiosities of value in all kinds ; he took much pleasure in planting groves and walks and fruit-trees ; he left off very early the wearing of anything that was costly, yet in his plainest negligent habit appeared very much a gentleman : upon occasions, though never without just ones, he would be very angry, yet he was never outrageous in passion. He hated persecution for religion, and detested all scoffs at any practice of worship, though such a one as he was not persuaded of it. Wherever he saw wisdom, learning, or other virtues in men, he honoured them highly. His conversation was very pleasant, for he was naturally cheerful. Scurrilous discourse even among men he abhorred. His whole life was the rule of temperance in meat, drink, apparel, pleasure." Milton, the poet of the Puritans, was a Hebrew, Greek, Latin, Syriac, and Italian scholar. Fairfax and Cromwell both gave manuscripts and books to the newly-founded Bodleian Library at Oxford. The Presbyterians, indeed, during their ascendancy, passed an order in Parliament, that all superstitious pictures in the king's collections should be burnt, the remainder sold. For the sale the Parliament has received more censure than it perhaps deserves. Charles himself would no doubt have denied that his valuable collection was in any sense the nation's property; but, in the year 1643, when the exigencies of the war were very great, it was hardly to be expected that the Parliament should hesitate to confiscate and sell the king's movables, more than those of any minor delinquent. It is said that Cromwell, on becoming Protector, tried to keep the remainder of the collection together, and put a stop to the sales.* Nor was this the only point in which his largeness of mind made him tread in opposite footsteps to the Presbyterians. Though unable to obtain the repeal of persecuting laws, yet when the executive came to lie in his own hand he often suffered them to be broken with impunity. Himself a lover of music, he placed an organ in the palace at Hampton Court, where he often retired for Sunday. Plays, written by Sir William Davenant, were performed at the cockpit in Drury Lane (1658), while strolling players again acted at country places, and in the houses of the nobility.†

Much of the savage violence of the middle ages still remained in the midst of the increased refinements of life that wealth and knowledge were bringing in their train. The custom of society did not require that the smallest effort should be made to control passion. Every gentleman wore his sword by his side, and was ready to draw it on provocation, and it was no uncommon occurrence for a man to be wounded in the presence of ladies in consequence of some drunken brawl. Amusements were cruel; bull-baiting, bear-baiting, and cock-fighting delighted all classes in town and country, till they were suppressed by Cromwell. The greatest subsequent advance of morality and refinement has been in this question of cruelty. There was then a general callousness to the sight of pain. The humanity of those who have signalized our own age by carrying laws to check the ill-treatment of animals, would then have had first to check the brutalizing

* Harris, Life of Cromwell.
† Evelyn, 198, 261; Chambers, 569, 599.

punishments which the law itself inflicted on men. The sight of human beings in torment failed to awaken feelings of indignation or of pain sufficiently strong to cause a reform of the criminal law. Women who had murdered their husbands were burned alive in Smithfield. Men were yearly hung by hundreds for paltry thefts. Prisoners were so neglected that they often died of disease and starvation before the time of their trial came on. Town and county gaols were miserable and filthy dens unfit for the habitation of man or beast. In the following century, Howard thus describes the gaol for the county of Cornwall at Launceston : "The prison is a room or passage 23½ feet by 7½ feet, with only one window 2 feet by 1½ ; and three dungeons or cages on the side opposite the window ; these are about 6½ feet deep, one 9 feet long, one about 8 feet, one not five feet ; the last for women. They are all very offensive ; no chimney, no water, no sewers, damp earth floors, no infirmary. The court not secure, and prisoners seldom permitted to go out into it. Indeed, the whole prison is out of repair, and yet the gaoler lives distant. I once found the prisoners chained two or three together. Their provisions were put down to them through a hole (9 inches by 8) in the floor of the room above, and those who served them often caught the fatal fever. I found the keeper, his assistant, and one prisoner all sick of it, and heard that a few years before many prisoners had died of it, and the keeper and his wife in one night." Though dungeons and fetters were, as a rule, reserved for felons, debtors were in some respects worse off than the highwayman, the housebreaker, and the murderer. To these last it was usual to allow a pennyworth or two-pennyworth of bread a day, but debtors and other offenders guilty of no criminal, often of no moral, offence were left to provide entirely for their own sustenance. In the London prisons a wealthy man, such as Sir John Eliot, by paying high fees could provide himself with the luxury of a bed and a separate room, but the ordinary prisoner slept on the floor in the common apartment, thankful if he could obtain of his keeper a little straw at a reasonable rate. As a rule, keepers and gaolers received no salaries, but made fortunes on the fees they extorted from prisoners. Men might be confined in prison for months, and then acquitted at the assizes, and, after acquittal, were still liable to be dragged back again and locked up because unable or unwilling to pay the exorbitant fees demanded. It was not seldom that the sufferings of the prison inmates were avenged in a fearful way. "The most pernicious infection," says Bacon, "next the plague, is the smell of the gaol where the prisoners have been long and close and nastily kept, whereof we have had in our time experience twice or thrice, when both the judges that sat upon the gaol and numbers of those who attended the business, sickened upon it and died." Between the years 1573 and 1579, 100 prisoners died in the King's Bench of 'a certain contagion called the sickness of the house.' Without knowledge of what the prison was, it is not possible fully to appreciate the cruelty of the sentences of the Star Chamber, nor yet the heroism of those who accepted an imprisonment of indefinite length, rather than pay an illegal fine. When this Court ordered Lilburne to be 'laid alone, with irons on his hands and legs, in the wards of the Fleet, where the meanest sort of the prisoners are put,' and forbade any to resort to him or give him money, the sentence was nothing short of a lingering death by disease and starvation. If it had been literally carried out for many months, the prisoner must have died.*

Credulity and ignorance walking, as they do, hand in hand, added to the cruelty of the age. Knowledge had not spread far enough to free the minds of men of a load of superstitious beliefs, handed down to them by their forefathers. The cavalier, afraid of no enemy in the field, would forebode evil to himself when a hare crossed his path, or the salt was overset. The clergyman of every parish was ready to exorcise the possessed. Ladies hung round the necks of the sick a charm, such as 'a spider in a nutshell lapped in silk,' with full belief in its efficacy to effect a cure. A belief in such amulets inspired hope, and probably saved many from falling by the hands of the country doctors of the time. An eclipse of the sun was so dreaded that hardly any would work or turn out of their doors for the day. During the war, astrologers on both sides published almanacs, foretelling events. King James prided himself on his learning in this subject,

---

* Though a committee of Parliament was appointed to investigate the state of prisons in 1729, no reforms were made for another half century. In 1773 John Howard began his tour of inspection. He lived to see many reforms introduced, both in the condition of prisons and the treatment of prisoners, the results of his own noble efforts.

and had an old woman tortured and put to death in Scotland, for raising a storm as he came from Denmark. He afterwards wrote a book on purpose to support the common belief in witchcraft; and in the second year of his reign a law was passed, making it felony to consult or employ any evil spirit. On one occasion at the Lancashire assizes nineteen witches were arraigned, and ten executed. The history of the witchcraft laws is the strongest homily on the necessity of diffusing such an education as will stimulate the intellect to independent thought. The vagaries of independent thought may be corrected by the conflict of minds, but bigotry with its narrow zeal cramps the development of all, while it deals murder or terror broadcast. Any withered decrepit old woman was liable to be at once feared and abused by her neighbours as a witch. Perhaps in her irritation she might curse "sometimes one, sometimes another, and that from the master of the house, his wife and children, to the little pig that lyeth in the sty;" then, did a sick cow die, she had bewitched it; did a child languish, she was causing its death, for she had been seen by one of her neighbours with a clay or waxen image of the child in her hands. Such proofs of witchcraft were quite sufficient to convince a jury that the accused was guilty. Men conceived that because an object was disagreeable and revolting to the eye, it must therefore have a sinister influence on their fortunes, just as conversely the beautiful wise women of the Norsemen were held to have a beneficial power. It was the common fallacy of inferring facts from feelings--of judging that there was necessarily some reality in nature corresponding to a feeling in the mind. Special delusions arise, when men shut themselves up in some little world of their own, and the conceptions of the Puritans made them peculiarly liable to this error. During their ascendancy, hundreds suffered death for witchcraft, for just as they believed in special providences for good, that is in God's continual interference with the ordinary course of the world for the support of His servants, so they believed in the immediate interposition of Satan with horn and hoof, and would as soon have denied the power of one man to make an agreement with another, as that of man or woman to form a compact with the devil. A common ordeal was to prick the witch with pins and needles, to find out if the devil had rendered any spot insensible : another was to throw her into a pond, and if she did not sink, it was held a clear proof that she was rejected by the baptismal element. In one year of the Presbyterian domination fourteen witches were found in a village of fourteen families, and twenty more were selected for burning in a place near.* About the same time, a man, by name Hopkins, travelled through the eastern counties in the character of a witch-finder, and caused sixty persons to be hung in Suffolk alone. His career at last was stopped short by some magistrate, who, wiser than his fellows, set the villain himself to the swimming ordeal. The belief in witchcraft was universal in Europe at the time. If a judge had no belief in witchcraft, he was obliged to conceal his opinion on the Bench, as otherwise the jury would have set him down as a man of no religion, and declared the accused guilty forthwith.†

Though the social system of the country showed a painful contrast between boundless wealth and hopeless poverty, and though the laws of debt and of trade caused a needless amount of misery, yet as compared with previous times, the barriers of privilege were not so unrelaxing, the lines between classes were not so hardly drawn. The Procrustean arrangement of the feudal system had long been gradually modified. The revolutionary spirit now tried to eliminate it from the law. The gentry were, in fact, eager themselves to change an honourable but irksome tenure into one that they had once looked upon as inferior, but the freedom of which they had now long coveted. The Long Parliament passed a resolution for the removal of feudal tenure (24th Feb.). Cromwell, when Protector, passed an Act of Parliament to the same effect. After the restoration, Cromwell's acts were held invalid, but Charles II. gave his consent to a similar act, converting feudal tenure into common socage. The king was then, indeed, not merely a nominal landlord. Feudal tenants had to pay him fines before entering upon their estates. If the heirs were minors he appropriated their rents until they came of age. A female ward was required to marry any person of suitable rank, proposed by the sovereign, under penalty of paying a heavy fine ; in fact this was one of the perquisites of favourites. Fines

---

* Whitelock, Mem., 450.
† Roger North, Life of Lord Guildford • Somers, iii.; Trial of Lancashire Witches.

were exacted when the sovereign's eldest son was knighted or his eldest daughter married.

The chief sources of the wealth of the nobles and richer gentry were the rents received from their tenantry and the wool of their sheep, which browsed by thousands on heaths and pasture lands. Their houses were large and commodious. Stag heads, muskets, swords, and coats of armour decorated the sides of their halls. The walls of their sitting-rooms were often painted with figures, hunting landscapes, or curious designs; tables, chairs, and cabinets, were richly carved. In the dining-room, the substitution of forks for fingers in eating was a notable advance in refinement. There were displays of plate for ornament, as well as for use. The households of some of the chief nobility consisted of as many as two hundred persons. At the Duke of Beaufort's house at Badminton, soap, candles, beer, and beds were all home-made. Outside their mansions the owners formed terraces, bowling-alleys, and tennis-courts, planted groves of elms, oaks, and walnuts, and enclosed large parks, which they stocked with deer. They laid out gardens adorned with statues, fountains, and aviaries, and cultivated what were then rare flowers and fruits—lilies, roses, cherries, pomegranates, and grapes. The eldest son inherited his father's dignities and estates. The younger passed into other employments, became barristers or merchants, held office at court, or sought their fortunes in foreign service. The girls were educated at home, and learnt, besides their letters, music, dancing, and painting.*

The ordinary country gentleman held land by knights' service of some superior lord, or of the crown. He lived the life of a farmer, looking after his corn and pigs and sheep. He seldom left his county, and a journey to London would be a leading event in his life. Besides cock-fighting and bull-baiting, hunting was his chief amusement. His table was plentifully supplied, and he was generally hospitable to his poorer neighbours. Sheep and cattle could not be fattened, as clover and turnips were not grown until the beginning of the next century, so that in winter time his fare consisted mainly of salted meat, fish, wild fowl, and rabbits. If he was justice of the peace, he had half the business of the parish upon his hands; to see that the peace was kept; to set children

* Life of Lord North; Beesley, Hist. of Banbury; Cullum, Hist. of Hawsted; Evelyn, Diary.

found growing up idle to work; to receive the accounts of the overseers of paupers; to punish rogues and vagabonds. But as in the army and the Parliament, so in the country parish, new men had risen into importance; and now, perhaps, some yeoman or Roundhead tradesman, a buyer of bishops' lands, was justice of the peace, in place of the Royalist knight or squire, who, having fought for King Charles, had been obliged to compound for his estate, and returned to his home to find himself a comparatively poor and uninfluential man. This was felt bitterly, for the Cavaliers who swelled Charles' armies, though not refined over their cups or in their amusements, were as proud of their descent as the greatest noble in the land. The children learnt their letters at home, or at the village school, some "little house by the churchyard side." The eldest son inherited his father's land; the younger became merchants, lawyers, sailors, and clergymen. The daughters, though getting a share of what education there was, for all that, often could barely read and write, but were brought up to be good housewives, to manage a dairy, to bake, to brew, to distil water from flowers and plants.

Small farmers, or freeholders, were numerous and independent. It was common for yeomen holding land by free socage* tenure to possess £40 or £50 a year. Of these petty proprietors, who farmed their few acres with their own hands, there were reported to be 180,000, a large proportion out of a population of 5,500,000. Their sons became tradesmen and lawyers, or entered the church. Sometimes very distinguished men rose out of their ranks. Thus the father of Selden, the lawyer and great Hebrew scholar, is said to have been a yeoman worth about £40 a year. The sectarian army, which conquered the Cavaliers, was mainly recruited from freeholders and their sons. Small farmers, proprietors of the soil, who once played this important part in English history, can no longer be said to exist as a class, large farms and hired labour having taken their place in the economy of the country. For more than a century preceding the time of the civil war, their
Decrease in numbers had been slowly decreasing. The demand for
numbers of small farmers. English wool in foreign parts was constantly rising, so that to keep sheep became a more profitable occupation than to grow corn. To convert arable into pasture land, landed proprietors would sometimes employ fraud, menace, or

* See p. 2.

actual violence, in order to dispossess the small farmers of their Naboth's vineyards. Whether these small farmers were tenants holding land for life or a stated number of years, or were copyholders, or even freeholders, it was no easy matter for the owner of a few acres to withstand the 'little tyrant of the fields,' who might possibly be justice of the peace, or even lord lieutenant of his county.

The following is an instance of landlord oppression in the reign of Charles I. :—Sir Edward Bullock, wishing to enclose land in Norfolk, informed his tenant, Blackhall, that unless he would consent to sell his lands and yield up his leases, he should be made to 'run the country.' Blackhall, in consequence of his refusal to part with his property, found his hedges broken down, his gates opened, and himself sued at law for trespass, because his cattle had strayed out upon the common. The verdict was given against Sir Edward, who vowed to be revenged upon Blackhall's witnesses. He caused the house of one to be pulled down, so that the owner's wife and children passed two nights in the streets, for nobody dared take them in; and they "being afterwards by a justice's direction received into a house, Sir Edward so threatened the owner, that he turned them out of doors, and all the winter they lay in an outhouse, without fire, so that the witness himself, his wife, and one child died." He caused a second witness, a woman, to be so beaten, that she could not put on her clothes for a month afterwards. The Star Chamber fined Sir Edward £1000 damages to the king, and £100 damages to Blackhall, 'out of which something was to be given to the children of the man whose house was pulled down.'* After such a tale of wrong, it is cheering to find that substantial justice was done, even by the Star Chamber, though it may be said that now the offences would receive a much severer punishment than a fine, and that the records of the court show it was only too glad to fine any rich man, as a means of recouping the exchequer, when the king had dispensed with Parliaments.

Although villeinage had long died out in England, and had been suppressed even in the western counties before the latter part of Elizabeth's reign (1574), the condition of the hired labourer was such, that, from a modern point of view, he could not fairly be called a free man. His employers, the landowners, passed

* Rushworth, Abr., ii., 191.

laws which kept him in a state of half-bondage to themselves. His wages were fixed by the justices of the peace, according to the price of food. If he refused to work at the wages offered, or went out of his county in search of higher wages, he became in the eye of the law a rogue and vagabond. The laws against such were exceedingly severe. Any person for the first time found 'wandering or roguing about,' was to be whipped on his naked back until his body was bloody, and then sent from parish to parish straightway to the place of his birth; or, if this was not known, then to 'the parish where he last dwelt for the space of a year (49th Eliz., 1597). "Poor Tom," says Edgar, in *King Lear*, when he plays the madman, "who is whipped from tything to tything, and stocked and punished and imprisoned." In order that the vagrant might be recognized, he was to be branded on the left shoulder with the letter R, and if a second time found begging or wandering about was to be adjudged a felon and hanged (2nd James I., 1604). This barbarous law, though probably not often enforced to its whole extent, was quite in keeping with the criminal legislation of the time, which condemned the thief, who stole any article above ten shillings in value, to die as a felon on the gallows.

Before the sixteenth century lords had naturally been expected to provide for the old age of their villeins, whose lives had been spent for their profit. But after villeinage became extinct, private charity was not openhanded enough to maintain the impotent poor, and the Government found it necessary to legislate in their favour. During the sixteenth century, the earliest of the poor-laws were passed. Statutes of Henry VIII. empower the justices of the peace to give licenses to impotent persons to beg within certain limits, and also order collections for the relief of the poor to be made in church on Sundays and holidays (22nd, 27th Henry VIII.). In the reign of Elizabeth, laws were passed, rendering these alms compulsory, and appointing in every parish overseers of the poor. These overseers were to consist of the churchwardens, together with three or four householders, to be appointed by the justices of the peace. The justices of the peace were further ordered to build houses of correction in waste places, where the impotent might be maintained, and the strong found idling or out of employ be set to work (5th, 43rd, 49th Eliz.). No means, however, were taken to see that these statutes were put into force; wanderers were branded, but workhouses were not built. "I have heard rogues and vagabonds," says a pamphlet writer, "curse the magistrates to their faces, for providing such a law to whip and brand them, when no place is provided to set them to work." These complaints were not ill-founded; and, in 1610, a statute was passed, that justices of the peace who neglected to build houses of correction should be fined £5 each. James I., in alarm at the beggars in London, usurped the legislative power, and issued a proclamation to the effect, that as rogues grew to be dangerous to himself and his court, they were to be banished to Newfoundland, the East and West Indies, Spain, or the Low Countries. Though the poor laws of Elizabeth and James do not forbid the labourer to remove from the place of his birth, they practically prevent migration by classing the man who is without a master, or refuses to work at the wages offered, under the same category as rogues and vagabonds. The Law of Settlement, passed immediately after the Restoration, actually bound the labourers to the soil (1662). It enacted that if any person came to settle in a parish and occupied a tenement under the yearly value of £10, the justices of the peace should have power to remove him back to the parish where he was last settled for the space of forty days. Roger North, writing in 1688, thus described the fatal effects of this pernicious law. "Surely, it is a great imprisonment, if not slavery, to a poor family to be under restraint by law, that they must always live in one place, whether they have friends, kindred, employment, or not. Such persons, if they had spirits, have no encouragement to aspire to a better condition, since being born poor and in a place which gives no means to be otherwise, they are not allowed to go and search it elsewhere; and if they find it, they are not permitted to entertain it. Then their spirits sink, and they fall into a sottish way of living, depend on the parish, who must however wretchedly maintain them." Two motives prevented the repeal of a law which was thus early allowed by intelligent men to be injurious—the one, the selfish desire of employers of labour to force the labourers to take work at the wages offered; the other, the selfish desire of ratepayers to limit as far as possible the number of poor in their own parish.* In the reigns of James and

* The law, having thus forbidden the labourer to move from his parish to seek work for himself, was compelled to provide for him. If the over-

Charles I., a labourer generally received from eightpence to one shilling a day, or from four shillings to six shillings a week, without board. As, however, four shillings then would buy as much as fourteen now, his living was not inferior to that of many agricultural labourers at the present time. So much land, moreover, still remained unenclosed, that he probably possessed a bit of garden-ground attached to his cottage, and fed his cow, or pig, or flock of geese, on the neighbouring common. His ordinary fare was rye-bread, barley-meal, onions, carrots, bacon, and beer. Vegetables common now, were then rarities. Potatoes, first brought from America by Hawkins, Drake, and Raleigh, sold at two shillings a pound. Articles of clothing, candles, salt, sugar, and wheaten bread, were all much dearer than they now are, though meat and beer were much cheaper. The wages of artificers and those engaged in manufactures were also fixed by the justices of the peace; and generally ranged at about one shilling a day. At Kidderminster there were few beggars, the common trade of stuff-weaving providing work for men, women, and children. 'But none were very wealthy, as the wages only served to provide food and raiment.'*

seers could not find him full employment, they were required to make up any deficiency in wages out of rates. In consequence of this system, farmers purposely underpaid their labourers, knowing the parish could not refuse relief, while the labourers themselves were deprived of any motive for self-exertion. As the overseers were not appointed by the ratepayers, there was no check upon the expenditure, and the poor-rates rose with extraordinary rapidity. In 1760, the population was 7,000,000; the rates were £1,250,000. In 1834, the population had rather more than doubled, being 14,372,000, the poor-rates had increased by more than five times, £6,317,235. In 1834, the Reformed Parliament passed the Poor Law Amendment Act. A central authority was created—a board of three commissioners, with power to regulate the administration of relief throughout England and Wales. Parishes were united into unions, directed by boards of guardians, of whom the majority were elected by the ratepayers. The commissioners put an end to the allowance system, only granting outdoor relief to the able-bodied poor in exceptional cases. This Act made no alteration in the Law of Settlement. The 35th George III. had already prohibited the removal from a parish of any newcomer, until he should have become actually chargeable (1795). The 9th and 10th Victoria prohibits the removal of any person who shall have resided five years in a parish without being chargeable. The 11th and 12th Vict. relieves the parish of the cost of maintaining persons who have so become chargeable, and lays it on the common fund of the union. The continuance of the Laws of Settlement to the present time is consequent upon the principle, that every parish, however poor itself, is bound to relieve its own poor. The entire abolition of these is still required, as well as the universal substitution of union instead of parochial chargeability; and, where necessary, an equalization of the poor-rates over wider areas than a single union presents.— NICHOLLS ON THE POOR LAWS. CHITTY'S STATUTES.

* Baxter's Life, 33.

Some of the master workmen got one shilling and eightpence a day. There were no large factories, as little machinery had been introduced, but weaving and other manufacturing processes were carried on in the poor people's homes by hand labour. Though the table of wages of the seventeenth century may not compare unfavourably with that of the nineteenth, in other respects a great improvement has taken place in the material condition of the working classes. In the seventeenth century the ravages of fire, disease, and famine often inflicted a greater amount of suffering than a war would now bring upon the country. Destructive fires took place periodically in most towns, for the houses were all of wood, and there were no appliances at hand with which to quench the flames. Whether the town were wholly or partially destroyed depended principally upon the direction of the wind at the time of the breaking out of the fire. Owing to an utter neglect of the laws of health, villages and towns were subject to the visitation of frightful plagues and diseases, for which no remedies were known. At such times the deaths in London would increase by several thousands a week.* Famines were common in England then, for the same reasons as they are now in India. The badness of the roads prevented any rapid communication from one part of the country to another, so that the people in Yorkshire might be near starving from lack of bread, while those in Kent possessed a superfluity of corn. It was customary to travel with a coach and four horses, not from ideas of grandeur or speed, but because otherwise there was no chance of getting through the bogs. Often a coach would be six or eight hours in going a distance of twelve miles. An overset was not the worst danger that might befall the traveller. He sometimes had to pass through gloomy forests and over far-stretching heaths without seeing a single enclosed field for a distance of forty or even fifty miles, and under these circumstances, it was a lucky chance if he came to his journey's end without being stopped by a band of highwaymen and robbed of money and goods. At the close of the civil war, many Cavaliers, finding they had ruined themselves in the service of the king, took to

Highwaymen.

* The deaths from plague in London were:—
 11,503 in 1592   35,428 in 1625   12,102 in 1636
 30,583 in 1603   1,317 in 1630   2,876 in 1637
                                   STATE PAPERS, 1667.

the road, and ended their lives on the gallows. Thus, in 1656, a notable highwayman was secured, the chief of a company which had robbed the carrier of York of £1500. "And it is reported," says the newspaper, "that he and his companions have, in little more than a twelvemonth's time, robbed to the value of £11,000; [and have taken] so great sums of money at a time, that, instead of telling it, they shared it by the quart pot."*

Post-office. Charles was the first to establish a post-office, to carry letters between London, Edinburgh, Chester, Holyhead, and other towns. The charge was twopence a letter on any distance under eighty miles. During the war, the post fell into disuse, but was re-established on the return of peace.

London itself was the centre of trade, wealth, and inte'ligence. It was, as it still is, a chartered or self-governed town. The city was Corporation divided into twenty-six wards. The householders or of London. freemen of every ward elected the members of a common council, which formed the legislative body of the corporation, making bye-laws and police regulations to be of force within the city boundaries. The aldermen were also elected by the householders, and these with the lord mayor were the principal magistrates. In the Old Bailey they had an independent criminal court for the trial of treasons, murders, and felonies, committed within the city of London and the County of Middlesex. The independence and power of the city have been shown in the previous history. The Guildhall was the asylum of the five members of the Parliament. Without the support of the corporation, that is to say, of freemen, common council, and city aldermen, the Parliament could never have commenced the war with the king; at a later hour, when the corporation went with the Presbyterians for the king, the Independent leaders, though backed by a veteran army, were greatly weakened by the defection. The city had supplied the sinews of war; indeed, from no other town in England could enough money have been borrowed to pay the troops of the Parliament. Had the king had the city at his back, he need never have been bankrupt, and might have checked the marauding habits of his army. It was in fact in London that the richest merchants of the kingdom were collected. The nobles themselves had not houses more magnificent, furniture more costly and collections of pictures and rarities more valuable. The

* Cromwelliana.

Thames served as a highway between the city and Westminster. There were numbers of public landing-places, where boatmen waited to ferry passengers to any part up and down the river, or over to Southwark. Old London Bridge was the one bridge that had then been built; the highway across, passing under gateways and flanked by houses, gave it the appearance of a castellated street. Some noblemen still lived in the Strand, and had gardens attached to their dwellings, sloping down to the river's edge, with private landing-places; but the more fashionable quarter was now further west, about Covent Garden and Drury Lane. Though London was then considered of enormous size, on the east it hardly extended beyond the Tower; on the west it touched the city of Westminster. In the north, around the old Convent or Covent Garden, Inigo Jones had lately designed new streets, connecting the City with St. Giles', then really a hamlet in-the-Fields. The old houses were all of timber, with high-gabled roofs, and stories jutting out one above the other. As few could read, not only every tavern, but every shop, possessed its signboard, and the streets presented a succession of Cross Keys, Three Pigeons, Golden Lambs, Ships, and Black Swans. The principal streets alone were paved, and these merely with little round jolting stones. The dirt was frightful. Into the kennel, or open gutter-like sewer, refuse was thrown out of houses and shops, and there rotted and reeked until it was carried away by the rain to Fleet Ditch and the Thames. Rain, in fact, did yeoman's service, though the pipes on the house-roofs first conducted their contents to the heads of passers-by. Kites and ravens were kept to act as scavengers, and the bonfires lighted on every occasion of rejoicing served a good purpose in occasionally consuming the rubbish. The streets, before the great fire, were rather to be called alleys; in some, friends could shake hands across from the projecting upper stories. Coaches had been introduced into England from Germany about 1580. Some enterprising man, a few years later, set up hackney-coaches in London, and in 1634 there were said to be 1900 such vehicles ready for hire in the streets. Sedan chairs followed. The first was brought by Buckingham from Spain. The street mob hooted at the hated favourite, regarding it as a 'mastering pride' in him to be borne upon men's shoulders; but the convenience of the conveyance overcame prejudice, and, like coaches, sedan chairs were soon in common use.

Hyde Park was a fashionable drive, where coach-races were sometimes held. Spring Gardens, opening into St. James' Park, was a favourite resort of ladies and gentlemen. There was drinking going on always under the trees, and quarrels took place two or three times a week. Cromwell, much to the discontent of Royalists, caused both gardens and park to be closed for some months.* Before the breaking out of the Civil War, St. Paul's Cathedral had been used as a daily lounging and meeting-place by people of every rank and profession. Its uses were, perhaps, less worldly when it became the stable of the sectarian horse during the war. The streets were always a Babel of sounds. Masters or their apprentices stood at the shop doors, touting for customers with cries of 'What d'ye lack, sir—what d'ye please to lack?' Fish-wives, orange-women, broom-men, chimney-sweepers, with the original costard-applemongers, passed up and down, crying their wares or services. Over this motley crowd hung the warning gallows, occupying a prominent position outside the Old Bailey on Ludgate Hill. Felons and others were hung there every Monday morning. Riots and scuffles often took place. We have seen how ready the populace of London was to rise, and how rival parties in Parliament raised mobs to intimidate their opponents. On all such occasions the apprentices took a leading part. There was a strong class feeling and close union amongst them. The apprentice was bound to his master for seven years, after which he might set up in business for himself, and rise if he could to be a member of the Common Council, a City Alderman, and even sworn Lord Mayor of London. If an apprentice were assaulted, he raised the cry of ''Prentices, clubs!' and out of every shop in the street rushed friends to the rescue. The students of the Inns of Court, mostly gentlemen by birth and Royalist at heart, felt themselves natural enemies of Presbyterian shopkeepers, and a standing feud produced frequent fights between Templars and apprentices. Like the athletic sports of the time—boating, bowling, shooting, football, cudgelling—the London street fights helped to form the raw material of a soldiery. Formerly the London train-bands had been famous for their archers. The Artillery Company had been originally formed in 1585 by volunteer citizens and officers, when the country was threatened with invasion ; and from this small beginning had developed the new

* Evelyn, Diary ; Knight, i. 191 ; Character of England, Somers Tracts, vii.

set of train-bands raised upon the breaking out of the Civil War. These, however, were not used as police, and the citizen of London had to trust in the strength of his own arm to defend his property and life from the assaults of thieves and robbers. There were no street lamps, though, indeed, an order existed for every householder to hang out a lanthorn over his door at night; and at stated times bellmen walked the streets, ringing their bells, and crying, 'Hang out your lanthorns!' The order, however, seems to have been but little observed, so that the city remained practically unlighted. Standing watchmen, who remained at their posts only till one or two o'clock in the morning, formed but an inefficient police, and, when it grew dark, even the chief streets grew dangerous for all but the well-armed. London was, indeed, the head-quarters of thieves and rogues of all descriptions, and the exercise of their profession required but little ingenuity or caution. The country gentleman was known to them at once by his manners, his accent, and the cut of his clothes. While he, a stranger in the great city, was gazing upon the new sights round him, thieves cut the string of his purse, which he wore, as was the custom, attached to his girdle. Sharpers prevailed upon him to enter taverns in their company, where his pockets were soon emptied of his cash. In the intervals of business, all rogues could find an asylum in Whitefriars, which took its name from a house of white-hooded friars; before the Reformation it had been a sanctuary for criminals, and still remained one for debtors. Accordingly, not only bankrupts and debtors, but highwaymen, false witnesses, robbers, and murderers herded together in Whitefriars and other congenial haunts, where the officers of justice dared not enter unattended by a guard of musketeers.*

A very slight comparison of the England of to-day with the England of the seventeenth century is sufficient to show what a vast advance has been made in the material condition of the country. Yet, because an efficient police system now renders roads and streets nearly as safe by night as by day; because the population has more than quadrupled; because towns have sprung up where once were villages; because trade has increased to an

---

* In 1697 an Act of Parliament was passed, abolishing the privileges of Whitefriars and of the Savoy, another haunt of the same kind. See Macaulay, chap. xxii.

extent far beyond the vision of the statesmen of the Long Parliament; because science has done much to prolong life and alleviate suffering—it would be a great mistake to suppose that, because of these things merely, future generations will regard the nineteenth century as superior to those before it. The men of the time of James I. and Charles I. are not now allowed any special credit, because in travelling they used coaches instead of riding on horseback; because they built better houses than their great-grandfathers, and slept on softer beds; because they had more wealth, more knowledge, and more refinement; all this was the result of work done before they were born. Material well-being must, in the first instance, spring from certain qualities of mind, and the people who, while they have inherited the well-being, have lost the qualities of mind which enabled their ancestors to bequeath it them, are far less likely to be at the highest than at the lowest stage of their career. The claim of any age to the respect and gratitude of posterity rests on the manner in which it dealt with its own special problems. Judged by this test, the patriots of the seventeenth century can never be found wanting. It has taken a course of two hundred years but to polish off the work that they rough-hewed. The material advantages now enjoyed spring in great part from the principles then so boldly maintained. Science cannot flourish in a land where men are imprisoned for speaking and writing what they believe; trade cannot flourish amid the shackles of monopolies and restrictive laws; abuses will rarely be reformed, or bad laws abolished, where the light of free discussion never penetrates. On the other hand, the mistakes of their age may be warnings for other generations: to take a single instance, the history of the witchcraft laws shows that education is vital to the morality of a state, and that the association of false theories with cherished beliefs is a means by which cruel and heartless oppression may win the support of religion and piety. The problems of the present century are distinct from those of the seventeenth, but, perhaps, no less important. Two or three hundred years hence it may be possible to form a fair judgment of the manner in which those problems have been treated. It may well be doubted whether future generations will allow that they owe us as great a debt of gratitude as we and they owe the men whose judgment, fortitude, and self-sacrifice alone prevented the establishment of arbitrary government in England.

CHAPTER XII.

TRIUMPHS OF THE COMMONWEALTH BY LAND AND SEA.— (1649—1652.)

True dispatch is a rich thing; for time is the measure of business, as money is of wares.—BACON.

THE Commons now formally abolished the House of Lords (19th March), and settled the government as a 'commonwealth or free state' (19th May, 1649). A Republican government is more or less democratical according to the number of those that are privileged to take part in it, either directly as rulers, or indirectly as electors. The government now established under the name of a republic was, in fact, a close oligarchy, and not so popular in constitution as the monarchy which it had overthrown. The body that exercised both the legislative and executive functions numbered about 120, and of these there were rarely more than fifty present at a debate. Though these members had been elected more than eight years ago, and represented but a small fraction of the nation, they had the power of refusing all share in the government to any but their own partisans, while they could not themselves be legally removed without their own consent. Yet, if the Republican ideal was to be carried into act, it had to be done by this remnant of a Parliament. The dissolution of the House involved too great a risk. If all the electors were allowed to take part in choosing a new representative, the majority of members would be Presbyterians and Royalists; if, on the other hand, Presbyterian and Royalist electors were disfranchised, the army officers would get an assembly which only represented themselves. Under these circumstances, both the honest men in the House and the self-interested were agreed in wishing to avoid a dissolution—the former, such as Vane, Martin, Ludlow, Hutchinson, and Bradshaw, because they thought that, in founding a republic, they were rendering their country an incalculable benefit; the latter, either through desire of power in the future, or fear of consequences for the past. "We slipped into circumstances by degrees," says the lawyer Whitelock, one of these followers with the stream, "by little and little plunging further in, until we knew not how to get out again."* To carry on the executive for the present a council of state was appointed, containing forty-one of the most influential men in the army and the House.

The Commonwealth had so many enemies that, but for the support of Cromwell and the army, it could not have stood for a day. At home it was threatened with danger alike from the country people and the Levellers: abroad it was threatened from Scotland, where the Prince of Wales had been proclaimed king of the three countries (Feb. 12th); from Ireland, where Ormond was still supreme; from the Channel, which Rupert held with the revolted ships; and from Europe at large, whose princes refused to recognize the rule of Republican rebels. The Emperor of Russia drove English merchants out of his dominions. The foreign representatives of the Commonwealth were assassinated. Dr. Dorislaus, the agent of the Republic to the States of Holland, was murdered by six Scotch followers of Montrose the very evening of his arrival at the Hague (May 3rd). A like fate befell Ascham, the agent of the Commonwealth to Spain. Two days after his arrival at Madrid, six men entered his chamber while he was at dinner, and, taking off their hats, saluted the company with the words, "Welcome, gallants, welcome!" Ascham rose, thinking them to be friends, and in another moment lay dead on the floor along with one of his companions. Out of the six criminals the Spanish government brought but one to justice. These disgraceful murders of "the things called ambassadors" were open subjects of rejoicing with Royalist exiles.

The Commonwealth, while thus attacked by its open enemies abroad, found no support among the masses at home. The immediate result of Charles' execution was to produce a revulsion of feeling in his favour. His faults were buried in his grave; his private virtues lived after him. A book was published, entitled Eikôn Basilikê, or the Royal Image, which professed to be written by Charles himself during his captivity at Carisbrooke Castle. In it the theory of Divine Right was pictured in its softest colours. Without abating one jot or tittle of

* Whitelock, Mem. 417.

the king's high pretensions as ruling by the will of God, Charles was portrayed as the father of his people, the lover of the established laws and of Parliaments, yielding in all points to the desires of his subjects, save where conscience and honour forbade. Against such a prince the people had taken up arms, misled by a few bold, bad men acting from love of power, blind party passions, and greed to satisfy their own necessities out of the lands and revenues of the Church. By these men the king's acts had been misrepresented, his good faith unreasonably questioned, but he remained frank and generously forgiving as ever. In his instructions to his son he is represented as bidding him entertain no dislike of Parliaments, but remember that the rebels had acted from misapprehension of their own good. In the prayers with which each chapter of the book closes, he is found beseeching God to bestow upon his enemies repentance and pardon, in place of punishment for the sin of fighting against God's anointed. For himself, let what would happen, he could still patiently submit to God's chastening hand, in the full assurance that his Saviour's crown of thorns was more precious than any crown of gold. Though in fact a forgery of Doctor Gauden, the book produced as great an effect as if it had proceeded from Charles' own hand. 48,000 copies of this Image of the Martyr-King were sold in a year.*

To increase the reaction in the king's favour, famine appeared in many parts of the country. The present Commonwealth and the late government of the two Houses were associated in the mind of the people with a standing army and heavy taxes ;† Charles' rule with the happy memories of unbroken peace. Tales of distress often came before the House—of a town reduced almost to penury, because the commander of the garrison, left unprovided by the government, was forced to allow the soldiers to live at free quarters ; of tumults against the tax-gatherers, in which the starving people declared "that they would leave their wives and children to be maintained by the gentry, for the bread was eaten out of their mouths by the taxes."‡

From all this discontent the Republicans had little to fear, so long as the army remained faithful. Discontent, however, was widespread there. A successful revolution, however much it

* Guizot, Hist. de la Répub. d'Angleterre, i. 28.
† P 233.   ‡ Whitelock, 464, 398, 421, 443 ; Carlyle, i. 345.

offends moderates, must disappoint extremes. Fifth Monarchists, Levellers, Anabaptists, found that neither the equality of men nor the millennium had come with the Republic. Petitions came that the House should dissolve in August; that new parliaments should be held every year; that excise and customs should be abolished; that the law and the church should be reformed; and, lastly, that none should pay rent or homage to fellow-creatures. Aroused by hunger or belief in natural right, bands of men began to dig and plant unenclosed lands. Pamphlets and papers were published supporting the principles of the Levellers. "The gentry," it was said, "held all authority and command, and drove on designs for their own interest and the people's slavery. The nobles, who had come in with William the Conqueror, had seized the lands of the people and forced the king to consent to laws necessary to preserve themselves, but had never acted from any love to the poor Commons." The impracticable Lilburne, the leader and mouthpiece of all the discontented, published tract after tract to stir up the soldiers to mutiny by attacking the ambition of the officers and the tyranny of the House. "The officers," he wrote, "are inferior to the essential part of the army, the soldiery, and ought to be controlled and overthrown when they try to overthrow and control the soldiery. We were before ruled by a King, Lords, and Commons; now by a General, a Court-Martial, and a House of Commons. We are but under an old cheat, the transmutation of names, but with the addition of new tyrannies to the old; and the last state of this Commonwealth is worse than the first."

The moment was critical. Prince Charles was invited to Ireland, and, should he land the Irish army in England in the midst of all this surging discontent, Presbyterians and Royalists might rise and defeat an army and party divided against itself. To meet the danger at its source, the Council of State appointed Cromwell commander-in-chief, with orders to make an expedition against Ireland. The soldiers, however, now refused to obey the orders of their officers, and broke out into open mutiny. In Oxfordshire, in Gloucestershire, in Wiltshire, bodies of men marched off from their head-quarters in arms. Fairfax, however, and his officers followed closely on the insurgents, who within a fortnight were all either taken prisoners or defeated and dispersed. The last body of mutineers had marched north from Salisbury, forded the Thames, and reached Burford, in Oxfordshire. Fairfax was at

Andover, but, by a march of fifty miles in the day, he surprised them the same evening in their quarters. The larger part of the army had, in fact, remained faithful to their generals, who could be tender, without being weak, stern, without being cruel, so that their soldiers loved and respected them accordingly. "Those," said Cromwell, "that thought martial law a burden should have liberty to lay down their arms, and be paid their arrears the same as those that stayed ; for the rest, the Parliament would in time do all that they desired." Of the Burford mutineers, out of 400 prisoners, every tenth man was condemned by court-martial to be shot. The sentence was only executed upon three ; the others felt grateful for the mercy extended to them : Cromwell's words brought them to their reason ; the men repented, and their leader confessed that many of his party "were so enraged against the Parliament that he did think (in his conscience) there would have been great cruelty exercised by these men, and that it was a happy hour they were surprised and prevented."

Meantime the Duke of Ormond had effected a peace with the Catholics in Ireland by promising them, in the name of Charles Stuart, the free exercise of their religion (Jan., 1649). He had further succeeded in uniting in the Prince's favour all four parties in the island—the Irish Catholics ; the Catholic descendants of the old English settlers ; English Episcopalians, whether fugitive Royalists or men whose fathers had been planted by Elizabeth and James on the lands of Irish rebels ; and, lastly, the Scotch Presbyterians of the Ulster settlement. Accordingly, when Cromwell arrived in Ireland at the head of 12,000 men, he found almost the whole country under the power of the Royalists (Aug. 15th). A Parliamentary garrison in Dublin itself had only escaped a siege by surprising the enemy on the banks of the Liffey (Aug. 2nd). The general first marched against Drogheda, then called Droghdagh or Tredah, and summoned the garrison to surrender. Sir Arthur Ashton, the governor, refused ; he had 3000 of the choicest troops of the confederates and enough provisions to enable him to hold out till winter should compel the enemy to raise the siege. But within twenty-four hours the English batteries had made a breach in the wall. Oliver, after twice seeing his soldiers beaten off, led them on in person and carried the breach. A terrible massacre followed. "Being in the heat of action I forbade them," Cromwell wrote in his despatch to the Parliament, "to spare any that were in arms in the town; and I think that night they put to the sword about 2000 men." Of these, one-half probably fell in the streets; the other half Cromwell describes as having been slain at early dawn in St. Peter's Church. This he looks upon as a judgment for their previous proceedings there. "It is remarkable," he writes, "that these people at first set up the mass in some places of the town that had been monasteries; but afterwards grew so insolent that, the last Lord's day before the storm, the Protestants were thrust out of the great church called St. Peter's, and they had public mass there; and in this very place near 1000 of them were put to the sword, fleeing thither for safety. I believe all the friars were knocked on the head promiscuously but two." Of the original garrison of 3000, many must have fallen in the defence; and of the remainder who escaped for that night, the officers were 'knocked on the head,' and the soldiers mostly shipped for Barbadoes. "I am persuaded," he further writes, "that this is a righteous judgment of God upon these barbarous wretches, who have imbrued their hands in so much innocent blood; and that it will tend to prevent the effusion of blood for the future, which are the satisfactory grounds to such actions, which otherwise cannot but work remorse and regret. The officers and soldiers of this garrison were the flower of their army. . . . That which caused your men to storm so courageously, it was the Spirit of God, who gave your men courage, and took it away again; and gave the enemy courage, and took it away again; and gave your men courage again, and therewith this happy success. And, therefore, it is good that God alone have all the glory."

Royalist accounts assert that many hundreds of women and children were slain in St. Peter's Church. It is, of course, possible that some of the townspeople, fleeing thither for safety, lost their lives in the general massacre of the garrison. There is, however, no trustworthy witness[*] for any lives being taken except

[*] Dr. Lingard gives credit to the story of Cromwell's massacre of townspeople—men, women, and children—but the only direct testimony is a story told by Thomas Wood (the brother of Anthony Wood, the historiographer of Oxford). This Thomas Wood had fought on the king's side, and after the king's death, "being deeply engaged in a Cavaliering plot in 1648, he, to avoid being taken and hanged, fled to Ireland," where, according to his brother's account, he got a command in the regiment of Ingoldsby, an old schoolfellow, and then a Parliamentary officer; and thus, having changed sides, "was engaged in the storming and assaulting" of Drogheda. He tells

those of soldiers and friars. Cromwell did not sanction the killing of any but those with arms in their hands, though he seems to have approved of the fate of the friars. The fanatical zeal of his letter, and the fact that he takes the full credit or discredit for the slaughter of the garrison, makes it improbable that he concealed anything; and this is substantiated by his subsequent declaration, in which he gives this challenge:—" Give us an instance of one man, since my coming into Ireland, not in arms, massacred, destroyed, or banished, concerning the massacre or the destruction of whom justice hath not been done, or endeavoured to be done."

With the enemy's troops Cromwell carried out the determined mode of warfare which he began at Drogheda. They were mostly scattered over the country, occupied in garrison duty. Before whatever town he came he demanded immediate surrender, or threatened to refuse quarter. Town after town opened its gates to this grim summons. Wexford, which refused to surrender, was stormed, and the whole garrison, 2000 in number, put to the sword (Oct. 11th).

While condemning these massacres we must remember, not only that there had been a terrible massacre of Protestants eight years before,* but that the Celts, whether Irish or Highlanders, failed themselves to observe towards others the rules of war obtaining among more civilized nations; and further that, even according to the rules of war of that time, the garrisons of places taken by storm were presumed to have lost their right to quarter; the Catholic generals on the Continent had, in fact, put to the sword, not only the garrisons, but the inhabitants of Protestant towns. Yet Cromwell was probably not so much influenced by precedents of his own day as by those drawn from "the wars of the Lord"

---

a tale, in Spenser's manner, of a "most handsome virgin, arrayed in costly and gorgeous apparel," whom a soldier treated as though he were Phineas and she a Midianitish woman; whereupon Wood, "seeing her gasping, took away her money, jewels, &c., and flung her clean over the works." His brother says "he had an art of merriment called buffooning," and he seems to have practised this on "his mother and brethren," to whom he often told this story. Ormond, writing from the neighbourhood, and speaking generally of great cruelty having been exercised for five days after the town was taken, makes no mention of a massacre of townspeople. The Catholic Council of Kilkenny, in the manifesto they published at Clonmacnoise at this time, make no mention of a massacre of townspeople at Drogheda, and even think it necessary to warn the Irish against being deceived by a show of clemency. It is in his answer to this manifesto that Cromwell makes the statement quoted in the text. Ormond Papers, ii. 412; Lingard, viii. Appendix. * See p. 104.

in his Bible. It is not the only time that religion has been made to seem at war with humanity through the mistaken idea, that usages tolerated among uncivilized nations 3000 years ago are a model for the observance of Christians. The history of the Indian mutiny, in our own time, shows that the danger of an uncritical interpretation of the sacred records is not past for us. It was only in the case of these two garrisons that Cromwell was merciless, but this blot on his character increased his difficulties in the next Scottish campaign by inspiring groundless fears in the civil population.

In other respects, while Cromwell's rigour and determination saved bloodshed in the end by the rapidity and completeness of his conquests, his conduct in Ireland contrasted favourably on many points with that of the Royalists there. His own soldiers, for ill-using the people contrary to regulations, were sometimes cashiered the army, sometimes hanged. When a treaty was made, he kept faithfully to its terms. Garrisons that yielded on summons were allowed either to march away with arms and baggage, or else to go abroad and enter the service of any government at peace with England. Before the war was over he had rid the country, on these terms, of some 45,000 soldiers. Taking advantage of the divisions of his enemies, he persuaded several garrisons of English soldiers to desert the cause of Charles Stuart for the Commonwealth. His conduct of the war was so successful that, during the nine months of his stay in Ireland, the forces of the Royalists were shattered, and the provinces of Leinster and Munster recovered for the Parliament. Cromwell returned to England in May 1650, leaving his son-in-law Ireton to complete the conquest of the country. The last garrisons in Ulster and Munster surrendered during the course of the ensuing summer and autumn. Ireton crossed the Shannon and drove the Irish back into the bogs and mountain fastnesses of Connaught, their last refuge, where fighting still continued for two years after all the rest of the country had been reduced (1651-2).

Cromwell had hastened from Ireland because a pressing danger now threatened England from Scotland. The Scots were divided into three parties—first, the Strict Covenanters, followers of Argyle, who had been placed in power by Cromwell after the defeat of Hamilton in Lancashire (1648); secondly, the Lax Covenanters, or Engagers, who had taken part in Hamilton's invasion;

thirdly, the old Royalists, headed by the Marquis of Montrose. Though the Strict Covenanters declined to fight for a king who refused the Covenant, they grew indignant at seeing Republicans and Sectarians triumph over Presbyterians in England; and, having hopes that the son would be less recalcitrant than the father, sent deputies to the Hague to offer Charles the crown of Scotland, on condition of his taking the Covenant, and promising to rule by the advice of Parliament and Kirk. At the time this treaty was being negotiated, Montrose was defeated and taken prisoner by the Covenanters. Charles, though he had given him a full commission, yet, not wishing to break off the treaty, basely disowned the earl, and caused word to be sent to Argyle that he felt no sorrow for the defeat of the man who had drawn the sword "contrary to the royal command." The outrages of Montrose's savage levies were long remembered in the Lowlands, and the Covenanters, in revenge, now determined to execute him with all the circumstances of shame they could devise. He was sentenced to be hung on a gibbet, thirty feet high, in the Grassmarket in Edinburgh, the place of execution for the lowest felons, his body quartered, and his limbs fixed on the gates of four towns in Scotland. Montrose, by the calmness and dignity of his bearing, cast back the scorn and the shame into the faces of his enemies. He had always loved to play the hero, and never had such a scene been offered him before. He walked calmly to the place of execution with a "grand air," magnificently dressed, as if he had been going to wait upon the king. His country honoured him in his death more than in his life (May 21st).

The Republican statesmen were aware that, if Charles Stuart reigned in Scotland, English and Scotch Presbyterians would unite in an attempt to place him upon the throne of England. They determined, therefore, to ward off the danger by being the first in the field. Fairfax, however, refused to command. The Republicans knew that the only man able to take his place was Cromwell. Cromwell's power they feared already, but it was in vain they begged and implored Fairfax to go; in vain Cromwell himself entreated him, which he did so earnestly that none could doubt his sincerity; in vain it was urged upon him that the Scots had already broken the Covenant by one invasion under Hamilton, and were now, without doubt, intending a second. Fairfax, however, refusing to march against the Scots unless they first actually entered England, resigned his command to the Commons, who appointed Cromwell commander-in-chief of the whole army in his stead (June 26th).

When Cromwell, at the head of 16,000 men, crossed the border (July 22nd), he found silence and desolation around him. The country people, frightened at horrible tales spread about of cruelties practised by the Sectarian soldiers, had obeyed the orders of the Scotch Parliament and fled for refuge to the towns, leaving behind them only a few women, who baked and brewed for the invaders. When Cromwell arrived at Musselburgh he found the Scotch army of 24,000 men occupying a long line of entrenchments, running from Leith to the hills called Salisbury Crags and Arthur's Seat, which lie to the east of Edinburgh Old Town. David Leslie, the Scotch general, had taken up this unassailable position with the intention of starving the English out of the country. His own army was amply supplied with provisions from all the north of Scotland lying at his back; while, the eastern Lowlands having been purposely laid waste, his enemies were entirely dependent for their supplies upon a fleet which had followed them from England.

Cromwell marched and countermarched, in hopes of drawing Leslie out of his fastness and bringing on a general engagement. But his efforts were in vain. As autumn approached the difficulties of the situation increased. The weather was wet and stormy, the soldiers fell sick, and the ocean was so rough that provisions were landed with difficulty. A council of war agreed to retreat to Dunbar, a town on the sea-coast, lying between Edinburgh and Berwick, which might, at the worst, be fortified, and afford some quarters for the winter (Aug. 31st). Accordingly the "poor, shattered, hungry, discouraged army" first shipped 500 sick men for Berwick, and then marched from Musselburgh through Haddingtonshire to Dunbar (Aug. 31st). Leslie, who mistakenly supposed that his enemies had put on board their great guns and a large number of troops, followed closely in pursuit, with the intention of putting himself between them and their communications with England. Having succeeded in passing them, he thus made it impossible for them to continue their retreat without cutting their way through his army, which now faced about to front them. They were cooped up between Belhaven Bay and the mouth of the Broxburn, on a strip of coast not above two miles long. Behind there was no shelter but the little fishing town of Dunbar. Immediately in front of this, barely a mile off, was Doon Hill, rising like a hog's back to a height of more than 500 feet, and forming the northern extremity of the dreary and boggy Lammermoor range. Upon the long level summit of this hill was stationed the Scots' army, commanding from its vantage ground the surrounding lowland country, and ready to seize any opportune moment to descend and annihilate the smaller force beneath it. In order the more completely to close the road to Berwick, Leslie's right wing of horse descended and occupied the undulating but comparatively level ground spreading between the foot of Doon Hill and the sea-coast. South of Doon Hill, the Lammermoors gradually approach closer and closer to the sea, until, at Copperspath, some eight or nine miles south of Dunbar, the road to Berwick runs through a narrow pass, "where ten men to hinder are better than forty to make their way," which was itself already held by the enemy.

To return westwards to Musselburgh was worse than useless. An attempt to escape in their ships was full of danger, as they would be open to attack from the Scots in their rear while embarking. To advance was destruction, as long as Leslie commanded the road to Berwick. To fight was impossible, so long as he remained upon the top of Doon Hill. Oliver prepared for the worst, but did not despair. He wrote to Haslerig, then governor of Newcastle, telling him to collect what forces he could, for the army was so blocked up he could not get out without "almost a miracle," and his soldiers were falling sick "beyond imagination." Neither did Oliver's men despair, to judge from the spirit of a musketeer with a wooden arm, who was taken prisoner in a skirmish. When asked by Leslie "if the army intended to fight," he replied, "What else do you think we came here for?" "Soldier, how will you fight when you have shipped half your men and all your great guns?" "Sir, if you please to draw down your men to the foot of the hill, you will find both men and great guns also." Leslie sent him back again free.

The Broxburn is a small stream which divides the foot of Doon Hill from the base of the little promontory upon which stands Dunbar. It flows in a glen with steep grassy banks between forty and fifty feet high, and as many apart. The easiest passage across is at a point about a mile from the sea-coast, near the

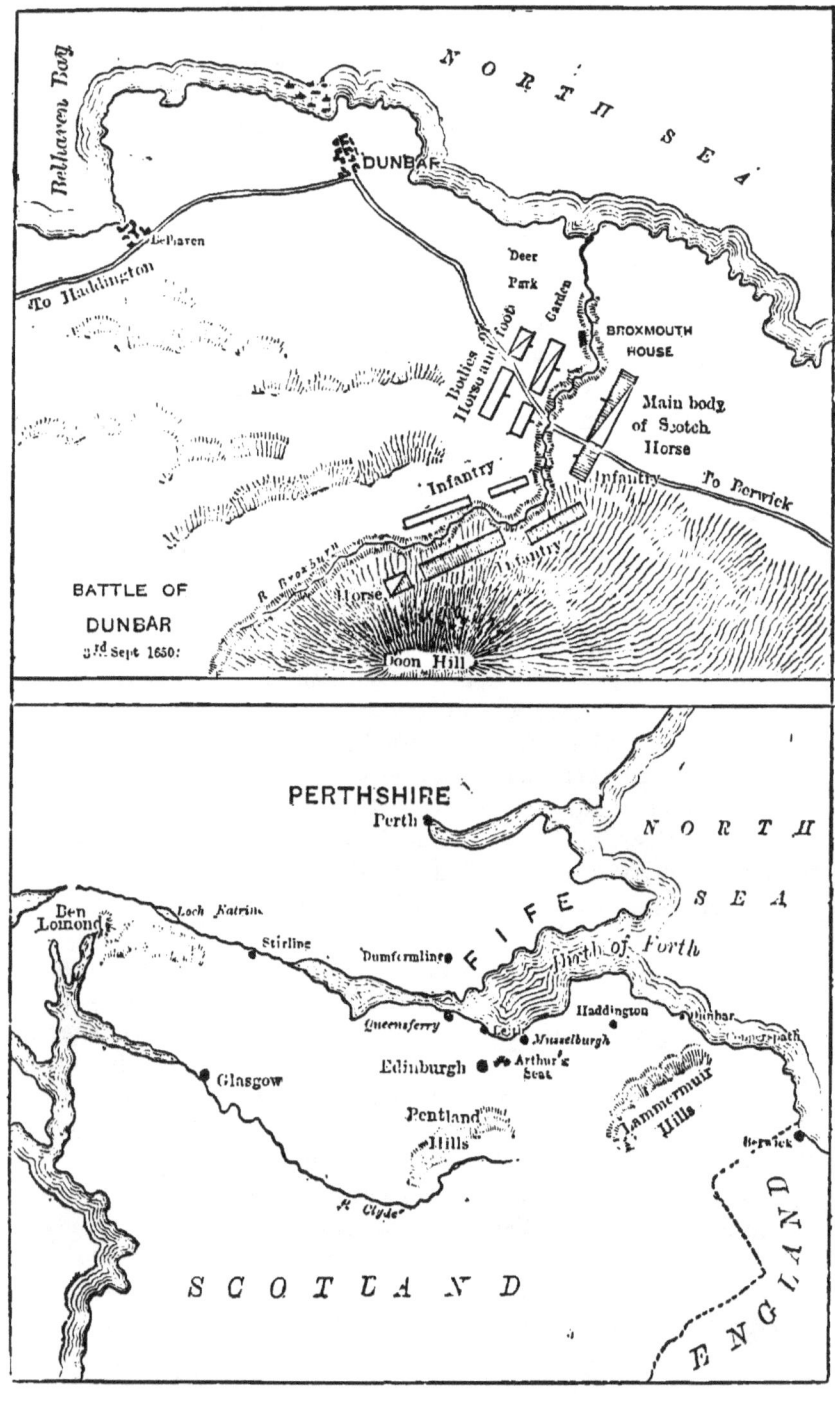

Duke of Roxburgh's seat, Broxmouth House, where the sides of the glen slope gently down to the water, and the high road to Berwick now crosses by a bridge. Oliver, about four o'clock on Monday afternoon (Sept. 2nd), was walking in the garden of Broxmouth House and watching the movements of the enemy upon Doon Hill, when he perceived that Leslie was actually bringing his whole army down below the steep part of the hill-side, strengthening his right wing, opposite the duke's house, with two-thirds of the cavalry from his left, and posting his infantry in the cornfields which sloped gently down to the Broxburn. What did this movement mean? Cromwell divined at once. Leslie's purpose was to seize the easy passage over the brook near Broxmouth House by a surprise, and then bring his forces over and fight at pleasure. Cromwell saw that, by attacking first, he might seize the passage, outflank Leslie's right wing, and drive it back upon the main body, and thus rout the whole army while hemmed up in that narrow space between the steep of Doon Hill and Broxburn glen. He suggested the plan to Lambert, who said he had meant to say the same thing, and the action was agreed upon for the morrow.

It was the Presbyterian Committee who had persuaded Leslie to abandon his masterly inactivity on the hill-top. They thought it a mistake to adopt a policy which would let the Sectarians surrender, and thus escape utter destruction. Moreover, while the English were provided with tents, Leslie's own men were absolutely without shelter, exposed to all the furies of wind and weather. Leslie himself, as his forces numbered 22,000 men, while those of Cromwell, supposing all the men had been in fighting condition, were not above 12,000, had no doubt of the event, and gave out in his camp that, by seven o'clock on the Tuesday, " they would have the army of the enemy dead or alive."

A misty morning followed a wet and tempestuous night. By four o'clock Cromwell had already set his troops in motion. Large bodies of horse and foot were massed opposite the Scots' right wing, while, for a mile along the bank of the Broxburn, great guns were stationed, and regiments of foot drawn up, in readiness to assault Leslie's main battle, now lying in the stubble of the reaped cornfields opposite. At six o'clock the trumpets sounded, the cannon fired all up the line, and the soldiers charged, shouting their word of battle, "The Lord of hosts—the Lord of hosts!"

The Scots' foot were hardly well awake, and had let their matches, then ropes of tow, nearly all out, so that they could not so much as return the fire that assailed them from the opposite side of the glen. Only at the passage, where the road to Berwick then went through the Broxburn, was the struggle fierce. For here the Scotch horse, themselves preparing for a surprise, returned the charge with spirit, and forced their enemies back over brook and hollow. Few, however, were their moments of triumph. Cromwell's own regiment of foot, coming up to battle, drove them back in turn at push of pike; two foot regiments, which had crossed the glen below Broxmouth House, took their wing in flank; the English horse, charging a second time, broke through horse and foot. Leslie's whole wing then turned and fled right back upon his own main battle, disordering the whole line, and trampling their friends to death beneath their horses' feet. For nearly an hour the whole scene was enveloped in mist; when at last the fog broke and the sun shone out upon the sea, Oliver shouted aloud the battle cry of Israel, "Now let God arise and scatter His enemies!" and, as the fog was more and more dispersed, and the battle-field more clearly revealed, he cried again, "I profess they run!" and there "was the Scots' army all in confusion and running, both right wing and left and main battle." In all directions they fled—some back towards Copperspath, some in mad panic northwards across the Broxburn to Dunbar itself, but the mass of the fugitives, horse and foot, along the skirts of Doon Hill westwards towards Haddington. Thus within one short hour the situation of the two armies was more than reversed. The English were victorious; destruction surrounded the Scotch. Before joining the chase, the general and those about him halted and sang Psalm cxvii.:—"O praise the Lord, all ye nations; praise him, all ye people. For His merciful kindness is great towards us, and the truth of the Lord endureth for ever. Praise ye the Lord." Such was the battle, or rather the rout of Dunbar. Upon the place, or near about it, 3000 men were killed or trampled to death; the chase was pursued for nearly eight miles; 10,000 prisoners were taken; the whole of the Scottish baggage and artillery fell into the hands of the conquerors (Sept. 3rd, 1650). Cromwell in his turn advanced; the town of Edinburgh opened its gates, and he laid siege to the castle.

After the defeat of the army of Strict Covenanters at Dunbar, the middle party obtained greater influence in the State. The members of this party were called Engagers, from their having entered into that 'Engagement' to free the king, which led to Hamilton's invasion in 1648. The Parliament met at Perth, and voted that not only Engagers, but Royalists, who submitted to public penance, should be allowed to serve in the army. Charles himself was crowned king at Scone (Jan. 1st), and made commander-in-chief of the army, which by the spring was again raised to a force of 20,000 men. Many Covenanters, however, could not hide from themselves the truth of reproaches cast upon them by Cromwell, that Charles hated the Covenant and sacrificed his conscience for love of a crown. The officers of a new army, raised during the autumn in the western Lowland counties, had presented a remonstrance, refused to fight for the king, and finally joined the invaders. The governor of Edinburgh Castle had shared the views of the remonstrants, and opened its gates to Cromwell (Dec. 19th, 1650).

Leslie and Charles, adopting the strategy of the former year, took up a strong position near Stirling, where they could not readily be attacked. Cromwell determined to starve them out. He crossed his army over the Firth of Forth at Queensferry, dispersed the force sent to oppose his landing, and thus gained possession of Fife, and shut Charles off from all the north of Scotland. Perth, the seat of the Scottish government, itself surrendered. Charles, finding his supplies cut off, and the road to England open, played the desperate game which Cromwell seems almost to have designed for him. Suddenly breaking up his camp (July 31st), and getting three days' start of the enemy, he marched straight into England, becoming in his turn the invader. He bent his course towards Gloucestershire, hoping that the people in the west would rise in his favour, and increase the size of his army before he turned upon London. But his friends were unprepared. Only a few partial risings took place, and, when the royal standard was raised at Worcester, his army barely numbered 16,000 men (Aug. 22nd). The Republicans despatched the militia, and every force that could be raised, to check his progress. Cromwell himself, having left 5000 men under General Monk, to complete the conquest of Scotland, followed fast in pursuit, and having effected a junction with the other

Republican forces, found himself by the time he reached Worcester, in command of a force of 30,000 men (Aug. 28th).

The city of Worcester, which stands on the eastern bank of the Severn, was then, as now, connected by a bridge with its western suburb of St. John's. The surrounding country, on either side of the Severn, was cultivated, and the numerous fields, lanes, and ditches rendered it all unsuited for cavalry fighting. West of the Severn a fruitful plain stretches away uninterruptedly as far as the Malvern Hills; but on the eastern side of the river the country is broken, and, at the distance of about a mile from the city, Red Hill, crowned by the Perry Woods, bounds the view. Around and within city and suburb Charles entrenched his army. On a small but abruptly rising eminence, which looks down on Worcester from the south-east, the Scots planted guns and raised an entrenchment, which they called Fort Royal. A bridge at Upton, some miles below Worcester, was broken down, to secure the suburb of St. John's from attack, by preventing the enemy from crossing to the Severn's western bank. The work, however, was not thoroughly done. Some of Lambert's soldiers straddled across a parapet left standing, and, after a fierce struggle, drove the Royalists out of Upton, and repaired and maintained the bridge. The next day, the 29th of August, Cromwell, advancing from Pershore and Whiteladies Ashton, occupied Red Hill and the Perry Woods with the main body of his army. On the 2nd of September, Fleetwood took over the repaired bridge at Upton a formidable force of 10,000 men. Several difficulties, however, remained to be overcome before he could approach St. John's, for the Royalists held the only bridge over the Teme at Powick, and had placed a strong detachment of troops in the village before it. To ensure a close communication with the other forces, from which he was now separated by the Severn, Fleetwood brought boats up from Upton and Gloucester, and made a bridge of them over the Severn. He then made a second bridge, within pistol-shot of the other, over the Teme, to be ready for use in case his troops could not force the Powick Bridge. Fleetwood began his march from Upton at five o'clock in the morning, but the bridges were not completed until about three in the afternoon. A furious assault was then made upon the Royalists' advanced guard at Powick, and, after a hard struggle, Fleetwood's soldiers succeeded in driving them from their position, and forcing a pas-

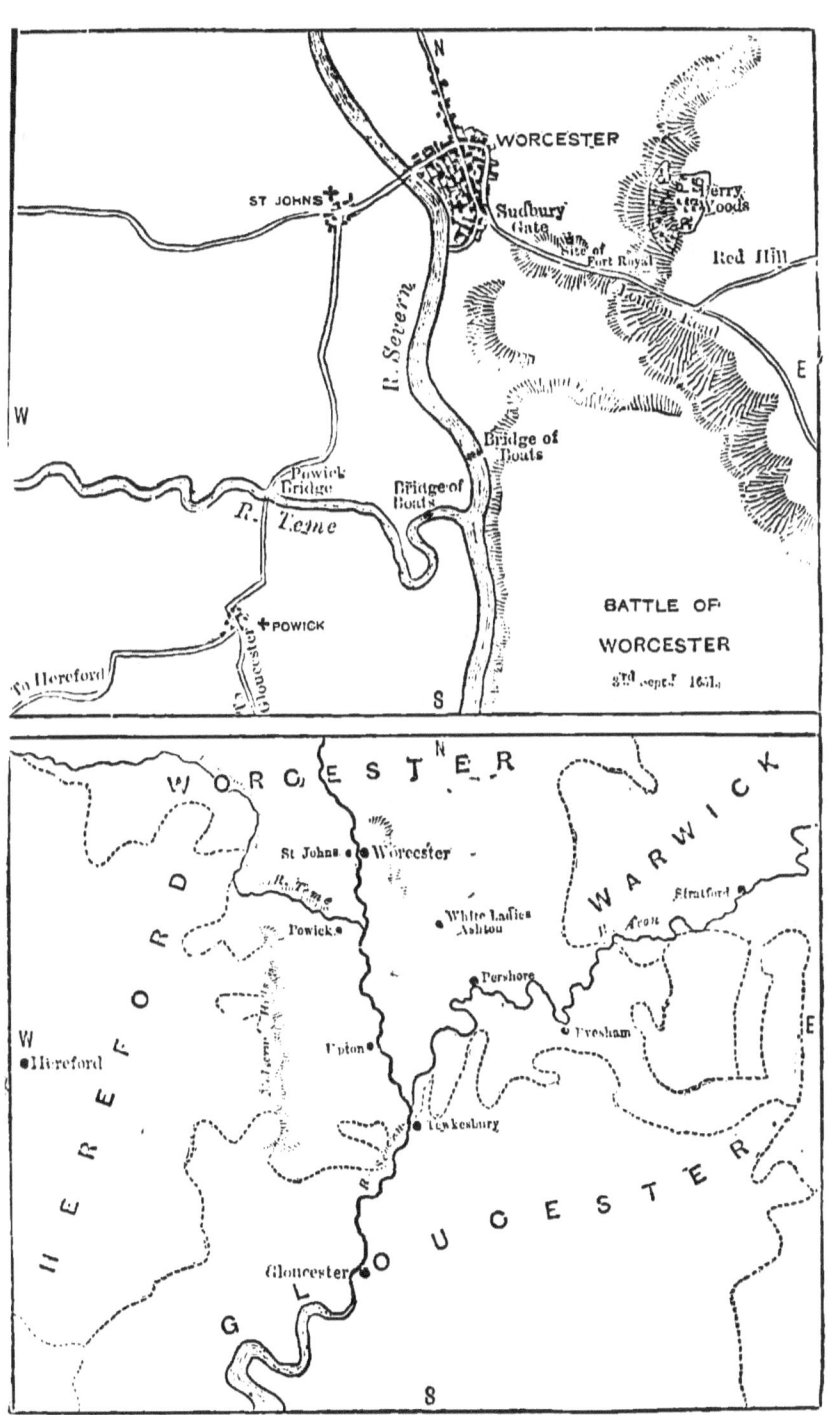

sage over the Teme. This success, however, was but momentary. On seeing the confusion of their friends, large bodies of horse and foot poured out from St. John's, and, charging furiously, forced the Parliamentarians back again upon the Teme. At this critical moment Cromwell brought several regiments of horse and foot across by the bridge of boats over the Severn. A body of Highlanders gallantly but vainly threw themselves in the way of their advance. Cromwell "led the van in person, being the first man that set foot on the enemy's ground." He effected a junction with Fleetwood's forces, and once for all turned the tide of battle on this side the river. "We beat the enemy," he says, "from hedge to hedge till we beat him into Worcester."

Charles, with his principal officers, was watching the operations from the tower of Worcester Cathedral. On seeing regiment after regiment of Parliamentarians stream across the bridge of boats to the western side of the Severn, he determined to assail the position of the forces still remaining on Red Hill. From the number of the enclosures which cut up the ground, the action was mainly confined to the infantry. The Royalists charged out of Sudbury Gate with even more than their usual gallantry, but could not succeed in breaking two of Cromwell's foot regiments, who bore the brunt of the shock. Before they had found time for a second charge, Oliver, with several regiments, had re-crossed the bridge of boats. He now charged himself, at the head of his veterans, and the fiercest struggle of all came on. The Highlanders, when their powder was spent, rather than retreat, fought with the butt-ends of their muskets; the artillery from Fort Royal played upon the ranks of the Parliamentarians; the king led his troops on in person again and again. Cromwell saw the position of the Royalists was really untenable; he "did exceedingly hazard himself, riding up and down in the midst of the fire; riding himself in person to the enemy's foot to offer them quarter, whereto they returned no answer but shot." In spite of the courage displayed by Charles and his troops, the battle necessarily ended in their complete discomfiture. Closely pursued by Cromwell, they were forced back into the city, where the bloody struggle was continued in the streets. About seven o'clock Fort Royal itself was stormed, and the guns turned upon Worcester. On the south-east side of the city, by Sudbury Gate, and on the west side, over Severn Bridge, the Parliamentarians pressed in at the same time. Charles, in despair, rode up and down the streets, now calling on the foot soldiers, who were throwing away their arms, to stand again; now imploring the horse to charge once more, crying that he would rather they should shoot him than let him outlive that fatal day. But his words were spent in vain; his troops were being pressed back to the north end of the town; the streets were becoming strewn with the dead bodies of men and horses; at last, to avoid falling into the hands of his enemies, he was obliged to fly hard out of the city's northern gate.*

Leslie himself was taken prisoner, but while prisoners of note, both Scotch and English noblemen, were captured daily, the Commonwealth's troops, though they scoured the country up and down, failed to light upon the greatest prize of all. Riding north from Worcester the night after the battle, Charles, early the next morning, reached Whiteladies, a house belonging to a Royalist gentleman. Here he changed his clothes for a peasant's dress; a coarse linen shirt, a pair of old green breeches, a coat of green, his own stockings with their embroidered tops cut off, and a pair of clumsy shoes, formed his apparel. His face and hands were dyed brown with walnuts. Richard Penderell, one of five brothers, tenants on the estate, clipped off the fugitive's long locks, and took him to a neighbouring wood for concealment. They had only left Whiteladies half an hour, when soldiers in pursuit came and searched the house. It was wet and cold in the wood, and Penderell sent his sister, Joan Yates, to the king with a blanket and a mess of milk, butter, and eggs. Charles started when she came. "Good woman," he said, "can you be faithful to a distressed Cavalier?" "Yes, sir," she replied; "I would rather die than betray you." At nightfall Charles left his retreat, hoping to get across the Severn and escape into Wales; but the bridges being all guarded, and no boat obtainable, he was obliged to retrace his steps to Whiteladies, where he spent a day, in company with a Cavalier, Captain Careless, in an oak, the thick foliage of which concealed the two fugitives from the sight of passers by. William Penderell and his wife gathered sticks near at hand, ready to give warning of danger, for occasionally soldiers came along the path near the tree, and looked about the surrounding woods and meadows.

* Cromwelliana; Carlyle; Boscobel Tracts; Personal Expenses of Charles II. in City of Worcester, communicated to the Transactions of the Historical Society by R. Woof.

After running many risks of discovery, Charles made his way through the country to the south coast, and, sailing from Brighton, was landed in safety at Fécamp, in Normandy (Oct. 16th). His escape spoke much for the good faith and loyalty of the English people. He had been a wanderer for forty-four days, and at the mercy of forty-five persons at least whose names are known—peasants, servants, gentlemen, women, Protestants, Catholics—of whom none were prevailed upon to betray him either by fear or greed; and this though the House of Commons had declared all his harbourers traitors, and offered a reward of £1000 for his discovery.

During the two troubled years in which Cromwell was reducing Ireland and Scotland, the Council of State had not neglected foreign affairs. Milton had been appointed their Secretary for Foreign Tongues (March 13th, 1649), and with Blake, Popham, and Dean for their admirals, they were engaged in strengthening the navy and raising England's power by sea. Prince Rupert, driven from the Channel and from Ireland, fled for refuge to the Tagus. Blake pursued him with eighteen ships of war, blocked up the mouth of the river, and inflicted so much damage on Portuguese merchants by seizing vessels coming home from the Indies, that the King of Portugal gave the prince orders to quit the coast (1650). Rupert sailed first to the Mediterranean, but when most of his vessels were destroyed by Blake he made with the remaining three for the West Indies, where being still pursued, wherever he went, by the Commonwealth's fleets, he at last gave over his pirate's calling, and sold his vessels to the King of France (March, 1652). His brother Maurice, who accompanied him, had been lost in a storm. By the end of the year 1652 there was hardly a corner of the British dominions that dared any longer openly support the cause of Charles. Guernsey was the last to give in, but Jersey, the Scilly Isles, and the colonies planted on the North American coast and in the West India Islands had all been visited by the Republican admirals, and had consented to recognize the authority of the Commonwealth.

After the victory of Worcester, foreign princes hastened to make friends of men who might prove formidable enemies, and no longer hesitated to recognize the Republic as the lawful government of England. Tuscany, Venice, Geneva, the Swiss cantons, the Hanseatic towns, German princes, sent and received agents; Sweden, Denmark, and Portugal sent extraordinary ambassadors. A Spanish ambassador, as early as December, 1650, received audience of the Commons. The aspirations of the Republican statesmen, Vane, Bradshaw, Martin, and their companions, rose with success. To foreigners they seemed "filled with pride," and vast schemes of advancing England's power and commerce were believed to float before their minds. "They intend," writes a foreigner, " to destroy the trade of Holland and usurp it to themselves. The Dutch must serve on board their fleet, and all the shipwrights, sailmakers, and ropemakers will be obliged to go and earn their living in England. Then they will turn their arms against Denmark, and will oblige Norway to sell their wood to no other nation than England. They will send their fleets against Spain and Lisbon to destroy their trade with the East Indies, and usurp the trade of all the European nations. All the earth must submit to them, work for nobody but them, and they will, from time to time, come into their ports and sweep away all their treasure. All commodities will be worked up in England, so that the best artificers will flock thither; and, if they will have any fine linen or good cloth to wear in another country, the flax and wool must be sent to be manufactured in England."*

When the King of Portugal sought a treaty, the Republicans demanded a very large sum as indemnity for the expenses England had incurred in fitting out the fleet against Rupert. The ambassador, on hesitating to agree to such terms, was peremptorily ordered to quit the country (May, 1651). Louis XIV. had allowed French vessels to join with those of Rupert in seizing English merchantmen. The Republicans were now in possession of the more powerful navy, and retaliated severely on the French for their former ill-will. There was no means by which Louis could come to more friendly relations but by sending an ambassador to England and making a treaty. But, though eager for England's support or, at least, neutrality in the war in which he was now engaged with Spain, his pride forbade him to recognize as lawful rulers the men who had driven his young cousin into exile, and put his uncle to death on the scaffold. The French merchants, in despair at the injuries inflicted on their

* Sorbière to M. de Courcelles at Amsterdam, 1st July, 1652, in Harris, Life of Cromwell, 270.

commerce, asked permission of the English Parliament to send an agent to London to treat privately. "I cannot," replied the Secretary of the Council of State, "procure for you a safe conduct to come in the capacity you propose. But, if the French Government will consider the wrongs by it committed, and will save us the necessity of seeking justice for ourselves, and treat with the Republic in the forms usual between sovereign states, I have no doubt that this State will be willing to entertain any honest and just propositions for the settlement of differences"* (Dec., 1650). Meantime Louis' delay not only affected the interest of merchants, but threatened the success of his own military expeditions. Agents from the revolted city of Bordeaux appeared in London, soliciting aid of the Republicans, and offering in return to place England in possession of a port it could secure for them on the west coast of France. The English fleet did not hesitate to seize some French vessels carrying provisions for the relief of Dunkirk, at the time besieged by the Netherlanders. The town, in consequence, was forced to surrender (Sept.); and, when the French government complained of the conduct of the English fleet, the Republicans replied that the act was merely a reprisal for damages inflicted on English merchants by French vessels in the Mediterranean. Thus pressed, Louis at last consented to send an ambassador to England, and formally recognized the Republican government (Dec.)

Though the Republicans, by the energy of their government, caused England to be feared and respected, yet their foreign policy was not marked by any true insight into the relations of states at the time. France, though a Catholic country, was no deadly enemy of Protestantism or of progress; the governments of Spain and Austria were distinguished for their fanatical and reactionary spirit. The Republicans, however, showed themselves inclined to support Spain against France, and now entered into a disastrous war with Holland, the enemy of Spain, a Protestant country, and their own natural ally. This war was, partly, the result of commercial jealousy. The aspiring spirit of the Republicans caused them to make unjust and unreasonable demands as the price of their friendship with the sister republic. We have before had occasion to notice the commercial rivalries existing between the

* Guizot, i. 448.

English and the Dutch, the cruel murders perpetrated in the East Indies, and the consequent depression of English trade.* The unfriendly feeling thus produced became still more pronounced after the execution of the king and the establishment of the Republic. The Dutch were afraid that England, now that it had a government like their own, would also turn its attention to commerce, and, by the superior size and resources of the country, eclipse the smaller luminary at its side.

On the other hand the Republicans had been so successful in founding and maintaining their new form of government, that now no designs seemed too bold for accomplishment. At first, trying fair means to prevent the Dutch from acting as their rivals on the sea and the destroyers of their commerce, they had sent two extraordinary ambassadors, Strickland and St. John, to Holland, offering the renewal of a former treaty of 1495, and proposing further that the two countries should unite in a kind of confederacy and have the same friends and enemies (Jan., 1651). The States of Holland, in place of a confederacy, proposed terms of their own for an alliance. Dutch statesmen foresaw that if England and Holland were confederated together, their country being the smaller and less powerful, would practically lose its independence, and in its foreign relations be forced to act in the interest of England. The negotiations were broken off, and the English ambassadors recalled (June, 1651). "My lords," said St. John to the States commissioners upon taking his leave, "you have your eye upon the issue of the affairs of the King of Scotland, and therefore have despised the friendship we proffered you; I will assure you that many in the Parliament were of opinion that we ought not to have come hither, or to have sent ambassadors till we had first overcome our difficulties, and seen an ambassador from you. I now see my fault, and perceive very well that those members of Parliament judged right. You will in a little time see our affairs against the King of Scotland despatched, and then you will by your ambassadors come and desire what we now so cordially come to proffer. But assure yourselves, you will then repent you have rejected our kindness."†

After the battle of Worcester (3rd Sept., 1651), the victorious

---

* See p. 253.   † De Witt, Interest of Holland, 393.

Republicans passed the Navigation Act, the heading of which briefly expressed its contents : "Goods from foreign parts; by whom to be imported." First, with a few exceptions named, it forbade any goods to be imported into England from Asia, Africa, or America, excepting in English ships, or in ships belonging to the English colonies; secondly, it forbade the produce or manufacture of any country in Europe, to be imported into England, except in English ships, or in ships of the country in which the goods were produced (9th Oct., 1651). The framers of this law had two ends in view. The first, to transfer part of the carrying trade* of the Dutch to Englishmen; the second, to increase the strength of the English navy. The first end was contrary to the principles of free trade. If the Dutch could import foreign goods into England cheaper than English merchants, the English consumer was benefited by the trade being in their hands, and a saving of labour was made. The second end, however, that of national defence, may, perhaps, then have partly justified the law. English merchants were practically compelled to build vessels in order to import the goods formerly imported by the Dutch; and from the merchant marine came the sailors, and often the ships, that guarded the coasts and caused foreigners to hesitate before insulting the English government. The usage English traders had experienced in the East Indies from the Dutch, in the West Indies from the Spaniards, had proved the necessity of England's possessing a powerful navy, if she was either to extend her trade or protect her colonies.

The Dutch sent ambassadors to resume the negotiations, and obtain the repeal of the new law, but so unfriendly was the feeling existing between the two nations, that while the ambassadors were still in the country, the English and Dutch admirals, Blake and Van Tromp, engaged with their fleets in the Downs (19th May). Each admiral accused the other of having been the aggressor, and war with Holland was now declared (19th July.) Blake sailed to the eastern coast of Scotland, where he surprised 600 Dutch fishing vessels, and exacted from them the tribute of the tenth herring. Meanwhile Van Tromp was prevented by a contrary wind from approaching a small fleet of fifteen vessels, left in the channel under the command of Ayscue to guard the

* See p. 252.

English coasts. He sailed north in search of Blake, but while in the German Ocean a violent storm so damaged his fleet, that he returned to Holland with his vessels reduced to a third of their former number. The Dutch, who thought themselves better sailors than the English, were deeply mortified at their misfortunes, which they ascribed to the " witch-wind" that prevented their admiral from attacking Ayscue. Nor were the English satisfied with such fortuitous successes. They remarked that the country had run great hazards during the summer, from which it had escaped rather by fortune of wind and weather than by the providence of committee or admiral. The committee of council which was at the head of the Admiralty, was, in the opinion of many, too large a body to conduct the affairs of the navy with the skill and expedition required in time of war. The council was now informed that "they were letting slip many fair opportunities, and were like to play a very dangerous after-game, for the Dutch were preparing a great fleet, and would pass through the channel to convoy their merchantmen, when the best of the English ships would be called in for want of victuals."* These fears proved not unfounded. Some of Blake's ships were under repair, while twenty others had been despatched to the Mediterranean, when Van Tromp, with 95 vessels, passed down the channel. Though Blake had only 37, he preferred fighting to retreating down the channel, and thus leaving the coast towns unguarded. An engagement took place off Dover, which lasted from eleven in the morning until dark. Although the fleets were so unequal in numbers, Blake under cover of the night, succeeded in reaching the Thames in safety with the larger part of his damaged fleet. Two vessels fell into the hands of the Dutch, the " Garland " and one other merchantman, which, when the rest made off, were left fighting 'board and board' with Van Tromp's own flagship (29th Nov.).

On news of this defeat great discouragement prevailed amongst the seamen, great fear amongst the people. General Monk was associated with Blake and Dean in command of the fleet, and four or five special commissioners of the Admiralty were appointed, with Vane at their head. Vane's name itself was sufficient to serve as a guarantee for an honest administration. The commissioners made every effort to repair the fleet and place it in a flourishing condition.

* Colonel Thompson's Notes upon the Dutch War in Bodleian MSS.

"They sent letters to all vice-admirals and mayors of sea towns to stir up seamen to engage in the service. The best and ablest commanders that could be heard of were invited to the service and entertained, if they were men of courage and civil conversation, and keeping good order in their ships. No fee or gratuity was suffered to be given or taken by any man for their places. The seamen were well paid; the wives and children of the slain were provided for; pensions were given to the wounded. Inquiry was made after misdemeanours in officers, and of embezzlements of stores and prize goods, and such officers were removed whose actions appeared to be ill. The commissioners sat daily at Whitehall, both early and late, and were private in their debates."*
Early in the spring Van Tromp, convoying on their return voyage up the channel more than 200 laden merchantmen, fell in with the English admirals off Portland Isle. On three successive days the two fleets, each of 80 or 90 sail, were engaged. The battle, begun off Portland Isle, extended to the coast of Holland. The Dutch were entirely defeated, and compelled to seek refuge in the shallow waters of the Texel, whither the English vessels, which drew more water than theirs, were unable to pursue. In this defeat the Dutch lost eleven men-of-war and thirty merchantmen (18, 19, 20 Feb., 1653).

* Colonel Thompson's Notes.

CHAPTER XIII.

FALL OF REPUBLICANS, AND BAREBONES' PARLIAMENT
(1651—1653).

Nothing is good for a nation but that which arises from its own core and its own general wants, without apish imitation of another; since what to one race of people, of a certain age, is a wholesome nutriment, may, perhaps, prove a poison for another.—GOETHE'S CONVERSATIONS WITH ECKERMANN.

CROMWELL, in his despatch to the Parliament, called his victory at Worcester a *crowning mercy*, words which the Republicans understood in a double sense. Conscious that he adhered to their party rather by sufferance than on principle, they dreaded to what use he might turn his influence with the army, now that his sword was sheathed. There was certainly cause for fear. The size of the army had been gradually increased during the late wars, so that the forces in England, Ireland, and Scotland numbered upwards of 50,000 men. The character of the army, moreover, was to some extent altered from what it was in the year '48, when the soldiers nearly mutinied against their officers for treating with the king. Since Fairfax' resignation, Cromwell had used his position as commander-in-chief to weed out of the ranks violent agitators, supplying their places by any who were willing to enter the service, even old Royalists, so long as these proved themselves orderly and good soldiers. Thus the men, no longer accustomed to hold meetings, pass resolutions, and form plans of their own, had, as a rule, become more ready to obey the commands of their general without questioning his purposes; while the fanatical element which still remained, the Anabaptists and Fifth Monarchists, at this time placed a blind confidence in Cromwell, because they knew that he shared their desire of reforming the law and the Church.

A change was not only discernible in the character of the ranks, but also in that of the council of officers. Here also it was due to

Cromwell, who, unwilling that the government of the country should rest upon a small Republican faction, was always ready to advance merit wherever he met it, and constantly succeeded in attaching to his service men of contrary principles to his own. Lord Broghill, to whom the Commons had just voted £2000, had been a Royalist. He was a son of the Earl of Cork, and his Irish influence made him an important acquisition. He was passing through London, on his way to join Charles Stuart on the continent, when Oliver, about to proceed to Ireland, paid him an unexpected visit, and told him he must either go to the Tower, or accept a command in the Irish army. Broghill asked for a little time in which to make up his mind. "Impossible," replied Cromwell; "if I leave you, my offer rejected, you will be at once a State prisoner." The offer was accepted. General Monk, now commander-in-chief in Scotland, was also an old Royalist, who had once fought in the king's armies in Ireland. Men such as these, unlike the heroes of Marston Moor and Naseby, allowed their principles to be identical with their interests. Accepting facts as they stood, it seemed to them unreasonable to follow any other line of action than that of supporting whatever government was best able to support itself. Meantime, the one link that remained between the Republicans and Cromwell was gone, when Ireton died at the age of forty-one, with a burning fever upon him, while still acting as commander-in-chief in Ireland (Nov. 26th). Ireton had great influence with the army; he used to say to his soldiers and fellow-officers, 'You may not want to do a thing, but you must do it, because the good of the State requires it of you;' sternly just, and though fond of his own way, yet ready to yield to those that first yielded to him, as hard to himself as to others, he won obedience by the confidence he inspired in his men. The Republicans he inspired with an equal confidence, and when they distrusted Cromwell they still trusted Ireton. But now aware of the change produced in the army, the Republicans were indignant with Cromwell for having, as they said, turned out "godly men, and put in rascally turncoat Cavaliers, pitiful sottish beasts of his own alliance." Yet there could be no matter of doubt that Cromwell was right alike in rendering the army more submissive in temper, and in conciliating men of all parties, whatever their principles or views. An army that refuses obedience to its commanders necessarily becomes demoralized, and can only bring mischief upon the country it professes to serve. The Republicans, dreading the increased power of the general, forgot the danger with which their government had been threatened by the mutinies of the Levellers. The second point, that touched the necessity of conciliating political opponents, was more important still. No government, whatever its inherent merits, however honest and upright the men who conduct it, can hope to be lasting unless it conciliates a general support sufficient to make it rest on a national as distinct from a party basis. In this the Republicans had entirely failed. The dream of Vane, Bradshaw, Martin, Ludlow, and Hutchinson, of establishing a "free commonwealth, with the hearts and affections of the people to support it," was still as far from fact as on the day when Colonel Pride stood at the door of the Commons and turned Presbyterian members back from the threshold. The Republicans had, in fact, made a capital error in abolishing the two established institutions of monarchy and an Upper House in obedience to a theory. No single form of government can be said to be good for all nations without regard to circumstances of climate, race, progress, and the history of the past. To alter a form of government, to change the relations which the executive, judicial, and legislative powers hold to one another, is a most delicate operation. Governments grow with the growth of nations, and shape themselves according to the circumstances of the national history. Hence a government rooted in the past is strong in the affections of a people, while a constitution transplanted or written on paper rarely lasts beyond the particular exigency which called it forth. Reforms, therefore, which, in an advancing state of civilization must always be needful, ought never to be introduced by means of violent changes, but, as far as possible, under the disguise of those old forms to which a people is already accustomed. A despotism, it is true, can rarely be changed into a free government without, as it were, setting the axe at the root of the tree, and planting a new constitution in the place of one man's will. This was the case in France at the time of the Revolution. But her history ever since has been a warning of the danger of snapping the chain that connects the past with the present. It has been well said that those who do so must prove that their work produces more good than evil. The men who established a republic in England in the seventeenth century failed to prove the good they did was greater than the good they undid. The English constitution they upset was distinctly free, though certain reforms were needed to shear the crown of prerogatives which in bad hands were fatal to liberty. Part of the work had been done by the laws passed by the Long Parliament; there remained the second, and possibly more difficult part of finding a king who would consent to allow his ministers to be responsible to Parliament. The foresight of Pym had provided for the emergency. There is little doubt that when he invited to London Charles Louis, the elector palatine, and elder brother of Rupert, he thought he had found such a king, and contemplated a change of succession. But Pym was long dead and gone, and there had now risen a race of politicians who drew their statesmanship from Biblical or classical models, and not from the study of English constitutional history. The scheme of the Republicans happened unfortunately to be utterly incapable of fitting on to old institutions. They would not hear of a government consisting of two Houses of Parliament, with a president bearing the name of king, though such a government might have been made practically Republican. What they proposed to establish was government by a standing assembly, re-elected or recruited at stated intervals; and to this it was impossible that the nation should give a willing adherence. They might have accomplished more for their country, had they laid to heart the weighty sentences of the great philosopher of their youth. "It is true," says Bacon, "that what is settled by custom, though it be not good, yet, at least, it is fit; and those things which have gone long together are, as it were, confederate within themselves, whereas new things piece not so well; but, though they help by their utility, yet they trouble by their inconformity; besides, they are like strangers, more admired and less favoured. It were good, therefore, that men in their innovations would follow the example of time itself, which, indeed, innovateth greatly, but quietly, and by degrees scarce to be perceived, for otherwise whatsoever is new is unlooked for; and ever it mends some and *im*pairs other; and he that is holpen takes it for a fortune, and thanks the time; and he that is hurt for a wrong, and imputeth it to the author. It is good also not to try experiments in states, except the necessity be urgent, or the utility evident; and well to beware that it be the reformation that draweth on the change, and not the desire of change that pretendeth the reformation."*

The dislike of nobles, gentry, lawyers, the Presbyterians, the masses, to the new government was mainly one of sentiment, arising from the abolition of monarchy and the House of Lords. With those who were moved by these constitutional feelings, any attempt at conciliation would probably have been useless. The Republicans, however, despite their numerical weakness, made a second error, and did not try to conciliate even the democratic party beneath them by granting the reforms desired in the law and the church. In fact, the character of their government towards all parties alike was harsh and revolutionary. Nor was this a matter of surprise, for the form of that government was intrinsically bad. The Commons were sole legislators; they appointed executive officers out of their own number; they often took upon themselves to act as judges; they were not held in check by fear of a dissolution; they were, in fact, in possession of absolute power. It is hardly possible for a body of men, thus emancipated from the control of constituents, to act the part either of just or moderate rulers. The selfish, cruel, and avaricious will number as many as the generous and upright. Temptations will be great, and the indifferent, sheltering themselves behind numbers, will consent to deeds which they would blush to own, were they acting on their sole responsibility. The treatment Royalists experienced from this body was not such as to allay enmity, or heal wounds yet green. <i>Treatment of Royalists.</i>

Following the bad precedent set at the trial of the king, High Courts of Justice were constantly instituted to try those suspected of treason against the Commonwealth. The Duke of Hamilton and two other leaders engaged in the Royalist risings and the Scottish invasion of the year 1648, were put to death by the sentence of one of these revolutionary tribunals. During the second war with the Scots there were in England four Royalist and Presbyterian plots, and twenty-seven persons engaged in them were executed in thirteen months.† Lilburne hit the weak points of the government in one of his seditious pamphlets. ' When," he wrote, "I came to hear Capel make his defence before the High Court of Justice, and cite statutes to prove all treasons should be tried by the rules of the common law, looking

* Bacon's Essays, xxiv., of Innovations. † Guizot, i. 152.

round about him and saying, 'I am an Englishman, and the law my inheritance, and the benefit of the Petition of Right my birthright;'—and looking upon the president, 'where is my jury? I see none of my jury; I demand the right of my jury, without verdict of whom I cannot in law be condemned;'—bringing forward their own declarations to maintain the fundamental laws of the nation;—but when all was to no purpose, I confess my heart was ready to sink within me, and I had much ado in the open court to contain myself from an avowed detestation of their abominable wickedness."*

In order to provide funds for the war, Cavaliers who had hitherto escaped were hunted out and forced to compound. In 1651 seventy Cavaliers had all their lands and goods confiscated; in 1652, the year after the battle of Worcester, twenty-nine suffered in the same manner, while 682 had to pay to the republic one third part of the value of their lands and goods. Where the sufferers had really fought against the government, no exception could be taken to the severity used, though it was not likely to conciliate; but too often estates were confiscated and fines imposed with gross injustice, and the 'Commonwealth men' grew rich on spoils unfairly wrung from their prostrate enemies.† Cromwell's indignation rose as he saw " poor men driven like flocks of sheep by forty in a morning to the confiscation of goods and estates, without any man being able to give a reason why two of them had deserved to forfeit a shilling."‡

Levellers, like Royalists, received harsh measure. Lilburne, *Lilburne banished.* as concerned in the mutinies of the soldiers, was tried by jury for high treason, and, much to the discontent of his accusers, acquitted (Oct., 1649). It was not long, however, before he was again in trouble. His uncle, George Lilburne, was deprived of some coal mines in Durham by sentence of the county committee for sequestering delinquents' estates. An appeal was made to 'the Committee of Parliament for the composition of delinquents' estates,' and a second time the cause was decided against George Lilburne. Hereupon 'Freeborn John' presented the House with a petition containing a fierce attack upon Haslerig, as the chairman of the county committee. The House, upon the report of a committee appointed to investigate

* Fund. Liberties of England vindicated (1649).
† Hutch., 353, 355; see also Hallam, i. 657. ‡ Carlyle, iii. 44.

the case, negatived the charges stated in the petition, and voted that Lilburne should pay £3000 to the republic, £2000 to Haslerig, be banished for life, and in case of return suffer death as a felon. As he refused to kneel at the bar of the House and hear his sentence read, an Act of Parliament, embodying its contents, was drawn up and passed against him. The irregularities of this course are obvious enough. In the first place county committees are found still sitting and taking the place of proper courts of justice, as in the confessed revolutionary times preceding the king's execution ; in the second, the Legislature is seen acting as a court of justice, and passing a sentence out of all proportion to the offence committed. Had Lilburne been tried for defamation, and found guilty by jury in a court of common law, the heaviest punishment that the judges could *by law* have inflicted upon him, would have been a fine and corporal punishment.* Those who condemned him to banishment for life were not unbiassed judges, but political enemies, who acted as jury by declaring him guilty of crime, as judges by passing sentence upon him, as legislature by embodying their sentence in a law. Nor was Lilburne's a solitary case.†
"The House," says Whitelock, "took upon them and exercised

* Godwin, iii. 337.

† The discoverer of unsequestered property belonging to 'delinquents' received 1s. in the £. By the warrant of county committees, the property of any who had rendered the slightest service to the royal cause was liable to be sequestered. For instance, John Browne, a gentleman owning estates in Herefordshire, being a minor and left destitute of the means of subsistence, was "forced to seek out his guardian and go into the king's quarters, whereby he became a delinquent." He did, indeed, bear arms as a Royalist, but atoned for this by serving afterwards for three years in the Parliament's army. Petitioning on that account to be admitted to compound for his estate, he was still fined a-tenth of his property. A Lancashire husbandman, for simply supplying a cheese to the soldiers at a Royalist rendezvous, (where he was summoned on pain of death by Lord Derby's officers), had his property sequestered, though he ever after lived in the Parliament's quarters, submitted to their committees, and took the covenant. Members of these committees were often paid the debts owing to them by Parliament out of delinquents' estates. "God of His mercy grant," says a journal of the time, "that for the future, it may never see a perpetuity added to the two Houses of Parliament ; nor committees to manage the justice of the kingdom and sit judges of men's liberties, estates, and fortunes, admitting not the law for their rule, but their own arbitrary, revocable, disputable orders and ordinances." It was said, indeed, that if a man had a single enemy on a committee, it was impossible to obtain justice, for 'against malice there was no fence.'—Military Mem. of Col. Birch, 63, 96, 219, 236 ; Sir Roger Twysden's Journal, quoted in Bisset, Omitted Chapter of English History.

all manner of jurisdiction, and sentenced persons at discretion, which was disliked by many lawyers of the House (of which I was one); and we showed them the illegality and breach of liberty in those arbitrary proceedings."

While the House treated Royalists and Levellers harshly, it passed over lightly the offences of friends. For instance, a certain Lord Howard of Esrick, was proved to have been bribed by Royalists to give them easy terms in compounding. Though sentenced to be fined and imprisoned, he was kept in confinement but a very short time, and his fine remitted. Many of the members themselves took advantage of their position to secure salaries or grants of land from their party. Even in the matter of religious toleration, the House fell far short of the principles of the best men in it; Catholic priests taken in the country were banished, and the Long Parliament's laws enforced, which forbade Episcopalians the exercise of their own forms of worship. It must not, however, be supposed that unjust sentences and harsh votes were passed without opposition; Martin would seek to save the life of a Royalist, urging what was, perhaps, the only argument that could have weight in such a House, the old adage that 'the blood of the martyr would be the seed of the church:' and there were others beside him who still remained faithful to the great principle of liberty of conscience. Vane showed the pecuniary incorruptibility which is the boast but not always the practice of republican virtue: he was the first to break through the iniquitous usage by which the commissioners of the navy received a percentage on the money expended; after refunding vast sums and securing a fixed salary for his agent, he worked himself for nothing. Yet members such as Vane, Martin, Bradshaw, and Ludlow, in spite of their integrity, noble intentions, and high principles, were unable to drag along the dead weight behind them. The House was judged by the votes and acts of the majority, and the government of this absolute Parliament was as much detested as that of any single tyrant.

Cromwell took a line of his own. The Republicans had always complained he was not hand and glove with them; they now doubted whether he would give them even a passive support. His aim as well as theirs had been the establishment of a free government, which should win the nation's trust and regard. Their means to this end had been tried and had failed. Their failure Cromwell had foreseen from the first, but at the time of the establishment of the republic he had not been strong enough to oppose their wishes without endangering the common cause. Now he might hope, not only to head, but to some extent to guide, his party. The army was a far more obedient instrument to his hand than it had ever been before, while the feeling of the levelling and reforming party towards him was entirely changed. When he treated with Charles, they had joined with the Republicans against him; now they looked upon him as their own leader in the cause of popular reform.

Misgovernment, disorder, injustice, Cromwell detested as only a man can who is himself possessed of the genius to govern well. There may, therefore, be truth in the assertion that after the 'crowning mercy' at Worcester, he did determine in his own mind to bring the present government to an end. Yet he was no self-seeking intriguer, such as his enemies supposed him. Ambitious he was in the true sense of seeking a vantage-ground for good. Conscious of ability, he hears the voice of his suffering nation calling aloud for a physician. Unhasting, he can wait till more eager hands have tried and failed. If he desires power, it is to accomplish a task that none other can. Had Cromwell fallen short of this amount of ambition, he would have fallen short also of being the greatest man of his time. More, however, than his country's needs, more than the knowledge of his own capacity in some measure to relieve them, urged him on to the destruction of the republic. For in the long course of events that had raised him, who once lived as a country gentleman on his farm, to be now the most powerful man in the state, he saw the directing hand of God. When he would have treated with Charles and allowed him to retain the title of king, Republicans and Levellers had been given the power to force him from his path. Fairfax' resignation of the chief command, victory following upon victory, had invested him with extraordinary power. To use this power for, what he now believed, the good of his country, seemed a duty imposed upon him by God. If it was necessary to convert old friends into enemies, he must not sacrifice duty to friendship. "I need pity," he wrote in a private letter to the father of his daughter-in-law; "I know what I feel. Great place and business in this world is not worth the looking after; I should have no comfort in mine, but that my hope is in the Lord's presence.

I have not sought these things; truly I have been called unto them by the Lord, and therefore am not without some assurance that He will enable His poor worm and weak servant to do His will, and to fulfil my generation. In this I desire your prayers."* Standing in the midst of the universal discontent, Cromwell seemed to feel himself the friend and protector of all the oppressed. When the Catholics petitioned the House for relief, Vane spoke in their favour and was beaten: Cromwell, without heeding the votes, gave protection from persecution by his own hand and seal.† In the distribution of livings between Presbyterians and Independents, the Republicans unduly favoured the Independents; it was Cromwell, the Independent, who sent a guard to a church to prevent an Independent from taking violent possession of a pulpit belonging to a Presbyterian: he tolerated even the Presbyterian preachers who told his soldiers that they broke the covenant in making war upon the Scots. It was Cromwell who, when Royalists were being deprived in large numbers of their estates, persisted in making the House pass an Act of Oblivion for the pardon of offences committed before Worcester (24th Feb., 1652): the Republicans had looked to the confiscations as a support for the Dutch war, but Cromwell thought funds for a foreign war were ill bought by stirring the embers of civil strife at home. And, lastly, it was Cromwell who could be trusted to attack the abuses which made the Anabaptists cry out for reform in the church, and who could sympathize with plain-dealing soldiers like Colonel Pride who "wished to see the lawyers' gowns hanging up in Westminster Hall by the side of the colours and trophies taken at Dunbar."

It was certain that the present relation of parties could not last. Since the Commonwealth was first established, the House had been repeatedly called upon by the officers to do two acts, to reform the law, and to fix a time for a dissolution. Though committees upon both questions were appointed, they did not advance quickly in their work. Through the opposition of the lawyers, a strong and influential body in the House, little reform was effected in the law beyond the passing of an act that all law-books should be translated out of Latin into English, and that all law proceedings should be conducted in the English

* Carl., ii. 161. † Harris, Life of Cromwell.

language. Members again were by no means anxious to divest themselves of the supreme power they possessed, and up to the date of the battle of Worcester (3rd Sept., 1651), the House had come to no decision whatever on the question of its own dissolution. When, however, the general and his officers entered London, as the victors of Dunbar and Worcester, and demanded with voices not to be gainsaid, that they should know for how long the present government was to continue, the House, by a very small majority, passed a vote that it would dissolve on the 3rd Nov., 1654, thus giving itself three more years of life (17th Nov., 1651). The date proposed was so distant that the vote gave no satisfaction. The eager reformers of law and church looked to Cromwell to bring matters to a speedier conclusion. The officers, generally, had no intention of allowing a clique of some fifty politicians to remain sovereigns for three years longer. Before the time of Pride's Purge, they had petitioned in favour of elective monarchy, by which they meant the kind of government afterwards represented by the Protectorate. They now simply petitioned for a Dissolution Bill providing for the calling of a new Parliament. Themselves preferring a Republic, they were, nevertheless, too practical in their aims to care more for the form than the substance, and were likely to be content with any government that assured influence to themselves, and a safe existence to the army. Thus pressed, the Republicans consented to introduce a bill for a new representative (13th Aug.), but at the same time were careful so to frame it that they themselves should still remain in exclusive possession of sovereign power. The next House of Commons was to consist of 400 members; all members, however, of the present House were to keep their seats, and be able at pleasure to reject newly-elected members. The officers held repeated conferences with members of Parliament about the bill that was now being hastened through the House. "This is no dissolution," they said, " nothing but a perpetuating of yourselves; we want men who will reform the law, and you were three months settling what a single word, 'incumbrance,' meant; reform will never get on at that rate." "You must go," said Oliver; "the nation loathes your sitting." The members, however, far from being wrought upon to alter their bill, replied obstinately that in the House they had the right of their yeas and their noes.

On the 19th of April, a conference held at Whitehall ended with an agreement that the objectionable bill should be laid aside until a second meeting had been held the following afternoon at the same place. The members, however, who made this agreement had no real power to bind the House. The next day, while about forty officers and members were discussing the question of dissolution, messages were brought to the general that the objectionable 'Perpetuation Bill' was being hurried through the House, and would shortly be made law. Cromwell left the conference, and ordering a company of his own regiment of musketeers to follow him, led the way to Westminster. Leaving the soldiers at the Commons' door, he entered the House, not in uniform, but "clad in plain black clothes and gray worsted stockings, and sat down, as he used to do, in an ordinary place." He listened for some time with interest to the debate, but when the question was about to be put 'That this bill do now pass,' he whispered to Major-General Harrison, "This is the time ; I must do it," "rose up, put off his hat, and spoke, at first in commendation for their pains and care of the public good, but afterwards he changed his style, told them of their injustice, self-interest, and other faults." "Perhaps you think," he said, "this is not Parliamentary language ! I confess it is not, neither are you to expect any such from me." "The first time," said Sir Peter Wentworth, rising, "I ever heard such unbecoming language given to Parliament ; it is the more horrid in that it comes from our servant, and that servant whom we have so highly trusted and obliged." But as he was going on, the general stepped into the midst of the House, "Come, come, I will put an end to your prating," and "clapping on his hat," walked up and down the floor and chid them roundly, saying, "You are no Parliament ; I say you are no Parliament ;" and looking and pointing at one member, said, "There sits a drunkard," and then pointing at a second gave him a bad word, though without mentioning names, while to Harrison he called out, "Bring them in." And then entered some thirty musketeers, ready to obey their general, whatever his orders might be. "This is not honest," cried Vane from his seat ; "yea, it is against morality and common honesty." "What shall we do with this bauble ? Here, take it away," said Oliver, picking up the mace, and handing it to a musketeer. "Take him down," he then said, addressing Harrison, and pointing at the Speaker.

"Come down," said Harrison. "I will not come down, unless I am forced," replied Lenthall, frowning, and trying to rise to the occasion, as he had done when Charles in that same House had demanded the five members of him. "Take him down," repeated Oliver; whereupon Harrison pulled Lenthall by the gown, who descended from his chair, and the rest of the members, fifty-three in all, after a little pretence of resistance, followed their Speaker out of the House. When all were gone, the Lord General locked the door, and put the key in his pocket. By break of day the next morning some Royalist wit had stuck a placard on the Commons' door: "This house is to be let, now unfurnished."*

Thus the law that this Parliament should not be dissolved without its own consent was broken by one of those who had given his vote to its making.† The original justification of the law was that it secured the just rights of the nation against the violence of the king. That this was the original purpose was shown by the fact that it was passed within three months of a triennial bill, which it was intended to supplement rather than supersede. When it was diverted from this purpose, and was used to secure the selfish aims of the members against the just rights of the nation, it became at once unconstitutional. The Commons had received a definite commission, and had no right to enlarge this commission without a fresh reference to the people who had appointed them. Temporary trustees have no right to make their tenure perpetual. The Commons were temporary representatives, and had no right to make themselves life peers, still less to intrigue for a power of co-optation by demanding a veto on new elections. The temporary justification was gone. The king was no more; the House of Lords was no more; the House of Commons was no longer a representative body. Danger resulted to the nation from the continuation of the House, not from its dissolution. In conquering Charles it had saved England from the establishment of a despotism, but it had not shown itself capable of the necessary afterwork of reconstruction. The country was drifting into anarchy; the people submitted to the government solely through fear of the army; the army and the House were in collision. The so-called bill for a 'new representative' being really a perpetuation bill, was practically a *coup d'état*.

* Sydney Papers, 141; Whitelock, 554; Ludlow, ii. 18, 21.
† See p. 100.

Powers of State must have either right or might; this Parliament had neither. Still, to resort to armed force is a blot on the origin of any new power. The establishment of a government that should unite in itself the elements of order and of reform, and thus save the nation from a third civil war, could alone justify Cromwell's employment of military force against the civil power. The responsibility of the act does not rest specially on Cromwell. The officers were determined on a dissolution, and for some weeks past had only been restrained from effecting their purpose by the opposition of Cromwell himself, who to the last clung to the hope that the House would yet be persuaded to dissolve itself. "I speak here," he said, a few months later, "in the presence of some that were at the closure of the consultations, and, as before the Lord, the thinking of an act of violence was to us worse than any battle that ever we were in, or that could be, to the utmost hazard of our lives; so willing were we, even very tender and desirous, if possible, that these men might quit their places with honour."

A temporary executive was constituted at once. The council of officers, and a new council of State, composed of nine army men and four civilians, now conducted the government between them. Cromwell, all-powerful as he was, did not attempt to assume the position which at this time he, perhaps, felt must ultimately be his. He was pledged to the Fifth Monarchists and the Anabaptists for the reform of the law and the church, and it was accordingly in the hands of men really determined on reform that he now placed the government. Orders were sent out by the council of officers to Independents and other sectarian ministers in every county to consult with their congregations, and return the names of 'godly men,' fitted to sit in a new Parliament of saints. Out of the returns thus made certain persons were selected, to whom Cromwell sent, in his own name, writs of summons, bidding them attend him at Whitehall, as representatives of different towns and counties. Five members were chosen for Scotland, six for Ireland, six for Wales, 139 for England.

The new assembly is sometimes called the Little Parliament, sometimes by the nickname of Barebone's Parliament, from the name of one of its members, Praise-God Barebone, a leather-seller in Fleet Street. It has been represented by its enemies as composed of a set of ignorant fanatics. This, however, was not the case. Many members were gentlemen, most were men of some mark, if not able to boast of great fortunes or high birth. In it were General Monk and other distinguished officers; Admiral Blake; Lockhart, afterwards ambassador in France; Viscount Lisle, son of the Earl of Leicester; and Alderman Ireton, brother of the late Lord-Deputy of Ireland.

The first grand reform which the Parliament undertook was that of the law. The general administration of English law was then, as it still is, divided into two distinct branches, that of common law, administered by the three Courts of King's Bench, Common Pleas, and Exchequer, and that of equity, administered by the Court of Chancery.

English common law originated in the unwritten rules or customs, derived in part from Saxon times, in part from the feudal system as introduced by the Normans. These unwritten rules or customs were in the course of time embodied in the decisions of the judges, who were guided, not only by the customs already spontaneously observed by the people, and the analogy of previous decisions, but also, though not professedly, by their own studies in Roman law and their own ideas of right and expediency. The ideal of early times is a fixed law unaltered by those in power. There is little demand for an adjusting legislation and less supply. But as circumstances change, the justice of one generation becomes injustice to another. The present source of adjustment is mainly in statutes made by Parliament, but for a long time there was little adjustment at all, and what there was came mainly out of the breasts of the judges, who used legal fictions as their means of quietly modifying the law. Such fictions have been justly described as 'invaluable expedients for overcoming the rigidity of law,' but they do not adjust the law either rapidly or completely enough, and their use gradually loads a system with technicalities. It necessarily followed that English common law became a complicated system, not easily reducible to general rules, and not easily understood except by those who had received a special education. Complaints were raised by the reformers that the client was left at the mercy of his advocate, for none could understand the law but lawyers trained; that law-books were so many and so costly that few could buy them; that decisions of former judges were often contradictory; that the fees demanded by lawyers were excessive, the delays of justice intolerable, and costs so great that the poor were shut out from redress at law; while the punishments enacted were unnecessarily severe, and were often arranged so as to press heavily on the offences of the poor, and let the rich off easily. Bentham, as late as the beginning of the present century, repeats the complaints of the reformers of the seventeenth:—"It is the people's interest that delay, vexation, and expense of procedure should be as small as possible; it is the advocate's interest that they should be as great as possible. As to uncertainty in the law, it is the people's interest that each man's security against wrong should be as complete as possible; that all his rights should be known to him; that all acts which, in case of his doing them, will be treated as offences, may be known to him as such, together with their eventual punishment, that he may avoid committing them. . . . It is the lawyer's interest that people should continually suffer for the non-observance of laws, which, so far from having received efficient promulgation, have never yet found any authoritative expression in words. This is the perfection of oppression; yet propose that access to knowledge of the laws be afforded by means of a code, lawyers, one and all, will join in declaring it impossible. To any effect, as occasion occurs, a judge will forge a rule of law; to that same effect, in any determinate form of words, propose to make a law, that same judge will declare it impossible. It is the judge's interest that, on every occasion, his declared opinion be taken for the standard of right and wrong."*

The institution of Chancery arose from an attempt to make law advance of itself with the increasing complexity of civilization. It became the chancellor's duty to interfere when, through the rigidity with which the common law was administered, some wrong was done for which law gave no remedy. Thus, in the now common case of property being vested in a third person as trustee, the common law acknowledged only the title of the trustee, ignoring altogether the moral rights of the parties for whose benefit the property was held. In these and similar cases the Court of Chancery intervened, on this ground—that although not legally bound, yet in *foro conscientiæ* the trustee could not violate the trust or confidence reposed in him. Another example may serve to illustrate the adjusting power of the two kinds of law. By the rules of common law, a married woman received at

* Bentham, on Fallacies.

her husband's death, by inalienable right, a dower of one-third of all the lands which had ever formed part of his estate. As society advanced, and the inalienable right was found to hamper the transfer of property, the common law courts adjusted the difficulty somewhat at the expense of the woman's security, by tolerating a palpable evasion of the law of dower through a fictitious suit and a conveyancer's quibble. When Chancery stepped in, by a piece of judge-made law, it avoided the inconvenience without entirely losing the object in view, securing women's property by settlement, and yet making it transferable by trustees. As time progressed, the Court of Chancery became itself as much bound by technical rules as the courts of common law. From the fact that the chancellor was originally an ecclesiastic, the procedure of the Roman or civil law was adopted in his court. This procedure was in itself more complicated than that of the common law. A complicated procedure in itself causes delay, and in Chancery the issues themselves are complex; for suits may not merely require sentences with the simple 'Yes' or 'No' of common law, but involve administering large estates and assigning various rights to different interests. In this system there was little check on the abuses of judges and officials. Much was delegated to the masters in Chancery, and Coke says these bought their appointments and recouped themselves by extortions from suitors. Moreover, the court was peculiarly open to the charge of corrupt motives, as before a body of precedents was formed the decision of each case was supposed to rest largely on the discretion of the chancellor. Complaints were made "that there were 23,000 causes depending upon the court, some of which had been depending five, twenty, thirty years and more! that there had been spent therein thousands of pounds, to the ruin of many families! in one word, that the Court of Chancery was nothing but a mystery of wickedness and standing cheat!" Thus, while common law was felt to be harsh and technical, Chancery was still more disliked as both dilatory and corrupt. Many of the complaints raised were only too well founded, especially those that referred to the brutality of the criminal law,* and the delay and expense involved in the proceedings of all the courts. The reformers went boldly to work to remedy the evils of both systems. A committee without a single

* See p. 261.

lawyer upon it, was appointed to consider the reform of the law, and boldly undertook to reduce 'the great volumes of the law to the bigness of a pocket volume;' while a bill for the abolition of Chancery was ordered to be brought into the House.

A simple and uniform code is an invaluable boon to a nation. In attempting, however, in that early time, to limit the judge's discretion, and also to secure simplicity for civil and criminal code alike, the English reformers overlooked the necessities of a complex and changing state of society. In times of little legislation, it has been owing mainly to the allowance of discretion in the judges that English law has had the merit of advancing hand in hand with the needs of society. There is no reason, in the nature of things, why equitable principles should not have been recognized in the common law courts, so as to avoid the inconvenience of two different and conflicting systems. But the common law courts, having always had equity courts by their side to correct the shortcomings of their branch of the law, retained theories based on a totally different state of things, which would have caused monstrous injustice, had not the appropriate remedies been provided by Chancery. In the bill for the abolition of Chancery which was finally brought in and read twice, some provision was made for this need, at least for the time, by the appointment of commissioners to settle causes already before the courts, and, apparently, to deal with future cases of an equitable nature. What was wanted was a fusion of the two systems, not the abolition of equity.

After the law followed church reform, both tithes and the right of patronage being brought into question. Tithes were then, as at the present day, the legal endowment of all parishes in England and Wales, and were paid in kind, the farmer giving the tenth pig, tenth corn-sheaf, tenth gallon of milk, and the like. Abuses had arisen in early times. The monasteries had been treated as spiritual corporations, and as such had received the whole tithes, of which they paid only some small portion to the vicar or substitute who did the duty for them. When the monasteries were suppressed, the great tithes which had been kept by the spiritual corporations often fell into the hands of laymen, while the vicar still received only what were called the small tithes. The abuses were obvious, and the mode in which tithes were raised was itself burdensome, and a frequent source of quarrels in parishes. The reformers did not propose to remedy the abuses of this system, but to sweep it away. The spiritual life of the age had come from ministers whose support had been the free gifts of their congregations, while the tithe-supported clergy had opposed the political and spiritual interests of the people. The popular notion, therefore, was to abolish tithes, and substitute a voluntary system which would render the minister dependent on the parishioner.

The first point which the reformers dealt with was patronage, or the right of presenting ministers to livings; this right had often passed with the great tithes into the hands of laymen, which had proved a natural and fruitful source of nepotism, and had also caused the scandal of next presentations being offered for sale. These usages, anomalous enough at all times, were then especially liable to abuse. Lay patronage had been long allowed, but it had always been supposed that the Church in some way secured that none but duly qualified ministers should be presented to livings. The patron nominated, the Church, at least in form, approved. But now in most parishes the endowments remained while the check of an Establishment was gone. The Presbyterian Church, though established by ordinance of Parliament, had been only set up in Lancashire and Middlesex. Hence patrons, being unchecked by either bishop or presbytery, were at liberty to impose upon congregations any ignorant or drunken kinsman on whom they pleased to confer a living. The reformers in Parliament held, as did sectarians generally, that congregations ought to elect their own ministers, as the only security against abuse of patronage. The propensity of lawyers to treat public offices as private rights, has left a door open for abuse even now; how much more opening was there then? And though, in later times, the interests of laymen in church property, anomalous though they are, have, no doubt, often saved the Establishment when threatened, yet in that time of enthusiasm the existence of such anomalies only increased the desire of the reformers to uproot the whole system. "Some young artist from Oxford,' they complained, "enters and takes possession of the tithes, of the care and cure of souls, for this his father hath bought for him, and who shall say him nay? What a sad account have the most of these proprietors for the many thousand souls that have perished by their means!"* Accordingly they passed a vote that patrons should be deprived of their right of presenting to livings, and that the choice of the minister should be vested in the parishioners, and a bill was ordered to be brought in to that effect (Nov. 17th). The next question was that of the support of the minister, when chosen. A committee reported in favour of the continuance of tithes; it had, no doubt, seen that the interests involved were too complicated to be dealt with in the off-hand fashion which was in favour with the enthusiasts, who formed a majority of the House. Simply to sweep away tithes would have been to make a free gift to landowners, while there would have been many difficulties in diverting them to other uses. But the House, bent on a voluntary system, rejected the committee's report by a majority of two (Dec. 10th).

Besides these violent changes many useful reforms were proposed, which do honour to Barebone's Parliament, and show that, though rash in execution, its legislators were in most points nearly two centuries in advance of their age. Chief amongst these was an act for the relief of debtors. The laws of debt were such that they gave the creditor unlimited power over the person of his debtor, but little or none over his property. Hence bankrupts, guilty of no criminal, often of no moral offence, were liable, through the cruelty of their creditors, to be imprisoned for life; while fraudulent debtors, by not applying for release, could keep possession of property in defiance of their creditors. A 'humble petition of all the prisoners for debt within the several tyrannical dens of cruelty, prisons, gaols, and dungeons in this land,' says truly enough that "restraint of men and women's persons in gaol pays no debts, but defrauds the creditors, feeds the lawyers and gaolers, and murders the debtors; witness the many thousands that have thus perished miserably, as the gaolers' books and coroners' records do testify. Your poor enslaved brethren, therefore, humbly pray that there may be no more arresting nor imprisonment for debt." In every county in England and Wales commissioners were appointed by the Parliament to investigate the cases of those confined for debt. Debtors who were genuinely bankrupt, and perishing in prison only through the cruelty and obduracy of creditors, were to be granted their liberty, either un-

* Somers, Tracts, ii.

conditionally, or for a limited space of time, at the discretion of the commissioners; on the other hand, the commissioners were empowered to order to close imprisonment those well able, but unwilling to pay. To protect prisoners from extortion, the act enjoined that wholesome provisions should be sold them at a reasonable price; that a table of moderate fees should be hung up in every prison; and that gaolers transgressing such tables in any particular should forfeit fourfold to the party injured, and be set in the pillory. This act was at once carried into execution, and 300 persons were let out of London prisons alone. Another important enactment which this Parliament made was one for the registration of births, marriages, and deaths: this occurred as a clause in an act making civil marriage before a magistrate compulsory, the religious ceremony apparently being added or not at the discretion of the parties; some change was no doubt necessary after the disestablishment of the Episcopal Church, but so violent a change can hardly have been otherwise than unpopular. Bills were also prepared for a new system of workhouses and provision for the poor, for fixing the fees of lawyers and clerks, for the prevention of bribery and the delay of justice, for checking the greediness of the courts by paying judges by salary and not by fees, for establishing a registry for deeds affecting land, and county judicatures to make justice accessible to the poor.

Excellent as many of these reforms were, they failed of their accomplishment. By voting the destruction of the Court of Chancery, and by proposing the abolition of tithes, which would have deprived the clergy of regular stipends, the reformers had shown they were not fit to be rulers, for they went much faster than the nation would follow. They had cut the knots instead of untying them. Abolishing equity was a violent mode of reforming the Court of Chancery; making all ministers dependent upon their parishioners, a needlessly radical means of providing that livings should only be bestowed upon men of good character. Such measures especially enraged the lawyers, whose feelings could not be disregarded, for their support had always been one of the chief pillars of the Commonwealth. Besides lawyers—Royalists, Presbyterians, patrons, ministers—all whose interests were attacked, or who felt, as most men do, attachment to old customs, regarded the innovators with hate and scorn, and looked up to Cromwell as the man who alone could stop the rash course

21—2

of the Parliament, and act in time to prevent its votes from being turned into laws.

In fact, even now supreme power belonged rather to Cromwell than to the Parliament. Ambassadors from Sweden, from Holland, and from France, were ordered to present themselves to Cromwell, their governments already recognizing the future monarch in the victorious general. The course which the Dutch war took in this summer served incidentally to increase his renown as commander-in-chief of the English forces. In the first engagement, the Dutch admirals, Van Tromp, De Ruyter, and De Witt, met Blake, Dean, and Monk off the North Foreland. The battle raged for two days. Admiral Dean was killed by a shot, and fell at Monk's feet, who flung a cloak over the body in order that the sailors might not be disheartened by knowledge of their loss. In the end, the Dutch were entirely defeated; nineteen of their vessels were destroyed, and 1300 of their sailors taken prisoners (2nd June).

Again, before the end of July, Van Tromp, who was once more on the water in joint command with De Witt of a fleet of nearly 120 sail, met Monk off the coast of Holland. Though Monk had only ninety vessels, yet after a desperate fight of nine hours, the struggle ended in the complete defeat of the Dutch, whose brave admiral, Van Tromp, was killed by a shot as he walked the deck, sword in hand. The Dutch vessels were pursued right up to their own coasts, 26 men-of-war were destroyed, and 1200 sailors were picked up as prisoners from the wrecks. The English only lost two ships, but 500 sailors, besides several captains, were killed in the action (31st July). After this second defeat the Dutch no longer thought of continuing the war. They had in the spring sent ambassadors to Cromwell to open negotiations, and now only endeavoured to obtain fair terms of peace.

While the nation had reason to be proud of its generals and admirals, it had no sympathy with its Parliament. There had always been a considerable minority in that body itself, that opposed the violent votes carried by the reformers. On the morning of the 12th of December, members of this party took their seats early in large numbers, and proposed that the House should repair in a body to the Lord General, and deliver back into his hands the power they had received from him. The speaker, without venturing to put the question to the vote, left his chair, and attended by about forty members, went to Whitehall, where he and his companions signed a resignation of their power to Cromwell. Within two or three days, above eighty members—a majority of the whole Parliament—had consented to sign their names to the same instrument (12th Dec.) There was 'a drinking of sack, and a making of bonfires' at the Inns of Court, when the news was told that Barebone's Parliament had come to an end. Yet the despised fanatics were in many points wiser than the lawyers. Of the reforms proposed by them, the larger number have been adopted, while others have been held advisable, if not practicable, in the present century. That delays of justice should be prevented in Chancery as elsewhere, that the costs of transferring land should be diminished by the establishment of an effective registry for titles, are reforms still called for in England as they were in the time of Barebone's Parliament.*

A council, composed of the leading officers and some civilians, now brought forward an 'Instrument of Government,' in which Cromwell was given the title of Lord Protector of England, Scotland, and Ireland. The executive government was vested in the protector and a council of state. The councillors were named in the instrument, and were not removable at the pleasure of the chief magistrate, but were to sit for life. A Parliament was to be summoned to meet in nine months, the date fixed being the 3rd of September (1654). Until the meeting of this Parliament, the protector and his council were granted the power

* In justice to Barebone's Parliament, its reforms should be compared with the course of subsequent legislation. (i.) Parliament passed Acts for the relief of debtors in 1813 and 1813: by the Act of 1861, fraudulent debt was dealt with as a criminal offence, and imprisonment of common debtors abolished for the rich, though practically retained for the poor: Acts were also passed for the reform of prisons in 1774, 1823, and 1835; (ii.) After the Restoration, criminal legislation was retrograde, and between that time and the death of George III., a period of 160 years, the punishment for 187 more offences was made capital: by successive Acts between 1824 and 1861, the punishment of death was limited to murder and treason; (iii.) Since 1828, several reforms have been introduced, which diminish the delays, and to some extent the costs, of the courts of common law and the Court of Chancery: the establishment of county courts for the recovery of small debts has rendered justice obtainable by the poor (1846); (iv.) An Act for the registration of births, marriages, and deaths was passed in 1836; (v.) By Acts passed under William IV. and Victoria tithes were commuted into a rent charge upon land, payable in money, varying with the price of corn.

of making ordinances to have the force of laws. After this date the power of legislation was vested entirely in the Parliament, the protector having only a suspensory veto on bills for twenty days after their passing, at the expiration of which time they were to become law of themselves. Parliaments were to be dissolved every three years, according to the provisions of the Triennial Bill. On the occurrence of any vacancy in the council, the protector was to choose a new member out of six candidates nominated by Parliament. The protector was to have command of all forces by sea and land, but in questions of peace or war was only to act with the consent of his council of state, and Parliament was to be immediately summoned in case of war. On the death of the protector a successor was to be appointed by the council.

Cromwell was inaugurated Lord Protector in the Court of Chancery at Westminster Hall. He there took the oath tendered him to observe the articles of the New Instrument, and received from Lambert a sheathed sword to replace his own, as a sign that his rule was no longer military (16th Dec., 1653).

The great scheme of a parliamentary republic had failed both in its original form and in that of the provisional government which followed the fall of the pure Republicans. That of a presidential republic had now to be tried, when the republican ideal was already discredited by a double failure. It will be seen in the sequel how this had again to be modified till it approximated so closely to the old government that it became a monarchy in all but the name. We can see clearly enough the folly of the persistency with which the Republicans adhered to an experiment of which the failure was inevitable. Yet their errors were natural to their age. In judging them, men are too apt to forget that the history of the last two hundred years, which has revealed so much to us, was a sealed book to them. No instance of a government like that which now exists in England was then to be found. Greek and Roman history told the tale of tyrants overthrown, liberty and prosperity assured by the rule of republican assemblies. In Europe could be seen absolute monarchies, as in France and Spain on the one hand, or pure republics, as in Venice and Switzerland, on the other. The virtues of republican governments and the happiness of their citizens had formed the common talk of scholars since the revival of classical literature in the beginning of the previous century; while almost within living memory a republic had been actually founded in Holland. With no alternative before them, the most forward minds in an age of revolution naturally developed into the most uncompromising Republicans. Two men, however, the most remarkable of all, were not in the strict sense Republicans. At the beginning of the war, Pym had guided his followers towards the true land of promise, where kings should reign and not govern. Yet had Pym lived, it is doubtful whether even he, with all his vast Parliamentary influence and experience, could have stemmed the current of the prevailing fanaticism without being overwhelmed by those who had been his own supporters. Views which Pym might have set aside with a smile as impracticable dreams, had become the declared policy of men versed in public affairs, of great incorruptibility and of deepest conviction. These were the men whom Cromwell had to face. They were his friends, and had been his political chiefs, yet he had to prefer the safety of the State to private friendship and the ties of party. Had he been less than he was, he too might have been a Republican, and his name, like that of Vane, have passed as a model of integrity. Being what he was, it was inevitable that he should take a different path, but it augured ill for his government that its very foundations should have to rest upon the irreconcilable enmity of the noblest of his fellow-workers in the cause of freedom.

CHAPTER XIV.

THE FIRST THREE YEARS OF THE PROTECTORATE (1654—1656).

Heaven knows, I had no such intent,
But that necessity so bowed the state
That I and greatness were compelled to kiss.
HENRY IV., pt. ii., iii. 1.

I will discover to you a political secret, which must ere long be made public. Capo d'Istria cannot long continue to administer the affairs of Greece; he wants one requisite indispensable in that position—*he is no soldier*. There is no instance on record in which a mere statesman has been able to organize a revolutionary state, and keep under his control the military and their leaders. With the sabre in his hand, at the head of an army, a man may command and make laws, secure of being obeyed, otherwise the attempt is hazardous. Napoleon, if he had not been a soldier, could never have attained the highest power; and Capo d'Istria will soon be forced to play a secondary part.—CONVERSATIONS WITH GOETHE, TRANSLATED FROM THE GERMAN OF ECKERMANN.

CROMWELL held his power by will of the army. Though Anabaptists and Republicans were hostile to the new government, the larger number of the common soldiers, and all the principal officers—Monk and Lambert, the protector's son-in-law Fleetwood, and his brother-in-law Desborough—were well content to effect a final settlement of the kingdom by raising their general to be the head of the State. Milton, who, though a Republican, consented to continue in office as Secretary for Foreign Tongues to the Council of State, thus exhorted his "chief of men:"—'Recollect that thou thyself canst not be free, unless we are so ; for it is fitly so provided, in the nature of things, that he who conquers another's liberty, in the very act loses his own; he becomes, and justly, the foremost slave. . . . . . Thou hast taken on thyself a task which will probe thee to the very vitals, and disclose to the eyes of all how much is thy courage, thy firmness, and thy fortitude ; whether that piety, perseverance, moderation, and justice really exist in thee, in consideration of which we have believed that God hath given thee the supreme dignity over thy fellows. To

govern three mighty States by thy counsels, to recall the people
from their corrupt institutions to a purer and nobler discipline, to
extend thy thoughts and send out thy mind to our remotest shores,
to foresee all and provide for all, to shrink from no labour, to
trample under foot and tear to pieces all the snares of pleasure
and all the entangling seducements of wealth and power—these
are matters so arduous that, in comparison of them, the perils of
war are but the sports of children. These will winnow thy facul-
ties, and search thee to the very soul; they require a man sustained by a strength that is more than human, and whose medi-
tations and whose thoughts shall be in perpetual commerce with
his Maker.'*

Cromwell, who from the first had fought in defence of liberty
in Church and State, and who came of the same breed of men as
Eliot, Pym, Vane, and Milton himself, would have scorned to rule
a race of slaves. "Of the two greatest concernments," he says,
"that God hath in this world, the one is that of religion, and of
the just preservation of the professors of it, to give them all due
and just liberty; the other is the civil liberty and interest of the
nation, which though it is, and, indeed, I think ought to be, sub-
ordinate to the more peculiar interest of God, yet it is the next
best God hath given men in this world, and, if well cared for, it
is better than any rock to fence men in their other interests.
Besides, if any whosoever think the interest of Christians and the
interest of the nation inconsistent, I wish my soul may never
enter into their secrets."† Such was Cromwell's ideal of government—one which, while leaving a people free, was to work at
once for their material and moral improvement. In Cromwell's
mouth, the words 'interest of religion' did not mean the interests
of any sect: in his use of the term, he comprehended the whole
moral life of the nation; a good education, the suppression of cruel
sports, a reform of the criminal law—all that could tend to ele-
vate the minds of men, he classed under the category of the interest of God.

The protector certainly could not fairly be accused of having
overthrown the free institutions of his country. Except during
the dictatorship of the first few months, the powers he possessed were rather those belonging to the chief magistrate of

* Defensio Secunda (Godwin, iv. 20).   † Carlyle, iii. 222.

a republican state, than those exercised by former Kings of England. The executive was placed under the control of the legislature; the chief magistrate was denied a veto on laws; his office was rendered elective. "For myself," he said to his first Parliament, "I desire not to keep my place in this government an hour longer than I may preserve England in its just rights, and may protect the people of God in a just liberty of their consciences."* Yet there was much to hinder Cromwell in achieving his cherished object of establishing a free and constitutional government. Too much hung on a single life, and that one past its prime. Time, the great conciliator, could not do much for one who was already fifty-five. The mass of the people were sure to be long prejudiced in favour of their old line of princes. Excepting his own immediate supporters, no political party favoured his government. Old Royalists and Presbyterians denounced him as guilty of treason and rebellion. The Republicans, Vane, Bradshaw, Hutchinson, Ludlow, did not scruple to avow their hostility, and their intention of rising whenever a good opportunity should offer for the restoration of the Commonwealth. Fanatical Levellers and Fifth-Monarchists joined with Royalists in plotting against the new government, deluded enough to think that, after they had overthrown it, they should be able to crush their allies and set up a Parliament of their own. There was, however, a surer and readier means than insurrection by which the protector's enemies might attempt the accomplishment of their wishes—assassination. "There remains nothing for him to do," said the Swedish Chancellor Oxenstiern, when he heard of the establishment of the Protectorate, "but to get him a back and breast-plate of steel." A proclamation was drawn in the name of Charles Stuart, and secretly dispersed amongst malcontent Royalists, Fifth-Monarchists, and Anabaptists, to the effect that, a certain base mechanic fellow, by name Oliver Cromwell, having usurped the throne, whosoever killed him by sword, pistol, or poison should receive a reward of £500 a year (1654). The life and government of the protector were constantly endangered by the plots of Royalists and Levellers, or of both parties united. Cromwell, however, proved himself more than a match for his enemies. He made use of his insight into character to find the right men to serve as spies, and was generally in full possession of the plans of his

* Carlyle, iii. 84.

enemies. Conspirators, after having advanced with their preparations until within a few hours for the moment of action, found themselves suddenly swooped upon by the officers of justice, and lodged securely in prison.

When the protector met his first Parliament, at the appointed date (3rd Sept.), he was prepared with a good account of his nine months of rule. Much to the indignation of Republicans and Anabaptists, who still clung to the ambitious project of reducing the States and incorporating the two Republics, Cromwell had ended the ruinous war with Holland by granting peace on fairly moderate terms. The Dutch agreed to lower their flag to the English navy; to banish from their territories enemies of England; to restore to England the island of Poleron, in the East Indies, seized by them during James' reign; to pay £170,000 damages to the East India Company; and to give to the heirs of those massacred at Amboyna (p. 253) during the same reign a sum amounting to near £4000, together with a compensation of nearly £100,000 to English traders to the Baltic. With the Danes (July, 1654) and with the Swedes (April, 1654) the protector had also concluded treaties favourable to the interests of English merchants. Portugal, long in disgrace for harbouring Rupert's fleet of privateers, had only obtained a treaty by consenting both to refund the expenses incurred by the English government in consequence of this unfriendly act, and also to allow English merchants liberty of conscience to worship in chapels of their own, and to have free use of Bibles and other Protestant books throughout the Portuguese dominions.

So much for foreign affairs; at home the protector had made active use of the powers granted him by the Instrument of Government. He had had the right to make ordinances and impose taxes, with the assistance of his council, until the meeting of Parliament. No less than eighty-two ordinances had been passed. Amongst others were two for the reform of the Church. The first empowered thirty-eight commissioners, a body of laymen and ministers, commonly called 'triers,' to examine and approve every person, whether presented by a patron, or in any other way introduced to a living, before allowing him to take possession (March 20th, 1654). The second appointed from fifteen to thirty commissioners in every county to expel from their offices any ministers or schoolmasters who set the people a bad example by neglecting their duties, and passing their time in taverns, playing at cards and dice (28th Aug). Cromwell's principles of toleration, made him desirous of uniting Protestant sects, and he named, as commissioners upon these ordinances, Presbyterians, Independents, and Anabaptists. To their political opinions he was indifferent, so long as he thought them the right men to do the work required. Amongst them sat, not only Fairfax, though now at heart almost a Royalist, but Republicans who were bitter enemies of the protector. The great Presbyterian, Baxter, was a 'trier' himself, and, though he could never forgive Cromwell's usurpation, he admitted that good resulted from this reform. "And with all their faults," he says, "thus much must be said of these triers, that they saved many a congregation from ignorant, ungodly, drunken teachers, that sort of men who intend no more in the ministry than to patch a few good words together to talk the people asleep on Sunday, and all the rest of the week go with them to the alehouse and harden them in sin; so that, though many of them were somewhat partial to the Independents, Fifth-Monarchy men, and Anabaptists, many thousands of souls blessed God for the faithful ministers whom they let in."* By another of his ordinances Cromwell reduced the costs of suits in Chancery by simplifying the procedure and cutting down the fees of counsel and solicitors, one of those acts which few subsequent governments have been found strong enough to repeat.

A reform was carried out in the system of representation. This reform had been proposed by the Republicans, and was laid down in the Instrument of Government. In early times, when the Lower House was summoned solely for the purpose of granting the king subsidies, attention had naturally been paid to allotting members to places in proportion to population and wealth. But, in the course of years, inequalities appeared. Towns which returned members lost their trade, and decreased in the number of their inhabitants, while unrepresented villages became large and thriving cities. This evil was increased by the practice of the princes of the Houses of Tudor and Stuart, who, in order to maintain their authority in the Commons, created new boroughs out of mere villages, which returned members according to the directions of servants of the crown. Thus Elizabeth added sixty members to the House of Commons, the loyalty of petty

* Baxter, Life, 69.

Cornish hamlets being especially favoured in the distribution of these seats. An inequality had from the first existed in the county representation, since counties, however unequal in size, as Yorkshire and Rutland, had always returned two members each. According to the reform now made, the number of members returned for England and Wales was reduced from 500 to 400. The county members, or knights of shires, were increased to 261, Yorkshire returning twelve members, Essex thirteen, Warwickshire four, and other counties in like proportion. A large number of rotten boroughs, some of which contained only a few houses, were disfranchised, while members were given to a few rising places, such as Leeds, Manchester, and Halifax; 149 members were returned in all for the towns and boroughs.* The county franchise, formerly confined to freeholders possessed of lands or tenements to the annual value of 40s., was extended to any resident in the county, the capital value of whose property, real or personal, amounted to £200.† As the value of money now is one-fourth of what it was then, the constituency was not as democratic as the present; when owners of freeholds of the annual value of 40s., and occupiers of property of the rateable value of £12, are qualified as county electors.‡

The reformed Parliament was imperial, representative of the three nations, thirty members being summoned to sit for Scotland, and thirty for Ireland. Those who had borne arms against the Parliament since 1641 were rendered, by the Instrument of Government, incapable of voting at elections for the present Parliament or the three following triennial Parliaments. This disfranchised not only the Royalists, but some of the Presbyterians, who had joined in Hamilton's invasion, or in that led by Prince Charles. The House, however, contained many Presbyterians, besides Republicans and others opposed to the government. These proceeded to debate the question whether they should approve the government by a single person and a Parliament; in other words, to attack the Instrument of Government

* There had been 400 members for towns, 100 for counties (p. 2).
† After the Restoration (1660) the old system of representation was restored, and no reform was made until 1832.
‡ Reform Act, 1867, by which county votes were also given to owners of property other than freehold of the annual value of £5; and borough votes to all ratepaying householders, and even to lodgers who have occupied for a year rooms of the annual value of £10.

by authority of which they, as well as the protector, ruled. More than a week had been spent upon this subject of debate, when Cromwell summoned the members to the Painted Chamber, and there informed them that he was in possession of the government by a good right from God and man ; by Divine right, because it was by his hand that God had saved the nation; by human right, because they had come to sit there in virtue of his writ, and, therefore, could not call in question the authority by which the Parliament itself existed. They would now, before again entering the House, be required to sign their names to an engagement to be true and faithful to the lord protector and Commonwealth, and not to propose or consent to any alteration of the government as it was settled in one person and a Parliament (Sept. 12th, 1654). Though this engagement eliminated a hundred members who refused to sign it and so lost their seats, the enemies of the government still maintained a majority in the House, which did not offer the protector either the money bills necessary for the support of the army, or any others for his consent. Accordingly, as soon as five months were spent, the length of session required by the Instrument of Government, Cromwell did not delay a day in dissolving the Parliament. "Divisions and discontent," he told the members, "which, like briars and thorns, had nourished themselves under their shadow, had been more multiplied during the five months they had sat than in some years before. . . . I bless God I have been inured to difficulties, and I never found God failing when I trusted in Him. I can laugh and sing in my heart when I speak of these things to you or elsewhere. And though some may think it is an hard thing to raise money without Parliamentary authority upon this nation, yet I have another argument to the good people of this nation, if they would be safe, and yet have no better principle— whether they prefer the having of their will, though it be their destruction, rather than comply with things of necessity ? That will excuse me. But I should wrong my native country to suppose this" (Jan. 22nd, 1655).

The divisions existing between the Parliament and the protector gave courage to his enemies to plot murder and insurrection, whether these were Royalists on the one hand, or Levellers and Fifth-Monarchists on the other. The best of the Republicans—men such as Vane, Ludlow, and Hutchinson—refused to join in conspiracies of which the success was doubtful, while they scorned the thought of resorting to assassination as a means to overthrow the government. Several conspiracies, however, were formed in England and Scotland, but were nipped in the bud by the timely seizure and imprisonment of the ringleaders. Wildman, a Leveller, and member of the late Parliament, was seized sitting at his table, and dictating a declaration against 'The tyrant, Oliver Cromwell, Esq.' Several plots were laid against the protector's life, 'little fiddling things,' as he once called them. In March partial risings of the Royalists took place in several counties. A body of 200 Cavaliers rode into Salisbury in the middle of the night, and seized the persons of the judges who had come to hold the assizes (10th March, 1655). The townspeople, however, refused to compromise themselves by offering the insurgents any support. The town crier, being ordered by Penruddock, their leader, to proclaim Charles Stuart at the Market Cross, "made 'O Yes' (Oyez) four times, but still, when Penruddock said, 'Charles the Second, king,' he stopped, though much beaten by them, and said he could not say that word, though they should call for faggots and burn him presently." Within twenty-four hours of their arrival, the Cavaliers were obliged to ride hastily out of the town, in order to avoid meeting the protector's troops. The insurgents were overtaken and dispersed, and above fifty taken prisoners, among whom were their leaders, Penruddock and Grove. The prisoners were regularly tried by jury for treason. Of those condemned, seventeen were executed; others transported to the Barbadoes, and their services as slaves sold to the English planters there for a period of five years.* No Republicans or Levellers were brought to trial.

Cromwell, who had intimated not obscurely to his Parliament that rather than suffer his government to be overturned he would resort to arbitrary measures, now carried his threat into execution, with the determination to keep up the army and with it maintain order at any cost. He continued to enforce ordinances made in council, which the Instrument of Government had only granted

* This early form of transportation or penal servitude was first introduced by the Long Parliament, who applied it to some of the Scotch prisoners taken after the defeat of Hamilton at Warrington in 1648. Such treatment seems quite indefensible when applied to prisoners of war: insurgents are even now liable to the treatment of convicts, but the substitution of private masters instead of the State is an outrage to sentiment.

him power of making until the meeting of his first Parliament. Thus he passed an ordinance for the continuance of the monthly assessment of £60,000 for the support of the army. Of his sole authority he imposed on Royalists, whose estates exceeded the worth of £100 per annum, an income tax of ten per cent., and this whether they had been engaged in the late risings or not. He divided England into eleven districts, over each of which he placed in command a major-general, with power to call out the county militia for the enforcement of his orders (Aug., 1655).

Major-Generals. These major-generals were, in fact, military governors, who encroached on the duties of the ordinary justices of the peace and other civil authorities, and acted at once as judges and police officers. There was no appeal from their decisions, except to the protector and his council. They received instructions to suppress tumults and rebellion, to see that Papists and Royalists had no arms in their possession, to collect the income-tax imposed upon Royalists, to arrest and imprison suspected persons, to aid in ejecting scandalous ministers, to suppress horse races, cock-fightings, bear-baitings, and other sports at which the disaffected collected.

Some of the chief men in the army, as Fleetwood, Skippon, and Desborough, held office as major-generals. They do not seem to have abused the power entrusted to them, though no doubt they carried out Cromwell's instructions to the full, exacted the last penny of the income tax from Royalists, and required Royalist justices of the peace, mayors, and sheriffs, to make way for men friendly to the government. A severe ordinance was issued, forbidding any to take into their families ejected Episcopalian ministers as chaplains or school-masters (Jan., 1656). Many Royalists and Republicans, known malcontents, were imprisoned, or forced to confine themselves to one place of abode. The movements of both Vane and Ludlow were at one time or another thus placed under restraint. An order of council was issued that no paper should be published without permission from the Secretary of State; and all but two, out of eight, weekly papers were suppressed (Sept., 1655).

Whether we admit, or not, the 'tyrant's plea, necessity,' we must not fail to mark the difference of motive that caused Charles and Cromwell to exercise arbitrary government. Charles imposed taxes without consent of Parliament, and committed men illegally to prison, in order to break the spirit of the people, and convert a constitutional into an absolute monarchy. Cromwell really taxed the country for the country's good, because his own government was all he saw able to stand between anarchy on the one side and the loss of freedom of conscience on the other. History will always judge by very different standards the arbitrary acts that break up an existing order and those which restore order out of disorder. The king who tries to make slaves of a free people has none of the excuses of one on whose shoulders has fallen the herculean task of remaking a nation out of the chaos of a revolution. Cromwell was marked out as the pilot to steer the storm-tossed State into port, and nothing would induce him to quit the helm. "I can sooner be willing," he said, "to be rolled into my grave and buried in infamy than I can give my consent unto [it]."

Hence, unlike Charles, Cromwell never resorted to arbitrary measures, until either his government or his life were in real danger, and then he was never cruel; the imprisonments he inflicted were generally short; he never sought the ruin of his adversary. He counselled his son, Henry, when commanding in Ireland, not to let the discontent of some make too much impression upon him. "Time and patience may work them to a better frame of spirit, and bring them to see that which for the present seems to be hid from them; especially if they shall see your moderation and love towards them, if they are found in other ways towards you."

Tyrants who have been raised by an army to a throne have often proved themselves the most suspicious of mankind. But the protector's nature remained as generous and trustful as it had been in his earlier years, when none grudged the quiet country gentleman his life. He only took a few necessary precautions for his safety by looking closely after his guards, and letting a report spread that he wore a mail coat under his clothes. So far, indeed, did he seem removed from personal feelings of fear and revenge, that he would pass over insulting words and even outbursts of deadly hatred, as though they concerned him not, so long as he preserved his power intact. When he imprisoned men without showing legal cause, he had good reason to suspect their intentions. Republicans, Levellers, Anabaptists, even those of them who sought his life, he always looked upon as friends estranged rather than as enemies. A lesser man might have freed himself from the charge of tyranny, and at the same time made his own life more secure, by bringing traitors to the gallows, for there is little doubt Cromwell had evidence enough if he had chosen to use it. A true tyrant, still more one who was conscious he had deserted the cause to which he was first engaged, would have been slow to deal leniently with old Republican friends, whose conduct might have seemed as a perpetual reproach to his own. But of all the Levellers, Fifth-Monarchists, or Anabaptists, who conspired against the protector's life or government, only one suffered by the hand of the executioner.* Sexby, a Leveller, died in prison, but he was a fanatic who plotted with Royalists to take the protector's life, and sent to England some "strange engines to that purpose."† Though towards Royalists less mercy was shown, they admitted themselves that their condition was greatly improved from the time of the dissolution of the Long Parliament. A committee of officers restored to their Royalist owners, estates unjustly sequestered, and inflicted condign punishment on false informers.‡ In matters of life and death too, Royalists received far more lenient treatment. Not nearly so many Royalist

* The contrast of Bonaparte's conduct may enable us to appreciate more fully Cromwell's magnanimity. Bonaparte had also for enemies two implacable parties, Jacobins and Royalists. As he was driving to the opera an attempt was made to kill him by blowing up a barrel of gunpowder close to his carriage. The plot had been laid by the Royalists, and two of the assassins were brought before a court of justice, condemned, and executed. Bonaparte, however, though he knew the contrary, affected to believe that the Jacobins were guilty, five of whom lost their lives by sentence of a military commission, while 300 others were transported. Cromwell's government by major-generals for a year and a half, may again be contrasted favourably with the present French government, which keeps half France under martial law for more than three years because of a revolt of the capital.
† Clarendon State Papers, iii. 311.
‡ "On Saturday last, Faulkener, one of the Lord Craven's accusers, was condemned to the pillory for perjury; it is believed his lordship will have his estates cleared and the purchaser to be satisfied with other lands; here be many others that hope for right in the like case; some interpret this favour (for here it is a great one to have justice) as an inclination to oblige the royal party, but such plausible things could never be more seasonable" (27th May, 1653). "The committee of officers have restored several parties to their estates with reparation for what is past. Sir John Stowel is out of prison upon bail, and many such plausible things are done to stroke the poor easy Cavalier" (3rd June, 1653).—Royalist letters of intelligence among MS. Clar. Papers in Bodleian.

conspirators were put to death by Cromwell as by the Republicans, and a High Court of Justice, which he occasionally erected, never convicted any but undoubted traitors.*

Cromwell's government, even whilst arbitrary, was in many respects conciliatory. No oaths of allegiance were required to be taken to it, and none but those who conspired against it were shut out from holding office in the State. The protector, in fact, endeavoured to obtain for the service of his country the most able of her sons without inquiring too closely into their political antecedents. The Republican, Admiral Blake, still remained in command of the fleet. Milton continued in the post of foreign secretary. Lockhart, the English ambassador in France, was a Royalist and a Scotchman. The judges appointed by Cromwell were not partisans of his own, who might be ready to wrest the law to serve his will, but incorruptible men, of all parties, who dared administer the laws impartially, not only between subject and subject, but between the subject and the government. Sir Matthew Hale, the chief justice, refused obedience to the Lord Protector himself, when he would once have interfered in the trial of a criminal case; and there is no doubt that the men appointed to office by Cromwell and the Republicans introduced many beneficial reforms into the administration of the law.†

It was possible for the judges gradually to modify the procedure of the courts, where it was dependent only upon custom and precedent; but for a thorough reform of the law itself, the interference of the legislature was necessary. Cromwell was desirous of reforming the anomalies and harshness of the criminal code, as well as the dilatoriness and expense of the civil code. The object of punishment is the protection of society, the primary object being to deter men from committing criminal acts,

* Godwin, iv. 34, 91, 357.
† " The practice of questioning juries for their verdicts, the exclusion of oral testimony" [as was the case in Raleigh's trial, see p. 88], " and the use of torture, were wholly swept away during the ten years which succeeded the death of Charles I., and were never afterwards revived. Just and rational principles of evidence, sound views of the object of penal laws, and of the proper means of enforcing them, first sprang up during the early years of the Commonwealth. Under the wise and moderate superintendence of such minds as Hale, Whitelock, and Rolle, our judicial institutions underwent a total revision and reform."—Jardine's Reading on the Use of Torture.

the secondary object to act beneficially on opinion, and so remove the motives to criminal acts. To deter criminals, the main requirement is not that the penalty should be terrible, but that it should be inevitable. To act beneficially on opinion, it is necessary that the punishment should be approved as just by the general judgment of the community. A criminal code that lags behind the humanity of the age to which it belongs not only fails in acting on opinion, but often defeats its primary end as a deterrent. The criminal either escapes unpunished, because his jury, contrary to evidence, refuses to find a verdict of guilty ; or if he does go to the gallows, he dies an object of sympathy rather than of abhorrence. "There are wicked and abominable laws," Cromwell said to his first Parliament, "which it will be in your power to alter. To hang a man for six-and-eightpence, and I know not what ; to hang for a trifle, and acquit murder —is in the ministration of the law, through the ill-framing of it. I have known in my experience abominable murders acquitted. And to see men lose their lives for petty matters, this is a thing God will reckon for. And I wish it may not lie upon this nation a day longer than you have an opportunity to give a remedy, and I hope I shall cheerfully join with you in it." To effect a reform of the law, it was necessary to secure the co-operation of the lawyers. Lawyers, however, were averse to changes which were often hurtful to their pecuniary interests, or contrary to the prejudices of their profession. It was not without difficulty that they were brought to submit to the protector's Ordinance for the Reform of Chancery. A rule of but five years was too short to carry out reforms in the face of a most influential profession, which was strongly represented in Parliament. "The sons of Zeruiah," as Cromwell once said, "were too strong for him." Had his life lasted twenty years instead of five, he might have done as great wonders as a social reformer and legislator as he did as a ruler and administrator.

Nor were his interests merely practical. Though not learned himself, Cromwell both honoured and rewarded learning in others. He asked one Royalist, a celebrated scholar, Meric Casaubon, to write an impartial history of the civil war ; to the Royalist philosopher, Hobbes, was offered the post of secretary in his household ; he put men of ability at the head of the universities, and founded a new university at Durham.

Though the protector always kept up fitting state as ruler of England, his court at Whitehall was neither luxurious nor extravagant. His very enemies confessed "he had much natural greatness, and well became the place he had usurped." Nor did foreign ambassadors ever find him less than the peer of kings in the dignity of his bearing or the manner of their entertainment. Equal, however, to every occasion, the protector could unbend at times. "He would sometimes," says one of his councillors, "be very cheerful with us, and laying aside his greatness, he would be exceeding familiar with us, and by way of diversion, would make verses with us, and every one must try his fancy; he commonly called for tobacco, pipes, and a candle, and would now and then take tobacco himself; then he would fall again to his serious business."

Cromwell treated religious opponents in the same liberal spirit as political. But for the intolerance of the people, he would have allowed Catholics the public exercise of their worship. At one time he even formed a project of allowing a Catholic bishop to reside in England, and preside over the English Catholics. The severe ordinance he framed at one time against Episcopalians was only enforced as long as they were engaged in fomenting insurrection. Episcopalians preached publicly in London and in the country, and both Catholics and Episcopalians were left unmolested in their private worship.* No oath of fidelity to the government was imposed upon ministers; and the church was made wide enough to admit to her livings Presbyterians, Independents, and Anabaptists. "If a man of one form," said Cromwell, addressing one of his Parliaments, "will be trampling upon the heels of another form, I will not suffer it in him. But God give us hearts and spirits to keep things equal. Which truly I must profess to you hath been my temper. I have had some boxes and rebukes on the one hand and on the other; some censuring me for Presbytery, others as an inletter to all the sects and heresies of the nation. I have borne my reproach, but I have, through God's mercy, not been unhappy in hindering any one religion to impose upon another.†
. . . Here is a great deal of truth among professors, but very

* Guizot, Hist. de Rep., 643; Neal, 74, 124; Evelyn's Diary, passim.
† Carl., iii. 182.

little mercy. When we are brought into the right way, we shall be merciful as well as orthodox, and we know who it is that saith, 'If a man could speak with the tongues of men and angels, and yet want that, he is but sounding brass and a tinkling cymbal.'" The Republicans had passed a law for the punishment of blasphemous opinions; any person who said he was God, who taught that swearing, drunkenness, and murder are as holy and righteous as prayer, preaching, and thanksgiving, was for the first offence to suffer six months' imprisonment: for the second, to abjure the dominions of the Commonwealth, and in case of return to suffer death as a felon (Aug., 1650). If the enumeration of such opinions shows the prevalence of strange fancies in that revolutionary time, their prohibition shows how little the framers had learnt of the distinctions between the spheres of law and of public opinion. Though a merciful law as compared with that passed by the Presbyterians,* it was not in accordance with the professed principles of its framers. With a large Presbyterian element in it, Cromwell's Parliament was not likely to be more tolerant than the Rump. The plain-spoken protector exhorted them to moderation. "What greater hypocrisy," he says, "than for those who were oppressed by the bishops to become the greatest oppressors themselves, as soon as their yoke was removed?" There were several sects whose doctrines gave offence, and whom Cromwell could with difficulty save from suffering under the intolerance of men whose watchword had once been 'liberty of conscience.' The Quakers, for instance, were at this time special objects of persecution. Lord Say-and-Sele, a suppo ter of the Independents, turned some of his tenants, who held Quaker opinions, out into the streets. Their peculiar doctrines, that it is wrong under any circumstances to go to war or to take an oath, excited much indignation, and they often brought suffering upon themselves by pressing their views out of season. George Fox, the founder of the sect, went into churches and contradicted the teaching of the ministers, into markets and exhorted traders to sell fairly, into inns and bade drunkards reform their lives. Vain enthusiasts, men half deceivers, half deceived, copied the example of Fox, and went about the country preaching, pretending to work miracles, and

_{The Quakers.}

* See p. 203.

calling themselves inspired by the Spirit of God. Some dozen men and women believed that the Spirit of Christ dwelt in an old soldier called James Naylor, as it had never dwelt in any other man before. These walked by his side as he rode into Bristol, strewing garments in his path, and shouting, 'Holy, holy, holy, Lord God of Israel.' One woman declared that she had been restored to life by him, after having been two days dead. The protector merely confined the wilder fanatics until they promised to keep quiet and give up working miracles. But his Parliament was far less merciful, and but for its timely dissolution, would have passed an act shutting out Quakers and several other sects from toleration.* Cromwell wished to allow even the Jews a legal residence in the country, though they had been banished from England for four hundred years; and a conference was held in London between some citizens, lawyers, and clergymen, and some Jews of Amsterdam. The divines, however, objected to admitting the unbelievers; the citizens were divided in their opinions; and the conference closed without coming to any decision on the point.† The protector afterwards of his own authority permitted several Jews to reside in London, where they built a synagogue and worshipped without molestation. In regard to toleration, indeed, Oliver's views were so far in advance of those generally held in his time, that they were treated as a subject for apology rather than for praise, even by friends and admirers. "It is true, his heart being tender to all," writes one, "especially such as were peaceable, he did not use that severity ordinarily towards the Quakers, or others of that mind, as was by some expected. But what other considerations did therein sway him to so much lenity, I cannot tell, neither is it fit for every one to know, much less to judge; but this we know, that he was merciful to all."‡

In Scotland, as in England, order was established under the protector's government; justice fairly administered; liberty of conscience ensured. Both the Republicans and Cromwell desired to incorporate the two countries under the same government, and thus prevent a recurrence of the Scotch invasions of England, which had occurred twice within five years. The Republicans were deprived of power before they had carried out their purpose; but Cromwell passed an ordinance,

Fanatics.

Union of England and Scotland.

* Neal, iv. 91.   † Godwin, iv. 249—300.   ‡ King's Tracts.

which was confirmed by his second Parliament, establishing the union of England and Scotland (April 12, 1654). This union lasted till the Restoration, when there was again a separation till the union was finally effected in the reign of Anne, when it was sanctioned by the consent of both nations (1707). At the time of the Commonwealth, the national antipathy was so strong that, whatever the advantages of union, the Scots would not voluntarily have consented to abandon their independent government. Being, however, a conquered people, they were forced to submit to the will of their masters; and thirty members for Scotland were summoned to sit in each of the protector's Parliaments. The executive was administered in Scotland by General Monk, assisted by a Council of State, of which, out of nine members, only two were Scotchmen. The army was gradually raised to a force of 20,000 men, and the country heavily taxed for its maintenance.

The union, though so much disliked by the Scots, conferred upon them several undoubted benefits: freedom of trade with England, a boon unprecedented at that time; the abolition of feudal tenures, which had kept the Scotch people in a state of almost servile dependence upon their lords; a pure administration of justice; security not only from the plundering raids of the Highlanders, but also from the still more destructive strife of factions. For under it the two hostile camps of Presbyterians —those that owned and those that disowned Charles' right to the throne—were forced to live in peace together. Four Englishmen, assisted by three Scotchmen, were appointed to go on circuits and administer justice in place of the Scotch Court of Session, which was exceedingly corrupt. Their fairness was long remembered: "Deil thank them, a wheen (pack of) kinless loons," said a Scotch judge of the next century, when reminded of their impartiality. "During this period," says Burnet, himself a Scotchman, "Scotland was kept in great order; there was good justice done, and vice was suppressed and punished; so that we always reckon on those eight years of usurpation as a time of great peace and prosperity.'

Ireland. Act of Settlement. The Republicans in the Rump, while still in office, had passed a severe law for the settlement of Ireland. They had not entertained the idea of reconciling the Irish to English rule, regarding it as impossible that men who were Catholics and Royalists should ever give willing submission to a government carried on by Sectarians and Republicans. The Irish were accordingly treated as a conquered people. In the course of the Irish war, two and a half millions of acres in Ireland had been pledged to the "adventurers," who lent the Long Parliament money on the assurance that, when Ireland was subdued, they should be repaid with interest out of the lands forfeited by the rebels. In order to satisfy these State creditors, the act of settlement had dealt hard measure to Irish landholders. A free pardon was granted to the mass of the people, to husbandmen, ploughmen, labourers, artificers, and others of inferior sort, not possessed of lands or goods above the value of £10. All engaged in the massacre of 1641 were exempted from pardon of life or estate. So many, however, of the original rebels were either dead or undetected, that sufferers under this clause numbered only about two hundred.* Those who, though not engaged in the massacre, had fought against the Parliament in the war that followed, were to forfeit two thirds of their estates, and to receive lands to the value of the remaining third in such other parts of the country as the government should think fit to appoint. Those who had not favoured the cause of the Parliament were to forfeit one third of their estates, and to be assigned lands elsewhere to the value of the remaining two-thirds (Aug., 1652). The barren and boggy province of Connaught, laid desolate by the late war, was reserved for division amongst these ejected Irish landowners. In this province, they would have the Shannon as a barrier to prevent their attacking the newcomers, and settled there it was not likely that they could ever succeed again in overpowering the Protestant population. The lands thus taken from the Irish were granted to the 'adventurers,' and to soldiers who had fought in Ireland, and whose pay was in arrears (1653). A strong Protestant army, maintained in the country, compelled submission. Fleetwood, commander-in-chief of the forces in Ireland, Ludlow, lieutenant-general of the horse, and three other officers were appointed by the Republicans as commissioners to conduct the government. Their government was distinguished by its severity; they refused to allow Catholics the exercise of their worship in public or in private, and forbade them to live in a garrison town, to possess

* Godwin, iv. 433.

arms, or to travel without a licence. Priests and Jesuits found in the country were declared traitors, and the celebration of the mass was made a capital offence. This persecution is said to have been maintained for two years (1653-4).

The protector summoned thirty members for Ireland, to sit in each of his Parliaments. Fleetwood returned to England in 1655, and the government was entrusted by Cromwell to his second son, Henry, first as commander-in-chief of the army, and afterwards as Lord Deputy. The young man inherited some of his father's capacity for government, and Ireland prospered under his administration. He treated the Irish more mercifully than the Republican commissioners, and even saved some families from the terrible transportation into Connaught. He treated all religious parties with moderation, and refrained from persecuting Catholics. Absolute freedom of trade was granted, and all manufactures were encouraged, so that the country soon assumed a flourishing aspect, in spite of the desolation caused by the late war. "There were many buildings," says the Royalist Hyde, "raised for beauty as well as use, orderly and regular plantations of trees and fences, and enclosures raised throughout the kingdom, purchases made by one from another at very valuable rates, and jointures made upon marriages, and all other conveyances and settlements, executed as in a kingdom at peace within itself, and where no doubt could be made of the validity of titles."

CHAPTER XV.

THE LAST TWO YEARS OF THE PROTECTORATE.—1656 1658.

> Cromwell, our chief of men, who through a cloud
> Not of war only, but detractions rude,
> Guided by faith and matchless fortitude,
> To peace and truth thy glorious way hast plough'd;
> And on the neck of crownèd fortune proud
> Hast reared God's trophies, and his work pursued,
> While Darwin* stream, with blood of Scots imbrued,
> And Dunbar's field, resounds thy praises loud,
> And Worcester's laureate wreath. Yet much remains
> To conquer still; peace hath her victories
> No less renowned than war; new foes arise,
> Threatening to bind our souls with secular chains:
> Help us to save free conscience from the paw
> Of hireling wolves, whose gospel is their maw.
> MILTON.

DURING the year and a half that Cromwell ruled arbitrarily, his government took root, for whatever its faults, it at least assured to the country the blessings of order and peace. Royalists and Presbyterians either sullenly acquiesced in the change of dynasty, or at least deferred their hopes of restoring Charles Stuart, till after the death of the present protector. As soon as the need of arbitrary government was past, Cromwell wished his use of it to pass too. "When matters of necessity come," he had said to his Parliament, "then without guilt extraordinary remedies may be applied, but if necessity be pretended there is so much the more sin." He determined to meet a Parliament that should restore the government to a nearer approach to its old form, and confer upon himself the title of king. To secure this result he would have to stretch his prerogative once more to oust the Republican opposition, but after this the legitimate career he longed for might be open to him. The Instrument of Government, which had been drawn up merely by

---

* Joining the Ribble just south of Preston, the scene of battle of 17th August, 1648

a council of officers, an unconstitutional authority, wanted a legal sanction, and in place of lasting settlement, only opened to the view of the nation a dreary vista of military rulers, elected by the will of the army. The title of protector was strange and unacceptable to the people generally, nor did it conciliate the Republicans, who called a protector

'A stately thing,
That confesseth itself but the ape of a king.'*

Timid and time-serving supporters of Cromwell's government remembered that by a statute of Henry VII., all persons adhering to the king *de facto* were pronounced guiltless of treason. The protector, therefore, by receiving from a Parliament the title of king, might hope to calm the fears of many of his friends, to gratify the monarchical prejudices of the people, and even to establish a constitutional monarchy in England under kings of his own house. To ensure meeting an assembly favourable to his interests, he did not hesitate to resort to an arbitrary stretch of power. The Instrument of Government authorized the protector and council to make a scrutiny of the returns of elections, and examine whether persons returned were qualified to sit. This clause was intended as a precaution against the admission of any that had borne arms against the Parliament since 1641, and all members of Cromwell's first Parliament had accordingly received tickets from the council, certifying that they were duly returned. Parliament met on the 17th of December; without any legal ground of exclusion, a hundred members, Republicans or other opponents of the government, were for the time refused tickets by the council. When they complained to the Parliament, Cromwell's friends carried a vote by 125 to 29, that they must apply to the council for redress. The residue did not employ themselves very profitably at first. For the first three months of its sitting, the Parliament was almost solely engaged in debating upon the punishment due to James Naylor, the man who had ridden into Bristol, and was worshipped by his followers as divine. According to statute law, this fanatic could only have been imprisoned for six months, and in case of a second offence, banished from the dominions of the Commonwealth. But the Commons, imitating the refinements of the Star Chamber, sen-

* See the lines found among Col. Overton's papers, quoted in Guizot, ii. vi.

tenced him to be six times whipped, put twice in the pillory, have his tongue bored, his forehead branded, and then to be kept in solitary confinement on short rations. This was dealing hard measure to one at the worst half fool, half knave, and gave all liberally or mercifully minded men cause to regret the time when the House of Commons did not resolve itself into a court of justice and inflict arbitrary punishment at pleasure. The protector sent a letter to the House, desiring to be informed of the grounds of its proceedings. The question raised long debates, which resulted in the drawing up of a new instrument of government, called the Petition and Advice. Cromwell was to bear the title of king and to appoint his successor to the throne. New Parliaments were to be summoned once every three years, and were to be composed as formerly of two Houses. The Upper House was to consist of not more than 70 or less than 40 persons, who were to be named by the king. Members of council and officers of State were to be approved by Parliament. The chief magistrate was presumably allowed a negative voice on bills, as no clause was introduced to deprive him of a power hitherto always exercised by English monarchs. The command of the Army and Navy was to rest with the chief magistrate, with consent of Parliament. Thus this new instrument restored the ancient monarchy with some of those checks which the Long Parliament had sought to impose upon Charles I. The protector, who intended to govern in accordance with the articles of the Petition and Advice, encouraged his friends in the Parliament, to abolish both the office of major-general and the income tax of ten per cent. upon Royalists. The major-generals, however, to whom arbitrary government was not so distasteful as to their chief, took offence at their removal from office, and displayed their ill-will and jealousy by opposing the Petition and Advice in the Commons' House, and especially the first clause, which conferred on the chief magistrate the title of king. Their motives may have been selfish; they may have disliked to see their fellow-soldier raised so far above themselves, when before any might have entertained a hope of succeeding. Oliver in the office of Lord Protector. But the ground they publicly put forward was their attachment to the Republican ideal. Their feeling was shared by the army, and a deputation of a hundred officers waited upon the general, to pray him not to accept the

Petition and Advice.

title of king. The protector replied in words to the following effect: 'that the title king, a feather in a hat, is as little valuable to him as to them. But the fact is, they and he have not succeeded in settling the nation hitherto, by the schemes they clamoured for. That the nation is tired of major-generalcies, of uncertain arbitrary ways. That the original instrument of government does need mending in some points. That a House of Lords, or other check upon the arbitrary tendencies of a single House of Parliament, may be of real use; see what they, by their own mere vote and will, I having no power to check them, have done with James Naylor: may it not be any one's case, some other day?'* The officers agreed to withdraw their opposition to the Petition and Advice with the exception of the first clause. But in the House, councillors, lawyers, and other civilians, outnumbered the army men, and the insertion of the title was carried by 123 against 62 votes (29th March). Cromwell, however, dared not accept a crown at the risk of offending the army. After six weeks' delay, during which he vainly sought to overcome the prejudices of officers and soldiers, he informed the Parliament, that though he approved of all the other articles of the new instrument, he could not undertake the government with the title of king. Accordingly it was agreed that while retaining the title of protector, he should exercise the powers vested in the chief magistrate by the Petition and Advice; and thus virtually become King of England in all but name (25th May).

Though the union now existing between Cromwell and his Parliament was a great discouragement to insurrection, still Royalist exiles, and fanatical Levellers, continued to conspire against the government. Their hopes were cheered by a promise of aid from a new quarter. As soon as the protector's foreign policy was declared, and there was no doubt that he would unite with France against Spain, the Spaniards promised to assist Charles Stuart with a body of 6000 men, as soon as any English port declared in his favour (April). An invasion had been planned for the preceding winter (1656-7). But the Royalists and Presbyterians refused to rise, before Charles had actually landed in the country; the Spaniards were found readier at promises than at performance, while Royalist exiles and Levellers, in spite of their common desire to overthrow the government, were suspicious

* Abridged from Burton in Carl., iii. 217.

of one another's final intentions. Thus this grand political combination resulted merely in another attempt at assassination. Syndercomb, an old quarter-master, was supplied with £1600 from Spain, with which he engaged the services first of another old soldier, and then of one of Cromwell's life-guardsmen. These agreed to fire Whitehall, and kill his highness in the tumult that would follow. One evening after a public service, there was left upon the floor of the chapel at Whitehall, a basket, filled with combustible matter, to which were attached two pieces of lighted match, intended to serve as a train, which should fire it about midnight. The sentinel, however, smelling fire, discovered basket and train, and the guardsman confessed the whole plot (March, 1657). Syndercomb, who was tried by jury and convicted of treason, poisoned himself in prison to escape the execution of his sentence. On this the Leveller, Sexby, wrote a pamphlet entitled 'Killing no Murder,' which compared Synder- 'Killing no comb to Brutus, and justified all attempts to 'cut off' Murder.' the protector (May). The Royalist exiles approved of the treatise. "It is only," wrote Hyde, "to show the lawfulness and conveniency that he be presently killed."*

There was, indeed, no hope for the Royalists except in Cromwell's death. His government was now believed at home and abroad to be securely established for his life. His authority had been bestowed upon him by a Parliament in place of a council of officers. Though he still bore the title of Lord Protector, he possessed regal power, and was addressed in the same language and style as those employed to sovereign princes. He had parted on good terms with his Parliament, which, before its prorogation on the 26th of June, had granted him supplies of money, besides the confirmation of the ordinances he had made in council. Royalists dared not rise. His worst enemies could only shame their own cause by making vain attempts at assassination. Nor were his triumphs confined to his home government; abroad, as well, his policy had been crowned with success, and he had already taught foreigners to court the friendship and dread the enmity of England. "Your general," said Christina, Queen of Sweden, to the English ambassador, "hath done the greatest things of any man in the world. I have as great a respect and honour for him

* Clarendon State Papers, iii. 343.

as for any man alive, and I pray let him know as much from me." Though Cromwell was not regarded by most princes with as much favour as he was by the daughter of the great Gustavus, they held the same opinion of his abilities, and dreaded the consequences of his ambition. Even before the expulsion of the Long Parliament, Louis XIV. was frightened by a report that the General of the English Commonwealth intended to land in France at the head of his renowned troops, and assist the French nobles, then in arms against his government. But Cromwell, unlike Napoleon, had no aspirations for the glory a mere soldier might earn by leading on his countrymen to foreign conquest. In him was nothing of the adventurer. The object of his ambition at home, was to establish in England a free government in Church and State ; abroad, his single aim was to support the cause of freedom in Europe, by a coalition of progressive and Protestant States against the reactionary kingdoms of Spain and Austria. He would have scorned to rule a people reduced to a slavish condition ; he would have scorned to conquer without some deeper motive than the mere aggrandizement of himself or his country. Somewhat haughtily he bade the French ambassador set his master's fears at rest. " Looking at his hair, which is white, General Cromwell said, that if he were ten years younger, there was not a king in Europe whom he could not make to tremble ; and that, as he had a better motive than the late King of Sweden, he believed himself still capable of doing more for the good of nations than the other ever did for his own ambition."*

Europe, no doubt, at this time opened a field for new combinations. The Thirty Years' War had been long brought to a close by the Treaty of Westphalia (Sept., 1648). During the latter years of the war the religious object of the struggle had dropped out of sight, and the belligerents were chiefly influenced by political motives. The Swedes fought to gain a footing on the southern shores of the Baltic. The French from the first had assisted Protestants against the emperor, in order to extend their own territories at the expense of Germany. The Catholic princes of the German empire had become more eager to maintain their political rights against the increased power of the emperor, than to eradicate Protestant heresy. By the conditions of the Treaty

* Guizot, i 418 ; Forster, Biog. Essays

of Westphalia, Protestant princes of the empire were to be put on an equality with Catholic; Protestant subjects of Catholic princes, Catholic subjects of Protestant princes, were to enjoy any religious immunities they possessed before the war began; part of the Lower Palatinate was to be restored to Charles Louis, the brother of Rupert and Maurice, and eldest son of the unfortunate Elector Palatine, who married the sister of Charles 1. Though the German war was over, the struggle between France and Spain was continued with great animosity, each country striving to crush her rival, and become the first power in Europe. Both Louis XIV. and Philip IV. of Spain were bidding for the protector's support. Spain offered the possession of Calais, when taken from France; France, the possession of Dunkirk when taken from Spain (1655). Cromwell determined to ally himself with France against Spain. France, though a Catholic country, did not adopt a Catholic policy abroad, while at home she tolerated Huguenots, and did not suffer her progress to be impeded by a blind submission to the Papacy. With Spain, on the other hand, collision was almost inevitable. For while she aspired to the leadership of Europe, her principles were in direct antagonism to all the new ideas, religious or political, that after a century of strife had at last forced their way into the hearts and minds of men. With the exclusion of Protestantism she shut all free life out of her dominions; and the Spaniards were recognized as the most fanatical nation in Europe, burners of heretics, supporters of the pope and the Inquisition, the declared enemies of freedom of conscience. It was in the West Indies that the obstructive policy of Spain came most into collision with the interests of England. Her kings based their claims to the possession of two continents on the bull of Pope Alexander VI., who in 1493 had granted them all lands they should discover from pole to pole, at the distance of a hundred leagues west from the Azores and Cape Verd Islands. On the strength of this bull they held that the discovery of an island gave them the right to the group, the discovery of a headland the right to a continent. Though this monstrous claim had quite broken down as far as the North American continent was concerned, the Spaniards, still recognizing "no peace beyond the line," endeavoured to shut all Europeans but themselves out of any share in the trade or colonization of at least the southern half of the New World. They had imprisoned and murdered English traders, and had already exterminated one French and English colony at St. Kitts (1629), and two English settlements, one at Tortuga (1637), another at Santa Cruz (1650). Accordingly, when Spain sought an alliance, the protector required satisfaction for the blood of both the Republican envoy, Ascham,* and other murdered Englishmen; and demanded liberty of trade to the West Indies, and permission for English merchants and sailors to use their Bibles in any part of the Spanish dominions, unmolested by the Inquisition. "But," said Cromwell, addressing his second Parliament, "there is not liberty of conscience to be had; neither is there satisfaction for injuries, nor for blood. When these two things were desired, the ambassador told us, 'It was to ask his master's two eyes;' to ask both his eyes, asking *these* things of him!"† Nor was Cromwell's disdain expressed in words only. Two large fleets were fitted out by his orders, without any special purpose being assigned for them. The one sailed under Blake to the Mediterranean, with instructions to obtain redress from any nation bordering on that sea, that had committed injuries upon the English (Oct., 1654). This fleet touched other offenders but left Spain alone, for the present, as war had not yet been declared. The Duke of Tuscany paid £60,000 damages. The Dey of Algiers agreed to allow English captives to be ransomed. "The Algiers men-of-war," says a paper of the time,‡ "are become associates with the English; they take Sallee ships and others that have any English in them, and bring them to General Blake, who at this very instant rides triumphant in the Levant." The Governor of Tunis refused satisfaction. "Here are our castles," he said, "do what you can : do you think we fear the show of your fleet?" Blake replied by shattering the castles with two hours' bombardment, and then burning nine ships of war in the harbour. This example had its effect, and at Tripoli his demands obtained immediate compliance.§ The second fleet, consisting of thirty vessels, with 4000 troops on board, was despatched to the West Indies. On opening their instructions at Barbadoes, the commanders, Admiral Penn and General Venables, found they were to surprise the two important islands of St. Domingo and Cuba. Though war with Spain had not yet been declared, there

* See p. 278.   † Carl., iii. 164.   ‡ Ellis, Orig. Letters, 2nd series iii. 378.
§ Heath, 692; Thurloe, iii. 413.

was no breach of faith, as whatever the relations of the two governments at home, no peace was recognized beyond the line. Penn and Venables sailed first, as directed by the instructions, to the former island. But instead of boldly entering the harbour of the capital, St. Domingo, they landed the troops at a point forty miles distant, thus giving the Spaniards time to prepare for defence (April 14, 1655). It was a fatal error, and a period of terrible disaster followed. Two regiments of Oliver's old soldiers were engaged upon the expedition, but the troops mainly consisted of an undisciplined medley of Cavaliers, Levellers, and other unruly spirits from England, together with transported English, Scotch, and Irish Royalists from Barbadoes. The general and the admiral, the land and the sea forces, disagreed. There was a long march of forty miles under a burning sun. There was want of water and want of food. The soldiers nearly mutinied when forbidden to plunder, and from eating unripe fruits dropped down by hundreds sick and dead on their march. Two unsuccessful attempts were made to gain possession of the town. In the second the army fell into an ambuscade, when coming up a narrow path, flanked on either side by woods, where not above six could march abreast. The guns from a battery, raised by the Spaniards, fired right down the path; the foot fell back on the horse, and the whole army was thrown into confusion; the enemy fired from the woods on either side. "Never was anything so wedged as we, which made the enemy weary of killing."* A body of seamen at length drove the Spaniards out of the woods, and night ended the slaughter; 1000 men had fallen. As Penn and Venables dared not return home while they had only this disastrous tale to bring to the protector's ear, they agreed to sail for Jamaica, then in the possession of the Spaniards. Here their success was greater, for the colonists, about five hundred in number, taken by surprise, fled upon their approach, and the island was reduced without opposition (May 10, 1655). In face of many obstacles offered by the climate, and the reckless and improvident habits of the English troops, now turned into colonists, Cromwell set to work to render Jamaica a flourishing settlement. He sent out able men as governors, shipped arms, provisions, and soldiers, directed the building of fortifications, and the planting of plantations, and, in short, laid

* From collection of Thurloe, iii. 510.

the foundations of the future power of England in the West Indies.*

While war was now proclaimed with Spain, a treaty of peace was signed between France and England, Louis XIV. agreeing to banish Charles Stuart and his brothers from French territory (Oct. 24, 1655). This treaty was afterwards changed into a league, offensive and defensive (March 23, 1657), Cromwell undertaking to assist Louis with 6000 men in besieging Gravelines, Mardyke, and Dunkirk, on condition of receiving the two latter towns when reduced by the allied armies. By the occupation of these towns Cromwell intended to control the trade of the Channel, to hold the Dutch in check, who were then but unwilling friends, and to lessen the danger of invasion from any union of Royalists and Spaniards. The war opened in the year 1657 with another triumph by sea. During the summer of 1656, Blake had made a second expedition to the Mediterranean ; he was now engaged in blockading Cadiz, when he learnt that a fleet with bullion, from Mexico, had taken refuge in the bay of Santa Cruz, in the island of Teneriffe. The horse-shoe bay was defended by castles at the two points, and by seven forts round the shore, connected by lines, bristling with guns and manned by musketeers. Ten small vessels were moored close to the shore ; six large galleons farther out in the bay, their broadsides towards the sea. This position the Spaniards believed unassailable : they still thought that ships had no chance against forts. The master of a Dutch merchantman asked leave to sail out of the bay. "I am very sure," he said, "Blake will presently be amongst you." " Get you gone, if you will, and let Blake come, if he dares," replied the Spaniards.† The English fleet numbered five-and-twenty sail. A favourable wind carried them into the bay. They attacked forts, ships, and galleons at once. After four hours' fighting the forts were silenced, and all the Spanish vessels burnt with the exception of two, which were sunk. The English fleet started homewards the same day. Blake was worn out with hard service, and before he could receive from his countrymen the thanks and honours that were his due, he " who would never strike to any other enemy, struck his topmast to death," within sight of Plymouth (Aug. 7). It was said of this gallant seaman, that with him valour never missed its reward,

Thurloe, v. 130; Carl., iii. 129. † Heath, 721.

nor cowardice its punishment. Ever loyal to his country, all he said to his sailors when he announced a change in the government was, "'Tis not our duty to mind State affairs, but to keep foreigners from fooling us." The chief of the State, indeed, was not the man to let foreigners "fool" us. In accordance with the terms of the French League, Cromwell had sent 6000 of his best troops to the Netherlands. But Mazarin, instead of besieging Mardyke and Dunkirk, commenced operations in the interior of the country, and tried to put his ally off with promises. "Tell him," Cromwell wrote to Lockhart, his ambassador in France, "that to talk of what will be done next campaign are but parcels of words for children." "If the French," he wrote again, "are going to be so false as to give us no footing on that side the water, we must ask for satisfaction for our expense, and draw off our men."* The story went that Cardinal Mazarin changed countenance whenever he heard the protector named, and was not so much afraid of the devil as he was of Oliver Cromwell. He dared not trifle with him any longer. Mardyke was besieged, taken in ten days, and delivered over to the English (Sept., 1657). In the spring of the following year the siege of Dunkirk was commenced (May, 1658). The Spaniards tried to relieve the town, but were completely defeated in an engagement, called the Battle of the Dunes from the sand hills among which it was fought; the defeat was mainly owing to the courage and discipline of Oliver's troops, who won for themselves the name of "the Immortal Six Thousand." James Stuart, the future king, commanded the left wing of the Spanish army, and narrowly escaped with his life. Ten days after the battle Dunkirk surrendered, and the French had no choice but to give over to the English ambassador the keys of a town they thought *un si bon morceau* (June 25).† At this time no honour was considered too great to be paid to the protector's envoys. During the siege of Dunkirk, Lord Fauconberg, lately become Cromwell's son-in-law, arrived from England to meet Louis at Calais. The governor of the town, accompanied by many persons of quality, came to receive him on his landing; the king's own Switzers guarded his door; the king and queen's own officers attended him at meals. Louis held a private interview with him

Surrender of Mardyke and Dunkirk.

* Carl, iii. 311, 313.   † Thurloe, vii. 174.

and remained uncovered the whole time. Cardinal Mazarin after a conference accompanied him downstairs, and saw him into his coach, a courtesy he seldom paid to his own sovereign.* Catholic governments dared not molest the protector's subjects. An Englishman in Portugal was imprisoned by the Inquisition. Cromwell's resident at Lisbon expostulated. The king replied that he had no authority over the Inquisition. At their next interview the resident intimated, that since his majesty had no power over the Inquisition, the protector declared war upon it. The Englishman was released.†

Cromwell had not been content with protecting his own subjects only from persecution. While his friendship was still being courted by both France and Spain, the Duke of Savoy had ordered the Vaudois living in the valleys of the Savoy Alps to embrace the Catholic faith, or to quit their homes within three days (Jan. 25, 1655). It was the depth of winter, the people were slow to obey, and appealed for aid and advice to the Protestant cantons of Switzerland. The duke, to suppress discontent, quartered soldiers in the valleys. Quarrels naturally ensued, and horrible barbarities were committed by the troops upon the inhabitants of the valley of Lucerna, whose sufferings stand commemorated in Milton's noble sonnet. Cromwell appeared as their champion. For their immediate needs he started a subscription list with a donation of £2000. The heart of England was moved with sympathy : a regular canvass was made ; the soldiers gave freely, and for love or shame almost everybody subscribed. An agent was sent at once, by Cromwell's orders, to intercede with the Duke of Savoy in their favour. Milton, by his directions, wrote letters to the Kings of France, Sweden, and Denmark, to the Protestant cantons of Switzerland, and to the States of Holland, appealing to their feelings of humanity to take measures to put an end to these cruelties. The pope's interference was prevented by a hint that he might hear the thunder of English cannon off Civita Vecchia. The duke himself was an ally of Louis XIV., and no treaty would Cromwell sign with France unless the Vaudois were first protected from persecution. In vain Louis objected that he had no right to interfere with an independent prince, such as the Duke of Savoy. Finding Cromwell was not to be put off, he consented to mediate, and by his

* Thurloe, vi. 157. † Burton's Diary, Introduction.

advice the duke forgave his rebellious subjects, and confirmed their ancient privileges.* The disgraces of Buckingham's administration were wiped out by this vigorous policy, and the position of England abroad was even higher than it was in the memorable days of Elizabeth. The remembrance of these successes made the nation smart the more when the Restoration reduced her to the position of a dependent upon France.

Foreign policy, indeed, must be judged on other considerations than mere national glorification. No war can be approved that is undertaken merely for the sake of conquest, increased revenue, or personal aggrandizement. A nation, however, is often justified, not only in defending itself against insult and wrong, but even in entering on an aggressive war, when made either to preserve the liberty of other nations from foreign attack, or to wrest an advantage which belongs by right to all mankind from the grasp of some single power. Cromwell's policy was, in the main, confined to these ends. It was an act of self-defence to punish Spain for the wrongs she had committed upon English subjects; it was an act of public right in the widest sense of the term to deprive Spain of her unjust monopoly of trade with the West Indies. On the other hand, if it is said that England gained too much by the war for her motives in carrying it on to be regarded as perfectly pure, in the first place, it is natural that the most injured party should be chief prosecutor of wrong; and secondly, the best interests of the world were served by the protector's policy of making England the head of Protestant States, and upholding the cause of liberty of conscience. At least one half of Western Europe was governed by tyrants, who were bent on crushing free institutions and the free expression of opinion by imprisonment, banishment, torture, and the stake. Cromwell, representing all that was best and highest in the nation, declared eternal hostility to these powers of obstruction and reaction, and flinging the weight of England into the cause of freedom and progress, raised her, as much by moral as by material force, to the foremost place amongst European nations.

In judging the policy of wars defended on public or international grounds, three criteria may be applied; first, has the principle invoked been sanctioned by history as one really tending to the highest good of mankind? secondly, has the

* Guizot, ii. 529; Carlyle, iii. 108; Lingard, viii. 233.

attempt a fair chance of success? and, thirdly, is the war likely to entail a more than compensating weight of misery on the poor and struggling classes of the nation? Cromwell's policy has passed two of these tests, it will be seen that it passes the third too. The government which effected such great results was carried on at comparatively a small cost. No waste, no corruption, was allowed, and the protector offered to lay the accounts of the expenditure open to inspection. The tax for the support of the army and navy was reduced from £120,000 to £90,000, and afterwards to £60,000 a month.

The success of Cromwell's foreign policy, however glorious it rendered their country, yet failed to conciliate the Republicans, who seized the opportunity of the re-assembling of Parliament to display their enmity (20th Jan.). According to the terms of the Petition and Advice, this Parliament consisted of two Houses, with the second House composed, not of the old peers, of whom the majority were Royalists, but of lords newly created for the purpose by the writs of the protector. To create lords whose title to the peerage, like that of Oliver's to the throne, rested not on hereditary descent but on superior capacity, was an overbold attempt to return by a short cut to the old forms of the constitution. For the unquestioning, unreasoning respect given to the possessors of titles is of slow growth, and new creations can only pass muster, if few enough to be undistinguishable among the mass of the old. These new lords were regarded by high and low as impostors. Out of sixty-three persons summoned to the protector's Upper House some twenty declined. Even the Earl of Warwick refused to attend, though a personal friend, and the grandfather of Cromwell's son-in-law, Mr. Rich. The old earl said that he could not bring himself to sit in the same assembly with Col. Pride, once a drayman, and Col. Hewson, once a shoemaker. Members of the Commons no longer had to be approved by the council before taking their seats, for an article of the Petition and Advice required that, as in former times, persons chosen to serve in Parliament should not be excluded from sitting, except by the judgment of the House of which they were members. Thus, any of the opponents of the government, who were excluded before,* were now suffered to take their seats

* See p. 348.

without opposition, on swearing the requisite oath of allegiance to the protector. The violent Republicans, Scot, Haslerig, Bradshaw, and others took the oath without scruple, and then at once set to work to attack the government. Aided by the absence of many of Cromwell's ablest friends, who had been removed to the Upper House, they readily obtained a majority to follow their lead. First they debated what rights belonged to the 'other House,' and tried to prove that the Petition and Advice gave it no co-ordinate power with the Commons in making laws and imposing taxes. They then proceeded to dispute with the protector's party as to the name they should call the 'other House,' refusing to allow it that of 'House of Lords.' For three weeks, while they occupied their time in these useless debates, dangers multiplied around the government. Charles Stuart, to whom the Dutch had sold twenty vessels, came to Ostend, intending, if only the Royalists would first attempt a rising in his behalf, to cross the Channel at the head of several regiments of transported Irishmen. At home, all the disaffected began to engage in conspiracy, or in trying to get up petitions hostile to the government. There was one petition being prepared for the restoration of the Stuarts; a second for the reduction of Cromwell's authority ; while the Republicans were secretly publishing seditious papers, and tampering with the army, in which they still possessed considerable influence. The protector's passion rose. The Parliament, he said, represented all the bad humours of the nation, and had become the Parliament of the Republican, Haslerig.* Though it had sat but fifteen days, he determined to dissolve it ; its continuance would soon have led to anarchy and another civil war.

"That," he said, addressing the members of the two Houses, "which brought me into the capacity I now stand in, was the Petition and Advice given me by you ; who, in reference to the ancient constitution, did draw me to accept the place of protector. There is not a man living can say I sought it ; no, not a man nor woman treading upon English ground. But contemplating the sad condition of these nations, relieved from an intestine war into a six or seven years' peace, I did think the nation happy therein !......I can say in the presence of God—in comparison with whom we are but like poor creeping ants upon the earth—I would have been glad to have lived under my woodside, to have kept a flock of sheep, rather than undertaken such a government as this. But undertaking it by the Advice and Petition of your

* Whitelock, 672 ; Documents in App. to Guizot, ii. 629.

I did look that you who had offered it unto me should make it good.......I do not speak to these gentlemen" (pointing to his right hand), "or lords, or whatsoever you will call them. I speak not this to them, but to *you*" (gentlemen of the House of Commons). " You have not only disjointed yourselves, but the whole nation, which is in likelihood of running into more confusion in these fifteen or sixteen days that you have sat, than it hath been from the rising of the last session to this day, through the intention of devising a Commonwealth again, that some people might be the men that might rule all ! And they are endeavouring to engage the army to carry that thing. ...These things tend to nothing else but the playing of the King o Scots' game, if I may so call him ; and I think myself bound before God to do what I can to prevent it. It hath been not only your endeavour to pervert the army while you have been sitting, and to draw them to state the question" [*i.e.*, to petition] " about a Commonwealth; but some of you have been listing of persons, by commission of Charles Stuart, to join with any insurrection that may be made. And what is like to come upon this, the enemy being ready to invade us, but even present blood and confusion? And if this be so, I do assign it to this cause—your not consenting to what you did invite me by your Petition and Advice, as that which might prove the settlement of the nation. And if this be the end of your sitting, and this be your carriage, I think it high time that an end be put to your sitting. And I do dissolve this Parliament. And let God be judge between you and me" (4th Feb.).

Cromwell, in his noble zeal for liberty, had really attempted an impossibility. Parliamentary government is perfectly feasible after a mere change of dynasty, but after revolutionary forces have been allowed to run their course, time must solidify existing rule before it can be exposed to the rude dissolvents of discussion and debate. A real revolution decomposes a nation into numberless parties, each of which cannot be content with anything less than all it aims at, and in a free Parliament any two of these parties, however opposite in policy, may combine for the sole purpose of destroying any intermediate party which seems to be more represented by the ruler of the time. It was natural for intolerant Presbyterians to wish for the overthrow of the Puritan apostle of toleration, and natural for Republicans to hate the man who ruled where their oligarchy had failed ; but both showed an incapacity for discerning the possibilities of the time, and for recognizing facts under forms. The alliance of these two parties against the protectorate could only promote the Episcopacy which was fatal to the one, and that absolute monarchy which was the true enemy of the other.

The Parliament dissolved, Cromwell set his hand to crushing

the conspiracies that had sprung up around. "An old friend of yours is in town," he said to Lord Broghill,* now a councillor, "the Marquis of Ormond; he lodges in Drury Lane, at the Papist surgeon's; if you have a mind to save your old acquaintance, let him know that I am informed where he is and what he is doing." On this hint, Ormond, who had ventured across the Channel in order, if possible, to concert a rising, hastened back to Holland, and told his young master that his friends were far more ready to promise than to perform. The Royalists were, in fact, disconcerted at the dissolution of the Parliament, on which they had relied as the cat's paw to wrest the protector's power from him. They now refused to venture property and life on what seemed a hopeless cast. Several conspirators were already apprehended and in prison. Five Royalists, engaged in various plots, were tried by a high court of justice, and executed as traitors. Officers implicated in Republican plots were cashiered. Disaffection, however, had not spread far, and the larger part of the army remained devoted to their general. Summoning the officers to Whitehall, Cromwell explained to them the cause of the sudden dissolution of the Parliament, and the plots and conspiracies to which its sitting had given rise, and expressed a hope that if he should be forced to take money by arbitrary means, they would give him their support. "We will live and die with you," they shouted in reply.†

In spite of the prejudice of the nation in favour of its old line of princes, the peaceful and order-loving classes were beginning to dread any change of government. Englishmen, even if they disliked the usurper, could hardly fail to be proud of their great countryman, who had humiliated the Spaniards, and raised England to the first place among European powers. National pride could not fail to be gratified by the surrender of Dunkirk, and the unprecedented honours paid to England's ambassadors. The very energy and success with which plots were suppressed and political enemies disconcerted, itself awoke admiration. The protector's dignity, his lenity, the uprightness of his administration, forced respect even from unwilling subjects. He was now intending, within the course of a few months, to summon another Parliament, in order to avoid resorting to arbitrary means for the

* See p. 301.   † Thurloe, vi. 786; Guizot (Documents), ii. 610.

raising of money. By taking means to exclude the Republicans, he might have obtained one friendly to his government, and would perhaps again have been offered the title of king. There was a wide-spread feeling that the 'fall of the present government would be the occasion of great disasters to the nation.' The protector's popularity had been much increased by the possession of Dunkirk; petitions were even sent in by some counties, desiring him to take the title of king; and whether men feared or hoped, the expectation that he would be crowned was general throughout the country.*

But this expectation was never to be realized. Sorrows fell upon Cromwell in his own family, and these to him were harder to bear than the plots and machinations of his enemies. Death had already deprived him of two relatives— Robert Rich, lately married to his youngest daughter (16th Feb.), and the Earl of Warwick, a firm friend to himself, the young man's grandfather (19th April). And now his favourite daughter, Lady Claypole, "of excellent parts, civil to all persons, courteous, friendly,"† lay ill at Hampton Court, " under great extremity of bodily pain," dying in fact by some terrible internal disease. The protector was constantly by her bedside, and so overpowered with grief for his dying child, that he had but little attention to bestow on public business. The groom of his bedchamber relates how "his sense of her outward misery, in the pains she endured, took deep impression upon him, who indeed was ever a most indulgent and tender father."‡ He also relates how the text, 'I can do all things through Christ which strengtheneth me,' was what restored him from despair. For " this scripture," as Cromwell himself said, " did once save my life when my eldest son died, which went as a dagger to my heart, indeed it did.'§ Lady Claypole died (6th Aug.), and a fortnight after her death his own health, which had for some time past been failing, quite broke down. He was seized with a dangerous ague, and by advice of his physicians removed from Hampton Court to Whitehall (21st Aug.).

Men prayed for his recovery, looking into the dark future

* Thurloe, vii. 144; Guizot (Documents), ii. 631, 643.
† Whitelock, 674.   ‡ King's Tracts., 792; Carl., iii. 368.
§ Robert, who was buried at Felsted, in Essex, æt. 19, in 1639 (**Forster's Essays**, p. 54).

with dismay at the anarchy that might ensue, when the one man was gone who could hold the rival parties down and compel them to live in peace.* "His heart," says one who then attended him, "was so carried out for God and His people—yea indeed, for some who had added no little sorrow to him, that at this time he seemed to forget his own family and nearest relations." "He would frequently say, 'God is good, indeed He is,' and would speak it with much cheerfulness and fervour of spirit in the midst of his pains. Again he said, 'I would be willing to live to be further serviceable to God and His people; but my work is done. Yet God will be with His people.' He was very restless most part of the [Thursday] night, speaking often to himself. And there being something to drink offered him, he was desired to take the same, and endeavour to sleep, unto which he answered, 'It is not my design to drink or sleep; but my design is to make what haste I can to be gone.'"† The next day was the 3rd of September, his lucky day, the anniversary of his victories of Dunbar and Worcester, and at four o'clock in the afternoon of that day Oliver Cromwell lay dead.

Born the year before the century began, he had not lived out his sixtieth year, when he was thus called away, but the work he had done, the perils and privations he had faced, might well have taken even more than ten years from man's allotted term. It was nearly two centuries before justice was done to his memory. Strange that England should have been so long deluded into believing that the noblest of her sons could have been the 'great wicked man' that blind and bitter partisans depicted; he a mere revolutionary demagogue, who was the restorer of order at home, the terror of tyranny abroad; he a hard and selfish usurper, whose stout nerves quailed at last, not at the attempts of assassins, but at the agony of a daughter's sufferings; he a prince of hypocrites, who, in the last and 'thickest press of domestic anarchies,' found time and means to shield the poor Protestants of Piedmont,‡ and whose last half-conscious murmurings were of the goodness of God and of His presence with His people! The change in the current of opinion on this point has been mainly due to the publication of the letters and speeches of Cromwell.§ The peculiar value of Mr. Carlyle's

* Thurloe, vii. 55. † King's Tracts., 792.
‡ 26 May, 1658; Carl., iii. 302. § 1st ed., pub. Dec., 1845.

labours has been thus admirably stated by the closest student of those times, whose testimony is the more valuable, as that of one who had himself held a different view of the character and aims of the greatest of the statesmen of the Commonwealth. "To collect and arrange in chronological succession, and with elucidatory comment, every authentic letter and speech left by Cromwell, was to subject him to a test from which falsehood could hardly escape; and the result has been to show, we think, conclusively and beyond further dispute, that through all these speeches and letters one mind runs consistently. Whatever a man's former prepossessions may have been, he cannot accompany the utterer of these speeches, the writer of these letters, from their first page to their last, travelling with him from his grazing lands at St. Ives up to his protector's throne; watching him in the tenderest intercourse with those dearest to him; observing him in affairs of State or in the ordinary business of the world, in offices of friendship or in conference with sovereigns and senates; listening to him as he comforts a persecuted preacher, or threatens a persecuting prince; and remain at last with any other conviction than that in all conditions and on every occasion Cromwell's tone is substantially the same, and that in the passionate fervour of his religious feeling, under its different and varying modifications, the true secret of his life must be sought, and will be found. Everywhere recognizable is the sense, deeply inter-penetrated with his nature and life, of spiritual dangers, of temporal vicissitudes, and of never-ceasing responsibility to the Eternal. 'Ever in his Great Taskmaster's eye.' Unless you can believe that you have an actor continually before you, you must believe that this man did unquestionably recognize in his Bible the authentic voice of God; and had an irremovable persuasion that according as, from that sacred source, he learned the divine law here and did it, or neglected to learn and to do it, infinite blessedness or infinite misery hereafter awaited him for evermore."[*]

[*] Forster, Essays, p. 33.

CHAPTER XVI.

RICHARD CROMWELL.—ANARCHY.—THE RESTORATION.—
1658—1660.

Quand on se trompe dans quelque projet pour sa fortune, ce n'est qu'un coup d'épée dans l'eau; mais dans les entreprises de l'Etat, il n'y a pas de coup d'épée dans l'eau.—MONTESQUIEU.

CROMWELL, by uniting in his own person the offices of general and protector, had curbed the ambition of his military subordinates, while he established a government capable of winning the respect if not the affection of civilians. The standing army was a fact and a necessity against which it would have been vain for him to contend, but none the less was it a worm in the bud of the Protectorate. The retention of such an army in the hands of the executive must in time have proved fatal to liberty. It was indeed just possible that the new protector might possess both the ability and moderation of his great predecessor, be willing to rule as a constitutional king, and be able to bridle the army till he could dispense with it. But if these qualities were not found combined in the same man, the nation must expect shipwreck on one rock or the other. Should the new protector be capable without being moderate, he would use the army as an instrument of arbitrary power; should he on the contrary be moderate without being capable, his officers might depose him and inaugurate a vicious succession of ephemeral military governments.

The Petition and Advice gave the protector power to appoint his successor, and Richard Cromwell, Oliver's eldest son, now took office in right of his father's deathbed nomination. The young man was by nature not ill fitted to play the part of a con-

stitutional king in quiet times; he was unprejudiced and not
fanatical; his temper was mild; he was always ready to give
ear to counsel. On the other hand he was deficient in those
qualities which are most essential for a ruler in troubled times;
he had not the qualities which ensure obedience and respect; he
had no insight into character; no firmness, no power of command. Hence the ambition of the officers, combined with his
own weakness, produced a period of anarchy and misgovernment
which caused the Restoration of our English Bourbons to be regarded for a time as a blessing to the country.

At first, indeed, the shadow of Oliver's greatness shielded his
son; at home no faction dared raise its head; abroad foreign
governments recognized the new protector, and refused to hold any
communication with Charles Stuart. This tranquillity, however,
lasted but a few months. The Republicans scoffed at the
idea of a man of third-rate capacity maintaining a throne they
had been at such pains to overthrow; the soldiers despised a
general who had never led them to battle. The leading officers
were no admirers of privilege, and were unwilling to allow that
the weak and vacillating Richard gained any right to stand above
themselves from the mere accident of birth. Fleetwood wished
to divide the offices of protector and general and to govern as
general in Richard's name. Lambert was believed to aspire to
the protectorship itself. "I wish Lambert was dead," writes a
Royalist, "there is no small danger his reputation with the army
may thrust Dick Cromwell (who sits like an ape on horseback)
out of the saddle, and yet not help the king into it."* The meeting of Parliament was the signal for action to both Republicans
and officers (Jan. 27). Vane opposed Richard's right to the
protectorship in words winged to reach the hearts of both Republicans and soldiers. "The people of England," he said, "are
now renowned all over the world for their great virtue and discipline; and yet suffer an idiot without courage, without sense,
nay, without ambition, to have dominion in a country of liberty!
One could bear a little with Oliver Cromwell, though, contrary
to his oath of fidelity to the Parliament, contrary to his duty to
the public, contrary to the respect he owed that venerable body
from which he received his authority, he usurped the govern-

* Clar. State Papers, iii. 408.

ment. His merit was so extraordinary, that our judgments, our passions, might be blinded by it. He made his way to empire by the most illustrious actions: he had under his command an army that had made him a conqueror, and a people that had made him their general. But as for Richard Cromwell, his son, who is he? what are his titles? We have seen that he had a sword by his side, but did he ever draw it? And, what is of more importance in this case, is he fit to get obedience from a mighty nation, who could never make a footman obey him? yet we must recognize this man as our king, under the style of protector!—a man without birth, without courage, without conduct. For my part, I declare, sir, it shall never be said that I made such a man my master."* Richard, however, had many able friends in the House, such as the lawyers St. John and Whitelock, Thurloe his secretary, and other civilians and councillors, who hoped to establish an hereditary and constitutional monarchy under the house of Cromwell. These succeeded in obtaining a majority to follow them. Richard's 'right' to govern, though not his 'undoubted right' was recognized, and a vote was carried to transact business with Oliver's lords, the 'Other House.' The officers, however, desiring themselves to govern the country, and jealous of the influence which civilians exercised in Richard's counsels, determined on the dissolution of the Parliament. Desborough, acting as their spokesman, told the protector that if he would do as they proposed, the officers would take care of him, but if he refused, they would do without him and leave him to shift for himself. Richard yielded, and thus virtually surrendered his authority into their hands (April 22nd).

The struggle between the army and the civil power, which Oliver had closed by the establishment of the protectorate, was now renewed. Conscious of their own unpopularity with the country, instead of summoning a new Parliament, the officers restored the Rump (May 7th). At the request of this body, Richard retired from Whitehall and thus formally resigned his ten-months' dignity (July). The officers intended to govern in the name of their allies; the Rump on its part meant to rule the soldiery. But, in revolutionary times might is right, and the people fully understanding the terms on which this extinct Parliament was revived,.

* Guizot, Richard Cromwell, i. 54, 293.

only derided its assumption of power. "Do the men in the Parliament House signify any more," says a pamphlet, "than the man that stands upon the clock in Westminster Abbey with the hammer in his hand, and when the iron wheel bids him strike, he strikes : hath it not been so between the army and the Parliament, as it is called ?"* During Oliver's protectorate the Presbyterians with all their dislike to his rule would never unite with "malignants" for the restoration of Charles Stuart. But now the dread of military tyrants overcame fears and prejudices. The union of Royalists and Presbyterians, however, itself restored in turn a forced accord between the House and the officers, which for the time crushed the hopes of the rival coalition. The same spies whom Oliver had once employed now revealed to the new government the conspiracies of its opponents. Only in Cheshire did any considerable rising take place. Sir George Booth, who appeared at the head of 4000 men, was defeated by Lambert and brought a prisoner to London. After this success the old quarrel was renewed. The officers asked that a standing senate should carry on the government in conjun tion with a House of Commons ; and further that no commissions should be revoked without the consent of a court-martial. By the first demand they thought to place the government virtually in their own hands ; by the second to secure for the military a complete independence of the civil power. The House in its turn tried to keep the army dependent upon themselves for pay by voting it treason to levy money without consent of Parliament. Having thus as they hoped defended themselves against a sudden dissolution, they proceeded to cashier Lambert, Desborough, and six other colonels ; and to put the command of the army in commission, by reducing Fleetwood, whom they had appointed commander-in-chief to check Booth's rising, to the position of a mere president of a board of seven (Oct. 12th). These votes were equal to a declaration of war, and the next day Lambert marched to Westminster at the head of 3000 soldiers. He found a guard of several regiments, friendly to the Republicans, already stationed round Parliament House. These regiments refused to fight their old comrades in arms, and fraternized with Lambert's men. Lenthall, the Speaker, tried in vain to recall the troops

* King's Tracts.

to allegiance to the House. As the nominal head of the new government he had lately renewed the officers' commissions. " I am your general," he said, " I expect your obedience." " If you had marched before us over Warrington Bridge" (p. 229) " we should have known you," was the curt reply. The will of the army had been expressed, and the Rump discontinued its sittings.

The officers now conducted the government by a Committee of Safety, consisting of a few Republicans and a majority of their own party. These military rulers, however, were foiled in their turn. There was in Scotland another army and another commander-in-chief, whose consent had not been given to this *pronunciamento*. General Monk owed no allegiance to Desborough or Fleetwood; locked in his breast he had his scheme of a settlement for the kingdom. Setting his army in motion to march south, he astutely proclaimed his intention 'to stand to, and assert the liberty and authority of Parliament.' The Republicans understood that he came to restore the Rump; the Cavaliers and Presbyterians that he came to summon a free Parliament, and thus prepare the way for the restoration of the Stuarts. Republicans, Presbyterians, and Cavaliers all took courage and refused obedience to the Committee of Safety, and the country was practically without any government at all. A part of the fleet declared for the Republicans, and took custom duties of all ships passing up and down the Thames. The governor of Portsmouth admitted into the town some regiments of Republican troops. Taxes could only be levied by force, for all over the country the people refused to pay 'without consent of Parliament.' The support of Presbyterian London at the opening of the war had enabled the Parliament to make war upon the king. But Presbyterian London was now become strongly Royalist, and its hostility threatened to be fatal to the ascendancy of a divided army. Fleetwood and Desborough tried in vain to cajole the Common Council into advancing a loan of £30,000. Soldiers had to be quartered in the city to prevent the apprentices from rising; quarrels ensued, and lives were lost on both sides. The goldsmiths in Cheapside and Lombard Street closed their shops and concealed their money and goods. The courts in Westminster Hall ceased to sit, for the commissions of the judges had expired, and there was no authority competent to renew them. After having thus brought all

Monk marches from Scotland.

government to a standstill, the officers saw only two courses open to them—the one to join with the Presbyterians and restore the House of Stuart; the other to reinstate the Republicans. The latter was preferred, and the members of the Rump resumed their sittings (26th Dec.).

Monk, meanwhile, was advancing from Scotland at the head of 7000 men. Lambert some weeks previously had marched north to oppose his approach with a force of 10,000 men (Nov.). But when his force had reached Marston Moor, the great Yorkshireman, Lord Fairfax, emerged from his retirement in Wharfedale to decide the fate of England. Like other sincere patriots, he regarded the restoration of the Stuarts as the only means of saving his country from utter anarchy. He had already promised Monk to effect a rising and attack Lambert in the rear as soon as the Scotch army had engaged him in front. But his victory was bloodless. A message came that a whole brigade in the rear of Lambert's army was ready to join him the next day on Marston Moor. Upon his arrival the troops presented their old general with a petition in favour of a free Commonwealth and against a government by a single person. Fairfax in reply tore the paper in pieces, and placed himself at the head of his raw Yorkshire levies, as though with them alone he were ready to fight a veteran army. His decision produced a strange effect. Troop after troop, regiment after regiment, came over to his side. Lambert, almost entirely deserted, slunk away to a country house* (3rd Jan.). Monk was now able to march to London unopposed. When his troops were once securely quartered in the capital, he declared himself plainly for a 'free Parliament.' This meant the return of Charles Stuart, for which every four men out of five now longed (10th Feb.). The city went wild with delight. Bells were rung; loyal healths were drunk in every street; the whole heaven was made aglow with the light of hundreds of bonfires; hardly one without a rump roasting before it, 'for the celebration of the funeral of the Parliament.' That funeral was near at hand. The Republicans were still sitting when the old Presbyterian members, who were expelled by Colonel Pride eleven years before, were escorted by a guard to retake their seats at Westminster (21st Feb.). According

Monk declares for a free Parliament.

---

* Markham, Fairfax, 381

to promises made to Monk, these members carried the voluntary dissolution of the House, and named the 25th of April for the meeting of a new and free Parliament (16th March). This new Parliament is commonly described as a convention, being summoned without the royal writ. Conventions are, in fact, national assemblies held, when the constitution is in abeyance, for the specific purpose of establishing some form of government. The Lower House was filled with Cavaliers and Presbyterians so Royalist in feeling that the few Republicans who were returned hardly dared show their faces among their fellow-members. The House of Lords was represented at its opening by only ten peers, Presbyterians, who resumed their seats after an absence of eleven years. This Convention at once invited Charles Stuart to return to his kingdom. There was reason, however, to fear that his return might not be accomplished without bloodshed, for, though the nation was united, the national will was opposed by a body of 50,000 fighting men. Every precaution was taken by Monk to divide the army and raise a force that might be able to cope with it. The fleet had now declared itself on the side of the nation; the London trainbands alone numbered 20,000 men; the militia was being trained and organized in every county; the citizens spared neither wine nor money to secure the favour, or at least the neutrality, of Monk's troops, who were quartered amongst them. Yet men and officers would sooner have fought their new friends than feasted with them. 'They were like beasts,' they would say, when feasting in the city halls, 'set up a-fatting for the slaughter.' But the army, though numerous, was not capable of combined and decisive action. Numbers, even though backed by bravery and skill, can avail little without a leader. The position of Monk commanded the obedience of the soldiers, while the support of Fairfax conciliated their feelings. On the other hand, neither Lambert, Desborough, nor Fleetwood could inspire the confidence that where they led victory must follow Charles Stuart returned from his exile in peace and triumph. Yet on the day when the new king made his entry into the capital, and on his way passed through the army which was drawn up on Blackheath to meet him, the officers kissed the royal hand with evident reluctance, while the men, as they stood sullenly amidst rejoicing thousands, looked like some black thunder-cloud that might end the sunny day of triumph by dispersing the crowds of welcomers in terror to their homes (29th May).* The dangerous day of entry over, the standing army was within a few months disbanded. The enemies of the royal prerogative feared it might be remodelled into an instrument of tyranny; while zealous Royalists still dreaded the terrible troopers who had raised a Cromwell to the throne. The return of the Stuarts, therefore, benefited the country by saving it from the rule of military governors who might have tried to play the rôle of the great protector without his incomparable genius for statesmanship. The longer the struggle lasted, the fiercer and more sanguinary it must have become, and all peace-loving men dreaded the day when the Fifth-Monarchists, Anabaptists, and Republicans who filled the army should each in succession signalize a short-lived triumph by a proscription of political and religious opponents. The Stuarts or anarchy—that was the only choice. The Restoration may therefore justly be regarded as a necessity, but nevertheless the day that brought back the exiled race to our shores, was the beginning of a brief but dark period of decay. The reaction which follows a revolution is always a heavy drawback on the advantages which may ultimately spring from the triumph of the people in a struggle. With the return of Charles Stuart came a great reaction. An heroic age had gone by, and with it all noble aspirations. The government of Charles II. was the most shameless England ever endured. The leaders of the State and the leaders of society were alike venal and immoral. As in the worst days of the Roman empire, virtue and self-respect vanished together.† Avowedly governed by self-interest, cupidity, and mere sensual desires, they refused to believe in the existence of higher motives of action. The king and his courtiers alike lived profligate lives; the king and his ministers alike received pensions from France. The Episcopal Church again set herself to work to teach the divine right of kings and the duty of passive obedience, and repaid the Presbyterians for the active help they had given in the Restoration, by rejecting all proposals for accommodation and inaugurating an universal persecution of nonconformists. The House of Commons, in an excess of loyal zeal, undid much of the best work of the first years of the Long Parliament; it passed persecuting laws, which

* Macaulay, I. ch. i.   † Contemptu famæ contemni virtutes.—Tac.

continued for nearly two centuries to inflame the religious passions of the strong, and corrupt the morals of the weak; broke up the union which the united efforts of Vane and Cromwell had established between the three kingdoms; by repealing the Triennial Bill destroyed the only security then existing for the continuity of Parliamentary life; and, by returning to the old system of representation, placed in power a corrupt oligarchy representing but a mere minority of the nation, which tried to press down the most active forces of opinion, causing upheaval after upheaval, till the buried giants were at last rendered harmless by the outlet given through the Reform Bill of 1832.

The reaction which set in in favour of the Stuarts was a necessary consequence of the revolution itself. In the beginning of a struggle for freedom, the people start with fresh vigour, believing in the goodness of their cause and the great things they are about to accomplish. Civil war soon engenders strong feelings of partisanship, and these in turn errors and excesses. If the popular revolution is successful, a newly established government, not having prescription on its side, cannot pursue the same mild treatment of political offenders as if it rested on a foundation of centuries. Hence it has recourse to harsh or arbitrary acts, and brings into disrepute the great watchwords in the name of which the struggle for freedom commenced. A generation had now grown up which knew nothing of the sentences of the Courts of Star Chamber and High Commission, or of the arbitrary acts committed under Strafford's policy of "thorough;" while even in the minds of older men the remembrance of all this had been dimmed by the changes and troubles of the past sixteen years. The erection of high courts of justice, the sale and transportation of freeborn Englishmen, government by major-generals, not to mention the forced observance of Sundays and fast days, with the suppression of old-established games, these seemed after all to be the outcome of Republican liberty and justice. If the apostles of liberty only declaimed against tyranny done for them, not by them, then indeed "all men were liars." It is by thus sowing the seeds of disbelief in the goodness of the best of causes that times of revolution produce immoral politicians. Men see acts of violence, which necessity itself finds hard to justify, constantly committed around them; what is held sacred on one day contemned on another; oaths required to which neither heart nor intellect assents. At last the pressure of the times makes self-interest the rule of action; personal security a point of greater moment than fidelity to friends or country. The career of General Monk, who shared in the government both before and after the Restoration, bears the stamp of his political training. His family was Royalist, and he originally served in the king's armies in Ireland. On being taken prisoner he changed his side, and received a commission in the Parliament's army. Cromwell, who noticed his military genius, advanced him to be commander-in-chief in Scotland, and he afterwards served as admiral on board the fleet, and shared with Blake the triumphs of the Dutch war. His fidelity Cromwell had never cause to suspect, and if Richard had had the strength to maintain his own power, and so guard the interests of his friends, Monk would not have withdrawn his support from the protectorate. But no principle bound him to any special form of government, or to the House of Cromwell more than to the House of Stuart. Foreseeing the issue of events, he determined to be the first to act for the king, and thus to gain the credit of the Restoration. His reward was a seat in the council, and the title of Duke of Albemarle. Together with many others, who had taken a leading part in the late government, he did not shrink from sitting as judge in a court of justice which condemned his late friends to death as traitors. Very different to this was the school in which the statesmen of the Long Parliament had been trained. During the first quarter of the century the nation, braced by its triumph over Catholicism and Spain, was nerved for a struggle to make its political liberties more secure, and 'reform reformation' in religion. The only weapons it possessed were those offered by a free constitution. A single deviation from principle, a single sacrifice of the cause of the nation for that of the man, a single violent and illegal action, might throw back the work for years if not for centuries. The triumphs of the past, the great future before them, the necessity of courage and self-sacrifice, bred a race of heroes, fired by a strong spirit of patriotism, and by a yet stronger sense of duty, till they were ready to lay down their lives for their country and their conscience. The 'men who produce revolutions' are, indeed, of a different stamp from the men 'whom revolutions produce.'

The general fall in the moral tone of the nation may be also in part ascribed to errors into which the Puritans were led through their intense earnestness. The Puritans held that it is one of the first duties of a government to attend to the subject's welfare as a spiritual and intellectual being. This truth was capable of a right and wise application, as well as a fanatical perversion. Protection of person and property touches the lower man only; to instruct his mind and soul concerns the ordering of his higher existence. Thus Milton's noble longing was that every faculty of a man's whole being should be educated, so that he might have liberty, and know how to use it. "Make it a shame," said Cromwell in the same spirit to one of his Parliaments, "to see men bold in sin and profaneness, and God will bless you. You will be a blessing to the nation; and by this, will be more repairers of breaches than by anything in the world. Truly these· things do respect the souls of men, and the spirits—which are the men—the mind is the man. If that be kept pure, a man signifies somewhat; if not, I would very fain see what difference there is betwixt him and a beast. He hath only some activity to do some more mischief."* With these feelings, Cromwell was specially careful of educational institutions; he fostered the old universities of the south, and founded a new one at Durham for the north; he reformed the character of the ministry—then the only educators—by exacting a strict inquiry before admission, so that the benefices of the Church might no longer be the refuge of the idle and the ignorant. The Long Parliament, when confiscating the property of bishops and 'delinquents,' spared any revenues that were devoted to educational uses. In the New England States, where Puritans held absolute sway, while the popular voice required the adoption of the foolish policy of punishing sins as crimes, yet the legislators really raised the level of society by enacting a law of compulsory education. But though the chief leaders of the Puritan movement were advanced enough to perceive the slow but sure effect of education in bringing about a real improvement in the morals of a people, the large majority of their followers were allured by the deluding appearances of immediate reform produced by a policy of coercion. Influenced by Hebrew precedents, these sanguine spirits hoped by their legislation to compel the nation to live up to a

* Carl., iii. 189.

higher and sterner ideal. Republicans, Independents, and Presbyterians alike took delight in fencing virtue about with penal laws, which often related to acts indifferent in themselves. In this they defeated their own end. Outward conduct was influenced, but the heart and intellect revolted at the interference. Had the Puritans wished to excite a desire of raising Maypoles, dancing on Sundays, and attending play-houses, they could not have done better than forbid any to take part in such amusements under pain of a fine or a whipping. To enact for swearing, drinking, and gambling, punishments out of all proportion to the offence, was the most efficacious means to create sympathy for offenders. Many, after figuring awkwardly as unwilling saints, as soon as the unnatural bonds were loosed, wallowed more than ever in vice, and scoffed at virtue as mere cant and hypocrisy. The mass of the nation, however, was not so much affected by this reaction as might be supposed from the profligacy of the court. The Puritan spirit had too much that was noble in it to be easily extinguished. It still lives as one of the great moral forces of the nation, and is still to be seen in its two aspects—in the consuming zeal of the far-sighted reformer on the one hand, in the narrow but elevating austerity of the unintelligent and uneducated on the other. It still helps men to prefer the higher to the lower, the future to the present. England would not have been what it is had the salt of the nation been transported elsewhere by a succession of 'Mayflowers,' or exterminated by St. Bartholomew massacres.

In the political sphere, again, although much failed of immediate accomplishment, the work of Cromwell and his compeers was never really undone. To use the words of Burke, "a great deal of the furniture of ancient tyranny was torn to rags." Taxation without consent of Parliament was never attempted after the Restoration. Torture was never employed in England after the meeting of the Long Parliament.* The temper of the nation

* Torture, though always illegal, was used to a great extent during the rule of the Tudors and the two first Stuarts. In the single year 1581 there are no less than six warrants entered in the Council Book. It was possible for persons to obtain, as a favour, warrants from the king or the council, to sanction, even in ordinary criminal cases, the illegal employment of torture, so that murder, embezzlement, and horse-stealing are found amongst the imputed offences for which torture is to be used. Since the end of Elizabeth's reign no instances have been found of its application to other than State crimes. The last warrant issued was in 1640, the year of the

never again could bear the jurisdiction of arbitrary courts of justice. Above all there remained in the recollection of the nation the precedent of the Great Rebellion. The signal successes of that rebellion were convincing proofs of the power of the people. In great crises the consciousness, that power lies in the last resort with the people, can remove aristocratic prejudices that seem to lie like lead on the minds of legislators. The glories of Louis Quatorze blinded the eyes of the French court till the lessons of the Revolution revealed the secret ; but to English legislators the secret was open, that beneath them lay an invisible force, which they might be allowed to trifle with, but never to trample on. Twenty-eight years after Charles II. was restored, James II. fled to France. A coward, a bigot, and a fool, unable to read aright his father's history, he endeavoured to establish in England at once arbitrary government, and the ascendancy of the Catholic religion. Even the natural supporters of the prerogative went against him. Ministers, courtiers, and nobles, while loudly avowing their detestation of treason and rebellion, turned against the tyrant who excluded from his council all but Papist converts and Jesuits. The clergy, though regardless of their country's liberties, turned against the spoiler of their Church. The people, detesting the tyrant and the bigot alike, were glad enough to see the upper classes do the work of resistance for them. The crown was declared vacant, and offered by Parliament to William and Mary of Orange. By the change of succession a fatal blow was given to the pernicious doctrine of divine right, and the law was, once for all, declared superior to the prerogative. William, by accepting the crown as a gift of Parliament, virtually admitted that he would reign as a constitutional king, holding sacred the authority of the law, and carrying out whatever reforms Parliament should consider essential for the welfare of the people. Thus

---

meeting of the Long Parliament. "In the days of the prerogative," says Jardine, " Magna Charta was an empty name, and trial by jury a mockery and a farce, when, upon the authority of a royal warrant, a man could be carried away to the prisons of the Tower, and after his body had been duly attenuated, and his spirit broken and subdued by the horrors of ' Little Ease ' and the ' Dungeon among the rats,' be brought into court to make a formal answer to evidence extracted by the cruelties of the rack, or the manacles, or the 'scavenger's daughter.' " The use of torture was not abolished in Scotland till 1708; in France till 1789 ; in Russia till 1801; in Hanover till 1822 ; in Baden till 1831.—Jardine on the Use of Torture.

was the Revolution terminated, after a struggle which had lasted for nearly all the ninety years of the Stuart régime. The executive was brought into dependence upon the legislature, and the government of the country fixed as a constitutional monarchy. Laws granting toleration to Catholics and to Puritans, laws securing the liberty of the press, laws securing the independence of the judges, are all fruits, that time has ripened, of the armed resistance offered by the Long Parliament to Charles I.

In estimating the debt of gratitude that England owes to the leaders of the Great Rebellion, the moderation with which they did their work must never be forgotten. Even in the heat of civil strife they respected constitutional forms. That they fought for the king, and not against him, was not a mere quibble, but the secret of their strength. It might, in fact, be not unfairly said, that in the first instance the rebels were not those who maintained the supremacy of law, but the supporters of the new theory of divine right and the usurpations they called prerogative. It is indeed remarkable how, throughout the whole course of English history, the cause of liberty has less often been advanced by the concession of new rights than by the ratification of old. Thus the Petition of Rights and the Bill of Rights, far from introducing any great change into the constitution, are mainly the reassertion of rights already recognized at law. Such a course of conservative progress was impossible in France, where the monarchy destroyed its own foundations by its excesses. The permanence of kingship in England is due to its association with a popular constitution. The French monarchy had its constitutional limits, till a centralized absolutism took the place of free institutions. Then when the crash came there was nothing known of the constitution except what was detested. Hence constitutional monarchs in France, instead of being looked on as representatives of an honoured past, are simply judged upon their own merits. The first storm of unpopularity drives them out of office as if their rule was no more than that of an English ministry. Thus, since the first break in continuity, no form of government in France has lasted for more than twenty years together. Again, the English revolution was far less sanguinary than the French, because its causes were not, as in France, social. In France an aristocracy, answering both to nobility and gentry in England, possessed many privileges, which appeared the more odious, because exercised by men who took no part in the government. In England the people were not ground down; taxes did not fall heaviest upon those who had least; a large portion of the nobles and gentry made common cause with the people; the watchwords of an absolute and envious "equality" never assumed any prominence in the struggle. There was no rising of a famine-stricken peasantry; no burning of châteaux; no flight of a whole aristocracy, to be avenged by foreign invasion. Had Strafford succeeded in establishing an arbitrary throne, supported by a standing army; had the English nobles and gentry, in compensation for the loss of political rights, obtained exemption from taxation and other exclusive privileges, the revolution might have been deferred indeed, but its character, when it came, might have been as violent and sanguinary as the French. Equality before the law, a free press, every political and social reform that our constitution has been found capable of adopting without any violent change of form, might then have been only obtainable by rooting up the old order of things, and severing all the links that now bind the present to the past. The nation, divided into factions, hating and fearing one another too much for conciliation or even for the preservation of political morality, might have fallen a prey to the ambition of military usurpers, and found itself incapable of constructing a free and lasting government. De Tocqueville justly remarks that the effect of two centuries of absolute government on the French was to make the nation so little prepared to act for itself, that it could not reform all without destroying all: and hence the same revolution, which destroyed so many institutions, ideas, and customs opposed to liberty, destroyed, at the same time, so many others which are the necessary conditions of liberty, that, like the monarchy, it destroyed its own foundations by its excesses. Such revolutions may be said, like Saturn of old, to devour all their own children except the one who is born the new tyrant to supplant themselves.

The moderation of the leaders of the Rebellion was remarkable enough, but their faith was even more remarkable; they did not know how to despair. "If Pope and Spaniard and devil and all set themselves against us," says Cromwell, "though they should compass us like bees, yet in the name of the Lord we should destroy them." A sort of spiritual pride, based on the cause for which they fought, was shared by these Puritan leaders with their less gifted followers, but the faith which engendered this pride inspired them also with a rare humility. Though they gave proof enough of remarkable abilities, they never regarded their own personal success and the success of their cause as bound up together. "It was a most indifferent thing to him to live or die," said Pym; "God could carry on His work by others." "Truly," said the Lord Protector, "I have, as before God, often thought that I could not tell what my business was, nor what I was in the place I stood in, save comparing myself to a good constable, to keep the peace of the parish." Cromwell's pre-eminent ability sufficed to ward off the Restoration, while he lived. But the same spirit of faith that in seasons of greatest peril 'shone in him like a pillar of fire,' did not fail in evil days to sustain and animate those who had been his companions in the camp and the senate-house. Evil days indeed there were to come, for though the transition itself was accomplished without bloodshed, the old leaders were not suffered to escape. The new king, before he left Holland, published a proclamation, commanding his father's judges to surrender themselves up within fourteen days, on pain of being excepted from any pardon or indemnity either as to their lives or estates. Ludlow, putting no faith in royal promises, escaped in time to the continent; his gravestone stands in the churchyard at Vevay, overlooking the Lake of Geneva, near which he lived on long enough to hear that the Revolution was consummated by the accession of William and Mary, though even then he found his presence was not tolerated in his country. Hutchinson, who surrendered upon the proclamation, died in prison in the course of a few months from the effects of confinement and bad air. Marten, after twenty years' imprisonment, died an old man of seventy-eight at Chepstow Castle, in Monmouthshire (1681). Through all his sufferings he never regretted what he had done. We are told that towards the end of his life, he was allowed to take walks with his guard beyond the castle walls. An inhabitant of a neighbouring village used to ask him to rest in his house, and one day put the critical question, whether, supposing the deed were to be done over again, he would again sign the king's death-warrant. The stern old regicide lost his entry to the house by his indomitable "Yes." The blind Milton suffered with the friends whose cause his pen had so ably defended. His losses he regretted no more than he had regretted the loss of the eyes he sacrificed in writing his defence of the king's execution against the attack of Salmasius—

> Cyriac, this three years' day these eyes, though clear
>   To outward view, of blemish or of spot,
>   Bereft of light, their seeing have forgot ;
> Nor to their idle orbs doth sight appear,
> Of sun, or moon, or star, throughout the year,
>   Or man or woman. Yet I argue not
>   Against Heaven's hand or will, nor bate a jot
> Of heart or hope ; but still bear up and steer
> Right onward. What supports me, dost thou ask?
>   The conscience, friend, to have lost them overplied
> In liberty's defence, my noble task,
>   Of which all Europe rings from side to side.
> This thought might lead me through the world's vain mask
>   Content, though blind, had I no better guide.[*]

Nine of the king's judges were executed as traitors, besides Cook, the solicitor at the High Court of Justice, Hacker and Axtell, the commanders of the guard on the day of the execution, and Hugh Peters, the Independent minister, through whose good offices Juxon had been allowed to attend the king during his last hours. They all died bravely, expressing confidence in the justice of their cause. Amongst their judges sat the Presbyterians, Denzil Hollis and the Earl of Manchester ; the Independent, Lord Say-and-Sele ; and even Monk himself, now Marquis of Albemarle, and Sir Antony Ashley Cooper, afterwards Earl of Shaftesbury, both of whom had been leading members of the government under the protectorate, but were now trying to efface the memories of their own acts by the severity of the measures they dealt to their old friends and accomplices. Well might Lord Fairfax indignantly exclaim, that 'if any man must be excepted, he knew no man

---

[*] Taine, Hist. of English Literature, i. 419, attributes the sonnet to this time, but it manifestly belongs to an earlier date. The great French scholar, Claude Saumaise, or, as he is more commonly called, Salmasius, wrote a Latin treatise in defence of the divine right of kings, and in vindication of the memory of Charles I. (1649.) Milton wrote an answer to the *Defensio Regia*, also in Latin (1651). He had lost the sight of one eye in 1651, and became totally blind not long afterwards. His enemies taunted him with his blindness as being a judgment for having written in defence of the king's death. He lived on for fourteen years after the Restoration.

that deserved it more than himself, who was the general of the
army at the time.' Not satisfied with wreaking their vengeance
upon the living, the Royalists insulted the remains of the dead.
The remains of the historian May, the two victorious admirals,
Blake and Popham, the great constitutional statesman, John
Pym, and even those of the protector's mother, and his daughter, Lady Claypole, were torn out of their graves in Westminster Abbey, and flung together into a pit near the back-door
of one of the prebendaries' houses at Westminster; while the
bodies of Bradshaw, of Ireton, and of Cromwell himself, the
greatest ruler that England ever produced, were dragged to Tyburn and there hanged on gibbets.

But of all the enormities of the Restoration, the most iniquitous was the trial and execution of Sir Henry Vane. Charles
and Hyde, now Lord Chancellor Clarendon, had obtained the
exception of Vane's name out of the Act of Indemnity, as
passed by the Convention Parliament, by promising that if
he were attainted, his sentence should be remitted. In 1662,
that Parliament had given place to one more reactionary and
more sanguinary; the ruse had served its turn; and while
renegades obtained life and pardon by giving false witness
against the living and defaming the dead, the noble Republican statesman was accused of high treason against Charles
II. for having exercised civil and military functions under the
usurping government. A law of Henry VII., drawing a distinction between the king *de facto* and the king *de jure*, had assured
indemnity to all persons who obeyed the king for the time being
on the throne. Vane, therefore, could fairly defend himself by
arguing that the Parliament being the government for the
time being, there was no treason in acting under it, since this
law limited the word 'king' in the statute of treasons to a
king actually on the throne, and declared, in fact, there could
be no treason in acting against one who was merely king *de jure*.
He also pleaded the undoubted fact that he had opposed the act
of the regicides at the time, and refused approbation afterwards. He was not, however, suffered to escape because law
and justice were on his side. The chief justice was reported
to have said, "Though we know not what to say to him, we
know what to do with him." The court decided that Charles II.
had been king *de facto* as well as *de jure* from the moment of

his father's death, though "kept out of the exercise of his royal authority by traitors and rebels." Vane heard with composure that the Restoration was to be consummated by his death. "This dark night and black shade," he wrote to his wife, "which God hath drawn over His work in the midst of us, may be, for aught we know, the ground-colour to some beautiful piece that He is now exposing to the light." True to his principles, he ascribed his country's calamities to the imperfections of himself and her ministers, and gloried in his trial as a means of showing how death may be contemned by him who suffers in a good cause. " Ten thousand deaths," he said to his friends, " rather than defile my conscience, the chastity and purity of which I value beyond all the world ! I would not for ten thousand lives part with this peace and satisfaction I have in my own heart, both in holding to the purity of my principles and to the righteousness of this good cause, and to the assurance I have that God is now fulfilling all these great and precious promises, in order to what He is bringing forth. Although I see it not, yet I die in the faith and assured expectation of it." On the day of execution, Tower Hill and the roofs of the neighbouring houses were crowded with spectators. When Vane attempted to address them, the trumpets were ordered to blow, in fear of the impression his last words might make. " It is a bad cause," he said, " which cannot bear the words of a dying man." His last words at the block were : " Father, glorify Thy servant in the sight of men, that he may glorify Thee in the discharge of his duty to Thee and to his country." The crowd dispersed awe-struck, regarding his constancy as a "miracle." "He was great in all his actions, but to me he seemed greatest in his sufferings," wrote a friend of his family ; while a Royalist present at the scene remarked that " the king lost more by that man's death than he will get again for a good while." Such was the death of the great English stoic, a fitting close to the history of an heroic age

APPENDIX.

Page 48.—The story of the meeting of Pym and Strafford is told by Dr. James Welwood in his "History of the Last Hundred Years preceding the Revolution in 1688." More authentic illustrations of the close connection of Wentworth with the popular leaders before his acceptance of office are to be found in the Strafford Letters and Despatches. While Eliot was confined in the Tower, Lord Cottingdon wrote to Wentworth in Ireland that his 'old dear friend, Sir John Eliot, is very like to die.' Again, Laud, in one of his letters to Wentworth, communicates the following piece of intelligence : "When we came to this passage in your despatch, 'Again, I did beseech them to look well about, and to be wise by others' harms, they were not ignorant of the misfortunes these meetings' [i.e., Parliaments] had run in England of late years,' here a good friend of yours interposed, '*Quorum pars magna fui.*'" "It pierces my heart," says Strafford himself on his trial, "though not with guilt, yet with sorrow, that in my gray hairs I should be so much misunderstood by the companions of my youth, with whom I have formerly spent so much time." Wentworth's contemporaries certainly considered him as an apostate. An attempt has recently been made (Quarterly Review, April, 1874), to defend him from the charge. The article bears evidence of most careful research, and the writer certainly shows that in the Parliament of 1628, Wentworth differed from Eliot on details as to the best means to be employed in securing the liberty of the subject, but does not prove that he differed about the end in view. The main facts remain that Wentworth was imprisoned in 1627 for resisting a forced loan, that he was returned to the Parliament of 1628 as an extreme advocate of popular rights in the teeth of an opposition from the court, which made his supporters afraid to disclose their names. Wentworth's speeches in this Parliament, as quoted in the article itself, seem to tell their own tale. " I cannot forget the duty I owe to my country, and unless we be secured in our liberties, we cannot give (any supplies);" again he wished the committee "to draw into a law what may assure us of our liberty of our persons and propriety of our goods before we report the resolution of our gift;" and further, "some character must be put upon it (this law), and the council must not on every occasion leap out of it. Therefore, let some penalty be set on the violators thereof." When the king promised to observe Magna Charta, and to govern according to the laws and statutes of the realm, and wished Parliament to give up the proposed bill and trust to this declaration, Wentworth persevered against the king's express wish, and proposed to "confirm Magna Charta and those other laws, *together with the king's declarations*," by the objectionable bill. This was the man who became the king's minister without conditions, the chief enemy of popular rights, and the advocate of the policy of Thorough.

Page 69.—Out of the twelve judges, two only, Hutton and Croke, decided in favour of Hampden on the ground of principle, viz., the illegality of the tax. Denham, who was very ill, gave a short written judgment, expressing no opinion on the legality of the tax, but deciding in favour of Hampden on technical grounds, viz., that the action was brought in the wrong form. Bramston and Davenport both agreed that in time of danger the king had the power of levying the tax, and that he was sole judge of the danger. Like Denham, however, they gave judgment in favour of Hampden on technical grounds, viz., that it was impossible to give judgment for the king, because the writs issued to the sheriff for levying the tax did not state to whom the money was due. The trial took place during the months of November and December, 1637, but some of the judges did not deliver their opinions till after the following Easter.

The judgment of the majority, as that of the court, was delivered against Hampden, 12th June, 1638.

Ib. Cadmean [or suicidal] victory, see Hdt. i. 116.

Page 70.—12th December, 1638. Address of Anthony Champeney, dean of the secular Catholic clergy in England, exhorting them to pray for the king's success against the Scots. (From Clar. MSS. in Bodleian, No. 1158. Copy by Windebank.)

"Dearly beloved Brethren,—Though I doubt not but that you daily present your humble and earnest prayers unto Almighty God for his Majesty, according to St. Paul his exhortation in these words : Obsecro fieri orationes pro Regibus et omnibus qui in sublimitate sunt, ut quietam et tranquillam vitam agamus in omni pietate et castitate, hoc enim bonum est, et acceptum coram Salvatore nostro Deo ; yet, considering these broken times, I could not admit at this present to stir you up now earnestly to the performance of this your duty towards your sovereign, wishing you all and every one of you to exhort the Catholics with whom you converse, and you also yourselves, to have more frequent recourse to Almighty God by prayer, for the peace and quietude of his Majesty's dominions in these general troubles of all Europe, and for the prosperity of his Majesty, the Queen, and all the royal issue, begging of Almighty God in their behalfs that which the prophet Baruch did for the king and prince under whom he lived, 'ut sint dies eorum sicut dies cœli super terram, et ut det Dominus virtutem nobis, ut illuminet oculos nostros et vivamus sub umbra eorum et serviamus eis multis diebus.' And also that their subjects may be indued with the spirit of dutiful submission and obedience, for as St. Paul teacheth us, 'Non est potestas nisi a Deo, itaque qui resistit potestati, Dei ordinationi resistit. Qui autem resistunt, ipsi sibi damnationem acquirunt.'

" Considering the reports which are spread abroad concerning the discontented humours of some of his Majesty's subjects in Scotland, although I hope they are not so bad as the general voice doth make them, yet in regard that good subjects cannot be too zealous in that which concerneth his Majesty's service, I do earnestly entreat you all to exhort, move, and insist seriously with the Catholics that as the religion which they profess doth teach them next after God to honour and serve their Prince, and as they themselves have always professed to be ready to lay their lands and goods at his Majesty's feet, in witness of their allegiance and loyalty towards him, so they would at this present, of their own accord, without expecting to be called on, endeavour and think of some means, every one according to his hability, to make an efficacious and real expression of the same, to the end that his Majesty may understand that if he should have use of them, they are ready in all occurrences that may fall out to serve to the utmost, both with their fortunes and persons, according as his Majesty shall please to command or accept of their service in that kind."

Page 83.—Cromwell was already known to the government as a supporter of popular rights. The municipal government of the town of Huntingdon, Cromwell's birthplace, had been vested in a body of bailiffs and burgesses elected annually by the residents. By a new charter this body was changed to a mayor, alderman, and recorder, all elected for life. The people opposed the change, and were supported by Oliver Cromwell, who used some strong language against the new mayor and new recorder. The council was appealed to, and a messenger was despatched to Huntingdon with a warrant for the apprehension of Oliver Cromwell, who, on the 26th Nov., 1630, was brought before the lords of the council. After five days' detention, the case was gone into, and 'both sides had a long hearing,' but it was finally referred to the Lord Privy Seal, the Earl of Manchester, who owned Hinchinbrook in the neighbourhood of Huntingdon, until lately the residence of Sir Oliver Cromwell, the uncle of the future protector. Manchester's report is as follows:

"Whereas it pleased your lordships to refer unto me the differences in the town of Huntingdon about the renovation of their charter, and some wrongs done to Mr. Mayor of Huntingdon, and Mr. Barnard, a counsellor-at-law [the recorder] by disgraceful and unseemly speeches used of them by Mr. Cromwell of Huntingdon . . . I have heard the said differences, and do find those supposed fears of prejudice that might be to the said town by their late altered charter, are causeless and ill-grounded, and the endeavour used to gain many of the burgesses against this new corporation was very indirect and unfit, and such as I could not but much blame them that stirred in it. For Mr. Barnard's carriage of the business in advising and obtaining the charter, it was fair and orderly done, being authorised by common consent of the town to do the same, and the thing effected by him tends much to the good and grace of the town. . . . . For the words spoken of Mr. Mayor and Mr. Barnard by Mr. Cromwell, as they were ill, so they are acknowledged to be spoken in heat and passion, and desired to be forgotten; and I found Mr. Cromwell very willing to hold friendship with Mr. Barnard, who with a good-will remitted the unkind passages past and entertained the same. So I left all parties reconciled, and wished them to join hereafter in things that may be for the common good and peace of the town.

"December 6th, 1630." "H. MANCHESTER.

A few months after the earl's award, Cromwell sold his property at Huntingdon, and removed to St. Ives.—Calendar of State Papers, 1629—1631.

Page 84.—Browning's Strafford I., i. The words are put in the younger Vane's mouth.

Page 98.—Wentworth obtained from Charles enlarged powers for himself, as President of the Court of the North. A judge of assize acted in opposition to them, whereupon Wentworth wrote from Ireland to Lord Cottingdon as follows:

"I do most humbly beseech this judge may be convened at the Council Board, and charged with these two great misdemeanors . . . . and I am a most earnest suitor to his Majesty and their lordships, that he be not admitted to go that circuit hereafter; and indeed I do most earnestly beseech his Majesty by you, that we may be troubled no more with such a peevish indiscreet piece of flesh. I confess I disdain to see the gownmen in this sort hang their noses over the flowers of the crown, blow and snuffle upon them till they take both scent and beauty off them; or to have them put such a prejudice upon all other sorts of men, as if none were able or worthy to be intrusted with honour and administration of justice but themselves."—Strafford, Letters and Despatches, i. 129.

Following Wentworth's advice, Charles agreed to bestow upon the Lord Chief Justice and Lord Chief Baron of Ireland four shillings in the £ out of the first yearly rent raised upon the commission of defective titles. "Now," wrote Wentworth, "they do intend it with a care and diligence such as if it were their own private. And most certain the gaining themselves every four shillings once paid will better your revenue for ever after at least five pounds."—Ib., ii. 41.

"It is plain, indeed, that the opinion delivered by the judges, declaring the lawfulness of the assignment for the shipping is the greatest service that profession have done the crown in my time. But unless his majesty hath the like power declared to raise a land army upon the same exigent of State, the crown seems to me to stand upon one leg at home, to be considerable but by halves to foreign princes abroad. Yet sure this methinks convinces a power for the sovereign to raise payments for land forces, ... and if by degrees Scotland and Ireland be drawn to contribute their proportions to these levies for the public, *omne tulit punctum* . . . this piece well fortified for ever vindicates the royalty at home from under the restraints of subjects . . . settles an authority and right in the crown to levies of that nature, which thread draws after it many huge and great advantages more proper to be thought on at some other seasons than now."—Ib., ii. 62.

A description of Wentworth, written by Sir Thomas Roe to Elizabeth, wife of the Elector Palatine.

"My Lord Deputy of Ireland doth great wonders and governs like a king, and hath taught that kingdom to show an example of envy by having Parliaments and knowing wisely how to use them; for they have given the king six subsidies, which will arise to £24,000, and they are like to have the liberty we contended for, and grace from his Majesty worth their gift double; and which is worth more, the honour of good intelligence and love between the king and his people, which I would to God our great wits had had eyes to see. This is a great service, and to give your Majesty a character of the man—he is severe abroad and in business, and sweet in private conversation; retired in his friendships, but very firm; a terrible judge, and a strong enemy; a servant violently zealous in his master's ends, and not negligent of his own; one that will have what he will, and though of great reason, he can make his will greater, when it may serve him; affecting glory by a seeming contempt; one that cannot stay long in the middle region of fortune, but *entreprenant:* but will either be the greatest man in England, or much less than he is; lastly, one that may——and his nature lies fit for it, for he is ambitious to do what others will not—do your Majesty very great service, if you can make him."

Page 107.—The decision of the question was deferred by a vote, which was carried, 'that this declaration shall not be printed without a particular order of the House.'

Page 139.—"A feat repeated by their Breton brethren at La Vendée."—See Alison's History of Europe, iii. 326, 342, 365.

Page 181.—Richard Symonds, a Royalist officer, and Sir Edward Walker, Garter-king at arms, both of whom were with the royal army, give the following account of the storming of Leicester :
On Thursday (29th May), the royal army sat down before the city. On Friday (30th May), Rupert raised a battery and sent a trumpeter to demand surrender. No satisfactory answer being returned, he caused the battery to play, which by six o'clock made a great breach in the wall. Between twelve and two o'clock at night the town was stormed and taken. Symonds says the garrison was 600 men ; Walker, that officers, soldiers, and townsmen in arms together amounted to 1200. Walker says the town was 'miserably sacked,' as do Symonds and Sprigge ; but Sprigge's account of the siege lasting four days seems wrong.

Page 203. — Milton's sonnet.—Edwards wrote " Reason against Independence and Toleration" (1641).

Page 221.—Morrice, chaplain to Lord Broghill, tells the well-known story how Cromwell and Ireton, in the disguise of troopers, found a letter of the king's to the queen, concealed in a saddle. He heard the story from Lord Broghill, who had heard it from Cromwell. Morrice says that in the letter "the king acquainted the queen that he was courted by both factions, the Scotch Presbyterians and the army, and which bid fairest for him should have him ; but he thought he should close with the Scots sooner than the other" (Morrice's Life of Broghill, prefixed to Orrery State Letters, 1743). The contents of the letter are usually taken from Richardson's account of a conversation he had with Lord Bolingbroke. "Lord Bolingbroke told us" [i.e., Pope and Richardson] (12th June, 1742), "that Lord Oxford had often told him that he had seen and had in his hand an original letter that Charles I. wrote to the queen, 'that she might be entirely easy as to whatever concessions he should make, for that he should know in due time how to deal with the rogues'" [i.e., Cromwell and the others], "'who, instead of a silken garter should be fitted with an hempen cord.'" Richardson merely says that those concerned awaited and intercepted the letter, without specifying persons or place. (Richardsoniana, by the late Jonathan Richardson, jun., 1776).

Page 242. *Sigebehrt*, King of Wessex, deposed (755) by his successor, Cenwulf, and the West Saxon Witan; *Æthelred* the Second (the Unready), deposed in favour of the invader, Swegen, (1013), and restored (1014). *Harthacnut* deposed from his West Saxon kingdom, while still uncrowned, because he insisted on remaining in Denmark (1037): afterwards re-elected to the whole kingdom of England (1040). See Freeman's Norman Conquest, i. p. 105, 358, 498.

Kemble's fifth canon is, 'The Witan had the power to depose the king, if his government was not conducted for the good of his people.'

Mr. Stubbs, however, limits the cases of real deposition to the Heptarchic period, a time of unexampled civil anarchy. The instances which he quotes in this period besides Sigebehrt of Wessex are among the Northumbrian kings. *Alcred* or *Ealhred* (774) deposed 'by the counsel and consent of his own people,' i.e., by the Witenagemot: his predecessor, *Ethelwald*, deposed at Wincenheale, the meeting-place of the Northumbrian councils (765); *Ethelred* displaced 779, restored 790, and 'murdered six years later by equally competent authority.' The fall of Ethelred the Unready he distinguishes as the result of defeat, and notices that the action of the Witan was more concerned with his restoration than with his deposition.—Stubbs' Const. History, i. p. 138.

Pages 274, 275.—For an excellent account of the times, see Sir W. Scott's Fortunes of Nigel, chap. i., and for Alsatia, ib. xvi., xvii.

Page 338.—Copies of Letters of Intelligence, from MSS. in Bodleian.

" 4th April, 1653, N.S.

"It was debated in the House a fortnight ago whether we should send an ambassador for Holland or no; they seemed much divided about it. . . . The same day the House debated this, the council of officers at St. James' had resolved to turn them out, and to have shut up the House doors, had not the general and Col. Desborough interceded, who asked them if they destroyed that Parliament, what they should call themselves, a State they could not be. They answered that they would call a new Parliament. Then says the general, the Parliament is not the supreme power, but that is the supreme power that calls it, and besides the House is now endeavouring a treaty with Holland (which is the only way that we have left for the destroying of the combination of our enemies, both at home and beyond sea), and if we destroy them, neither Holland nor any other State will enter into a treaty with us. This seemed to satisfy them at present, but they have met since, and are framing a petition."

"May, 1653.

"I will not trouble you with the names of our new Council of State, nor with the proclamation subscribed by the general, because they are in print. The people generally entertain and acquiesce in it, yet in the army are some divisions about it, and there is a party which menace a second purgation because some persons have been refused to sit at the helm whom they propounded. Our general is very sedulous to give satisfaction to all parties, and after he hath made a peace with Holland (which, if once they treat we doubt not of), he will cement all other differences. He is very kind to the old malignant party, and some have found much more favour since the late dissolution than in seven years' solicitation before. This hath been effected by the Court of Articles, where the honour of the army is much concerned. Mr. Bradshaw is president, who checked a councillor at that bar for saying the Parliament was dissolved, which many of the members will not acknowledge, terming it only a disturbance."

Page 290.—"Copperspath" (*i.e.* Cobburn's-path) is Cromwell's version of the Scotch Cockburn's-path.

INDEX.

Act of Settlement, 6; of Settlement for Ireland, 342; of Supremacy, 9; of Uniformity, 10; for triennial Parliaments, 99, 375; rendering Long Parliament indissoluble but by its own consent, 100, 315; abolishing illegal courts, 101; excluding ecclesiastics from civil office, 102, 108, 115; Navigation, 300; for conducting law proceedings in English, 312
Amboyna, 253, 331
America, 75, 253, 254
Anabaptists, 204, 308, 330
Areopagitica, 207
Argyle, Duke of, 227, 230
Armada, Spanish, 13
Armour, 125, 126
Army, remodelled, 178, 214, 217, 220, 224, 236, 371, 373
Ascham, 278
Ashburnham, John, 222
Assembly, of Divines, 150, 154, 195, 203; of Peers, 81
Astley, Sir Jacob, 193
Austria, 22, 65

Bacon, Sir Francis, 252, 262, 306
Balfour, 108
Barbadoes, 335
Bastwick, 73, 86
Batten, Admiral, 134
Baxter, 32
Berkeley, Judge, 85
Berkley, 222
Berwick, Pacification of, 78
Bill, Dissolution, 313; for command of militia, 114; bishops' exclusion, 114
Bills of Attainder, 91, 96, 98
Birch, Colonel, 233
Bishops, 11, 108, 109, 114

Blake, Admiral, 190, 296, 300—302, 317, 322, 339, 354, 356, 384
Booth, Sir George, 370
Bradshaw, 238, 239, 384
Brentford, 132
Bristol, 129, 248
Broghill, Lord, 304, 363
Brook, Robert Greville, Lord, 132
Brownists, 204
Buckingham, George Villiers, Duke of, 27—34, 40, 43, 45
Burton, 73, 86
Byron, Lord, 146

Cadiz, 33, 356
Calais, 353, 359
Calvort, Sir John, 19
Casaubon, Meric, 340
Catholics, 69, 70, 151, 312, 341. See Appendix
Cecil, Sir Edward, 33
Chambers, 59, 86
Charles I. visits Spain, 27; marriage treaty broken off, 28; refuses assent to Tonnage and Poundage Bill, 31; lends ships to Louis XIII., 32; imprisons managers of Buckingham's impeachment, 36; war with France, 37; demands general loan, 38, 39; answers to Petition of Right, 42, 43, 47; proclamation of, against Parliament, 50; education and character, 51; love of art, 256; court of, 29, 53; arbitrary government of, 54 59; attempts to establish Episcopacy in Scotland, 76, 78; foreign policy of, 78; summons Assembly of Peers, 80; conduct towards Strafford, 84, 96, 97; assents to Army Plot, 94; concessions in Scotland, 103; suspected of com-

plicity in Irish rebellion, 104, 105; reaction in favour of, 106, 197; guard at Whitehall, 108; attempts to seize five members, 110, 111; visits Guildhall, 112; prepares for war, 114; consents to Bishops' Exclusion Bill, 115; refuses Militia Bill, 116; refused admittance into Hull, 116; rejects York propositions, 118; raises standard, 119; deceit, cause of war, 120; at Edgehill, 124–131; attacks Brentford, 132; classes on side of, 134; answer to Oxford propositions, 136; success of forces, 139, 141; besieges Gloucester, 142; at Newbury, 145; habits of troops, 148, 153; cessation of arms with Irish, 158; Oxford Parliament, 157; defeats Waller, 160; forces Essex to surrender, 167–169; at Newbury, 172; breaks off Uxbridge negotiations, 177; at Naseby, 186; letters published, 187; treaty with Irish Catholics, 191, 192; goes to Scotch camp, 193; rejects Newcastle propositions, 197; removed from Holmby by Joyce, 215, 217; rejects army propositions, 219; flies to Isle of Wight, 222; treaty with Scots, 225; concessions at Newport, 235; hesitates to escape, 236; trial and execution, 238–247. See Appendix.
Charles Louis, elector palatine, 306, 353
Chillingworth, 211
Church, Episcopalian, 9–13, 20, 40, 69–75, 102, 150; Presbyterian, 10, 75, 202; Independent, 12, 195
Christina, Queen of Sweden, 35
Claypole, Lady Elizabeth, 364, 384
Clubmen, 188
Colchester, 227, 330
Colepepper, 106, 109, 181, 187
Colonies, 75, 251–254, 296
Companies, 250, 253
Confirmatio Chartarum, 1
Confiscations, 212, 233, 309
Cooper, Sir Antony Ashley, 388
Copyholders, 3, 267
Cotton, Sir Robert, 255
Council, King's, 7, 17, 101
Court, of Admiralty, 19; of Chancery, 6, 318–320, 332; of Exchequer, 6, 68, 74; of King's Bench, 16, 39, 57; of the North, 58; of High Commission, 7, 16, 72, 101; of Star Chamber, 7, 15, 59, 73, 74, 101, 267
Courts of Common Law, 6, 317–320; High Courts of Justice, 238, 307
Covenant, Scotch, 77; Solemn League and, 153
Covenanters, Scotch, 77–80, 227, 285, 291
Cromwell, Henry, 337, 346
Cromwell, Oliver, member for Huntingdon, 41; for Cambridge, 83; leader of Independents, 102; lieutenant-general of eastern counties' army, 155; character of troops, 156; at Marston

Moor, 163–166; quarrels with Manchester, 173; supports Self-denying Ordinance, 174; lieutenant-general of remodelled army, 182; at Naseby, 185; in west, 188; character and appearance, 209, 210, 341, 366; views of settlement, 216, 218, 221, 224, 226; suppresses mutinies in army, 224, 281; defeats Scots at Preston, 228–230; supports execution of king, 238, 246; in Ireland, 281–284; commander-in-chief of army, 285; in Scotland, 287; at Dunbar, 288–290; at Worcester, 292–295; political views of, 303–313; expels Long Parliament, 314; summons Barebone's Parliament, 316; protector, 227; ideal of government, 229; plots against, 330, 351, 363; reform of Church, 331; of Chancery, 332, 340; quarrels with Parliaments, 334, 348, 361; rules arbitrarily, 336; moderation of, 337–339; urges reforms of law, 340; encourages learning, 260, 340, 377; toleration of, 341–343; refuses title of king, 350; foreign policy of, 331, 352–359; protects Vaudois, 358; economy of government, 360; friends of government, 363; illness and death, 364–366. See Appendix
Cromwell, Richard, 367–369
Cropredy Bridge, 159
Customs, 15, 31, 157, 251

Davenant, Sir William, 260
Dean, Admiral, 296, 325
Debtors, 323
Denmark, 331
De Ruyter, 325
Desborough, 328, 336, 369, 370
Digby, Lord, 188
Dorislaus, Dr., 278
Dragoons, 125
Drogheda, 282
Dunbar, 288–290
Dunkirk, 353, 356, 357, 363

Edgehill, 126–131
Eikōn Basilikē, 278
Eliot, Sir John, 18, 19, 35, 50, 56, 57, 255
Elizabeth, Queen, government of, 8–14
Elizabeth of Bohemia, 14, 22
Engagers, 230, 291
Erastians, 200
Essex, Robert Devereux, Earl of, 94, 118, 128, 130, 133, 137, 141, 143, 145–147, 159, 167, 168, 212
Excise, 158
Exports, 253

Fairfax, Lord Ferdinando, 161
Fairfax, Lady, 239
Fairfax, Sir Thomas, 117, 161, 165, 180, 213, 215, 223, 227, 231, 233, 238, 244, 259, 280, 332, 372, 383

INDEX.

Falkland, Sir Lucius Cary, Lord, 82, 83, 103, 106, 110, 117, 136, 146, 255
Fauconberg, Lord, 357
Felton, 44
Fiennes, Nathaniel, 119, 139
Fifth-Monarchists, 204, 303, 330
Finch, Sir John, 49, 66, 85
Fleetwood, 190, 292, 328, 336, 344, 369
Fox, George, 343
France, 3, 38, 298. 353, 356, 359, 330, 381
Frederic, Prince of the Palatinate, 14, 21, 23, 25
Freeholders, 2, 121, 134, 264, 266

Glamorgan, Lord Herbert, Earl of, 190, 255
Gloucester, 143
Goring, Colonel, 163, 165, 181, 187
Government, three functions of, 1—6. See Appendix
Grenville, Sir Richard, 167, 181, 187
Gustavus Adolphus, 66

Habeas Corpus, writ of, 15, 16, 101
Hale, Sir Matthew, 339
Hamilton, James, Duke of, 227, 229, 307
Hammond, 222
Hampden, John, 68, 91, 107, 110, 113, 114, 119, 128, 130, 137, 138, 149
Harlech Castle, 212
Haslerig, Sir Arthur, 110, 119, 288, 308, 361
Henrietta Maria, 53, 64, 93, 97, 105, 111, 115, 158, 176, 196, 236
Heyworth Moor, 117
Highlanders, 170
Hobbes, 211, 340
Holland, 252, 253, 299, 300; war with, 301, 302, 325, 331, 361.
Hollis, Denzil, 49, 106, 119, 383
Hopton, Sir Ralph, 122, 139
Hotham, Sir John, 135
Howard, Lord, of Esrick, 310
Huguenots, 37, 40, 44—46
Huntingdon, Major-General, 231
Hutchinson, Colonel, 190, 203, 208, 245, 259, 382
Hyde, Edward, 82, 103, 106, 109, 113, 117, 181, 191, 258, 346, 351, 384

Impeachment, 34, 35, 37, 84, 85, 110
Imports, 253
Independents, 102, 154, 167, 195, 201, 234
India, 251, 253
Instrument of Government, 326
Ireland, 61, 63, 64, 104, 156, 278, 281—284, 316, 333, 345, 375
Irish troops, 157, 170
Ireton, Henry, 183, 185, 190, 209, 217, 219, 221, 230, 235, 237, 243, 245, 284, 304, 384
Ironsides, 156, 164, 166

Jamaica, 355
James I., government of, 14—28, 257, 262

Jermyn, Lord, 258
Jews, 343
Jones, Inigo, 256
Joyce, Cornet, 215
Judges, 6, 44, 68, 83, 323, 339

'Killing no murder,' 351
King, General, 163

Labourers, 270
Lamb, Dr., 41
Lambert, 289, 292, 362, 370, 372
Laud, William, Archbishop of Canterbury, 59, 72—75, 85, 178
Law, English common, 317—320, 339; martial, 40; see *Act, Ordinance*
Leeds, 248
Leicester, 181. See Appendix
Lenthall, William, 112, 219, 376
Leslie, Alexander, Earl of Leven, 157, 161, 164, 165, 167
Leslie, David, 161, 287—290, 291—295
Levellers, 221, 223, 235. 245, 280, 335, 337, 350
Lilburne, John, 73, 86, 221, 234, 307
Lindsey, Earl of, 128, 130
Loans, 5, 38, 39
Lockhart, 339, 357
London, 113, 117, 131—133, 135, 140, 151, 216, 220, 226, 248, 251, 272—275, 371
Lords, House of, 2, 117, 177, 238, 277, 349, 360, 373
Louis XIII., 33, 37, 78
Louis XIV., 298, 356, 357
Lunsford, Colonel, 107
Ludlow, Edmund, 190, 208, 219, 226, 336, 346, 382

Magna Charta, 2
Major-generals, 336, 349
Manchester, Edward Montague, Earl of, 110, 129, 155, 172, 174, 383
Manchester, 247
Mardyke, 356, 348
Marston Moor, 161—167
Marten, Sir Henry, Judge of Admiralty, 6
Marten, Henry, son of Judge, 152, 313, 382
Massey, 142
Maurice, Prince, 14, 119, 135, 139, 296
Mazarin, Cardinal, 193, 357
Mercantile system, 350
Mercurius Aulicus, 149
Militia, 114, 116, 118
Milton, John, 75, 132, 200, 203, 206—208, 259, 296, 328, 339, 346, 358, 377, 383
Monk, General, 291, 301, 304, 317, 325 371—373, 376, 383
Monopolies, 55, 67, 249
Montreuil, M. de, 193

Montrose, Marquis of, 170, 176, 189, 195, 285
Mountnorris, Lord, 64

Naseby, 182—186
Naylor, 343, 348, 350
Newcastle, Marquis of, 134, 141, 158, 160, 163, 165, 167
Newbury, 143—147, 173
Newspapers, 100, 149, 208, 336
Noy, 66
Nutt, Captain, 19

Ordinance, Self-Denying, 175, 177; for remodelling army, 175; for new Prayer-book, 202; for establishment of Presbyterian Church, 202; for suppression of blasphemies and heresies, 203; forbidding use of Prayer-book, 204; for High Court of Justice, 238; forbidding Episcopalian ministers to act as chaplains or schoolmasters, 336; for reform of Chancery, 332, 340; for union of England and Scotland, 344
Ordinances or proclamations made in council, 5; for suppression of vice and observance of Sundays, 151; for reform of Church, 331; for restraining unlicensed printing, 152, 207, 208
Ormond, Duke of, 156, 190, 192, 195, 235, 281, 363
Oxenstiern, 330
Oxford, 133, 135, 157, 158

Palatinate, 22, 353
Parliament, privileges of, 25, 232; classes represented in, 2, 3, 333; character of, in seventeenth century, 100; *of* 1621, 24; *of* 1625, 30—32; *of* 1626, Buckingham impeached, 35; *of* 1628, Petition of Right, 41—43; *session of* 1629, 48, 49; *Short Parliament of* 1640, 79; *Long Parliament*, meeting of, 83; proceedings against Strafford, 84, 87—93, 97; against delinquents, 83, 85; votes Scots £300,000, 94; reforms of, 99, 101; religious parties in, 102; debates on Grand Remonstrance, 106; five members impeached, 110; sits in Guildhall, 113; a war council, 117; constitutional attitude of, 122; classes on side of, 121, 133; peace party in, 135; peace propositions of Lords, 140; petitioned by mobs, 140; parties in, 152; armies of, 157; quarrels with army, 212—214; yields to army, 216; intimidated by Presbyterian mob, 219; fugitive members restored, 220; votes no more addresses to king, 225; reverses votes, and negotiates with Charles, 231; causes of unpopularity, 231—234; financial administration of, 233; accepts king's concessions, 237; purged by Pride, 237; *Rump* erects high court for trial of king, 238; establishes Republic, 277; raises a powerful navy, 296; government recognized abroad, 297; foreign policy, 297—299; war with Holland, 299—302; severity of government, 307—310;

eform of law, 312; bill for new representative, 313; expelled by Cromwell, 314; restored by officers, 370, 371; Presbyterian members restored by Monk, 372; votes own dissolution, 373. *Barebone's*, reforms of, 317—325; *First of Protector*, 333, 334; reformed representation, 333; *Second of Protector*, sentence on Naylor, 348; Petition and Advice, 349; *Second Session*, 'new House of Lords, 360; dissolved, 362; *of Richard Cromwell*, 368; *Convention* 373 *Oxford Parliament*, 157.
Patronage, 323
Pembroke Castle, 227
Pendereels, 295
Penn, Admiral, 354, 356
Pennington, Captain, 32
Penruddock, 334
Peters, Hugh, 383
Petition and Advice, 349, 360, 367
Petition of Right, 42
Pilgrim Fathers, 75, 254
Pirates, 32, 66
Poor Laws, 268—270
Popham, 296
Population, 248
Portugal, 296, 331, 358
Post Office, 272
Prerogative, royal, 5, 29, 42, 51, 68
Presbyterians, in England, 10, 102, 150, 151, 155, 178, 189, 192, 195, 202, 214, 231, 237, 307, 330, 362; in Scotland, 11, 76, 153, 201
Preston, 227—230
Pride, Colonel, 237, 312, 360
Prisoners, 149, 335
Prisons, 261, 323, 325
Proclamations, 55
Propositions, of York, 118; of Oxford, 136; of Uxbridge, 176; of Newcastle, 195; of army, 217; of Newport, 235
Prynne, 73, 236
Puritans, 9, 12, 20, 22, 70—74, 256, 258, 377, 378
Pym, John, 42, 48, 84, 91, 95, 102, 103, 106, 109, 160, 116, 123, 154, 306, 382, 384

Quakers, 342

Raleigh, Sir Walter, 23
Regicides, fate of, 382, 383
Remonstrance, Grand, 110, 120
Republicans, 152, 205, 225, 299, 234, 244, 304—307, 327, 330, 334—337, 348, 361, 368, 370
Rich, Robert, 360, 364
Rochelle, 32, 40, 44, 46
Royalists, 121, 134, 136, 139, 149, 157, 167, 227, 273, 307, 335, 338, 350
Royal Revenue, 53
Rubens, Peter Paul, 256
Rupert, Prince, 14, 119, 126, 128—134, 135, 138, 139, 142, 149, 159, 161—167, 181, 185, 188, 296

INDEX.

Salmasius, 383
Santa Cruz, 354
Savoy, Duke of, 358
Say-and-Sele, Lord, 342
Scots, 77, 80, 94, 154, 190, 193, 198, 225, 227, 229, 284, 285—291, 316, 333, 344, 375
Sectarians, 12, 135, 152, 204
Selden, 201
Sexby, 338, 351
Seymour, William, 17
Sheffield, 247
Ship-money, 66, 68, 83. See Appendix
Shrewsbury, Countess of, 17
Sidney, Algernon, 190, 238, 244
Skippon, 118, 133, 185, 213, 244, 336
Socage tenure, 2
Spain, 22, 28, 33, 37, 350, 353, 355—357
Statute of Winchester, 114
St. Domingo, 355
St. John, 110, 299, 303, 369
St. Kitts, 354
Strafford, Sir Thomas Wentworth, Earl of, 42, 47, 52, 60—65, 78, 85, 87—92, 95, 97. See Appendix
Strickland, 299
Strode, 110
Stuart, Lady Arabella, 17; Lady Elizabeth, 217, 240; Charles, Prince of Wales, 130, 181, 192, 227, 256, 278, 285, 291—296, 350, 361, 363, 370; James, 357, 379
Subsidies, 15, 30, 158
Superstitions, 262
Sweden, 331
Syndercomb, 351

Taylor, Jeremy, 211
Teneriffe, 356
Thirty Years' War, 22, 65, 352

Tithes, 320, 321, 325
Tom Tell-Truth, 26
Tortuga, 354
Torture, 5, 44, 378
Trade, 249—254
Travelling, 271
Treason, law of high, 87
Tunis, 354

Uxbridge, 174—177

Valentine, 49, 56
Vandyke, 256
Vane, Sir Henry, the elder, 79, 89
Vane, Sir Henry, the younger, 91, 153, 205, 207, 244, 277, 301, 310, 312, 314, 336, 369, 384, 386
Van Tromp, 300—302, 322
Vaudois, 355
Venables, General, 354, 355
Verney, Sir Edmund, 122

Waller, Sir William, 122, 139, 157, 159, 167, 172
Waller, the poet, 137
Warwick, Robert Rich, Earl of, 360, 364
Westphalia, Treaty of, 353
Wexford, 283
Whalley, Colonel, 223
Whitelock, Bulstrode, 278, 369
Wildman, 335
William III., 242, 379
Williams, Archbishop of York, 103
Wilmot, Colonel, 128
Witchcraft, 263
Worcester, 291—295
Wroth, Sir Thomas, 225

Yeomen, 2, 266
York, 116, 118, 158, 160, 167

THE END.

DILLING AND SONS, PRINTERS, GUILDFORD, SURREY.

www.ingramcontent.com/pod-product-compliance
Lightning Source LLC
Chambersburg PA
CBHW022114290426
44112CB00008B/673